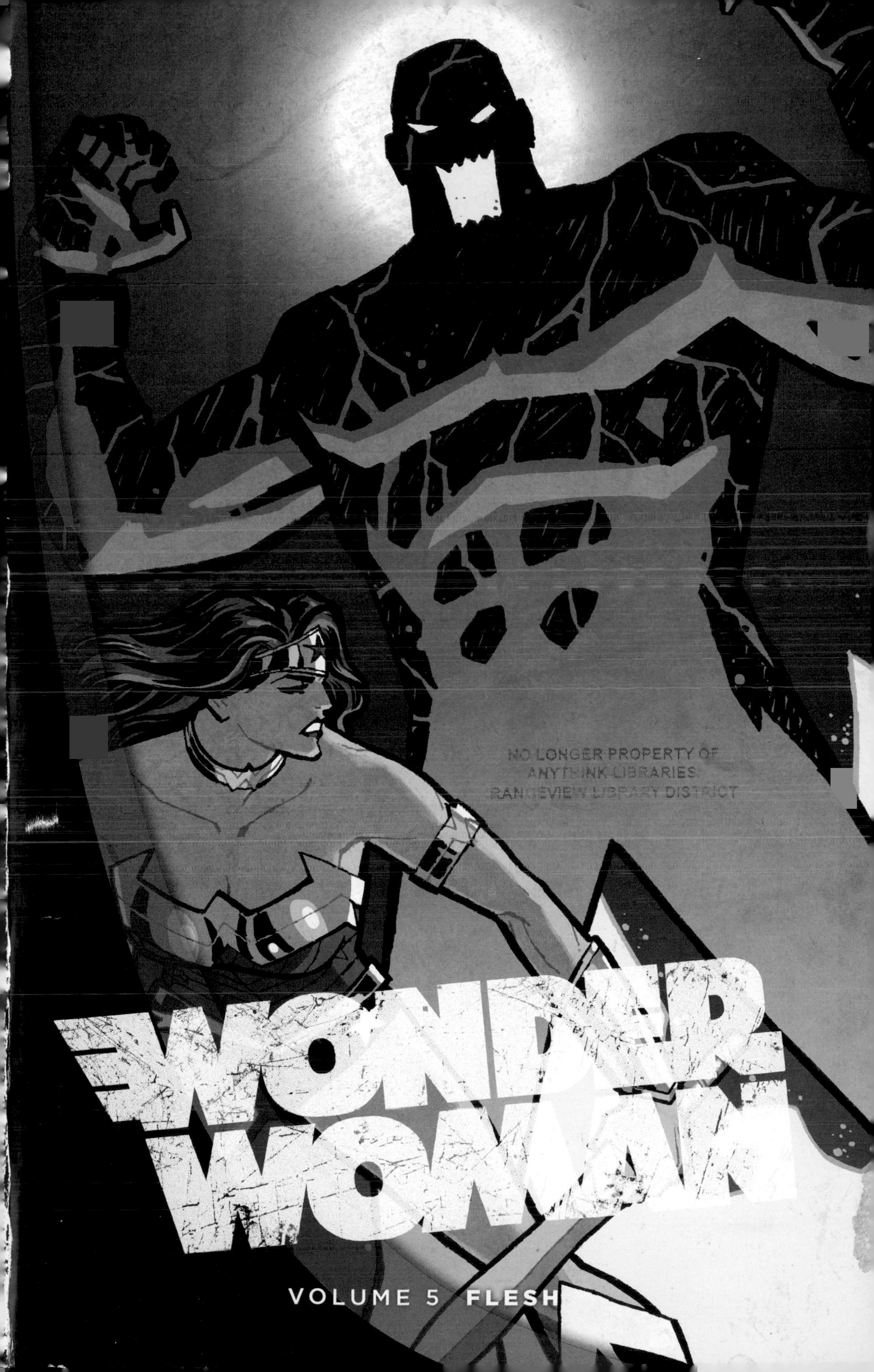
WONDER WOMAN
VOLUME 5 FLESH

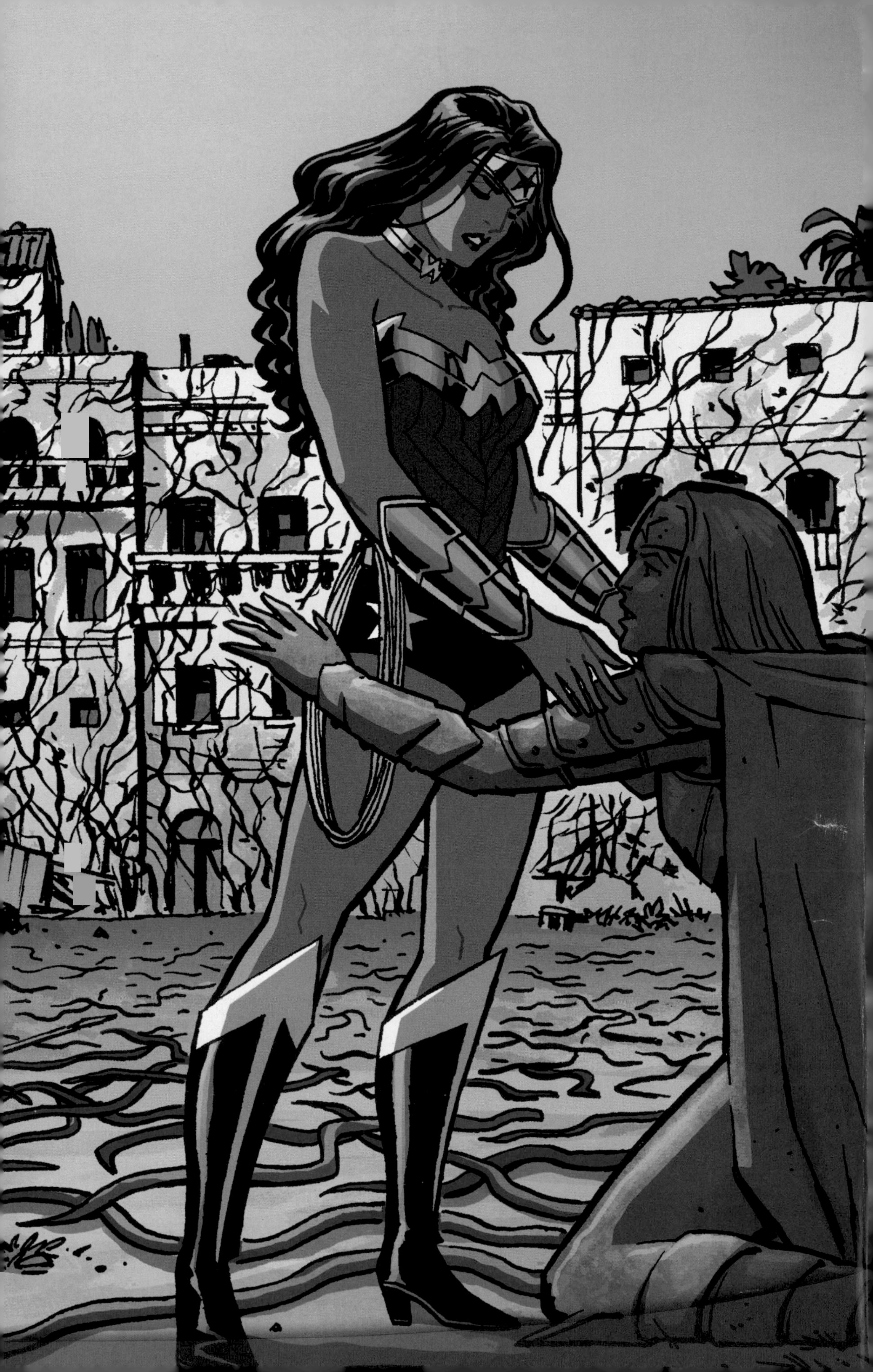

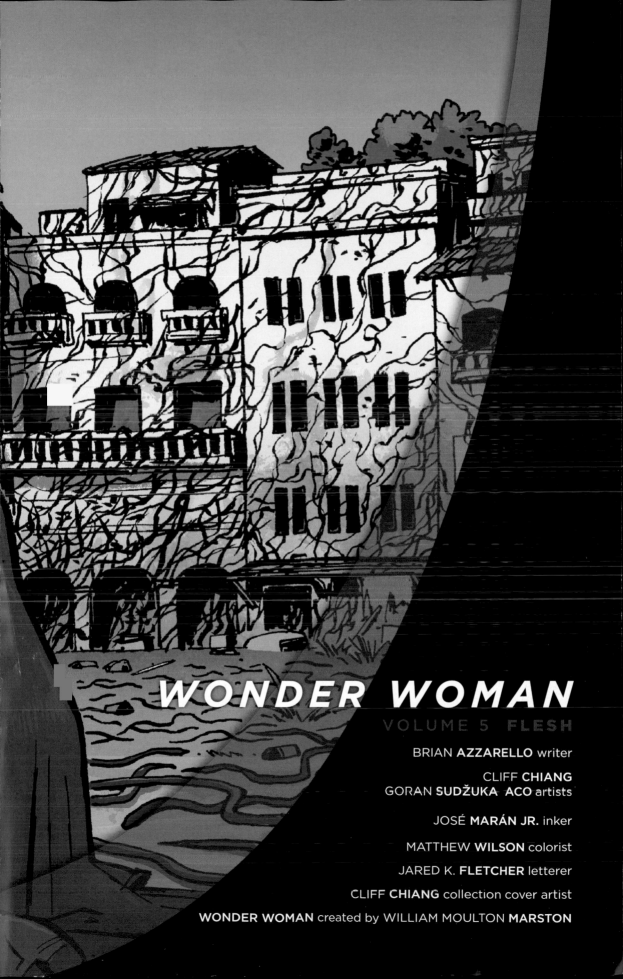

# WONDER WOMAN

## VOLUME 5 FLESH

BRIAN **AZZARELLO** writer

CLIFF **CHIANG**
GORAN **SUDŽUKA** **ACO** artists

JOSÉ **MARÁN JR.** inker

MATTHEW **WILSON** colorist

JARED K. **FLETCHER** letterer

CLIFF **CHIANG** collection cover artist

**WONDER WOMAN** created by WILLIAM MOULTON **MARSTON**

MATT IDELSON Editor – Original Series  CHRIS CONROY Associate Editor – Original Series
RACHEL PINNELAS Editor  ROBBIN BROSTERMAN Design Director – Books
ROBBIE BIEDERMAN Publication Design

BOB HARRAS Senior VP – Editor-in-Chief, DC Comics

DIANE NELSON President  DAN DIDIO and JIM LEE Co-Publishers  GEOFF JOHNS Chief Creative Officer
AMIT DESAI Senior VP – Marketing and Franchise Management
AMY GENKINS Senior VP – Business and Legal Affairs  NAIRI GARDINER Senior VP – Finance
JEFF BOISON VP – Publishing Planning  MARK CHIARELLO VP – Art Direction and Design
JOHN CUNNINGHAM VP – Marketing  TERRI CUNNINGHAM VP – Editorial Administration
LARRY GANEM VP – Talent Relations and Services  ALISON GILL Senior VP – Manufacturing and Operations
HANK KANALZ Senior VP – Vertigo and Integrated Publishing  JAY KOGAN VP – Business and Legal Affairs, Publishing
JACK MAHAN VP – Business Affairs, Talent  NICK NAPOLITANO VP – Manufacturing Administration  SUE POHJA VP – Book Sales
FRED RUIZ VP – Manufacturing Operations  COURTNEY SIMMONS Senior VP – Publicity  BOB WAYNE Senior VP – Sales

WONDER WOMAN VOLUME 5: FLESH

DC Comics, 1700 Broadway, New York, NY 10019
A Warner Bros. Entertainment Company.
Printed by RR Donnelley, Salem, VA, USA. 8/29/14. First Printing.
HC ISBN: 978-1-4012-5097-3
SC ISBN: 978-1-4012-5349-3

SUSTAINABLE FORESTRY INITIATIVE

Certified Chain of Custody
20% Certified Forest Content,
80% Certified Sourcing
www.sfiprogram.org
SFI-01042
APPLIES TO TEXT STOCK ONLY

Library of Congress Cataloging-in-Publication Data

Azzarello, Brian, author.
Wonder Woman. Volume 5 / Brian Azzarello, Cliff Chiang, Goran Sudzuka.
pages cm.
ISBN 978-1-4012-5097-3 (hardback)
1. Graphic novels.  I. Chiang, Cliff, illustrator. II. Sudzuka, Goran, illustrator. III. Title.
PN6728.W6A995 2014
741.5'973—dc23
                           2014015079

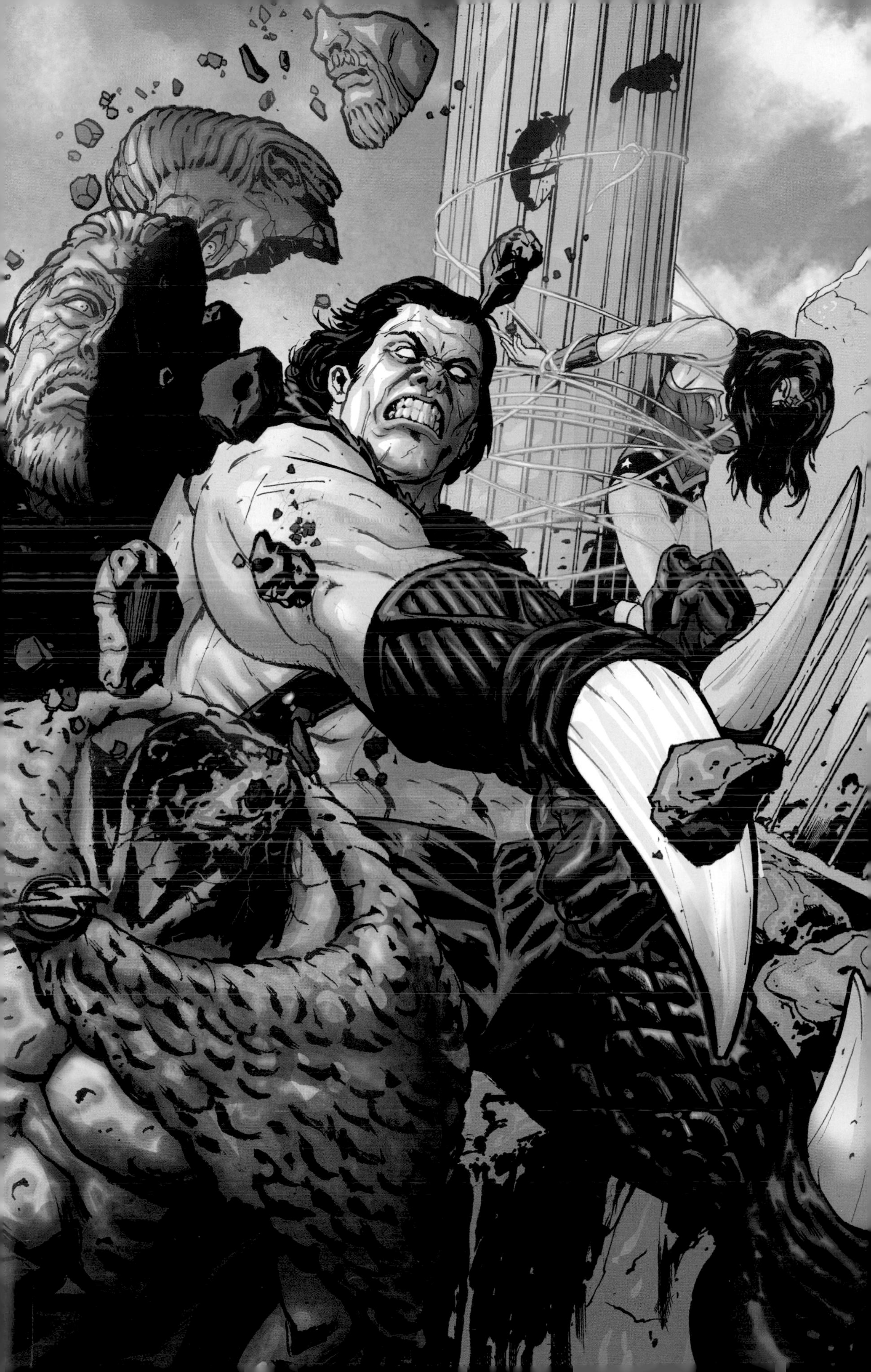

Cover art by VICTOR IBÁÑEZ

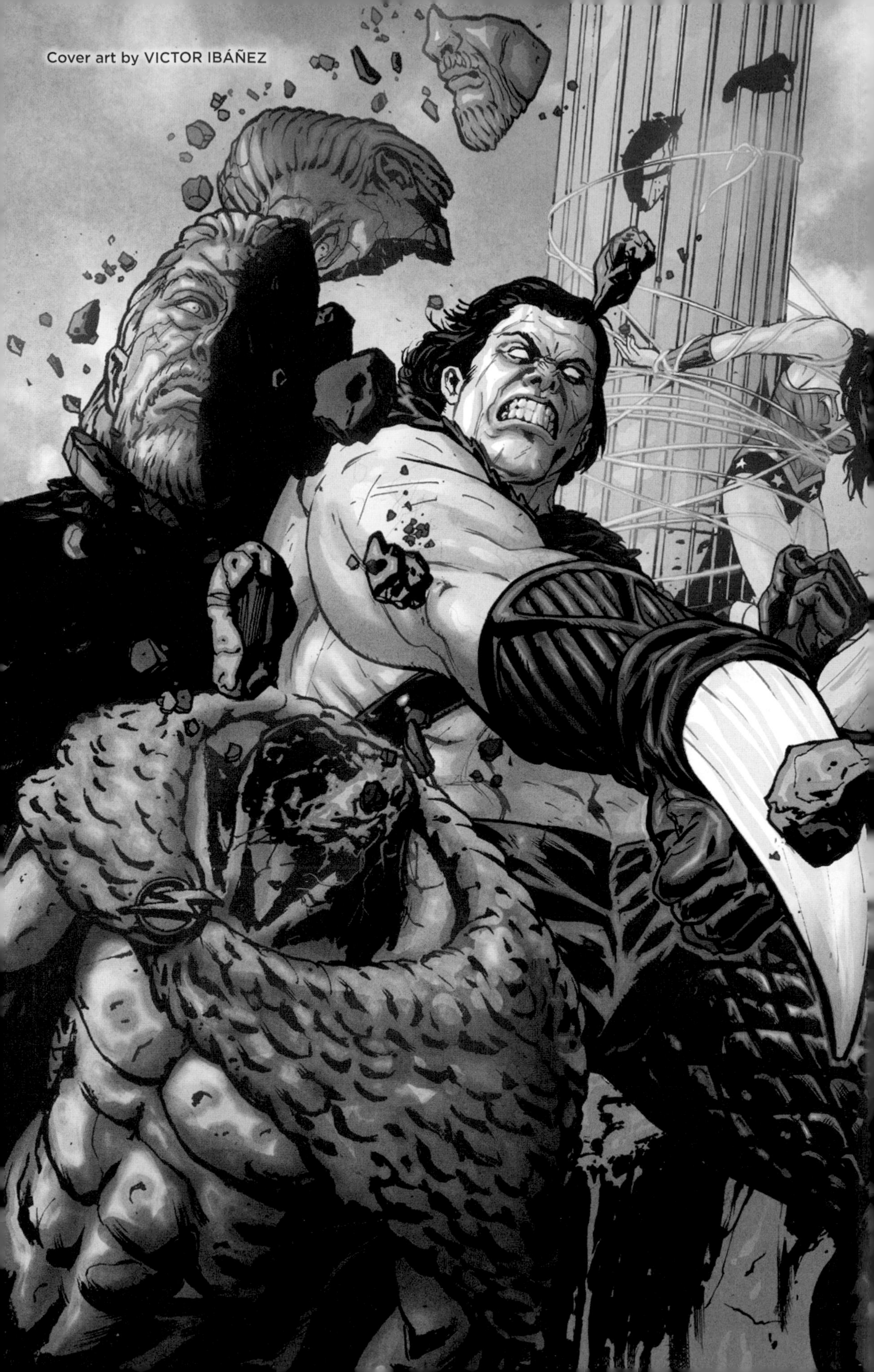

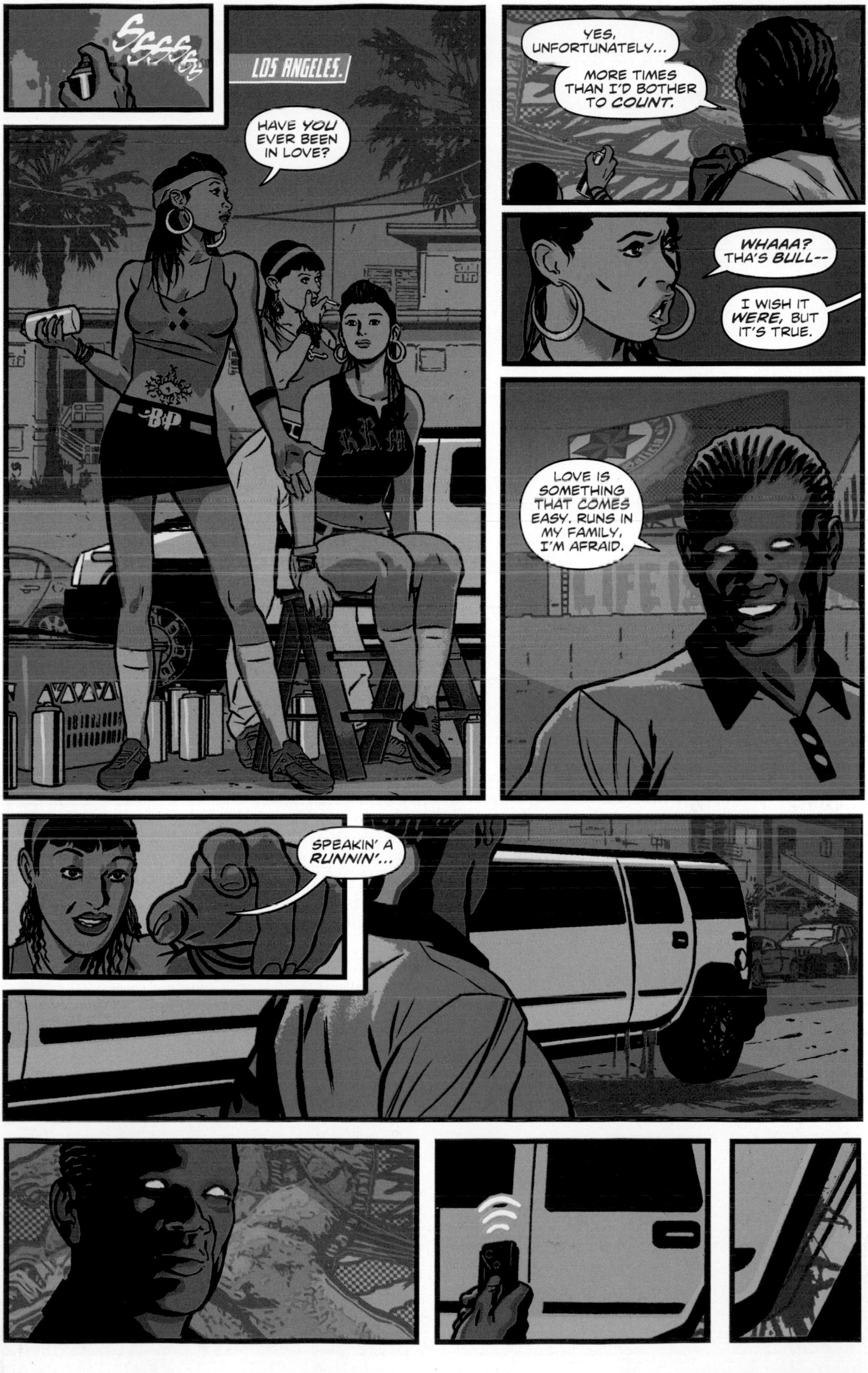

SSSSSS
LOS ANGELES.
HAVE YOU EVER BEEN IN LOVE?
YES, UNFORTUNATELY...
MORE TIMES THAN I'D BOTHER TO COUNT.
WHAAA? THA'S BULL--
I WISH IT WERE, BUT IT'S TRUE.
LOVE IS SOMETHING THAT COMES EASY. RUNS IN MY FAMILY, I'M AFRAID.
SPEAKIN' A RUNNIN'...

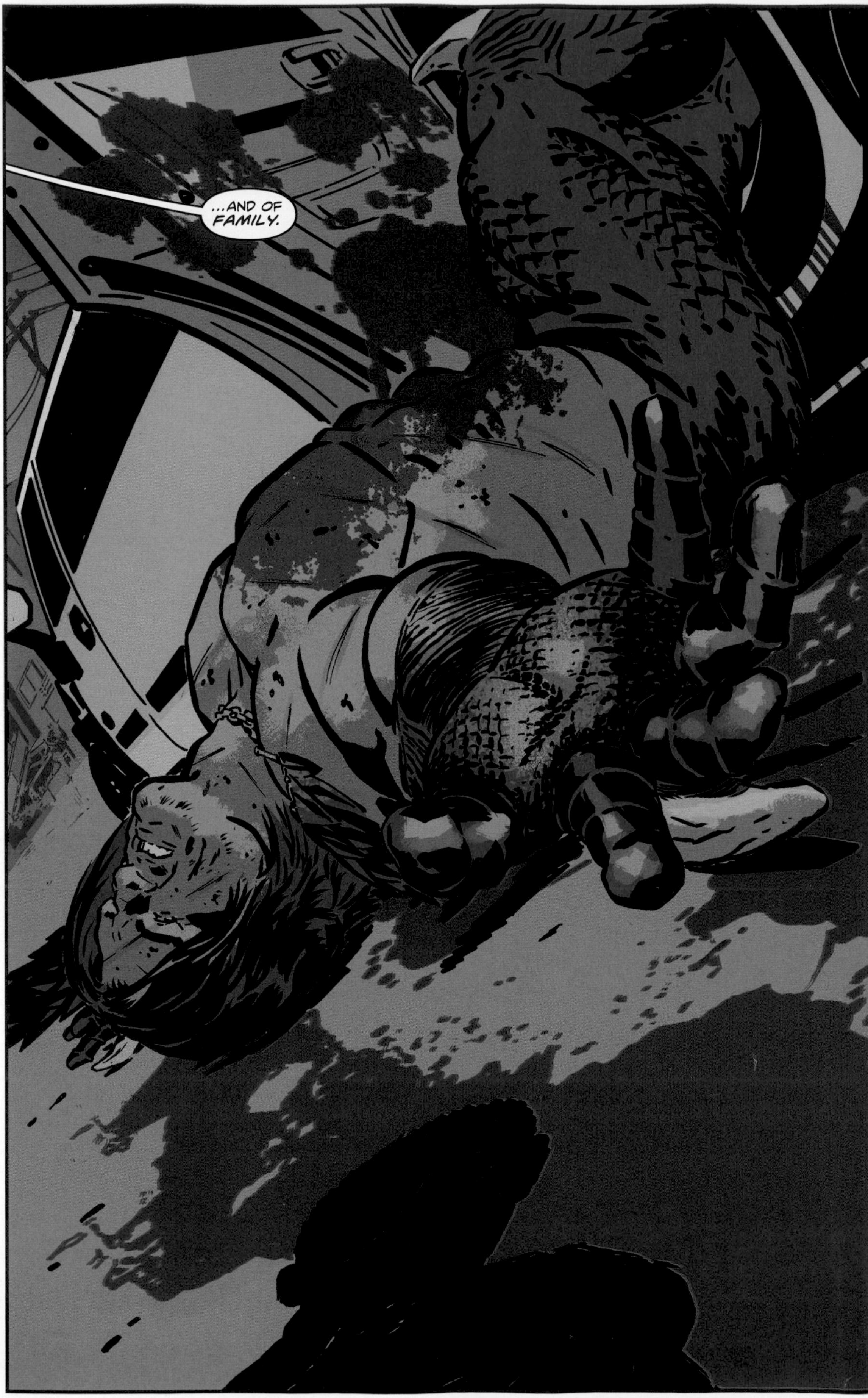
...AND OF FAMILY.

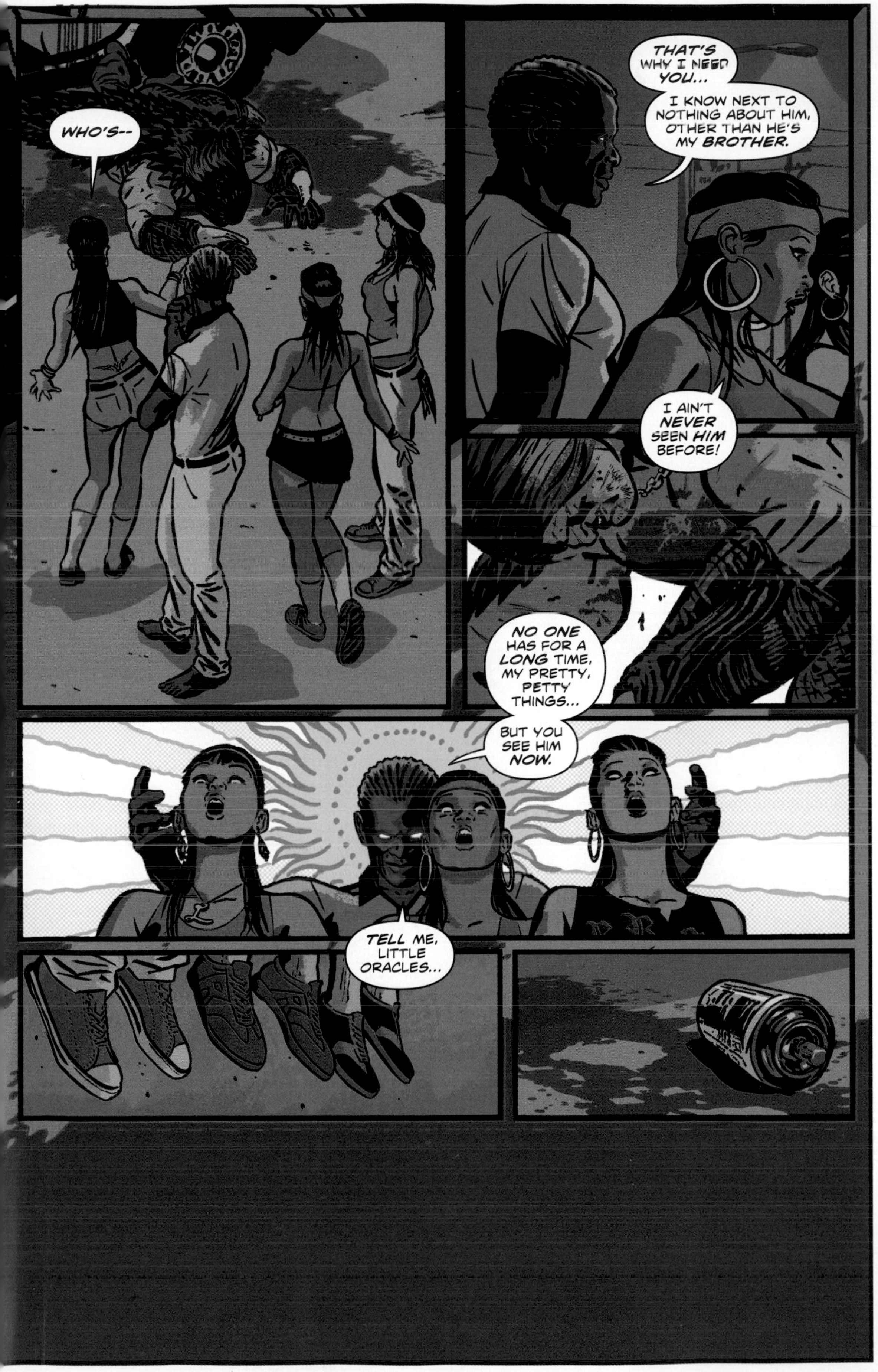
WHO'S--
THAT'S WHY I NEED YOU...
I KNOW NEXT TO NOTHING ABOUT HIM, OTHER THAN HE'S MY BROTHER.
I AIN'T NEVER SEEN HIM BEFORE!
NO ONE HAS FOR A LONG TIME, MY PRETTY, PETTY THINGS...
BUT YOU SEE HIM NOW.
TELL ME, LITTLE ORACLES...

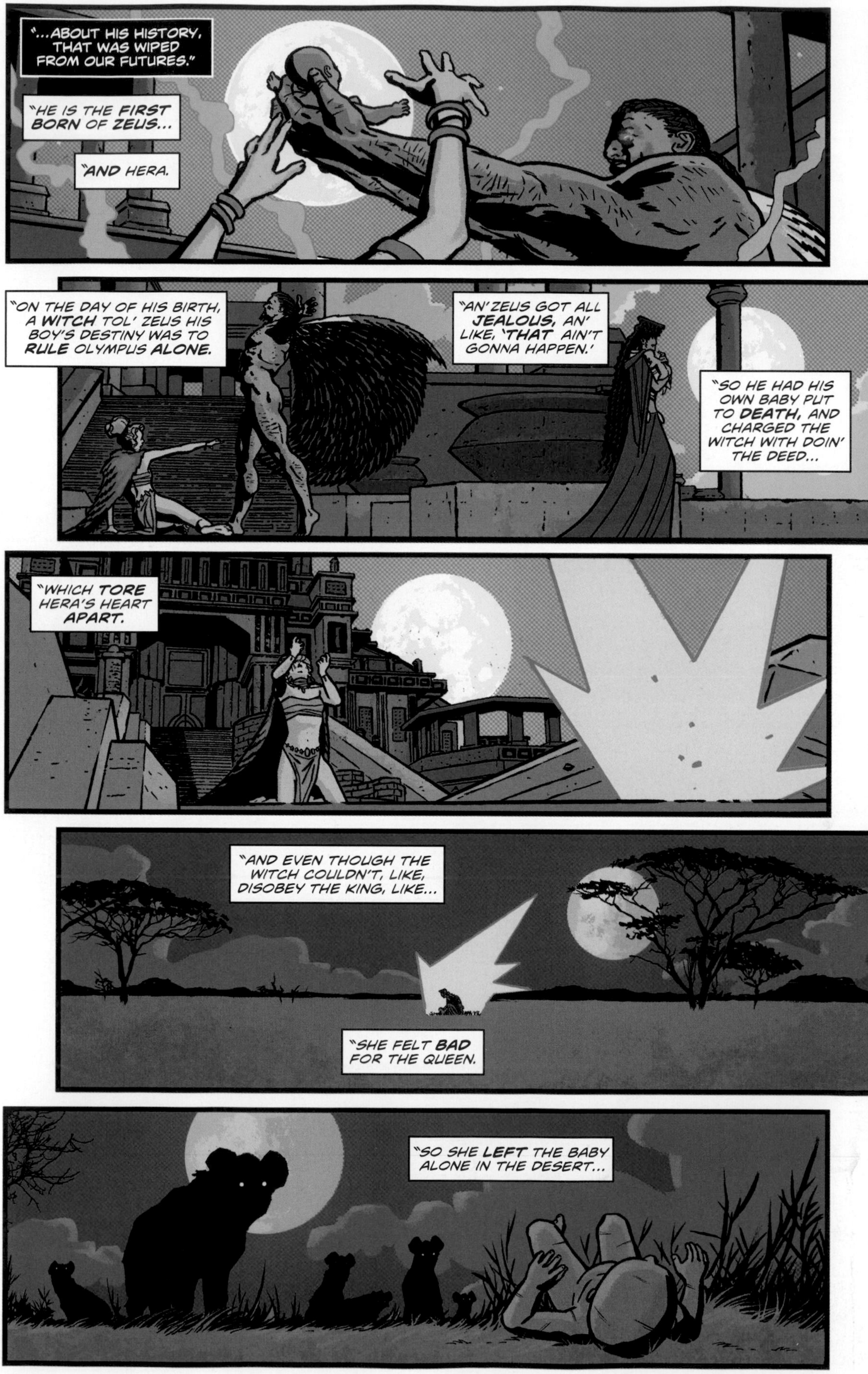
"...ABOUT HIS HISTORY, THAT WAS WIPED FROM OUR FUTURES."
"HE IS THE FIRST BORN OF ZEUS...
"AND HERA.
"ON THE DAY OF HIS BIRTH, A WITCH TOL' ZEUS HIS BOY'S DESTINY WAS TO RULE OLYMPUS ALONE.
"AN' ZEUS GOT ALL JEALOUS, AN' LIKE, 'THAT AIN'T GONNA HAPPEN.'
"SO HE HAD HIS OWN BABY PUT TO DEATH, AND CHARGED THE WITCH WITH DOIN' THE DEED...
"WHICH TORE HERA'S HEART APART.
"AND EVEN THOUGH THE WITCH COULDN'T, LIKE, DISOBEY THE KING, LIKE...
"SHE FELT BAD FOR THE QUEEN.
"SO SHE LEFT THE BABY ALONE IN THE DESERT...

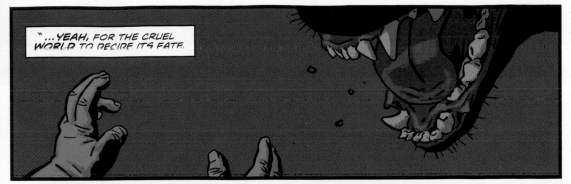

"...YEAH, FOR THE CRUEL WORLD TO DECIDE ITS FATE.

"LIFE'S A *BITCH*.

"AND THE FIRST BORN *OWES* HIS LIFE TO ONE.

"HIS CRIES DIDN'T FALL ONLY ON *HUNGRY* EARS.

"BUT ON A *MOTHER'S*.

"GAME *OVER*.

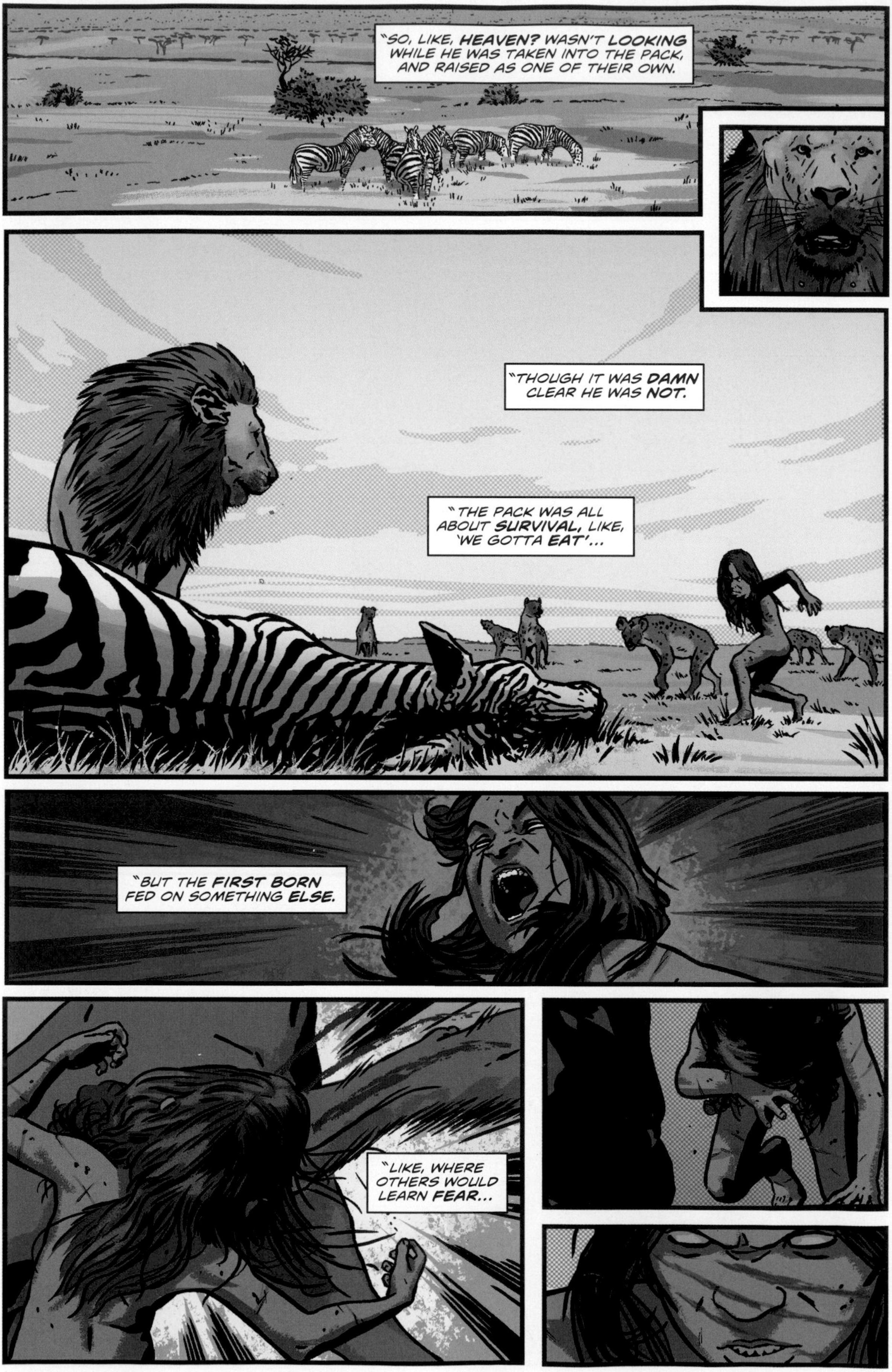
"SO, LIKE, HEAVEN? WASN'T LOOKING WHILE HE WAS TAKEN INTO THE PACK, AND RAISED AS ONE OF THEIR OWN.
"THOUGH IT WAS DAMN CLEAR HE WAS NOT.
"THE PACK WAS ALL ABOUT SURVIVAL, LIKE, 'WE GOTTA EAT'...
"BUT THE FIRST BORN FED ON SOMETHING ELSE.
"LIKE, WHERE OTHERS WOULD LEARN FEAR...

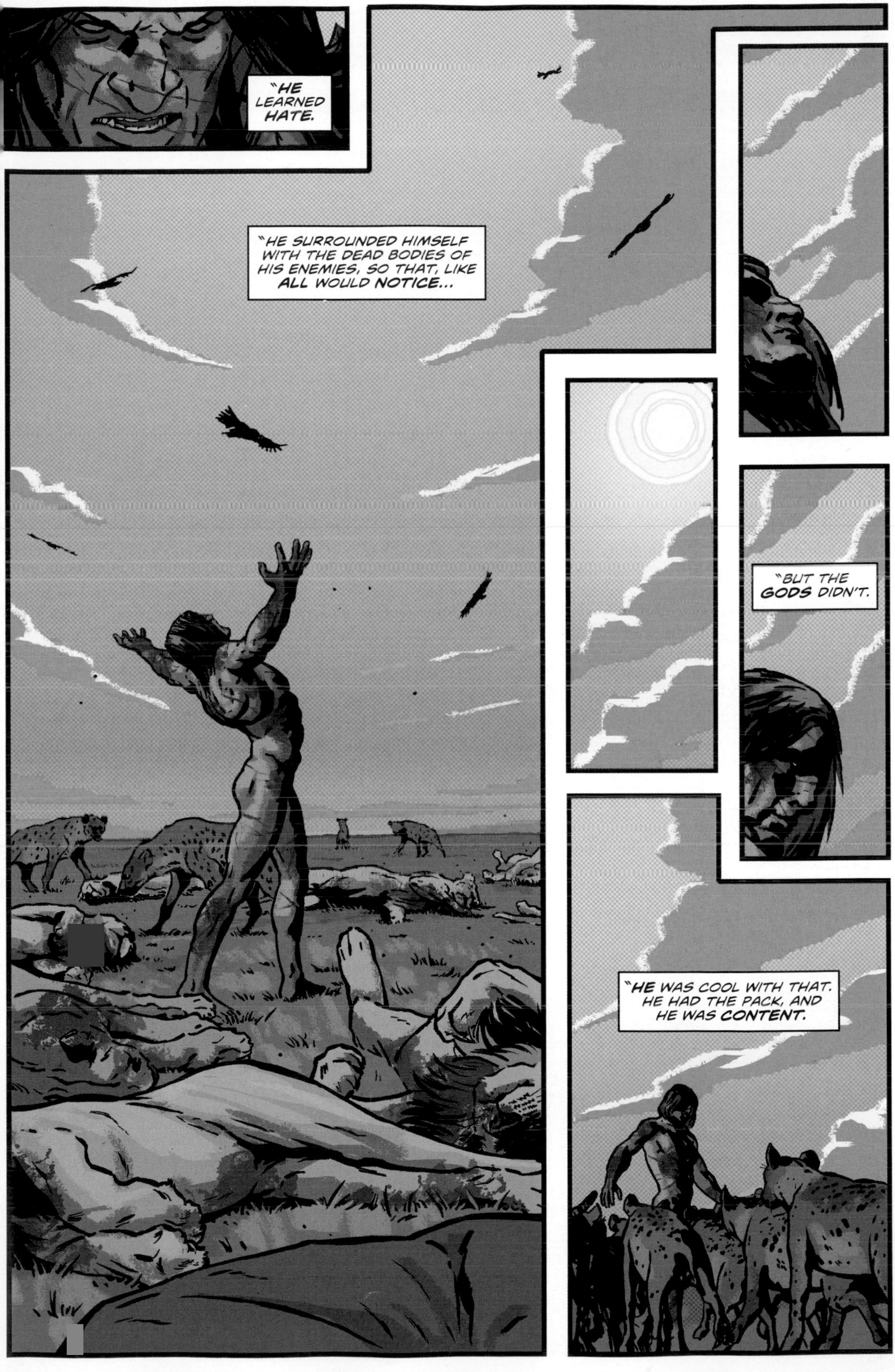
"HE LEARNED HATE.
"HE SURROUNDED HIMSELF WITH THE DEAD BODIES OF HIS ENEMIES, SO THAT, LIKE ALL WOULD NOTICE...
"BUT THE GODS DIDN'T.
"HE WAS COOL WITH THAT. HE HAD THE PACK, AND HE WAS CONTENT.

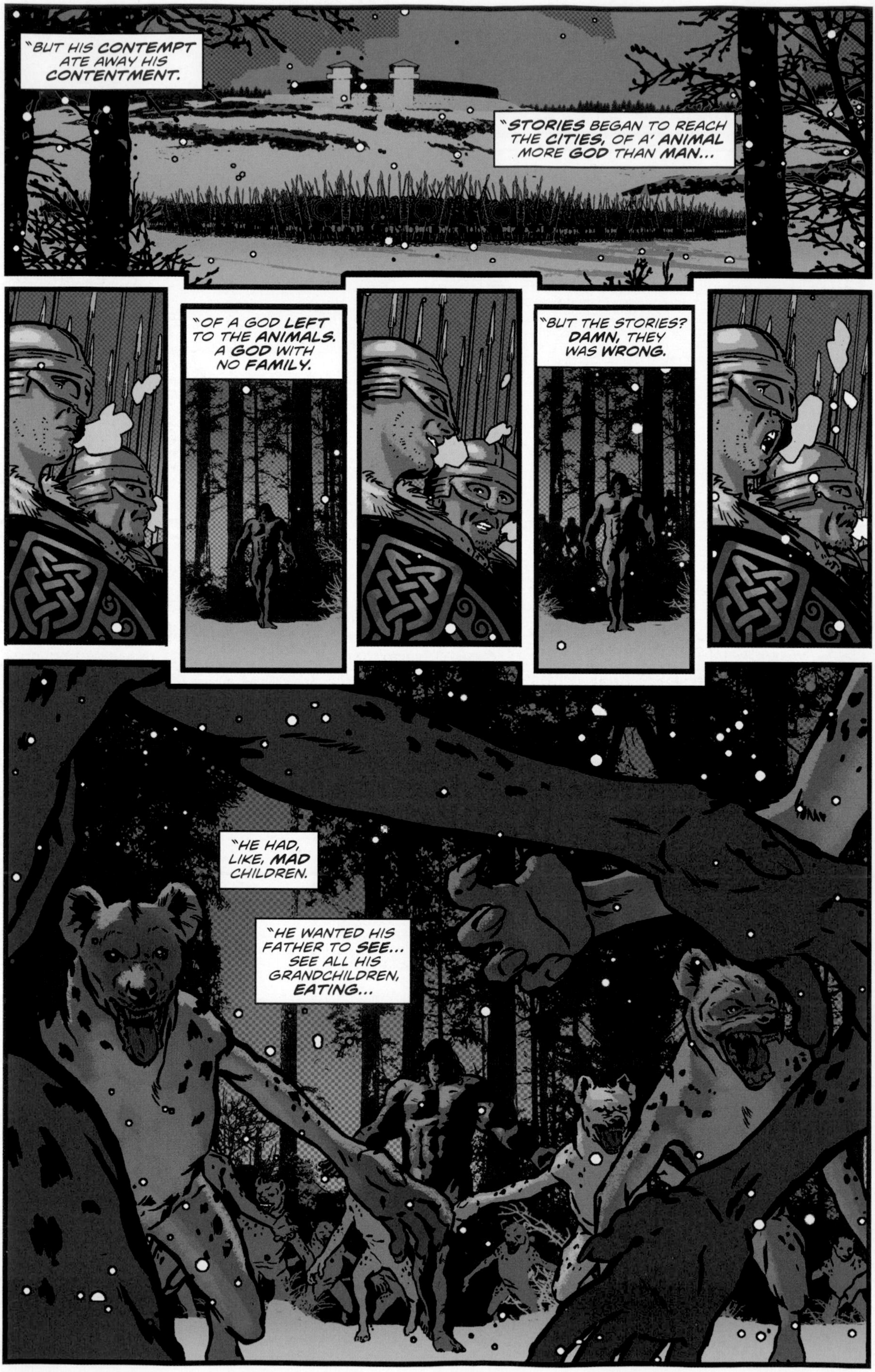
"BUT HIS CONTEMPT ATE AWAY HIS CONTENTMENT.
"STORIES BEGAN TO REACH THE CITIES, OF A' ANIMAL MORE GOD THAN MAN...
"OF A GOD LEFT TO THE ANIMALS. A GOD WITH NO FAMILY.
"BUT THE STORIES? DAMN, THEY WAS WRONG.
"HE HAD, LIKE, MAD CHILDREN.
"HE WANTED HIS FATHER TO SEE... SEE ALL HIS GRANDCHILDREN, EATING...

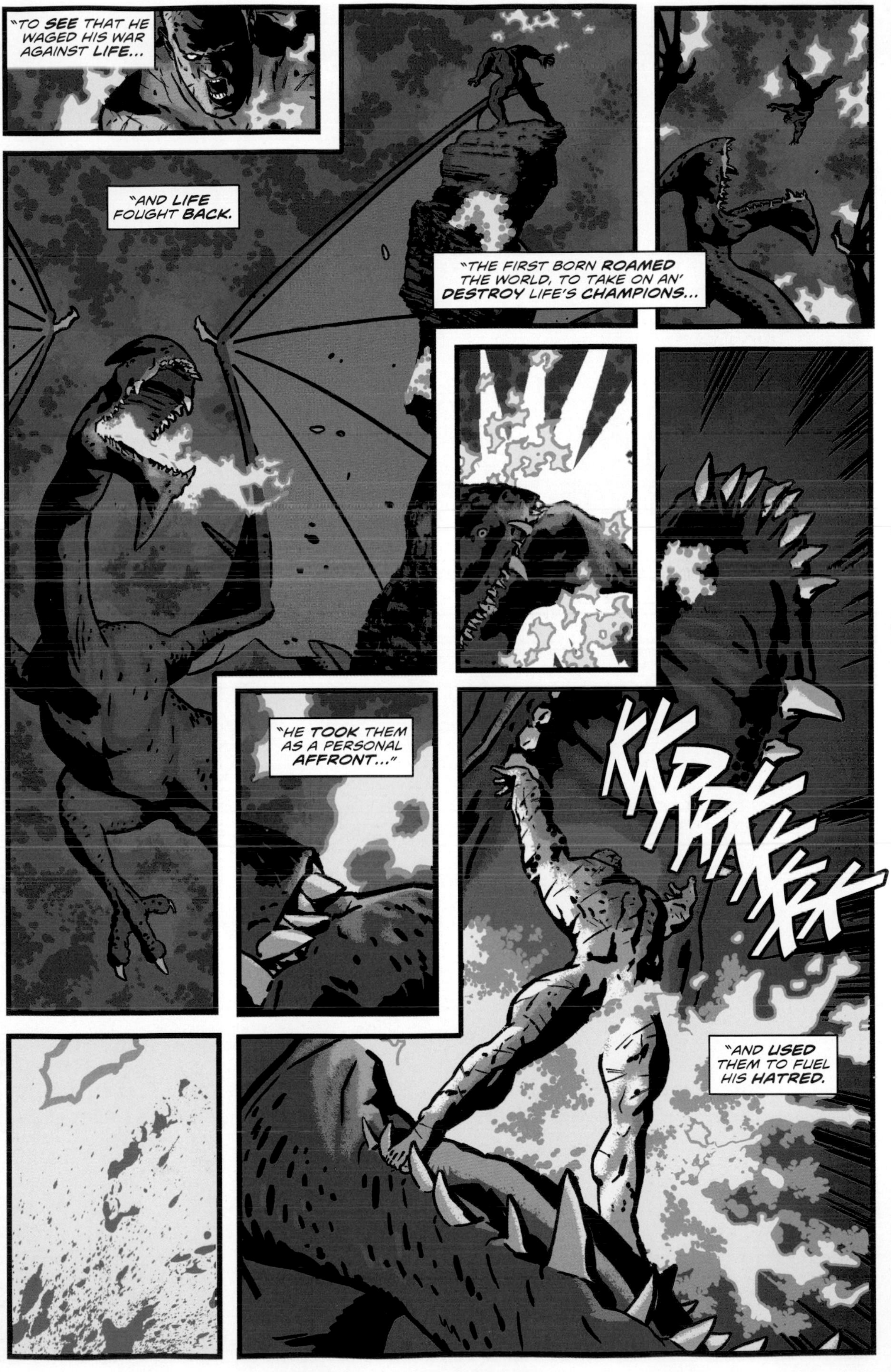
"TO SEE THAT HE WAGED HIS WAR AGAINST LIFE...
"AND LIFE FOUGHT BACK.
"THE FIRST BORN ROAMED THE WORLD, TO TAKE ON AN' DESTROY LIFE'S CHAMPIONS...
"HE TOOK THEM AS A PERSONAL AFFRONT..."
KKRRKKKK
"AND USED THEM TO FUEL HIS HATRED.

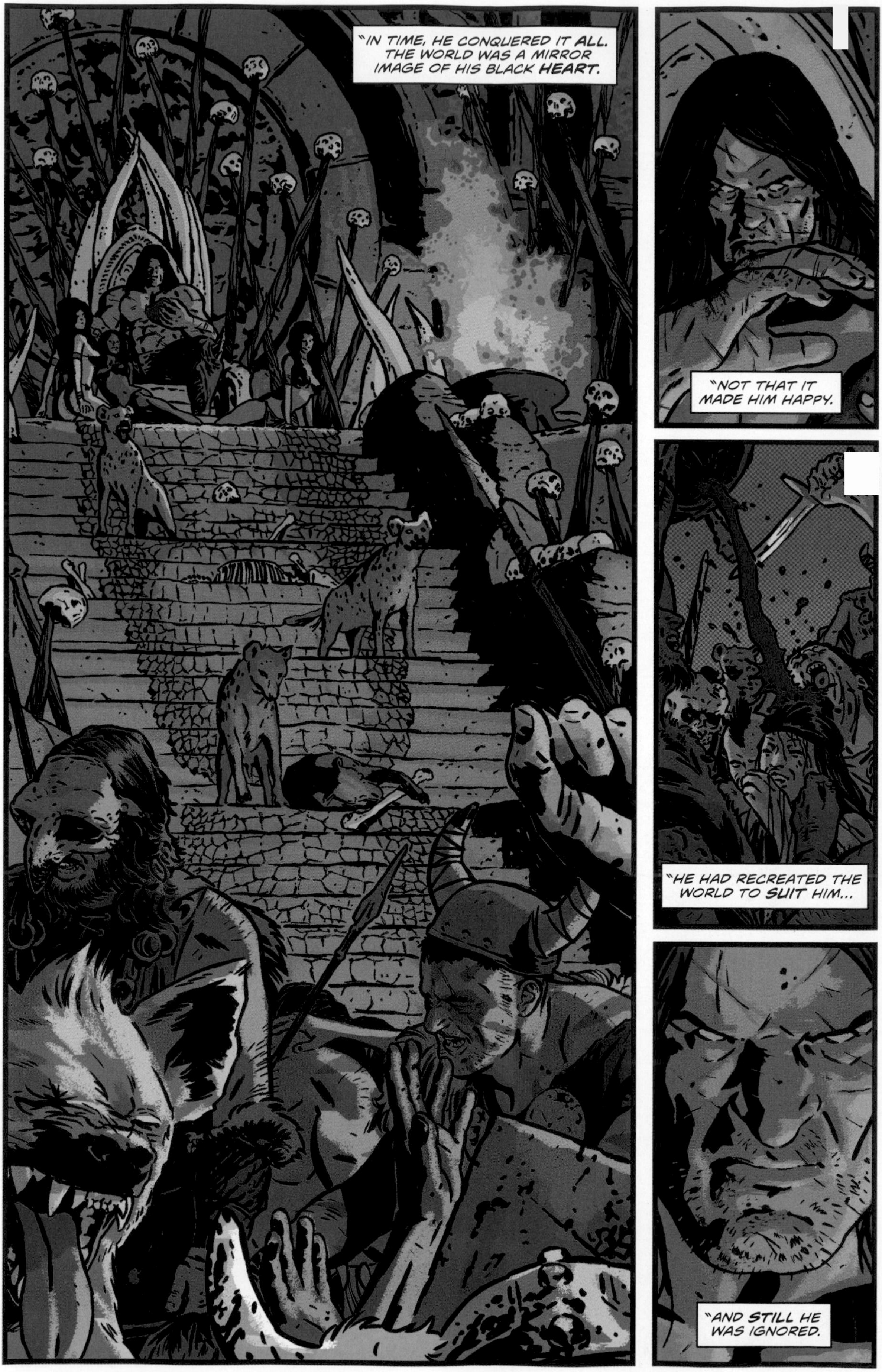
"IN TIME, HE CONQUERED IT ALL. THE WORLD WAS A MIRROR IMAGE OF HIS BLACK HEART.
"NOT THAT IT MADE HIM HAPPY.
"HE HAD RECREATED THE WORLD TO SUIT HIM...
"AND STILL HE WAS IGNORED.

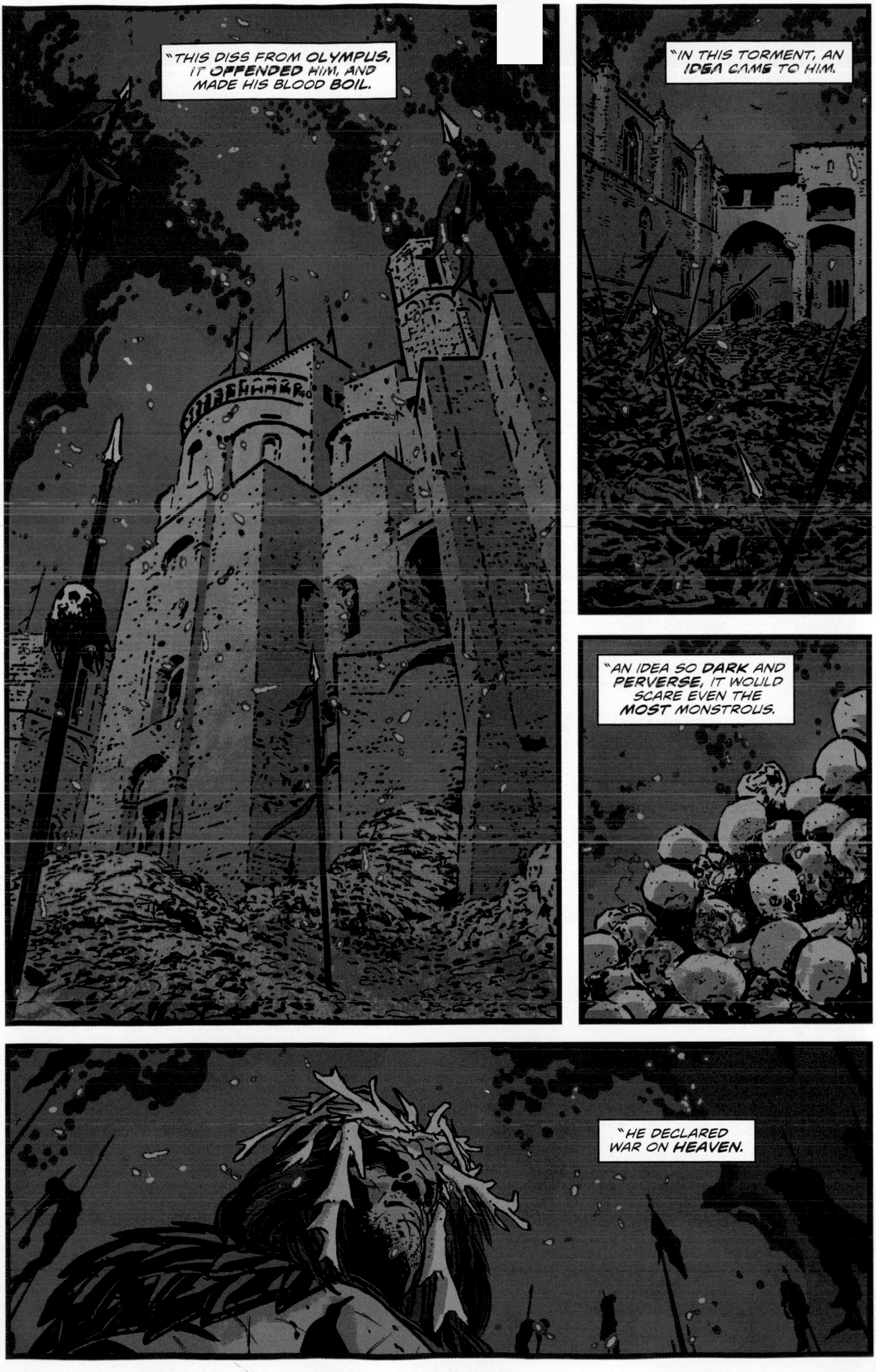
"THIS DISS FROM OLYMPUS, IT OFFENDED HIM, AND MADE HIS BLOOD BOIL.
"IN THIS TORMENT, AN IDEA CAME TO HIM.
"AN IDEA SO DARK AND PERVERSE, IT WOULD SCARE EVEN THE MOST MONSTROUS.
"HE DECLARED WAR ON HEAVEN.

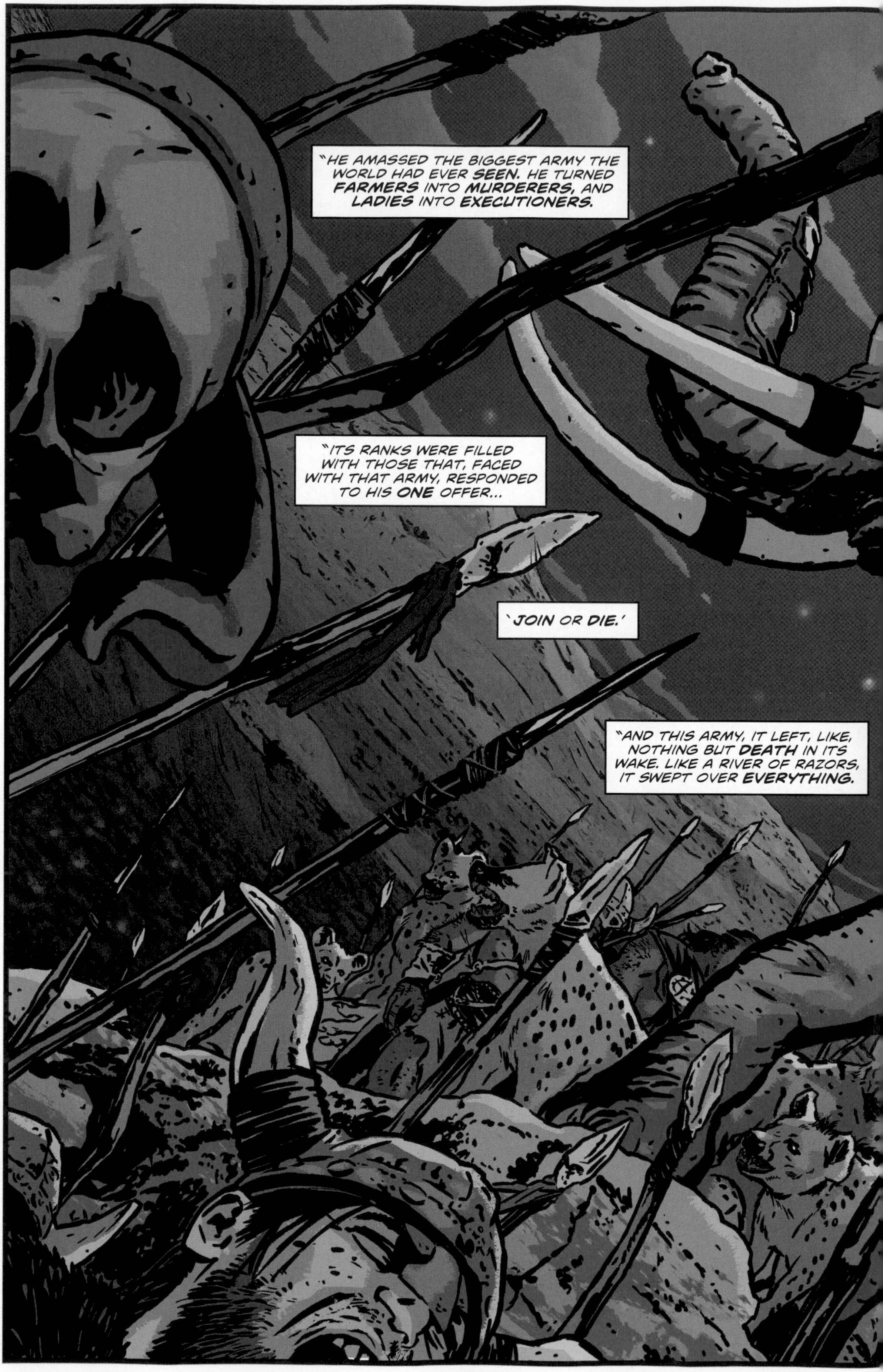
"HE AMASSED THE BIGGEST ARMY THE WORLD HAD EVER SEEN. HE TURNED FARMERS INTO MURDERERS, AND LADIES INTO EXECUTIONERS.
"ITS RANKS WERE FILLED WITH THOSE THAT, FACED WITH THAT ARMY, RESPONDED TO HIS ONE OFFER...
'JOIN OR DIE.'
"AND THIS ARMY, IT LEFT, LIKE, NOTHING BUT DEATH IN ITS WAKE. LIKE A RIVER OF RAZORS, IT SWEPT OVER EVERYTHING.

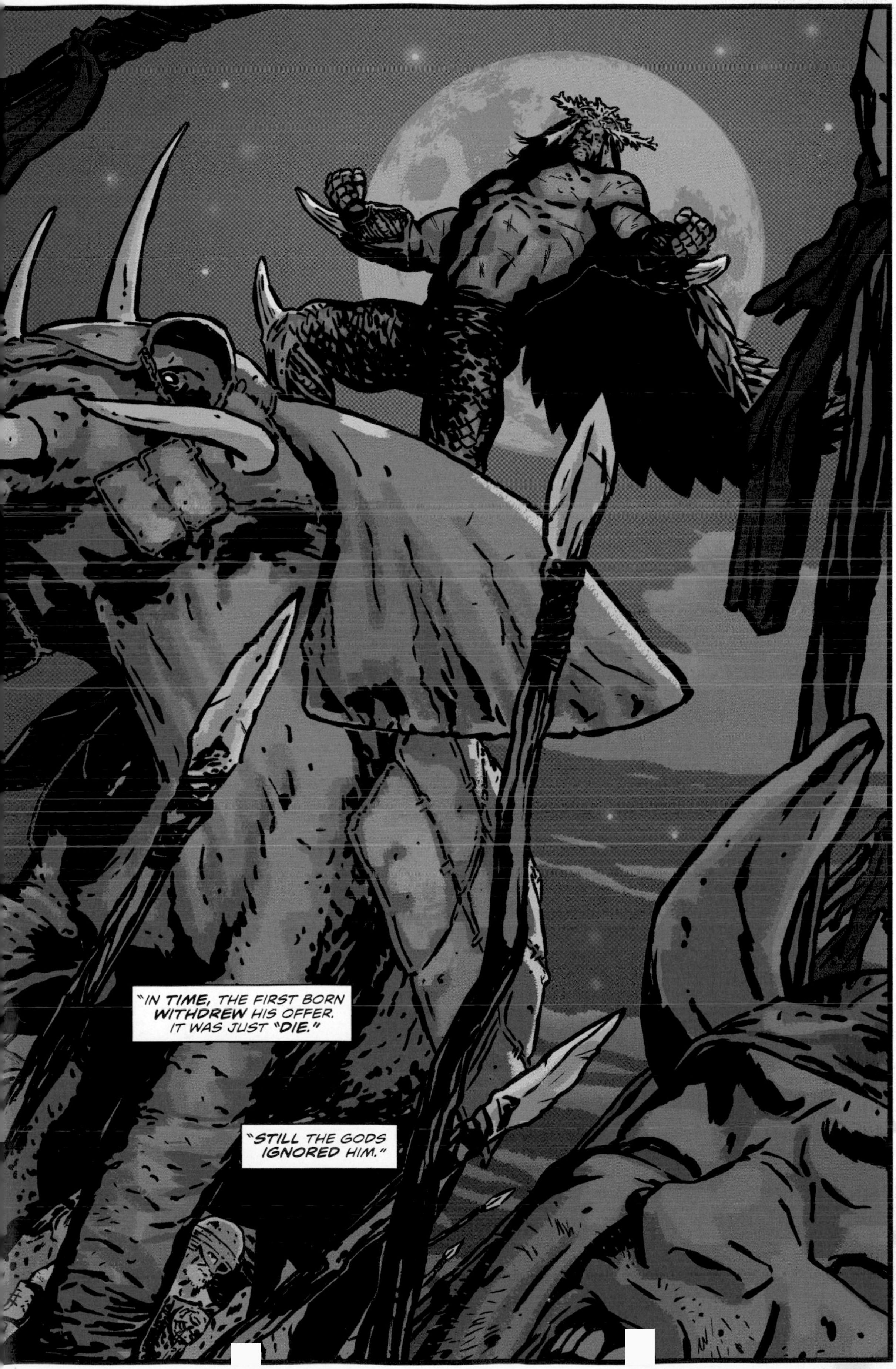
"IN TIME, THE FIRST BORN WITHDREW HIS OFFER. IT WAS JUST "DIE."
"STILL THE GODS IGNORED HIM."

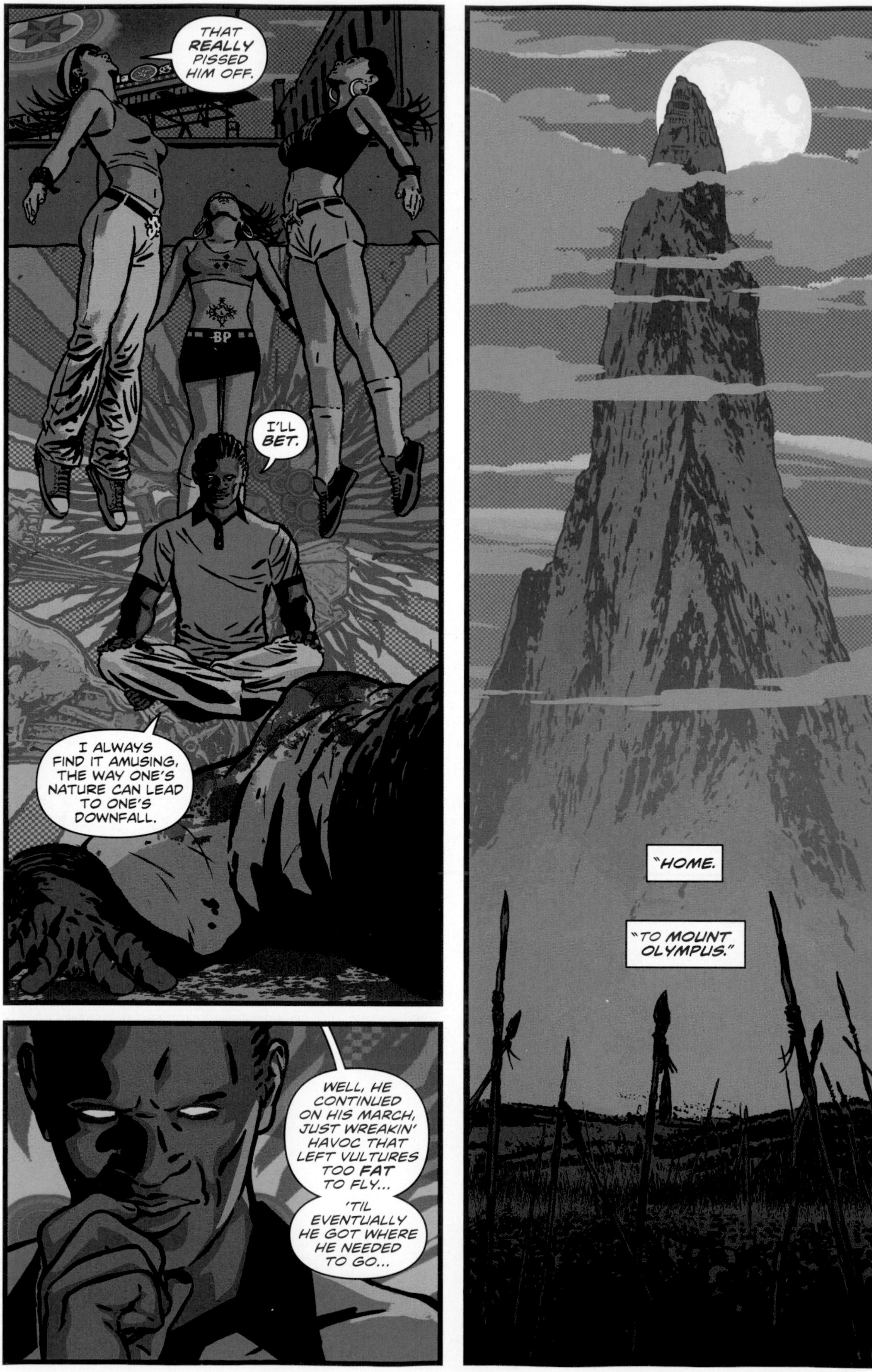
THAT REALLY PISSED HIM OFF.
I'LL BET.
I ALWAYS FIND IT AMUSING, THE WAY ONE'S NATURE CAN LEAD TO ONE'S DOWNFALL.
WELL, HE CONTINUED ON HIS MARCH, JUST WREAKIN' HAVOC THAT LEFT VULTURES TOO FAT TO FLY...
'TIL EVENTUALLY HE GOT WHERE HE NEEDED TO GO...
"HOME.
"TO MOUNT OLYMPUS."

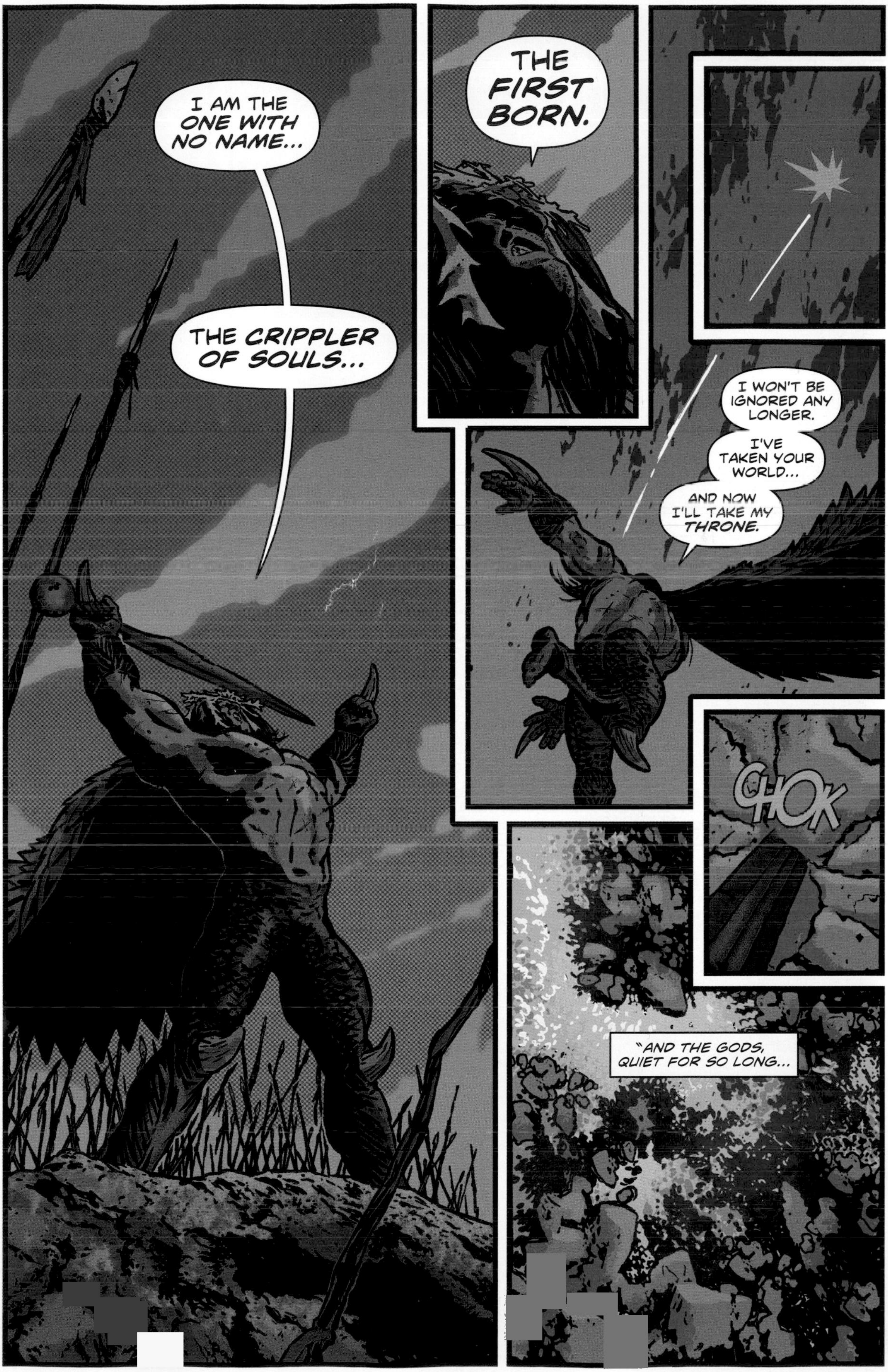

I AM THE ONE WITH NO NAME...
THE CRIPPLER OF SOULS...
THE FIRST BORN.
I WON'T BE IGNORED ANY LONGER.
I'VE TAKEN YOUR WORLD...
AND NOW I'LL TAKE MY THRONE.
CHOK
"AND THE GODS, QUIET FOR SO LONG...

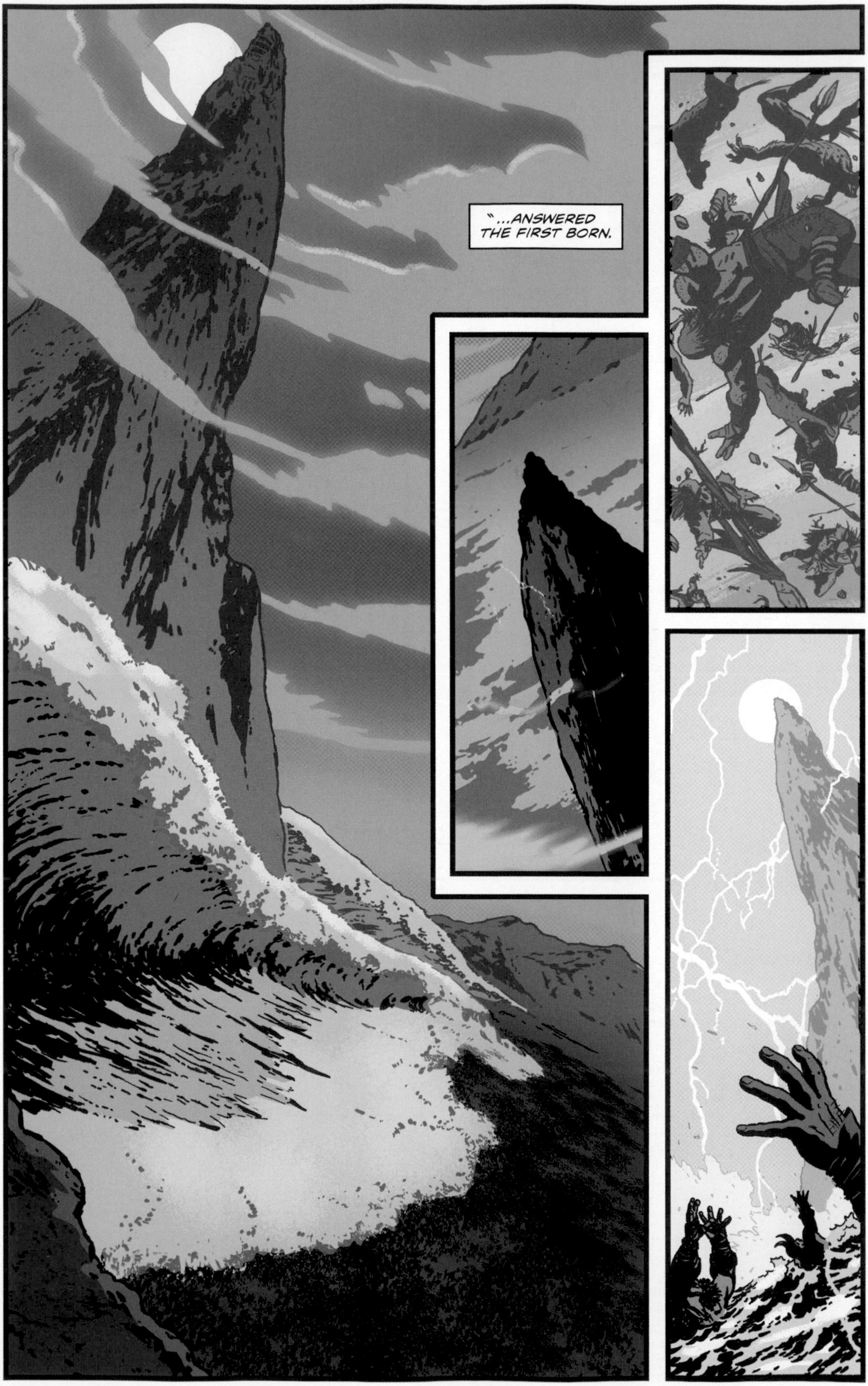
"...ANSWERED THE FIRST BORN.

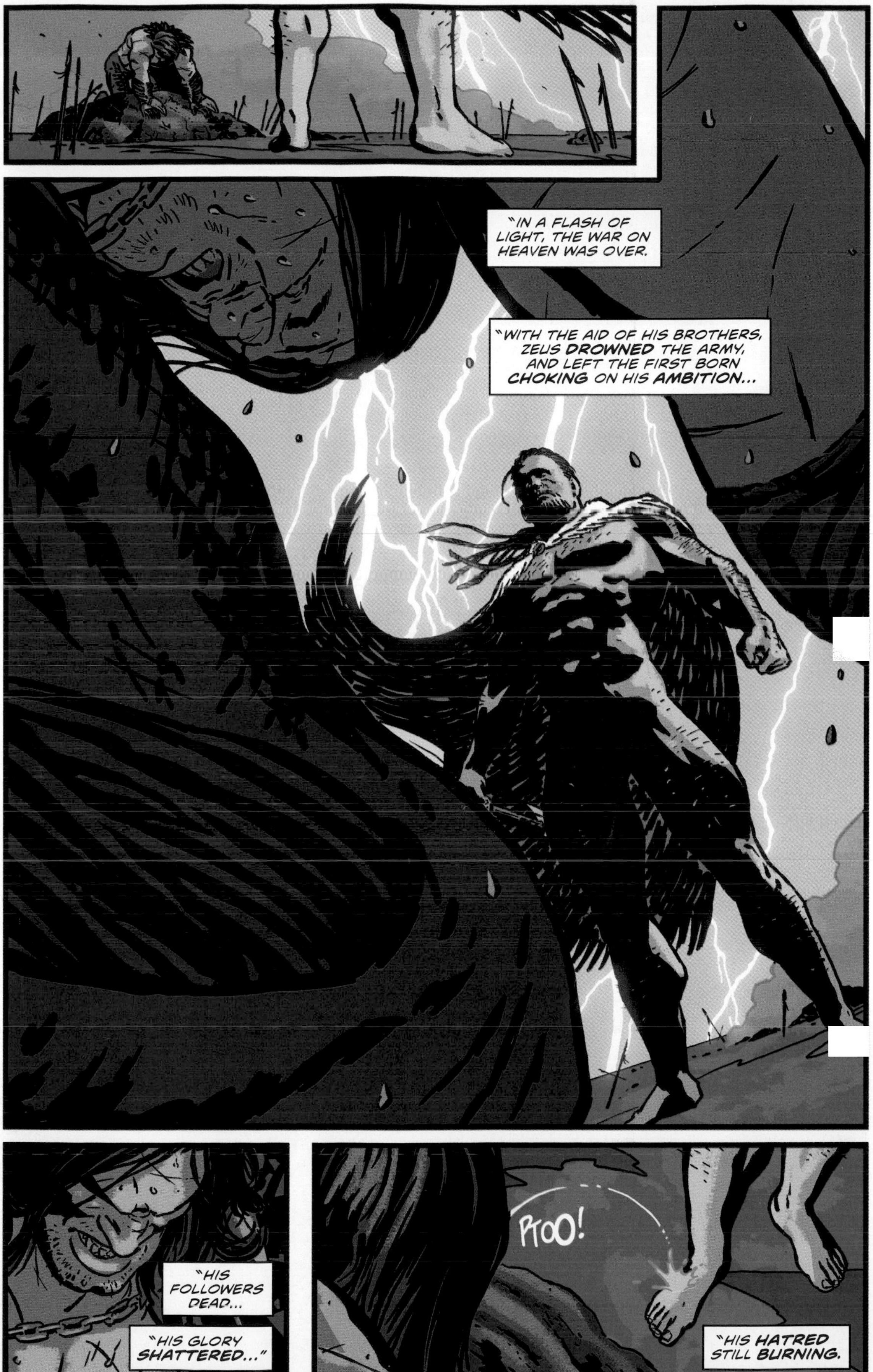
"IN A FLASH OF LIGHT, THE WAR ON HEAVEN WAS OVER.
"WITH THE AID OF HIS BROTHERS, ZEUS **DROWNED** THE ARMY, AND LEFT THE FIRST BORN **CHOKING** ON HIS **AMBITION...**
"HIS FOLLOWERS DEAD...
"HIS GLORY **SHATTERED...**"
PTOO!
"HIS **HATRED** STILL **BURNING.**

"IN THE FACE OF SUCH HATRED, ZEUS WAS ALL, '**HUH?**'

"...LIKE, HE WAS SEEING SOMETHING HE'D NEVER SEEN BEFORE. KINDA BLEW HIS MIND.

"SO RATHER THAN KILL HIS SON, HE **CONDEMNED** HIM. WIPED HIS EXISTENCE FROM HISTORY.

"HE TOOK THE FIRST BORN'S PRIDE-- HIS DRAGON SKIN AN' STUFF-- AND SPLIT IT WITH HIS BROTHERS. LEFT HIM ONLY WITH HIS HATE...

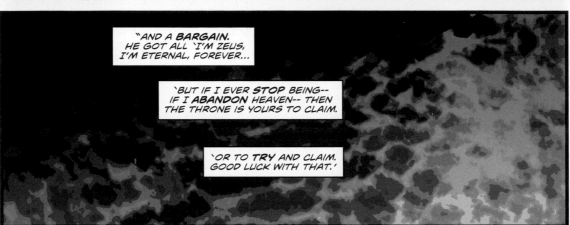

"AND A **BARGAIN**. HE GOT ALL '**I'M ZEUS, I'M ETERNAL, FOREVER**...

'BUT IF I EVER **STOP** BEING-- IF I **ABANDON** HEAVEN-- THEN THE THRONE IS YOURS TO CLAIM.

'OR TO **TRY** AND CLAIM. GOOD LUCK WITH THAT.'

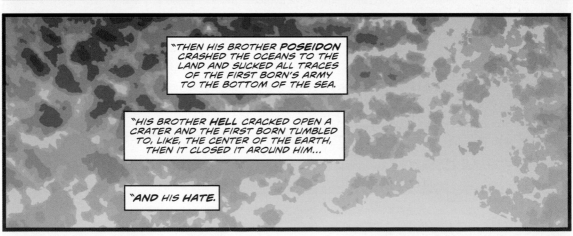

"THEN HIS BROTHER **POSEIDON** CRASHED THE OCEANS TO THE LAND AND SUCKED ALL TRACES OF THE FIRST BORN'S ARMY TO THE BOTTOM OF THE SEA.

"HIS BROTHER **HELL** CRACKED OPEN A CRATER AND THE FIRST BORN TUMBLED TO, LIKE, THE CENTER OF THE EARTH, THEN IT CLOSED IT AROUND HIM...

"**AND HIS HATE.**

"**AND HIS BARGAIN.**

"**AND THAT WAS ENOUGH.**"

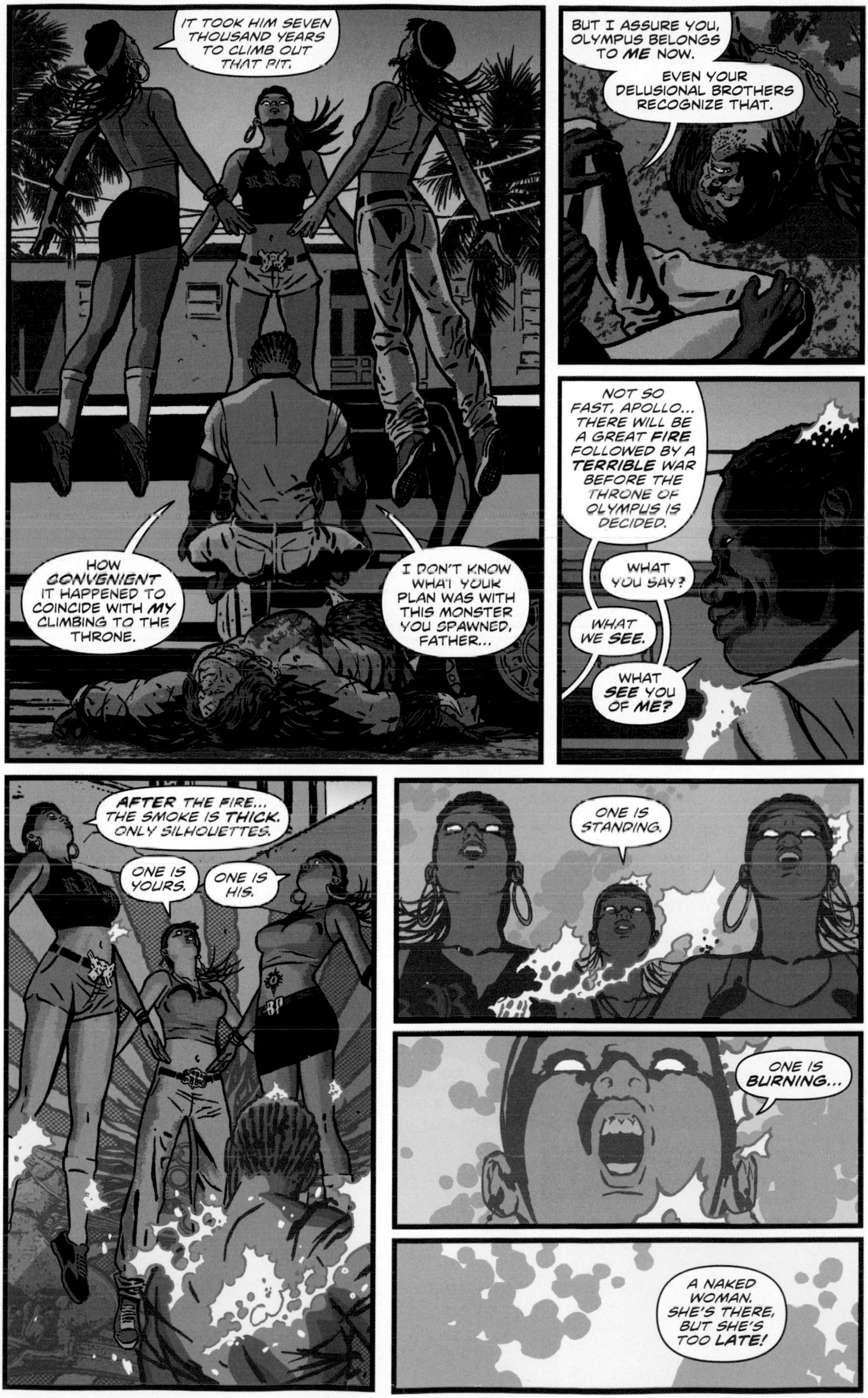
IT TOOK HIM SEVEN THOUSAND YEARS TO CLIMB OUT THAT PIT.
HOW CONVENIENT IT HAPPENED TO COINCIDE WITH MY CLIMBING TO THE THRONE.
I DON'T KNOW WHAT YOUR PLAN WAS WITH THIS MONSTER YOU SPAWNED, FATHER...
BUT I ASSURE YOU, OLYMPUS BELONGS TO ME NOW.
EVEN YOUR DELUSIONAL BROTHERS RECOGNIZE THAT.
NOT SO FAST, APOLLO... THERE WILL BE A GREAT FIRE FOLLOWED BY A TERRIBLE WAR BEFORE THE THRONE OF OLYMPUS IS DECIDED.
WHAT YOU SAY?
WHAT WE SEE.
WHAT SEE YOU OF ME?
AFTER THE FIRE... THE SMOKE IS THICK. ONLY SILHOUETTES.
ONE IS YOURS.
ONE IS HIS.
ONE IS STANDING.
ONE IS BURNING...
A NAKED WOMAN. SHE'S THERE, BUT SHE'S TOO LATE!

FOR?

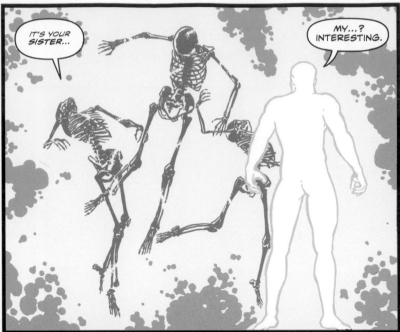

IT'S YOUR SISTER...

MY...? INTERESTING.

YOU AND I, FIRST BORN, WE'RE GOING TO GET TO KNOW EACH OTHER, I THINK.

SO YOUR LIFE, IT'S BEEN NOTHING BUT TORTURE?

WELL, I HAVE NEWS FOR YOU...

"IT'S JUST GETTING STARTED."

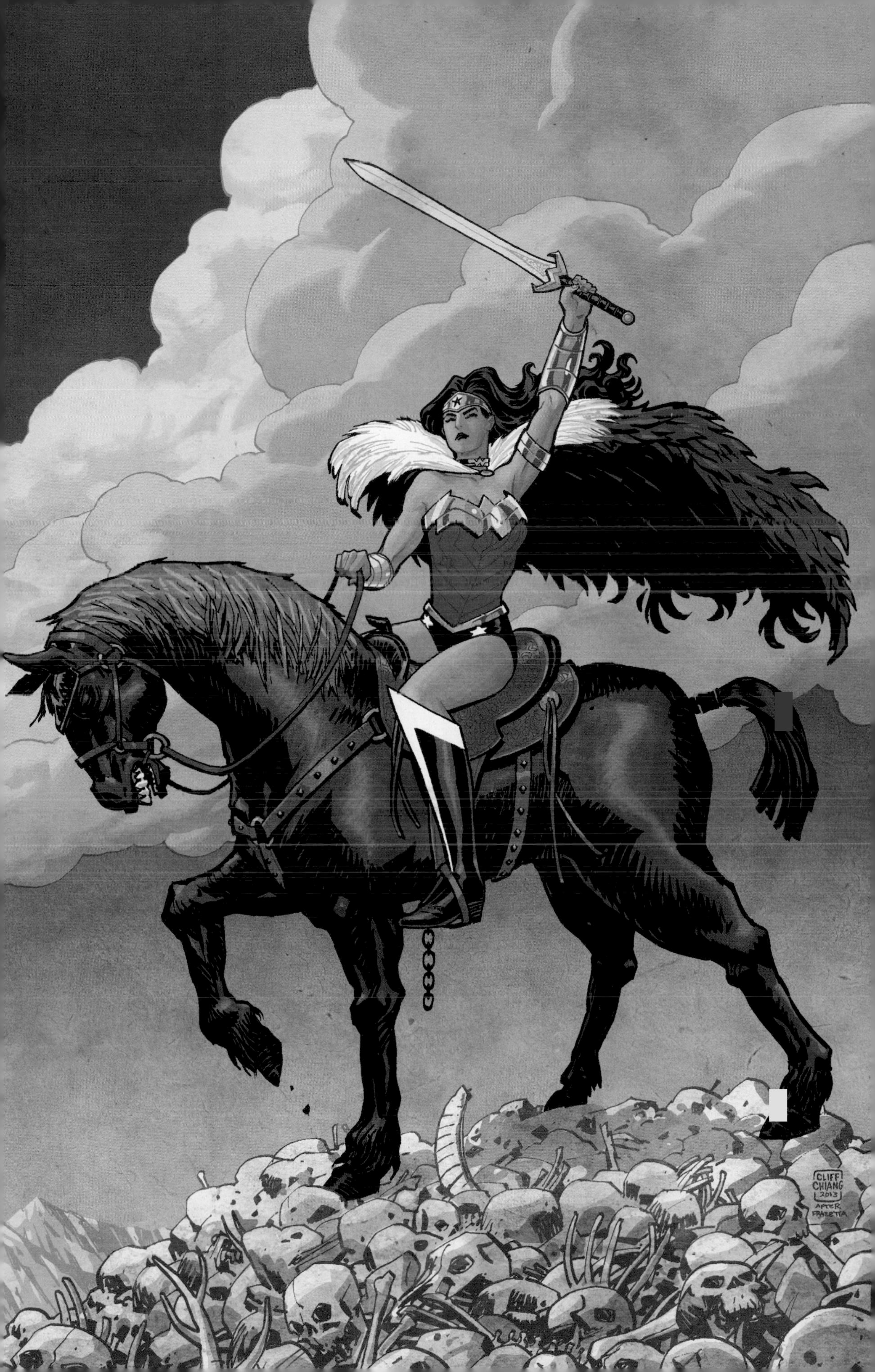
CLIFF CHIANG 2013
AFTER FRAZETTA

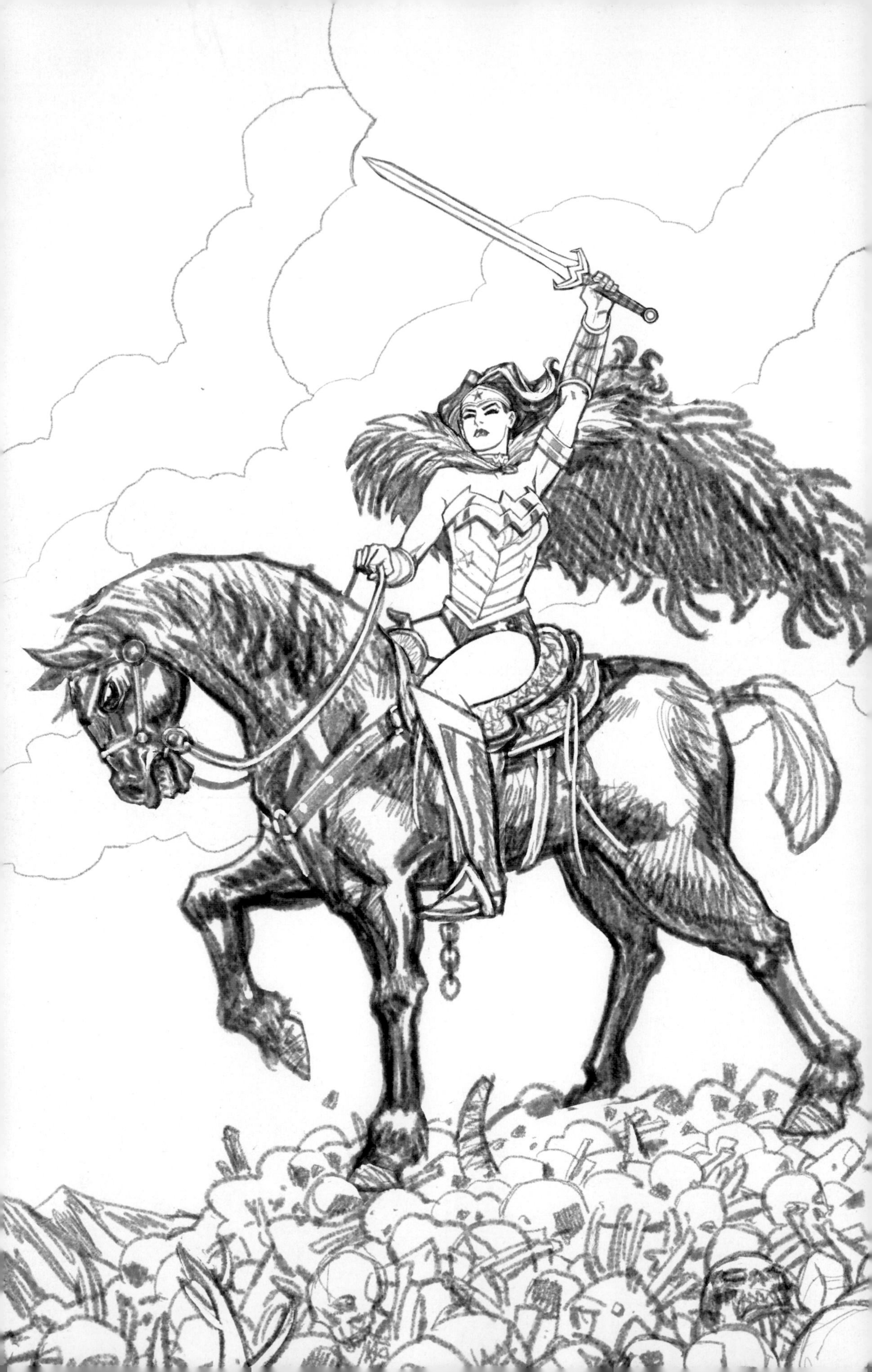

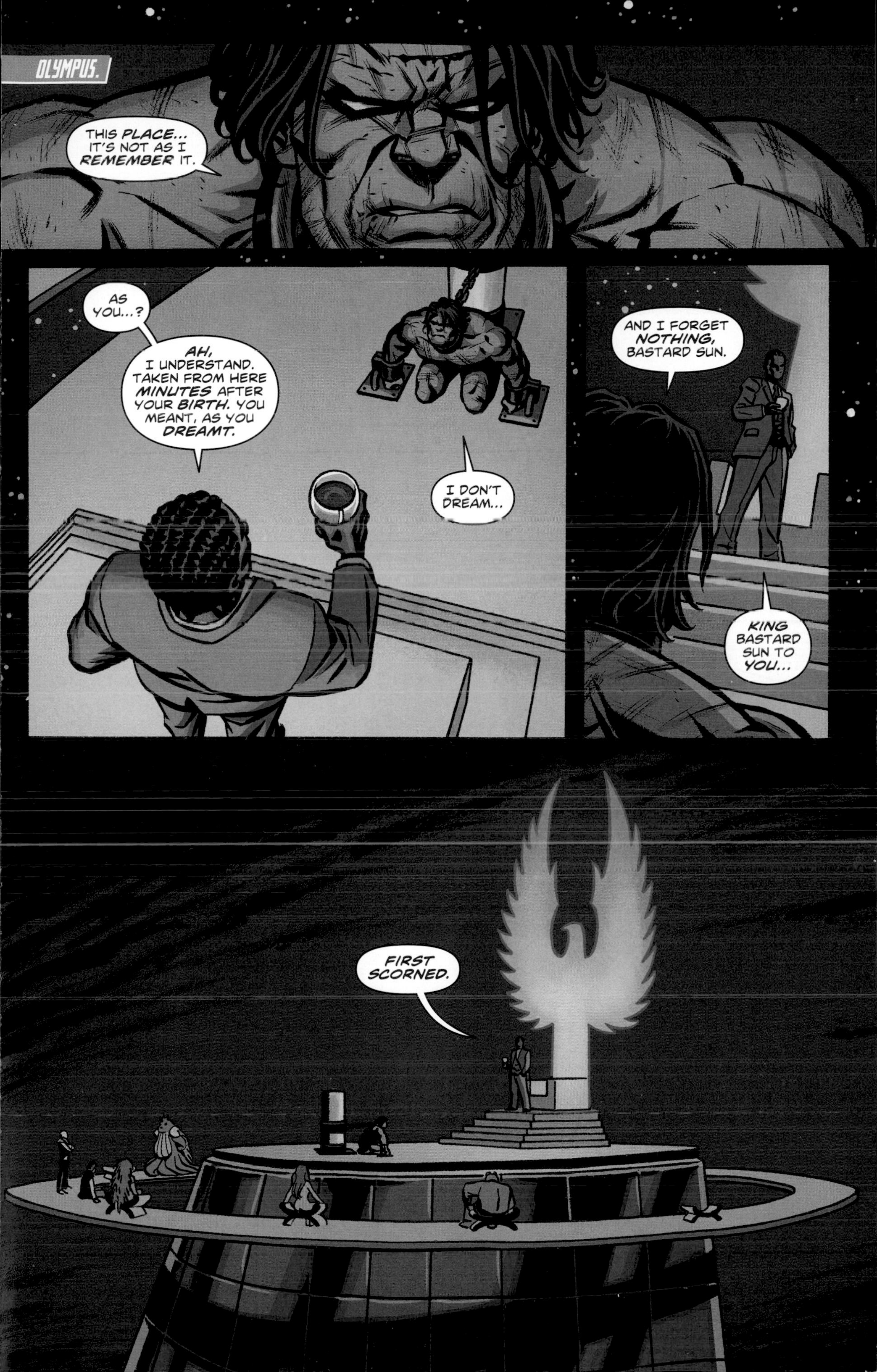
OLYMPUS.
THIS PLACE... IT'S NOT AS I REMEMBER IT.
AS YOU...?
AH, I UNDERSTAND. TAKEN FROM HERE MINUTES AFTER YOUR BIRTH. YOU MEANT, AS YOU DREAMT.
I DON'T DREAM...
AND I FORGET NOTHING, BASTARD SUN.
KING BASTARD SUN TO YOU...
FIRST SCORNED.

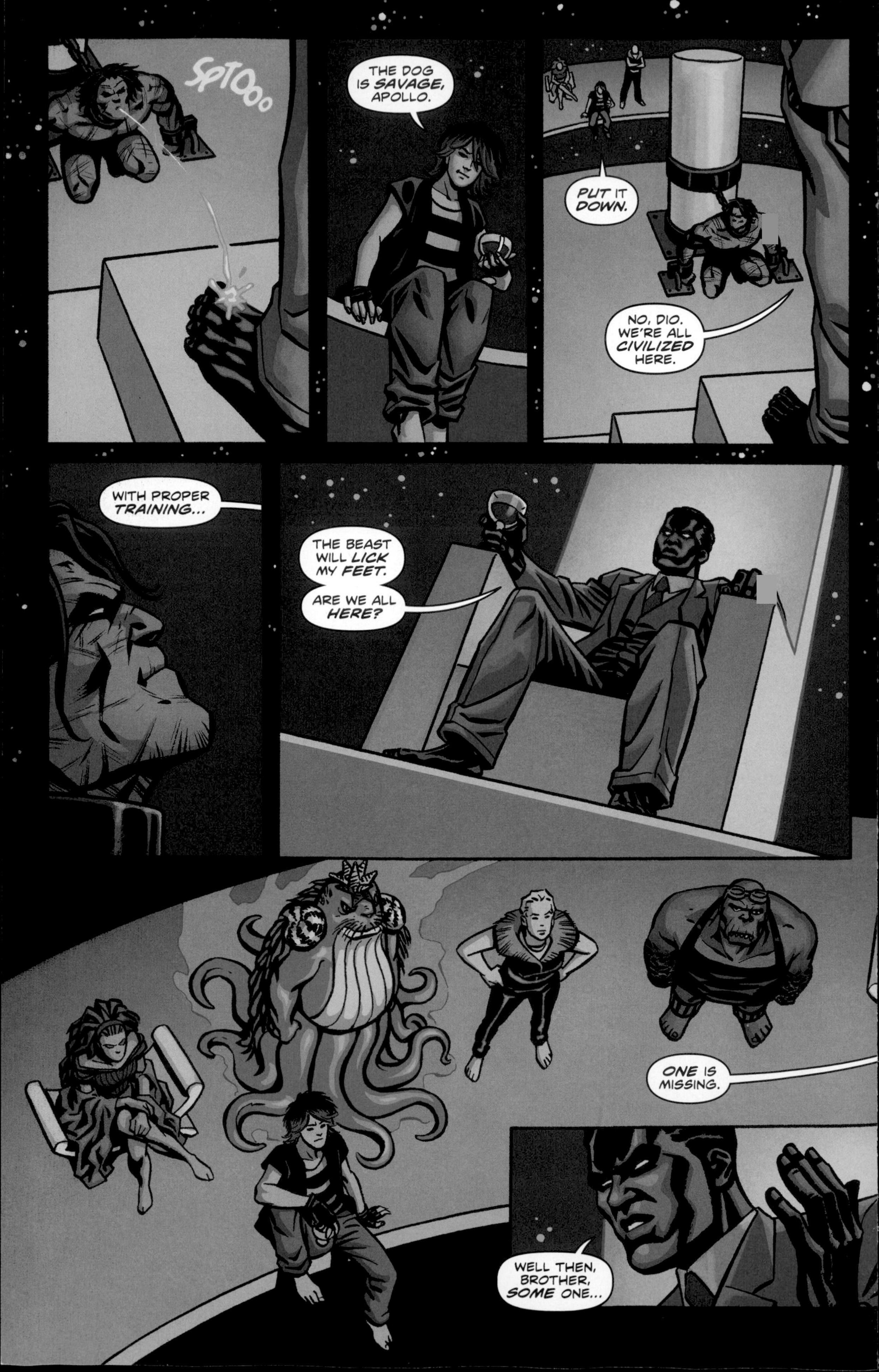
SPTOOO
THE DOG IS SAVAGE, APOLLO.
PUT IT DOWN.
NO, DIO. WE'RE ALL CIVILIZED HERE.
WITH PROPER TRAINING...
THE BEAST WILL LICK MY FEET.
ARE WE ALL HERE?
ONE IS MISSING.
WELL THEN, BROTHER, SOME ONE...

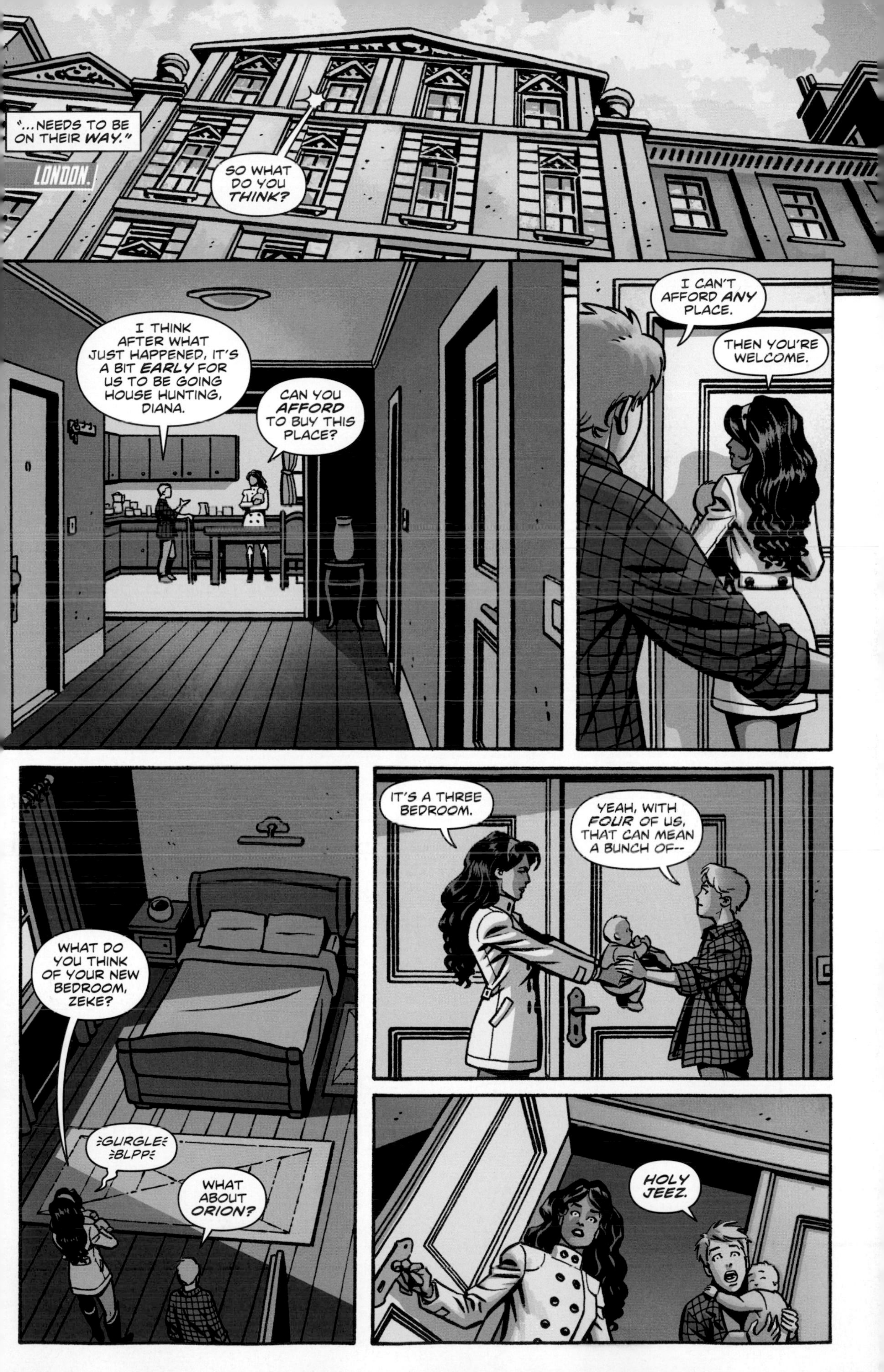
"...NEEDS TO BE ON THEIR WAY."
LONDON.
SO WHAT DO YOU THINK?
I THINK AFTER WHAT JUST HAPPENED, IT'S A BIT EARLY FOR US TO BE GOING HOUSE HUNTING, DIANA.
CAN YOU AFFORD TO BUY THIS PLACE?
I CAN'T AFFORD ANY PLACE.
THEN YOU'RE WELCOME.
WHAT DO YOU THINK OF YOUR NEW BEDROOM, ZEKE?
GURGLE BLPP
WHAT ABOUT ORION?
IT'S A THREE BEDROOM.
YEAH, WITH FOUR OF US, THAT CAN MEAN A BUNCH OF--
HOLY JEEZ.

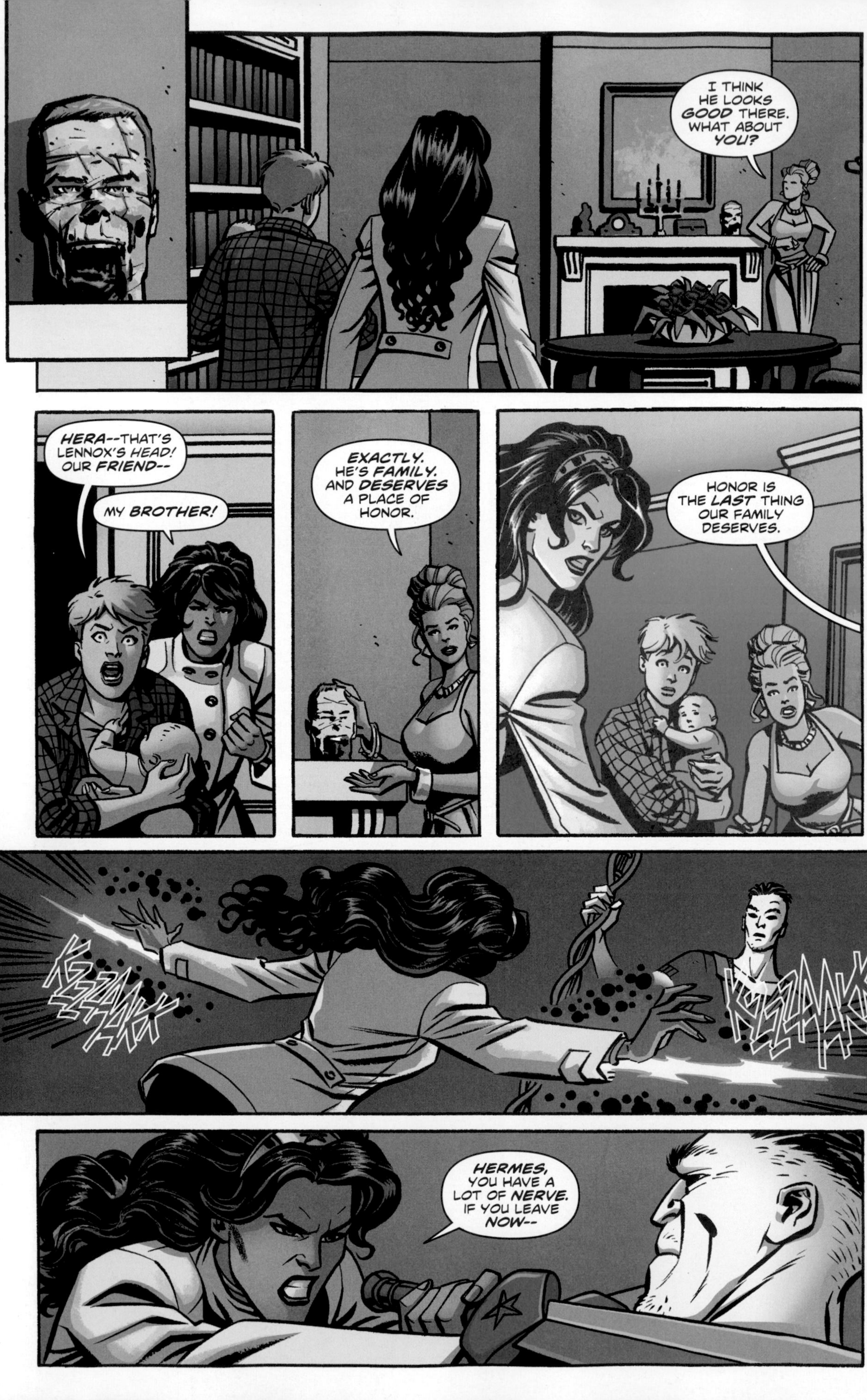
I THINK HE LOOKS GOOD THERE. WHAT ABOUT YOU?
HERA--THAT'S LENNOX'S HEAD! OUR FRIEND--
MY BROTHER!
EXACTLY. HE'S FAMILY. AND DESERVES A PLACE OF HONOR.
HONOR IS THE LAST THING OUR FAMILY DESERVES.
KZZAKK
KZZAKK
HERMES, YOU HAVE A LOT OF NERVE. IF YOU LEAVE NOW--

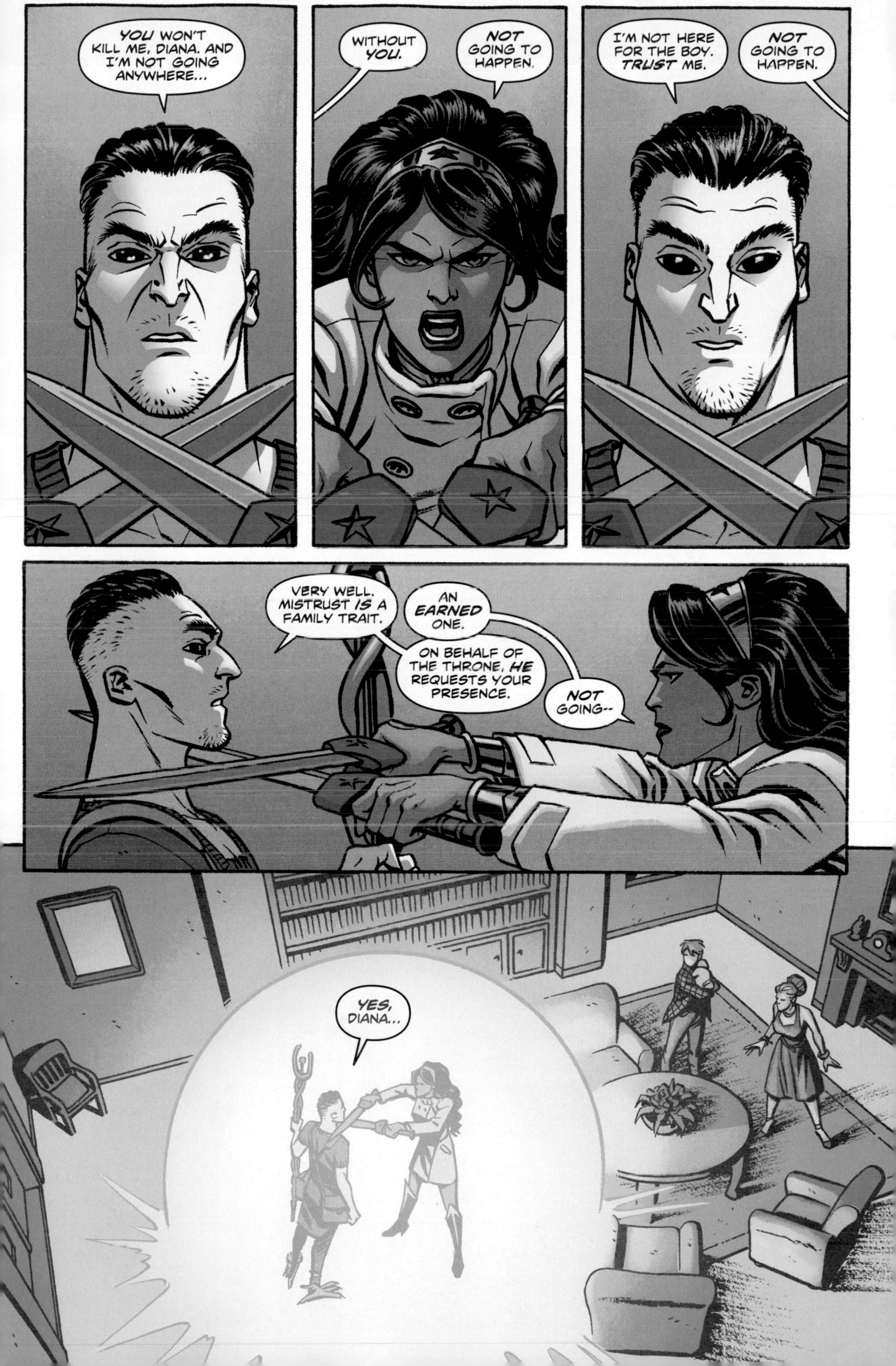
YOU WON'T KILL ME, DIANA. AND I'M NOT GOING ANYWHERE...
WITHOUT YOU.
NOT GOING TO HAPPEN.
I'M NOT HERE FOR THE BOY. TRUST ME.
NOT GOING TO HAPPEN.
VERY WELL. MISTRUST IS A FAMILY TRAIT.
AN EARNED ONE.
ON BEHALF OF THE THRONE, HE REQUESTS YOUR PRESENCE.
NOT GOING--
YES, DIANA...

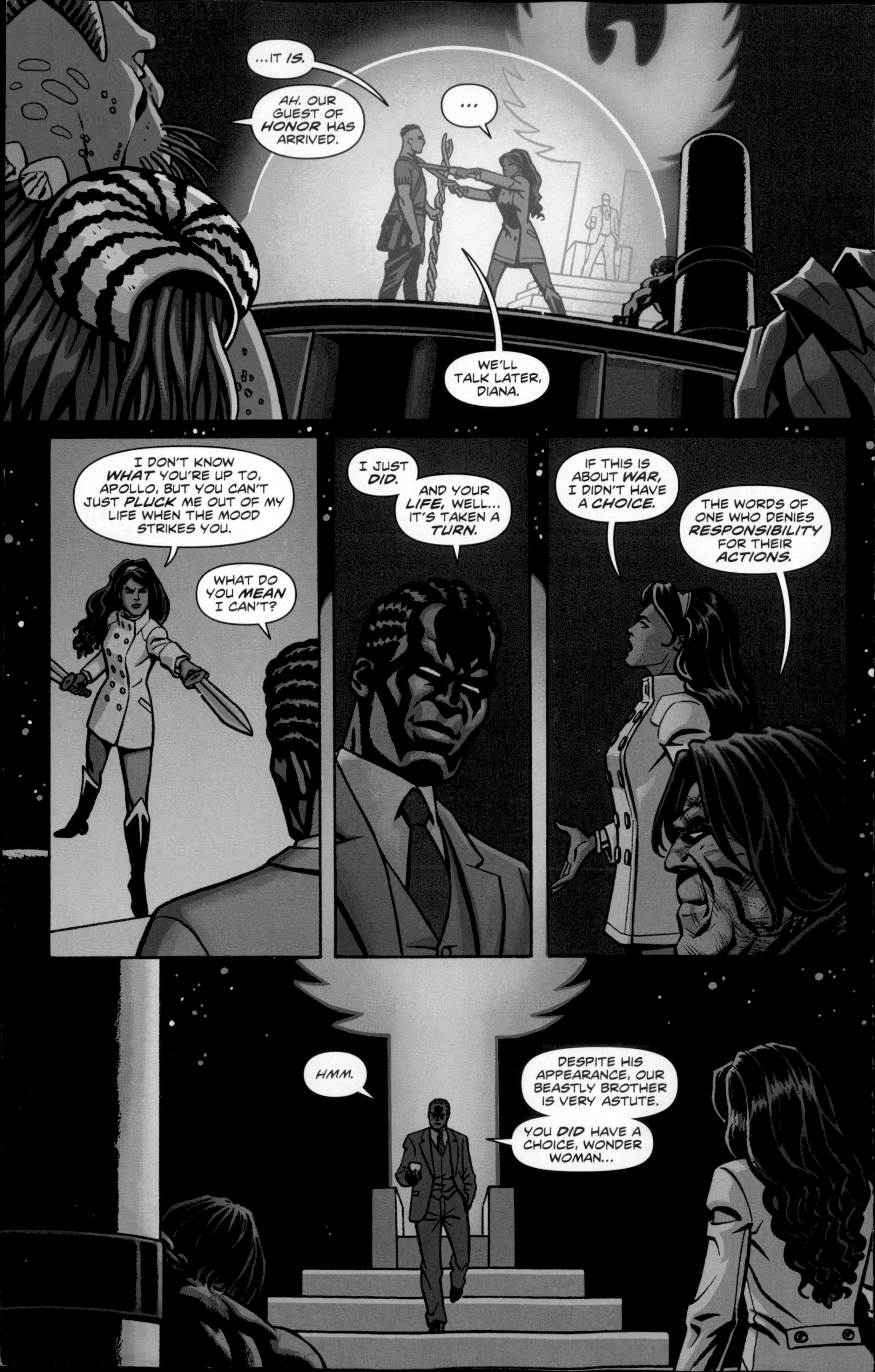
...IT IS.
AH. OUR GUEST OF HONOR HAS ARRIVED.
...
WE'LL TALK LATER, DIANA.
I DON'T KNOW WHAT YOU'RE UP TO, APOLLO, BUT YOU CAN'T JUST PLUCK ME OUT OF MY LIFE WHEN THE MOOD STRIKES YOU.
WHAT DO YOU MEAN I CAN'T?
I JUST DID.
AND YOUR LIFE, WELL... IT'S TAKEN A TURN.
IF THIS IS ABOUT WAR, I DIDN'T HAVE A CHOICE.
THE WORDS OF ONE WHO DENIES RESPONSIBILITY FOR THEIR ACTIONS.
HMM.
DESPITE HIS APPEARANCE, OUR BEASTLY BROTHER IS VERY ASTUTE.
YOU DID HAVE A CHOICE, WONDER WOMAN...

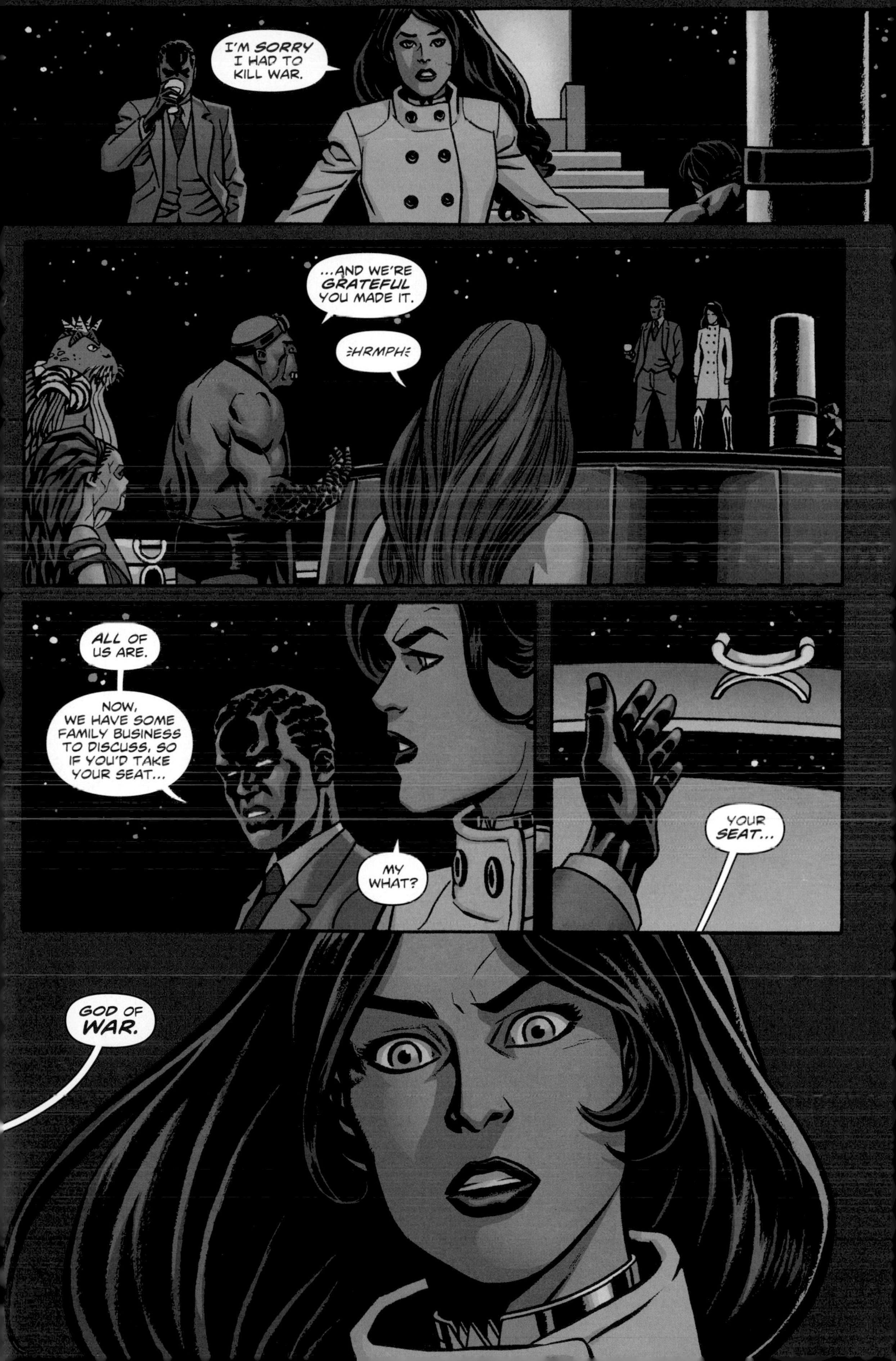
I'M SORRY I HAD TO KILL WAR.
...AND WE'RE GRATEFUL YOU MADE IT.
HRMPH
ALL OF US ARE.
NOW, WE HAVE SOME FAMILY BUSINESS TO DISCUSS, SO IF YOU'D TAKE YOUR SEAT...
MY WHAT?
YOUR SEAT...
GOD OF WAR.

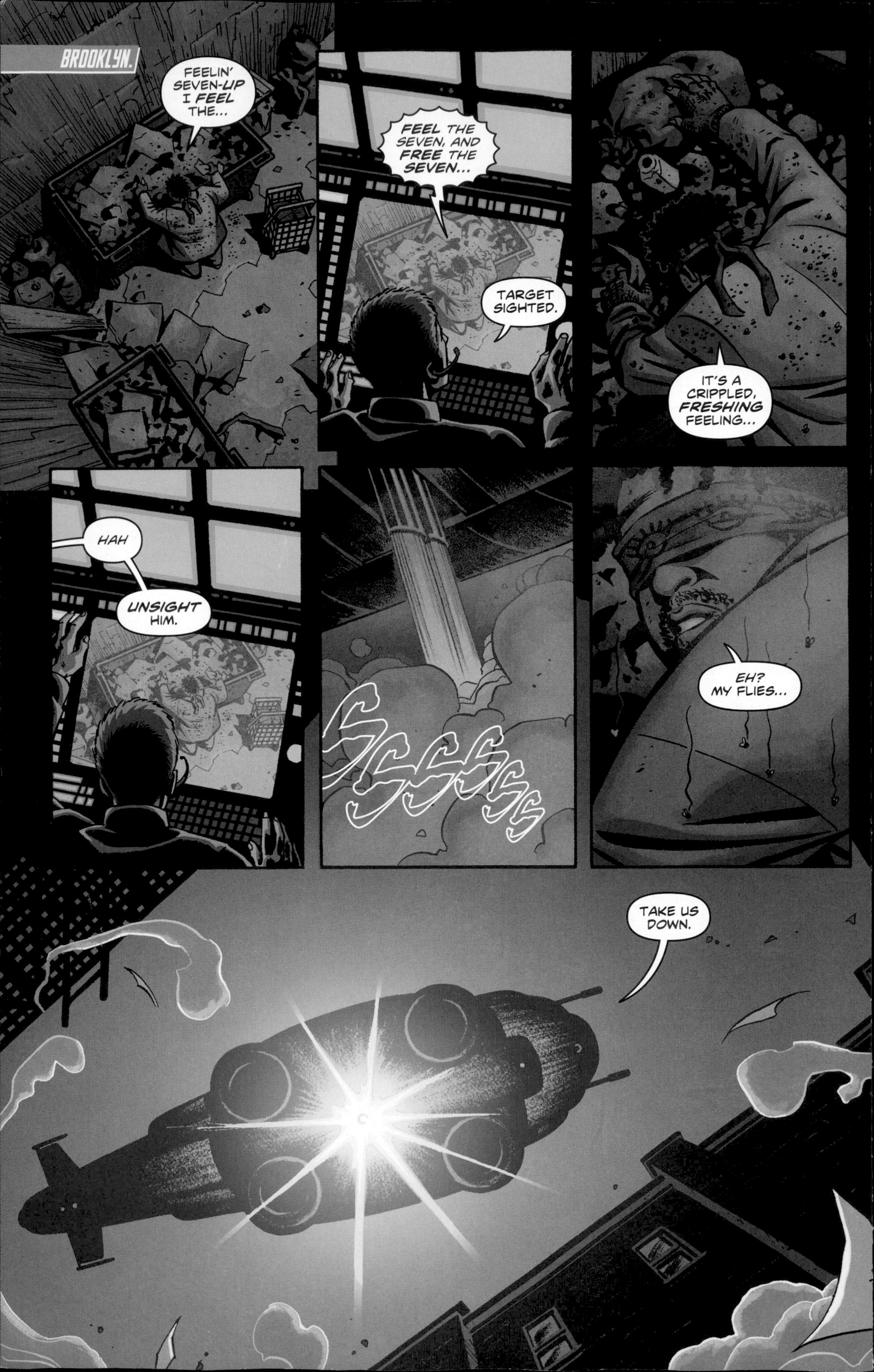
BROOKLYN.
FEELIN' SEVEN-UP I FEEL THE...
FEEL THE SEVEN, AND FREE THE SEVEN...
TARGET SIGHTED.
IT'S A CRIPPLED, FRESHING FEELING...
HAH
UNSIGHT HIM.
SSSSSS
EH? MY FLIES...
TAKE US DOWN.

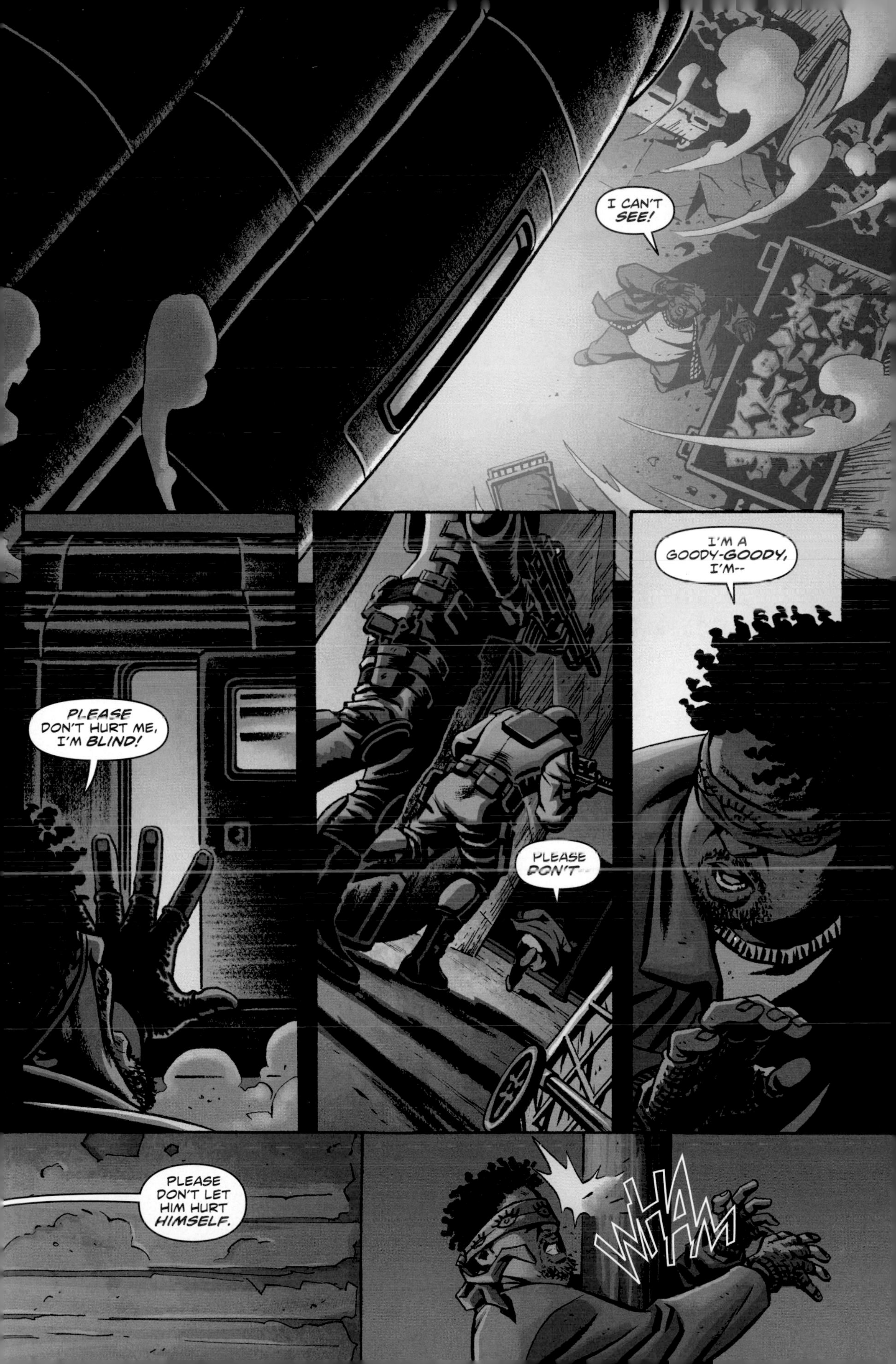
I CAN'T SEE!
I'M A GOODY-GOODY, I'M--
PLEASE DON'T HURT ME, I'M BLIND!
PLEASE DON'T--
PLEASE DON'T LET HIM HURT HIMSELF.
WHAM

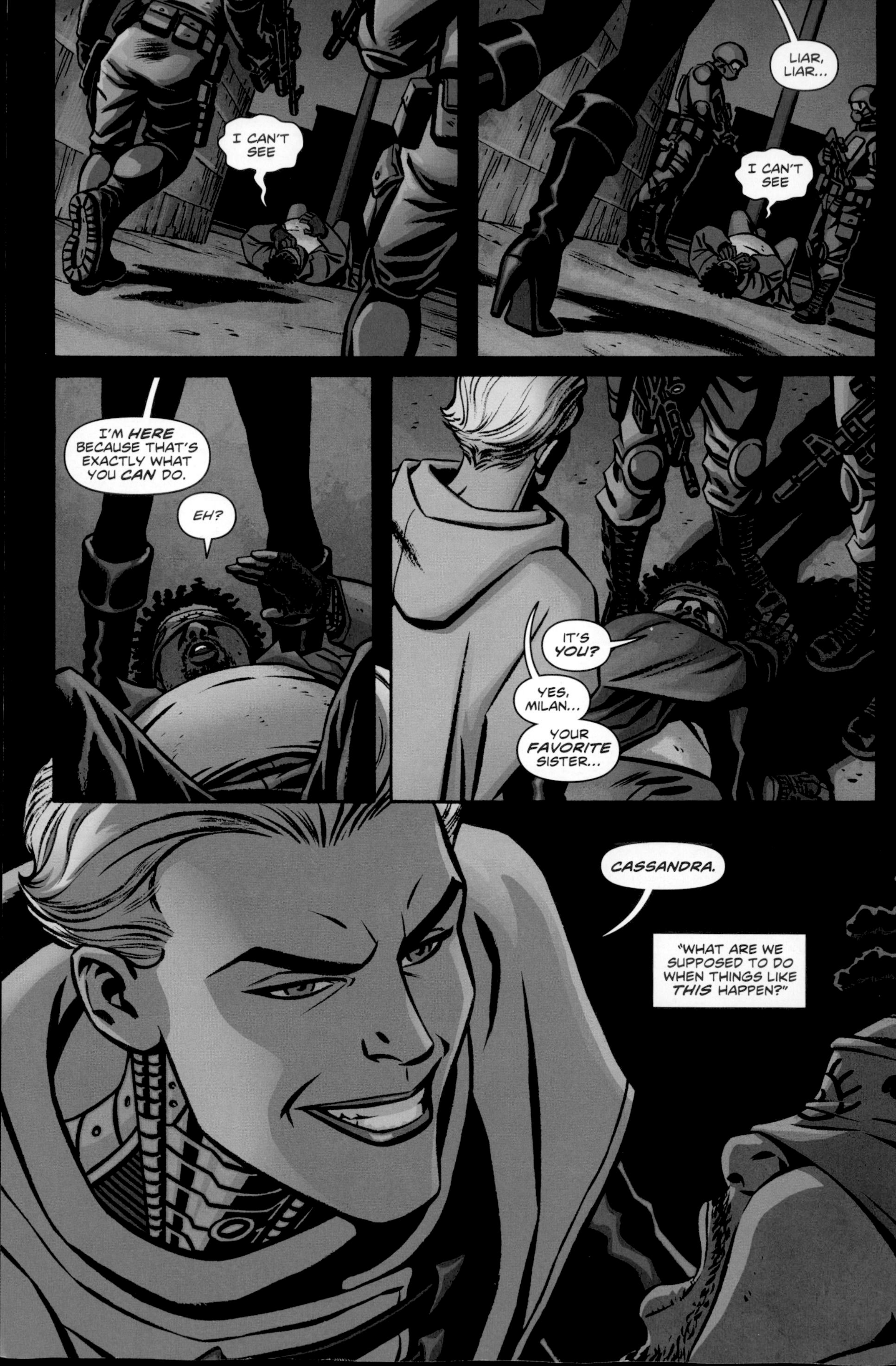
I CAN'T SEE
LIAR, LIAR...
I CAN'T SEE
I'M *HERE* BECAUSE THAT'S EXACTLY WHAT YOU *CAN* DO.
*EH?*
IT'S *YOU?*
YES, MILAN...
YOUR *FAVORITE* SISTER...
*CASSANDRA.*
"WHAT ARE WE SUPPOSED TO DO WHEN THINGS LIKE *THIS* HAPPEN?"

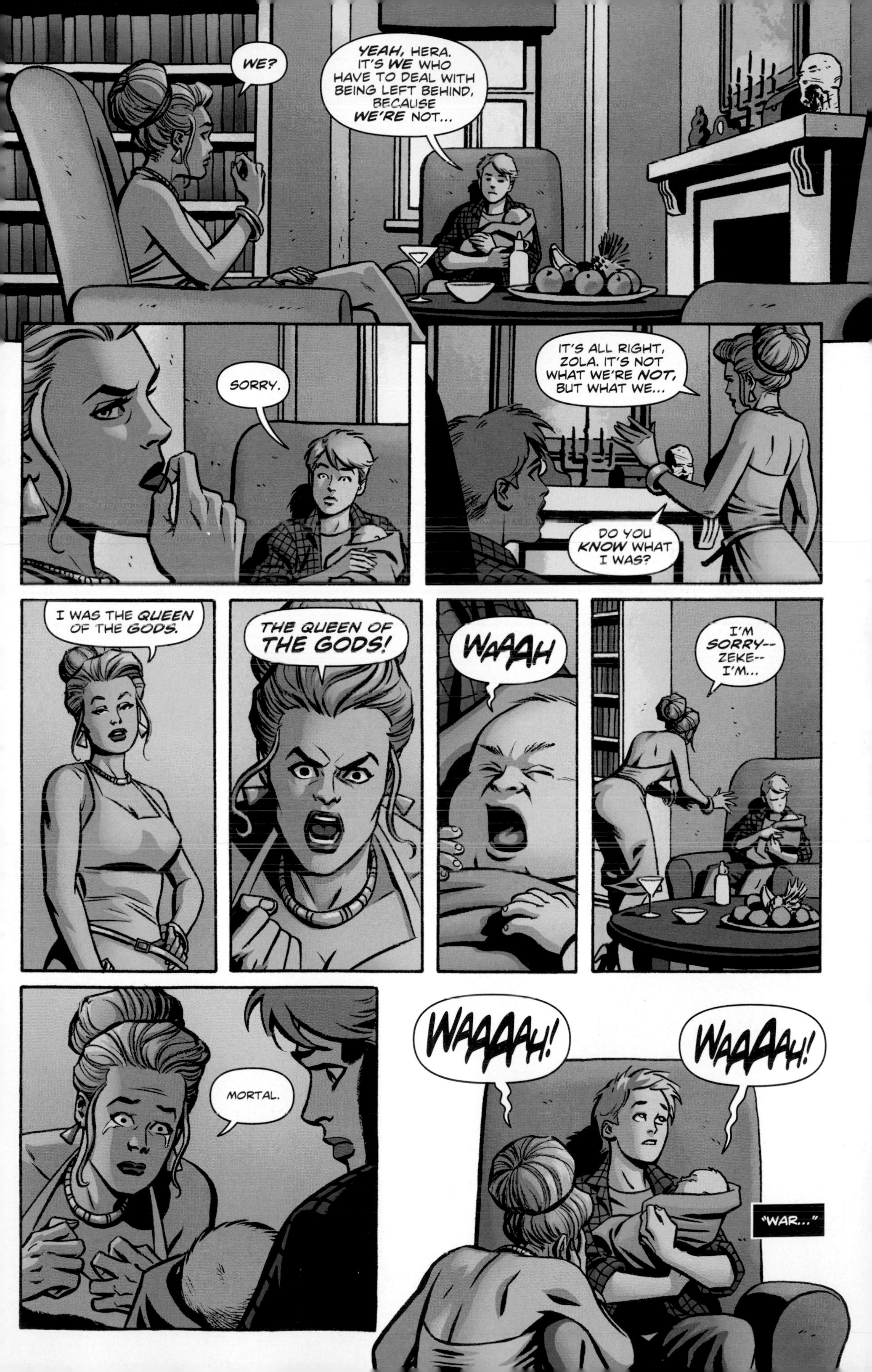
WE?
YEAH, HERA. IT'S WE WHO HAVE TO DEAL WITH BEING LEFT BEHIND, BECAUSE WE'RE NOT...
SORRY.
IT'S ALL RIGHT, ZOLA. IT'S NOT WHAT WE'RE NOT, BUT WHAT WE...
DO YOU KNOW WHAT I WAS?
I WAS THE QUEEN OF THE GODS.
THE QUEEN OF THE GODS!
WAAAH
I'M SORRY-- ZEKE-- I'M...
MORTAL.
WAAAAH!
WAAAAH!
"WAR..."

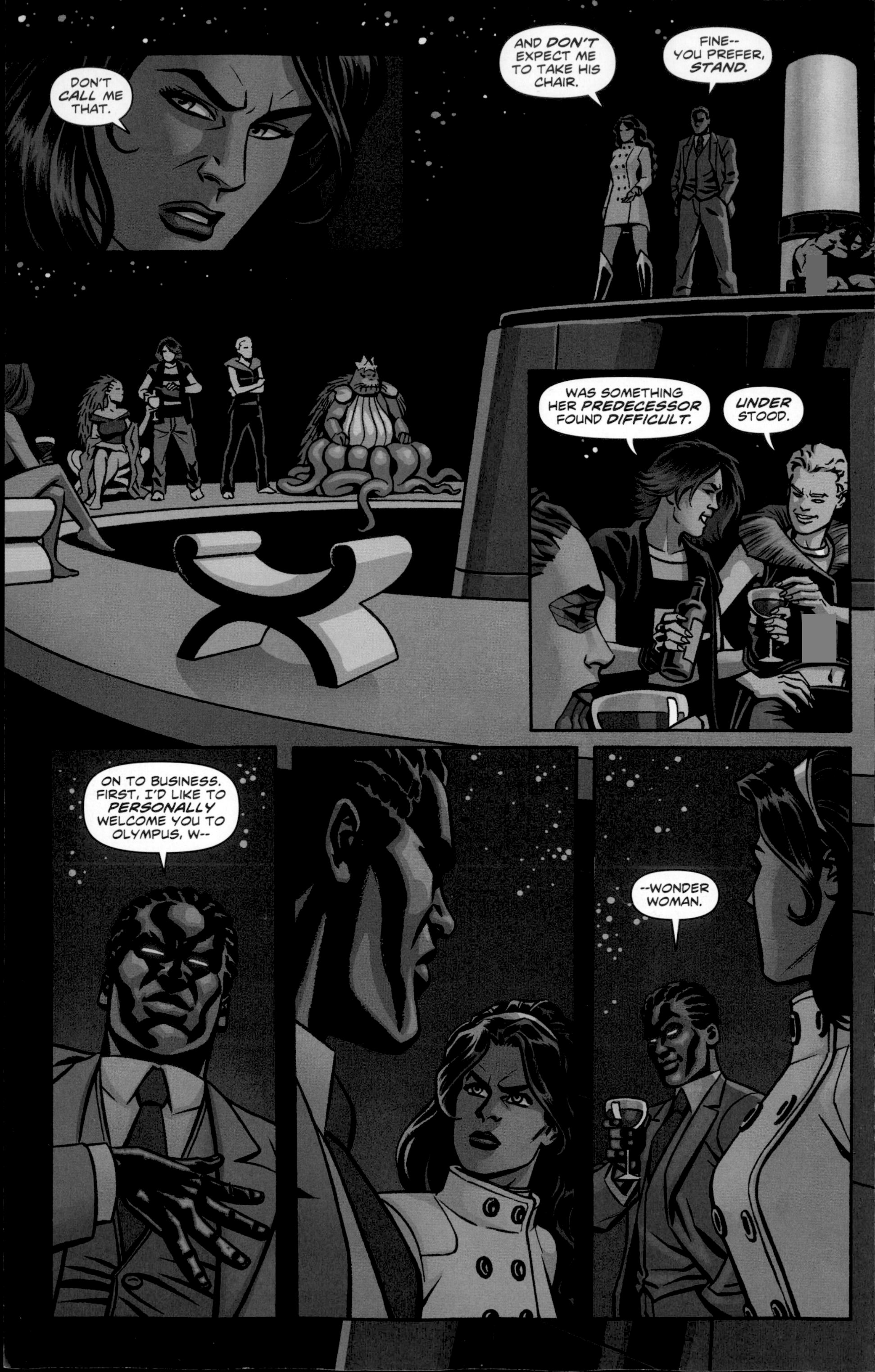
DON'T CALL ME THAT.
AND DON'T EXPECT ME TO TAKE HIS CHAIR.
FINE-- YOU PREFER, STAND.
WAS SOMETHING HER PREDECESSOR FOUND DIFFICULT.
UNDER STOOD.
ON TO BUSINESS. FIRST, I'D LIKE TO PERSONALLY WELCOME YOU TO OLYMPUS, W--
--WONDER WOMAN.

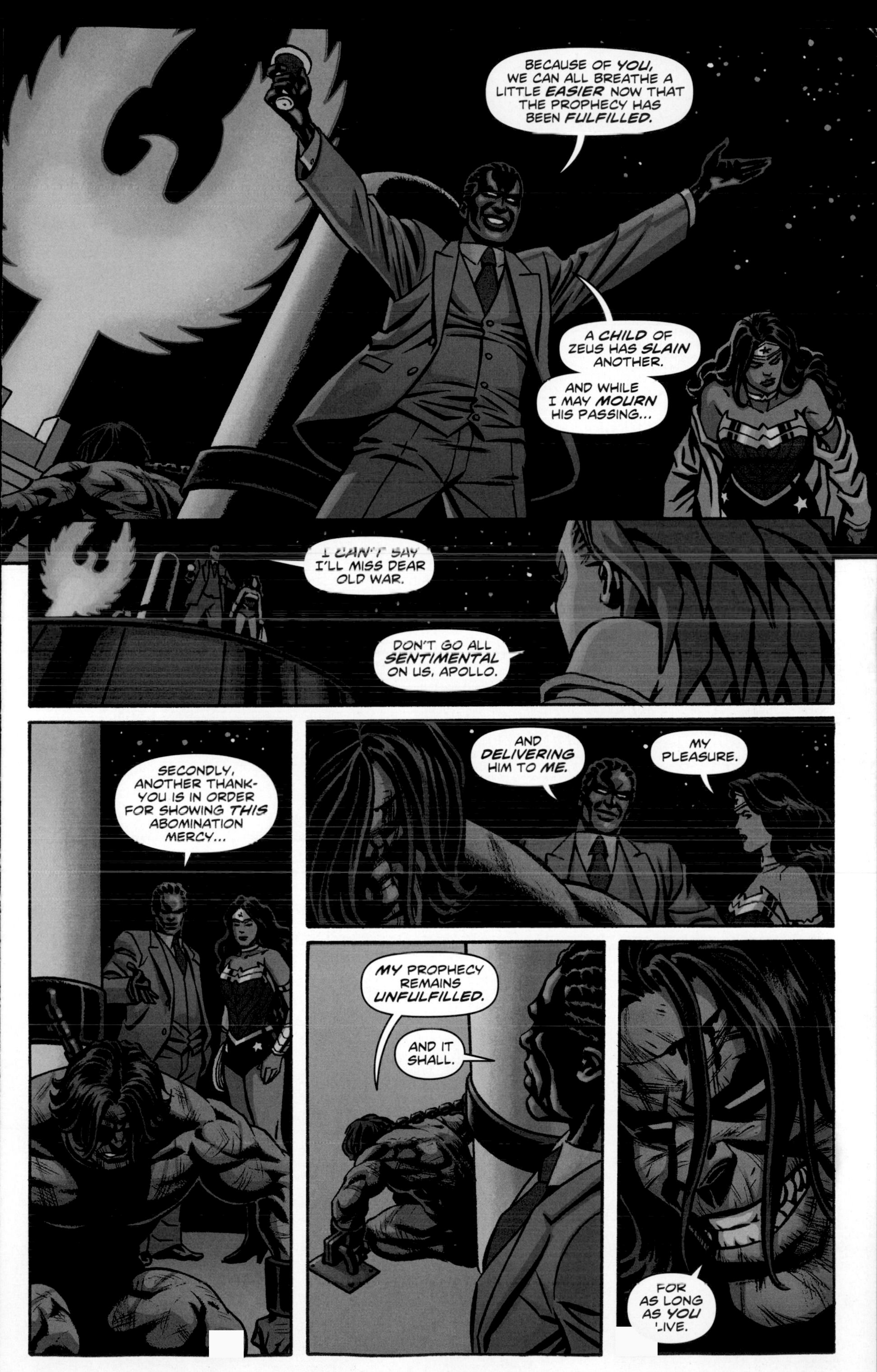
BECAUSE OF YOU, WE CAN ALL BREATHE A LITTLE EASIER NOW THAT THE PROPHECY HAS BEEN FULFILLED.
A CHILD OF ZEUS HAS SLAIN ANOTHER.
AND WHILE I MAY MOURN HIS PASSING...
I CAN'T SAY I'LL MISS DEAR OLD WAR.
DON'T GO ALL SENTIMENTAL ON US, APOLLO.
SECONDLY, ANOTHER THANK-YOU IS IN ORDER FOR SHOWING THIS ABOMINATION MERCY...
AND DELIVERING HIM TO ME.
MY PLEASURE.
MY PROPHECY REMAINS UNFULFILLED.
AND IT SHALL.
FOR AS LONG AS YOU LIVE.

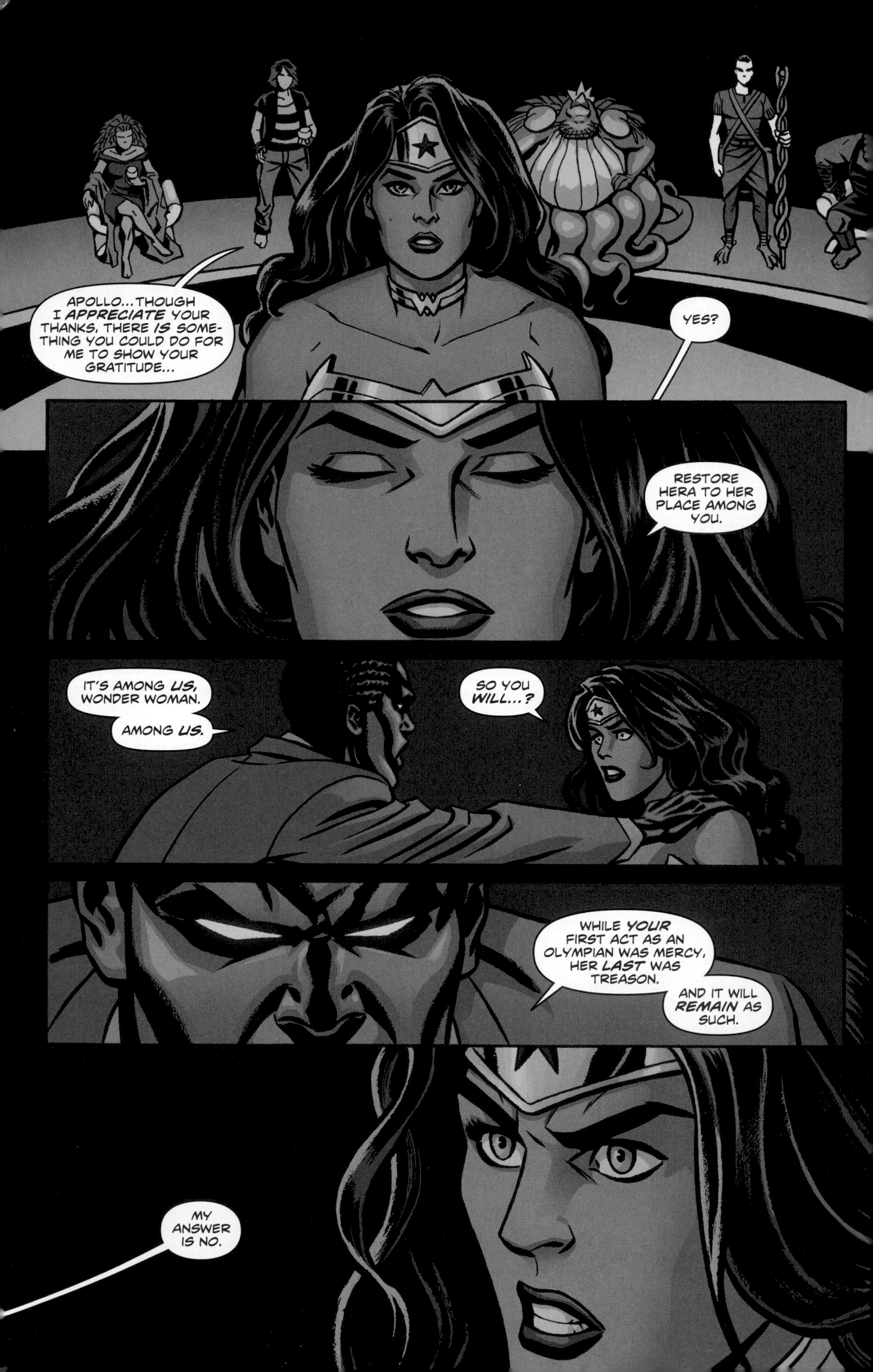
APOLLO...THOUGH I APPRECIATE YOUR THANKS, THERE IS SOMETHING YOU COULD DO FOR ME TO SHOW YOUR GRATITUDE...
YES?
RESTORE HERA TO HER PLACE AMONG YOU.
IT'S AMONG US, WONDER WOMAN.
AMONG US.
SO YOU WILL...?
WHILE YOUR FIRST ACT AS AN OLYMPIAN WAS MERCY, HER LAST WAS TREASON.
AND IT WILL REMAIN AS SUCH.
MY ANSWER IS NO.

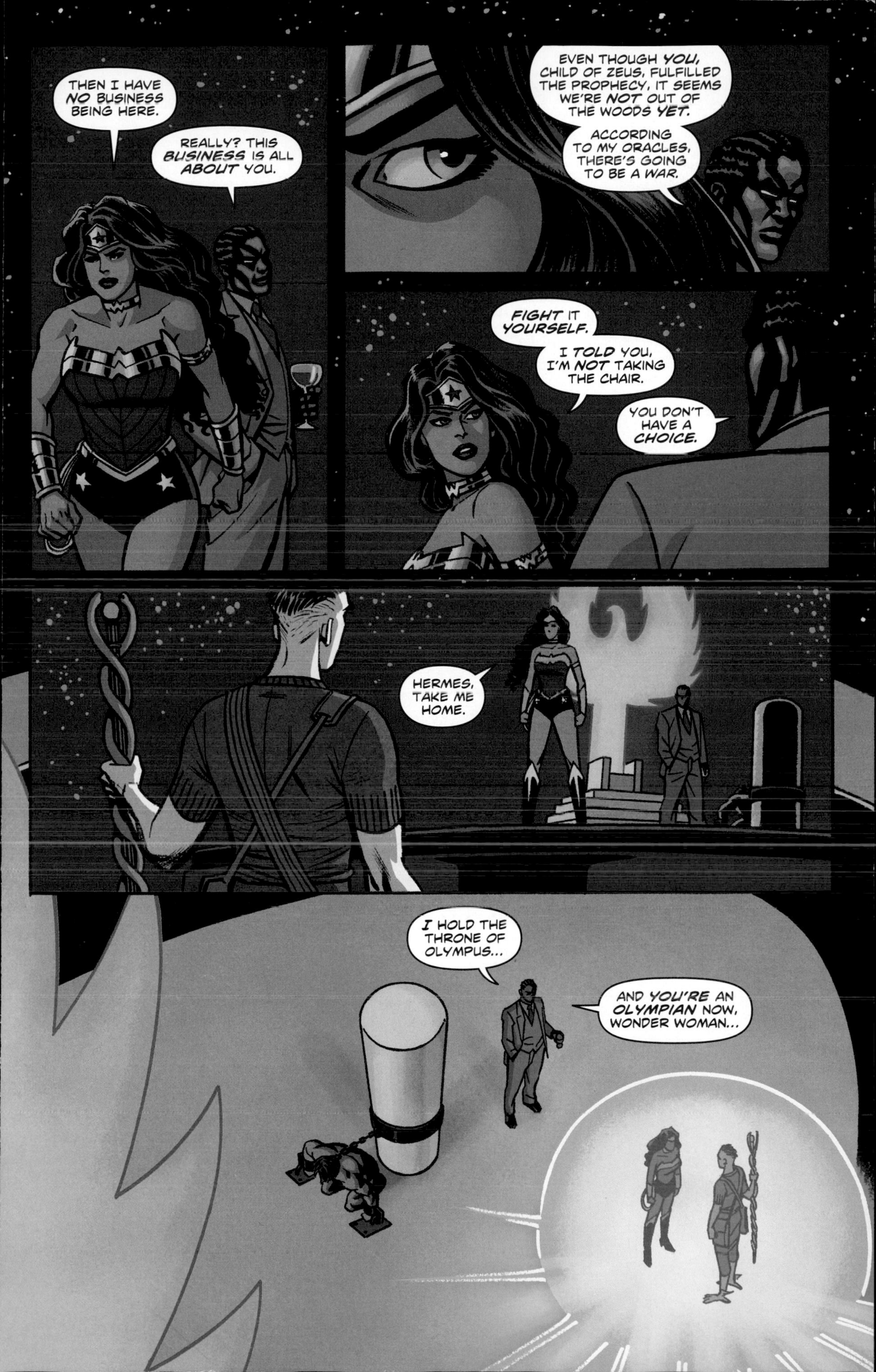
THEN I HAVE NO BUSINESS BEING HERE.
REALLY? THIS BUSINESS IS ALL ABOUT YOU.
EVEN THOUGH YOU, CHILD OF ZEUS, FULFILLED THE PROPHECY, IT SEEMS WE'RE NOT OUT OF THE WOODS YET.
ACCORDING TO MY ORACLES, THERE'S GOING TO BE A WAR.
FIGHT IT YOURSELF.
I TOLD YOU, I'M NOT TAKING THE CHAIR.
YOU DON'T HAVE A CHOICE.
HERMES, TAKE ME HOME.
I HOLD THE THRONE OF OLYMPUS...
AND YOU'RE AN OLYMPIAN NOW, WONDER WOMAN...

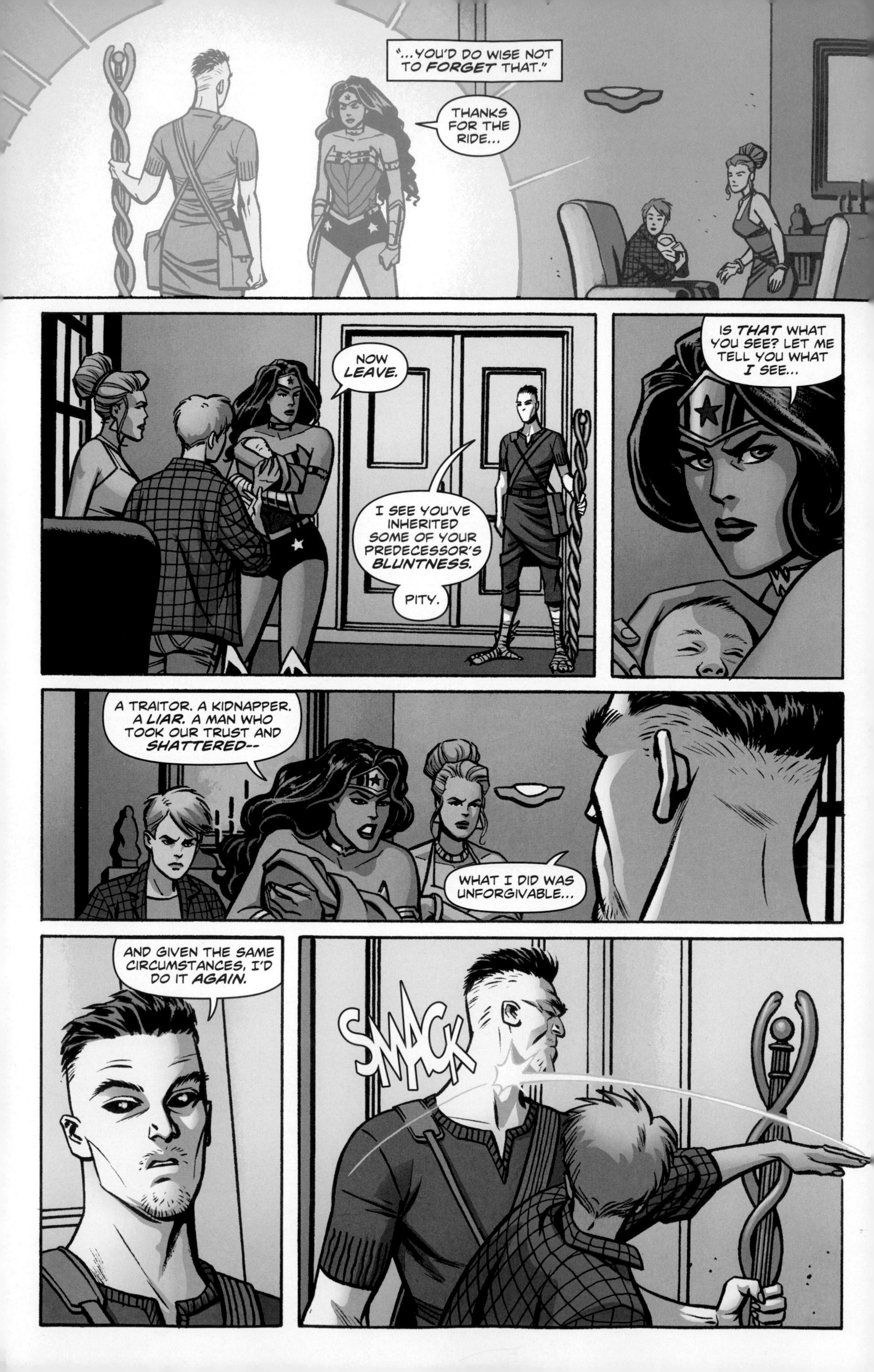
"...YOU'D DO WISE NOT TO *FORGET* THAT."
THANKS FOR THE RIDE...
NOW *LEAVE*.
I SEE YOU'VE INHERITED SOME OF YOUR PREDECESSOR'S *BLUNTNESS*.
PITY.
IS *THAT* WHAT YOU SEE? LET ME TELL YOU WHAT *I* SEE...
A TRAITOR. A KIDNAPPER. A *LIAR*. A MAN WHO TOOK OUR TRUST AND *SHATTERED*--
WHAT I DID WAS UNFORGIVABLE...
AND GIVEN THE SAME CIRCUMSTANCES, I'D DO IT *AGAIN*.
SMACK

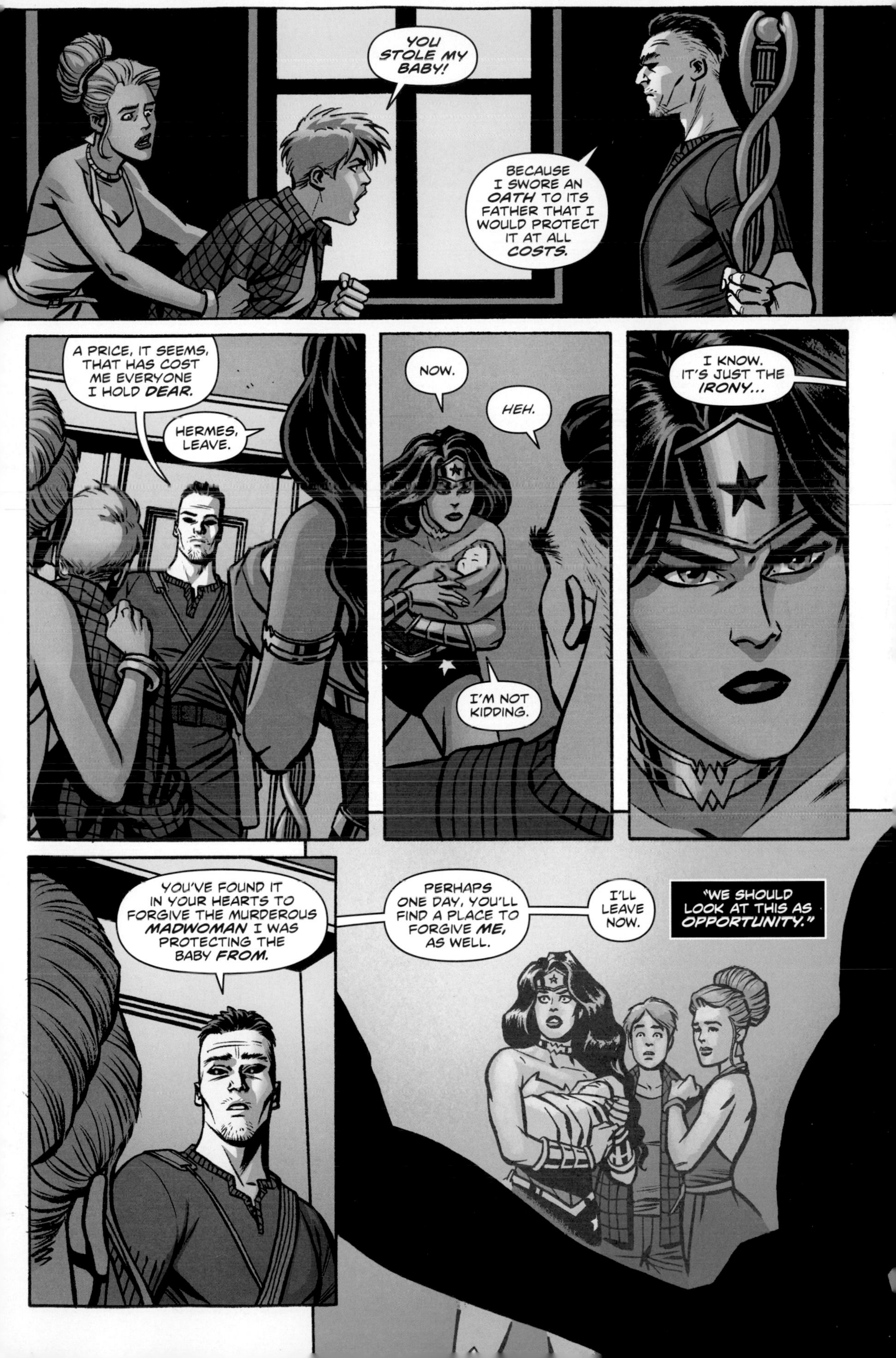
YOU STOLE MY BABY!
BECAUSE I SWORE AN OATH TO ITS FATHER THAT I WOULD PROTECT IT AT ALL COSTS.
A PRICE, IT SEEMS, THAT HAS COST ME EVERYONE I HOLD DEAR.
HERMES, LEAVE.
NOW.
HEH.
I'M NOT KIDDING.
I KNOW. IT'S JUST THE IRONY...
YOU'VE FOUND IT IN YOUR HEARTS TO FORGIVE THE MURDEROUS MADWOMAN I WAS PROTECTING THE BABY FROM.
PERHAPS ONE DAY, YOU'LL FIND A PLACE TO FORGIVE ME, AS WELL.
I'LL LEAVE NOW.
"WE SHOULD LOOK AT THIS AS OPPORTUNITY."

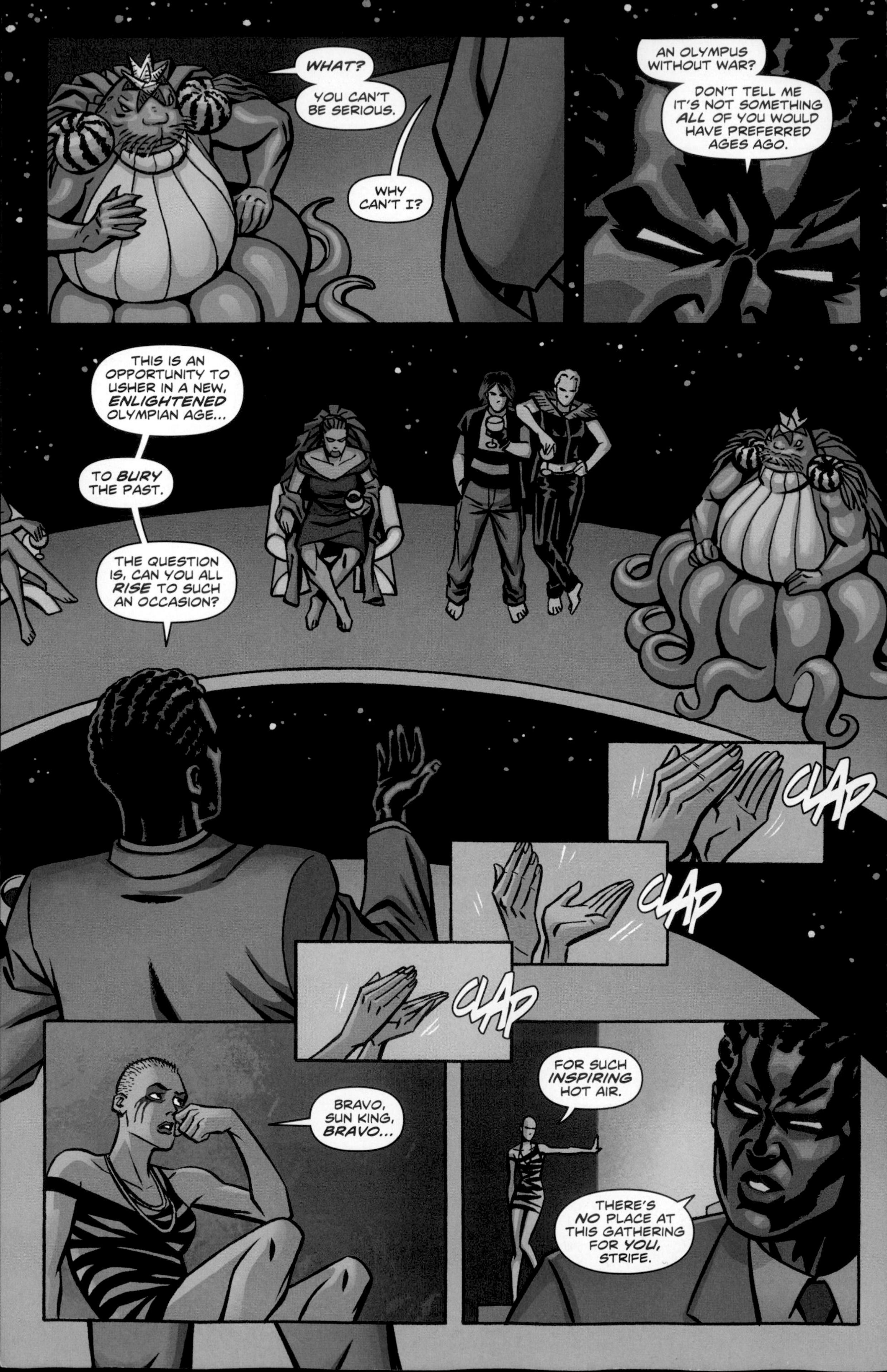
WHAT?
YOU CAN'T BE SERIOUS.
WHY CAN'T I?
AN OLYMPUS WITHOUT WAR?
DON'T TELL ME IT'S NOT SOMETHING ALL OF YOU WOULD HAVE PREFERRED AGES AGO.
THIS IS AN OPPORTUNITY TO USHER IN A NEW, ENLIGHTENED OLYMPIAN AGE...
TO BURY THE PAST.
THE QUESTION IS, CAN YOU ALL RISE TO SUCH AN OCCASION?
CLAP
CLAP
CLAP
BRAVO, SUN KING, BRAVO...
FOR SUCH INSPIRING HOT AIR.
THERE'S NO PLACE AT THIS GATHERING FOR YOU, STRIFE.

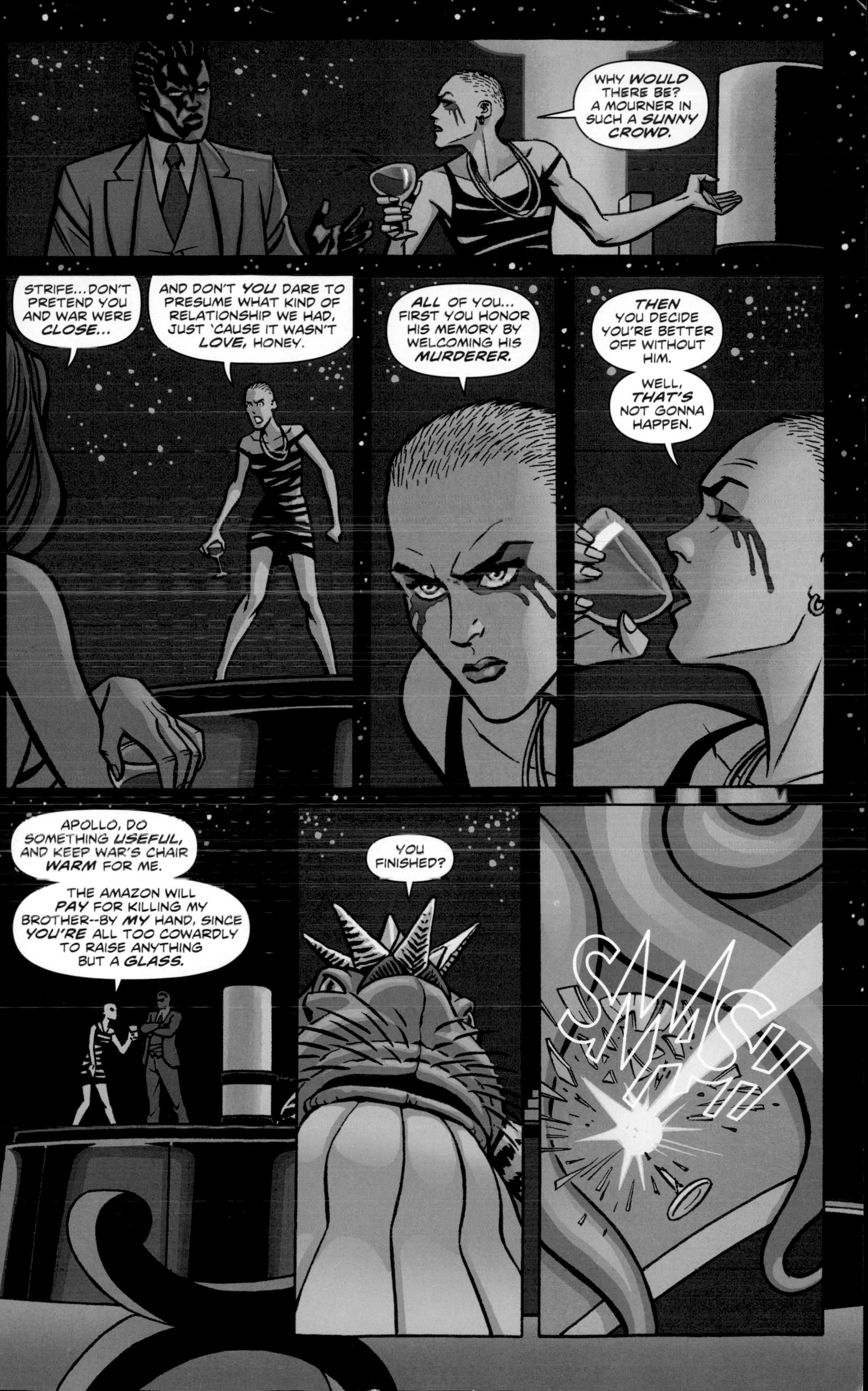
WHY WOULD THERE BE? A MOURNER IN SUCH A SUNNY CROWD.
STRIFE...DON'T PRETEND YOU AND WAR WERE CLOSE...
AND DON'T YOU DARE TO PRESUME WHAT KIND OF RELATIONSHIP WE HAD, JUST 'CAUSE IT WASN'T LOVE, HONEY.
ALL OF YOU... FIRST YOU HONOR HIS MEMORY BY WELCOMING HIS MURDERER.
THEN YOU DECIDE YOU'RE BETTER OFF WITHOUT HIM.
WELL, THAT'S NOT GONNA HAPPEN.
APOLLO, DO SOMETHING USEFUL, AND KEEP WAR'S CHAIR WARM FOR ME.
THE AMAZON WILL PAY FOR KILLING MY BROTHER--BY MY HAND, SINCE YOU'RE ALL TOO COWARDLY TO RAISE ANYTHING BUT A GLASS.
YOU FINISHED?
SMASH!!

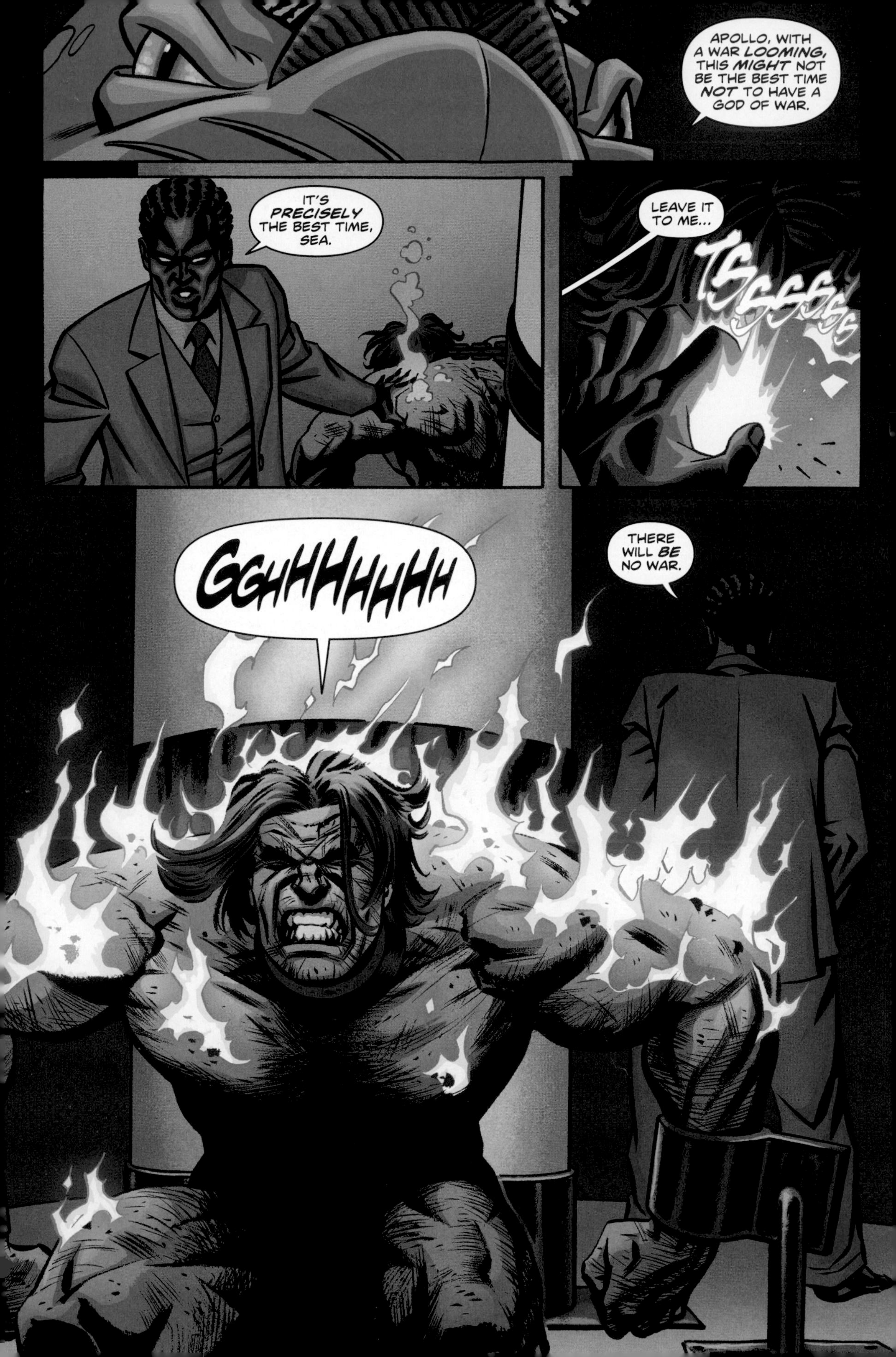
APOLLO, WITH A WAR *LOOMING*, THIS *MIGHT* NOT BE THE BEST TIME *NOT* TO HAVE A GOD OF WAR.
IT'S *PRECISELY* THE BEST TIME, SEA.
LEAVE IT TO ME...
TSSSSSS
GGHHHHHHH
THERE WILL *BE* NO WAR.

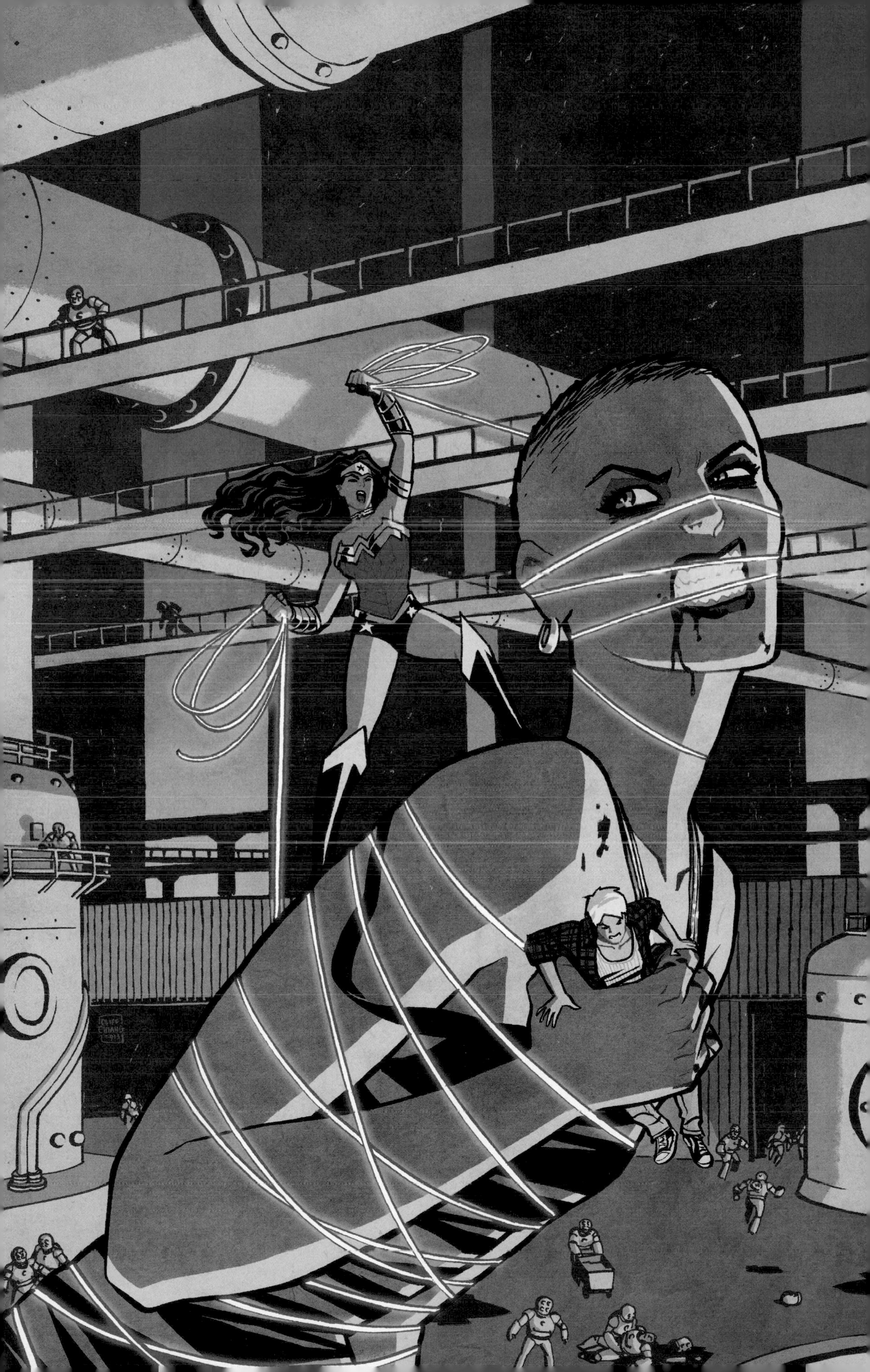

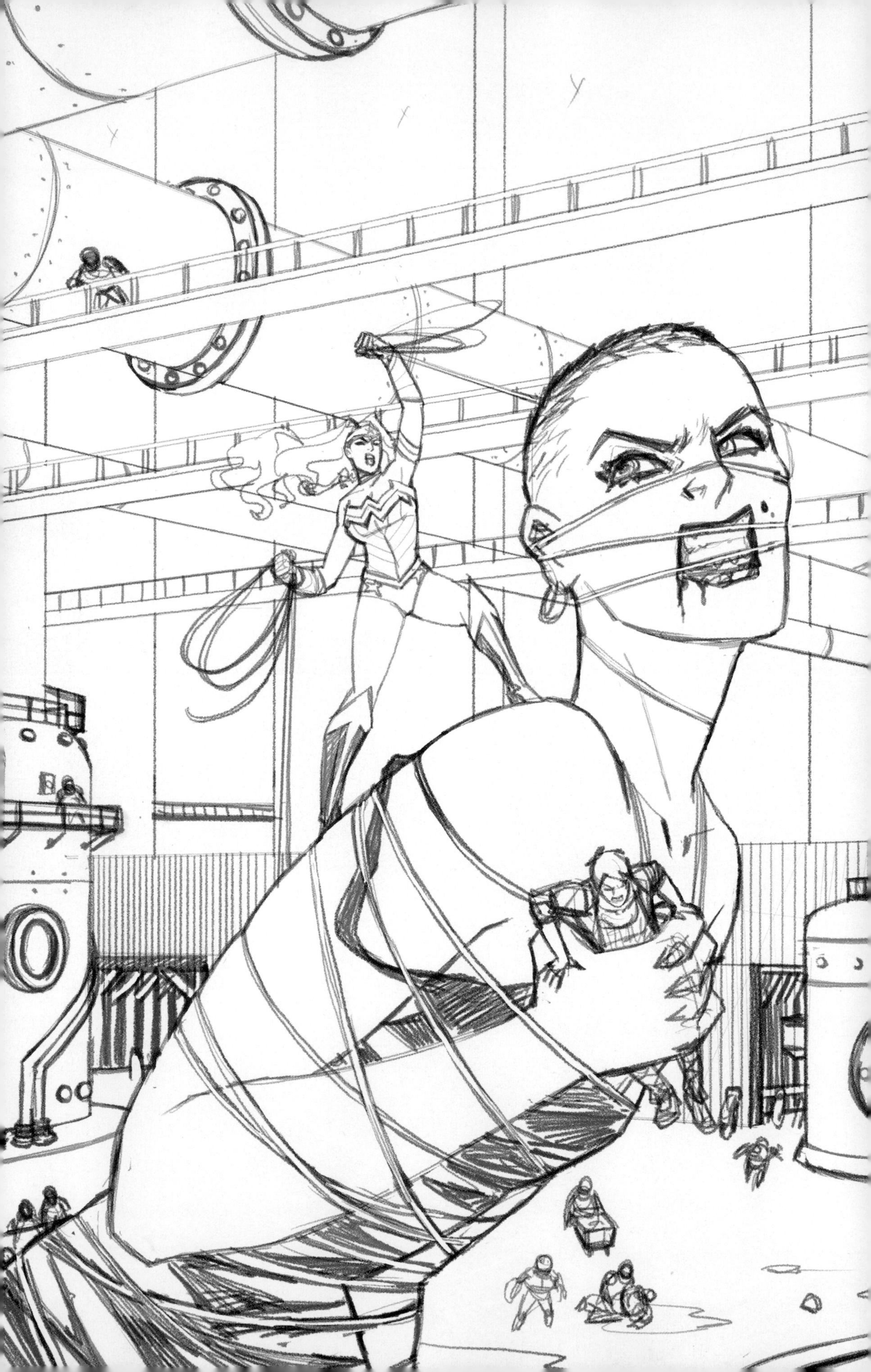

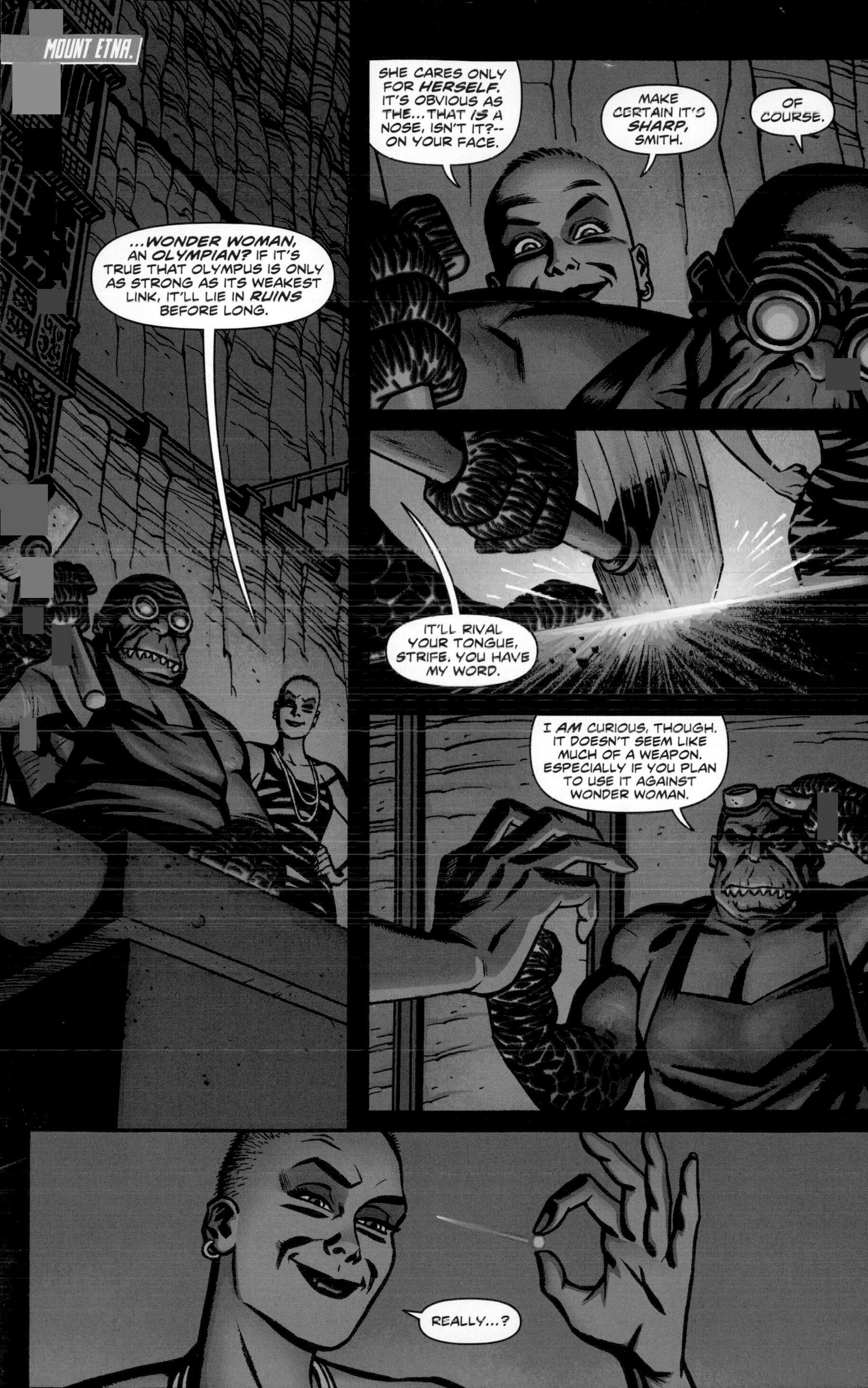
MOUNT ETNA.
...WONDER WOMAN, AN OLYMPIAN? IF IT'S TRUE THAT OLYMPUS IS ONLY AS STRONG AS ITS WEAKEST LINK, IT'LL LIE IN RUINS BEFORE LONG.
SHE CARES ONLY FOR HERSELF. IT'S OBVIOUS AS THE...THAT IS A NOSE, ISN'T IT?-- ON YOUR FACE.
MAKE CERTAIN IT'S SHARP, SMITH.
OF COURSE.
IT'LL RIVAL YOUR TONGUE, STRIFE. YOU HAVE MY WORD.
I AM CURIOUS, THOUGH. IT DOESN'T SEEM LIKE MUCH OF A WEAPON. ESPECIALLY IF YOU PLAN TO USE IT AGAINST WONDER WOMAN.
REALLY...?

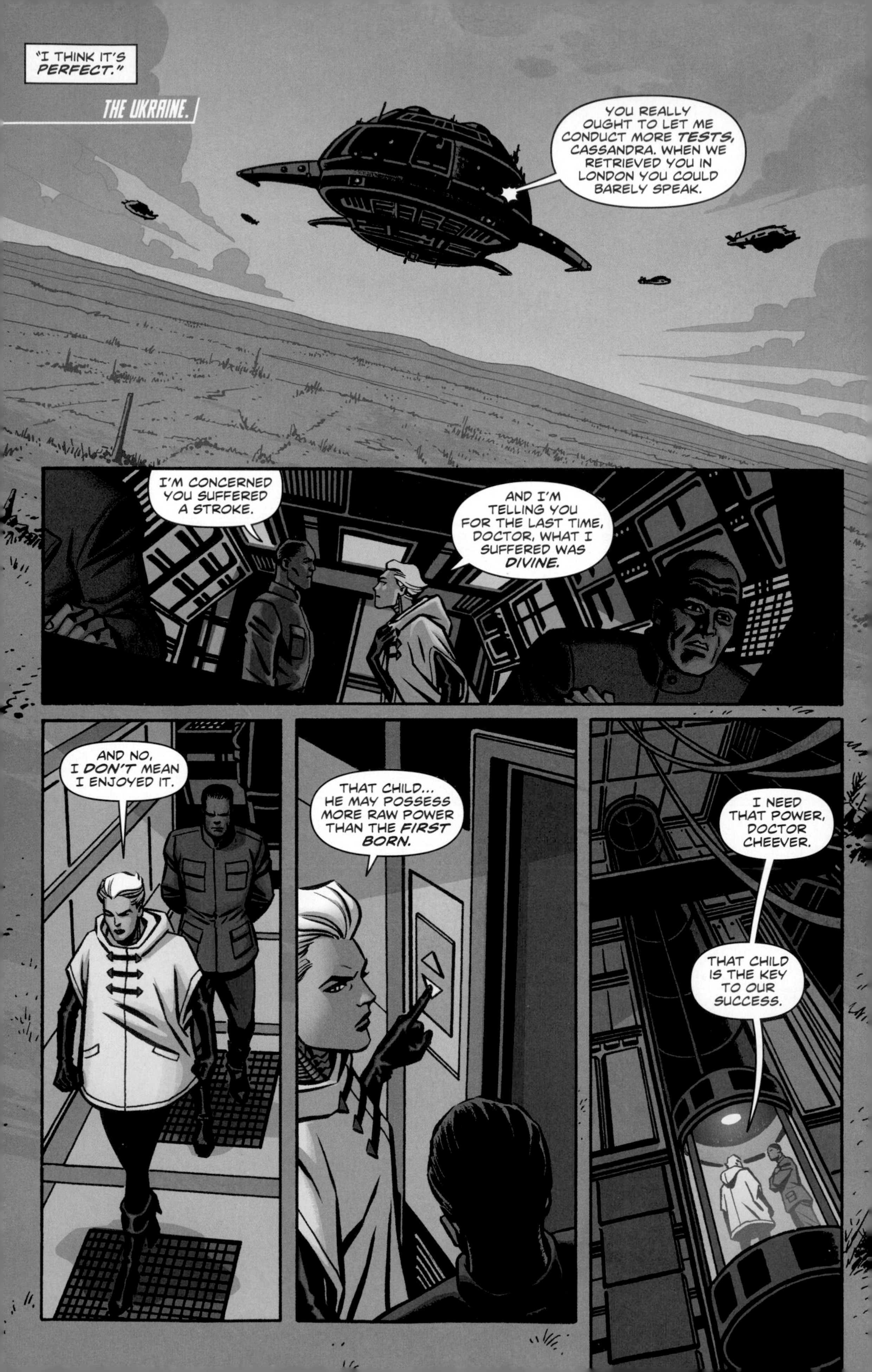
"I THINK IT'S PERFECT."
THE UKRAINE.
YOU REALLY OUGHT TO LET ME CONDUCT MORE TESTS, CASSANDRA. WHEN WE RETRIEVED YOU IN LONDON YOU COULD BARELY SPEAK.
I'M CONCERNED YOU SUFFERED A STROKE.
AND I'M TELLING YOU FOR THE LAST TIME, DOCTOR, WHAT I SUFFERED WAS DIVINE.
AND NO, I DON'T MEAN I ENJOYED IT.
THAT CHILD... HE MAY POSSESS MORE RAW POWER THAN THE FIRST BORN.
I NEED THAT POWER, DOCTOR CHEEVER.
THAT CHILD IS THE KEY TO OUR SUCCESS.

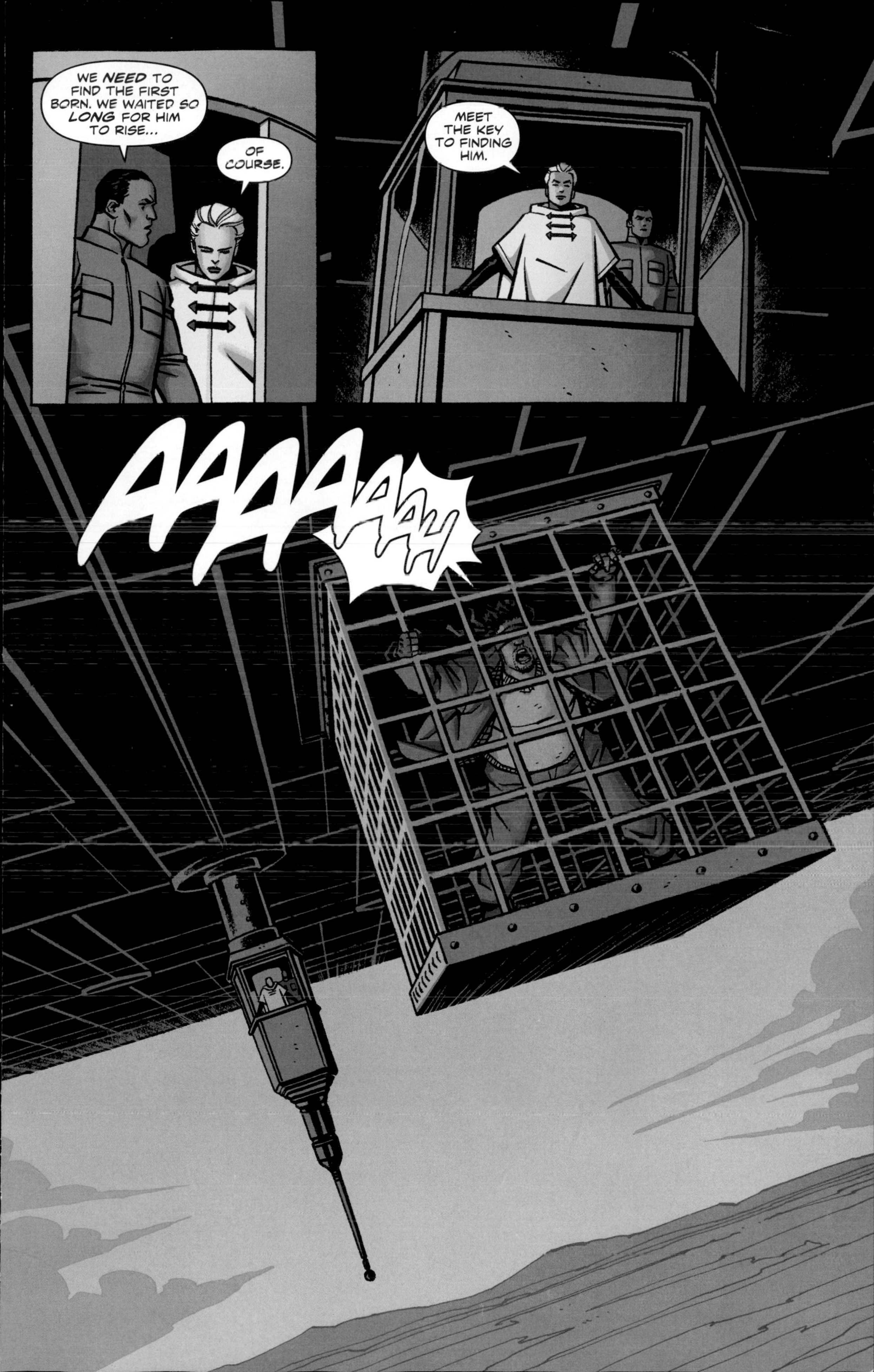
WE NEED TO FIND THE FIRST BORN. WE WAITED SO LONG FOR HIM TO RISE...
OF COURSE.
MEET THE KEY TO FINDING HIM.
AAAAAAAH

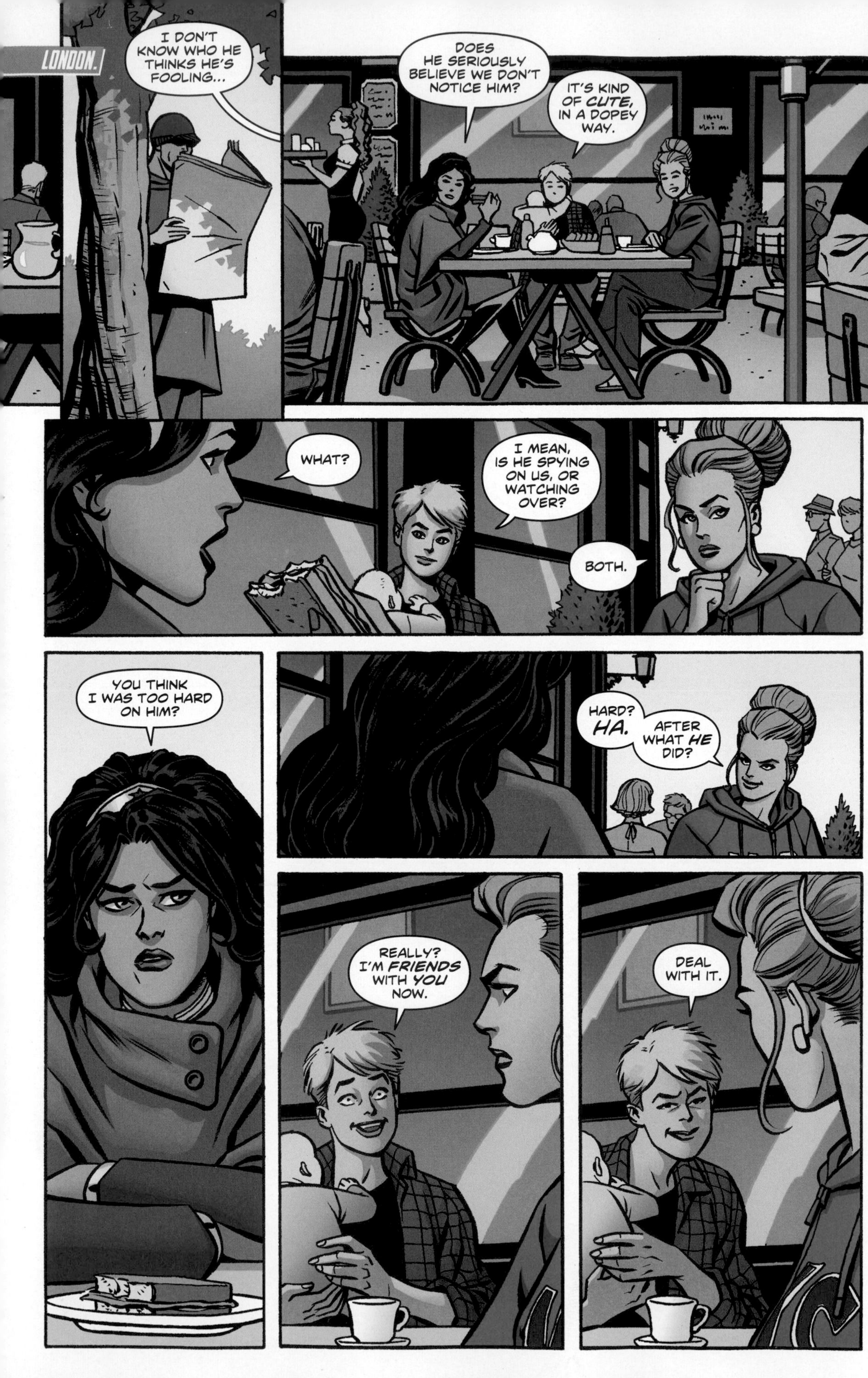
LONDON.
I DON'T KNOW WHO HE THINKS HE'S FOOLING...
DOES HE SERIOUSLY BELIEVE WE DON'T NOTICE HIM?
IT'S KIND OF CUTE, IN A DOPEY WAY.
WHAT?
I MEAN, IS HE SPYING ON US, OR WATCHING OVER?
BOTH.
YOU THINK I WAS TOO HARD ON HIM?
HARD? HA.
AFTER WHAT HE DID?
REALLY? I'M FRIENDS WITH YOU NOW.
DEAL WITH IT.

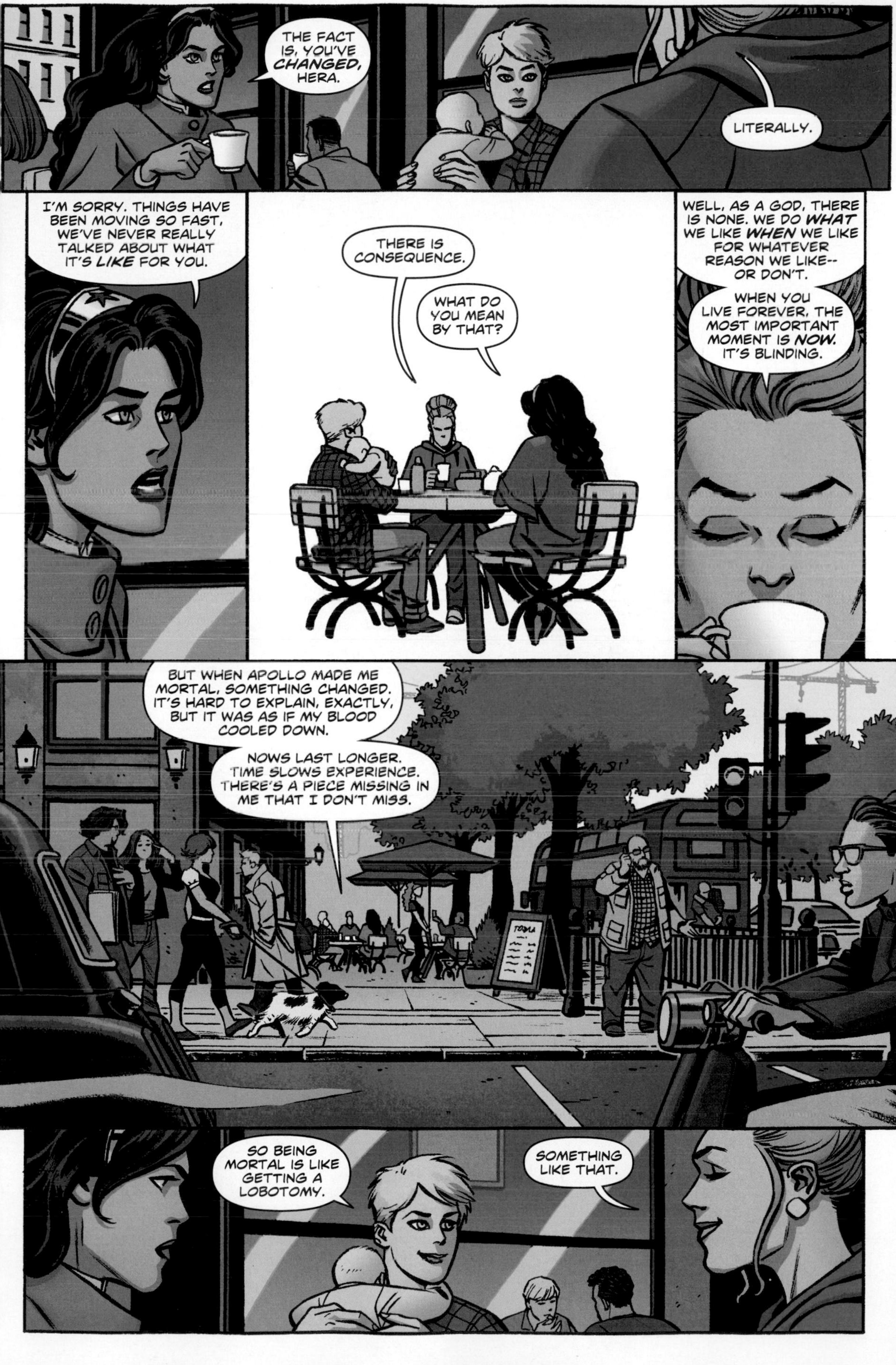
THE FACT IS, YOU'VE CHANGED, HERA.
LITERALLY.
I'M SORRY. THINGS HAVE BEEN MOVING SO FAST, WE'VE NEVER REALLY TALKED ABOUT WHAT IT'S LIKE FOR YOU.
THERE IS CONSEQUENCE.
WHAT DO YOU MEAN BY THAT?
WELL, AS A GOD, THERE IS NONE. WE DO WHAT WE LIKE WHEN WE LIKE FOR WHATEVER REASON WE LIKE-- OR DON'T.
WHEN YOU LIVE FOREVER, THE MOST IMPORTANT MOMENT IS NOW. IT'S BLINDING.
BUT WHEN APOLLO MADE ME MORTAL, SOMETHING CHANGED. IT'S HARD TO EXPLAIN, EXACTLY, BUT IT WAS AS IF MY BLOOD COOLED DOWN.
NOWS LAST LONGER. TIME SLOWS EXPERIENCE. THERE'S A PIECE MISSING IN ME THAT I DON'T MISS.
SO BEING MORTAL IS LIKE GETTING A LOBOTOMY.
SOMETHING LIKE THAT.

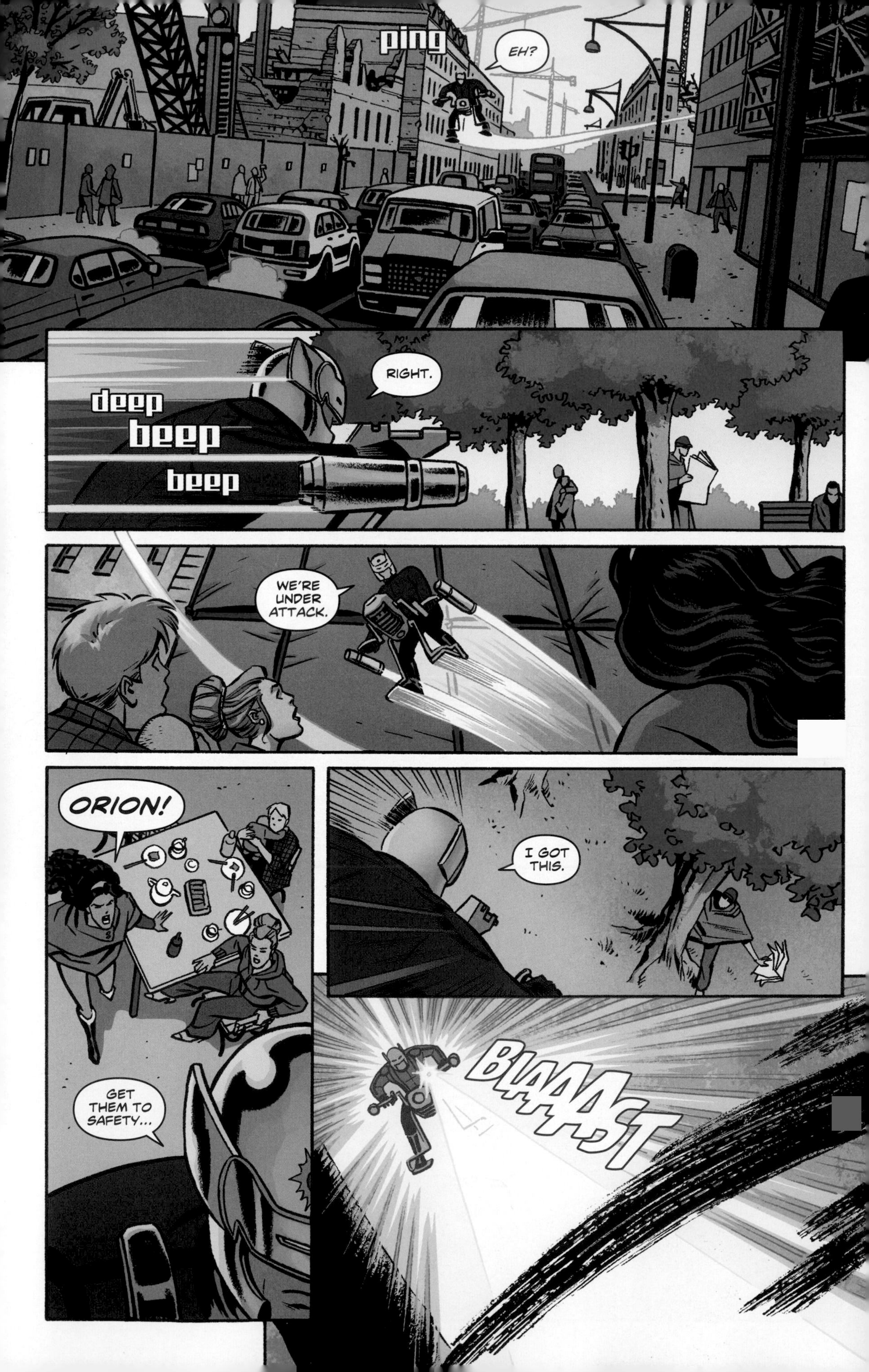
ping
EH?
RIGHT.
deep
beep
beep
WE'RE UNDER ATTACK.
ORION!
I GOT THIS.
GET THEM TO SAFETY...
BLAAAST

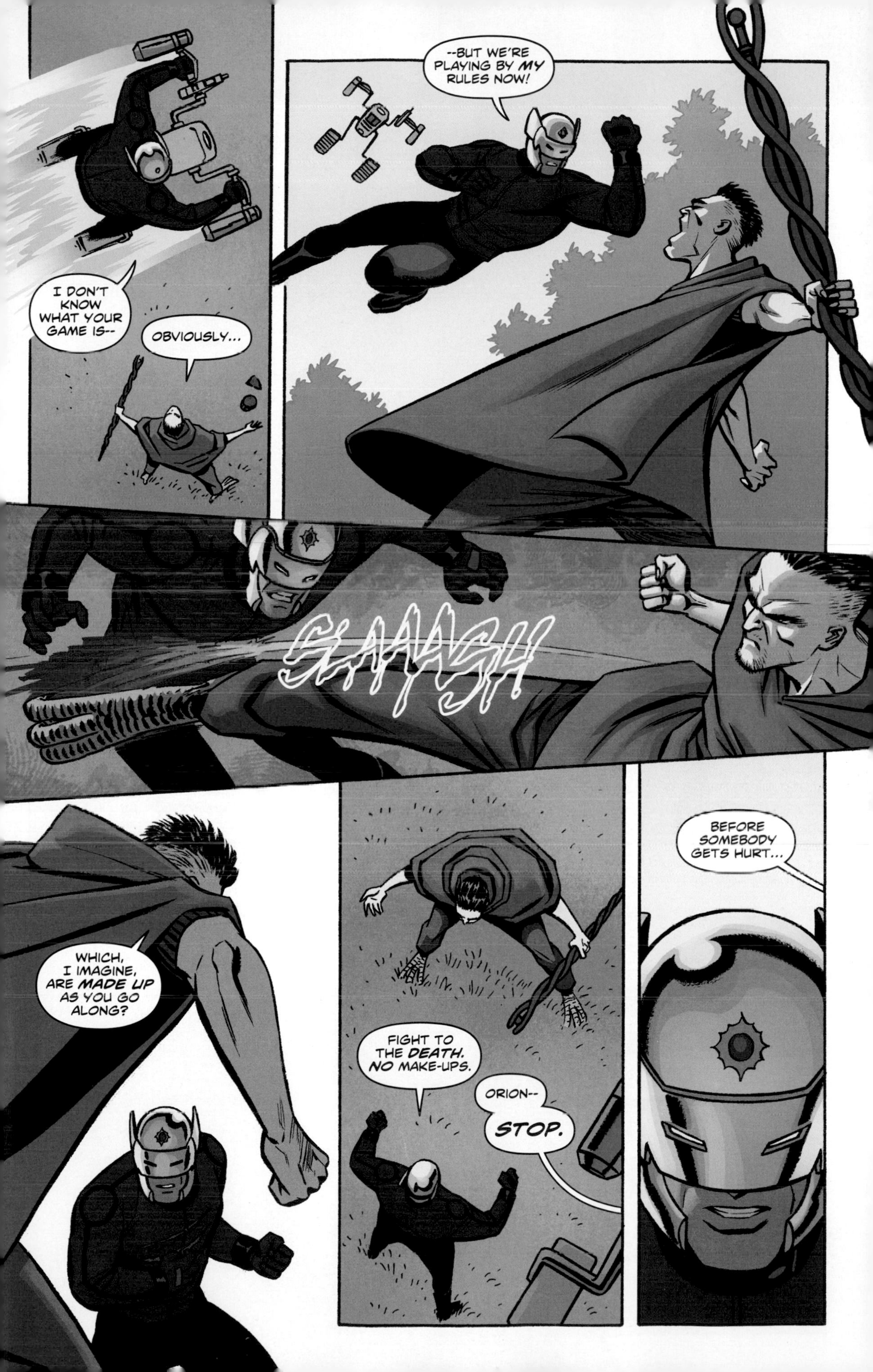
--BUT WE'RE PLAYING BY MY RULES NOW!
I DON'T KNOW WHAT YOUR GAME IS--
OBVIOUSLY...
SLAAAASH!
WHICH, I IMAGINE, ARE MADE UP AS YOU GO ALONG?
FIGHT TO THE DEATH. NO MAKE-UPS.
ORION-- STOP.
BEFORE SOMEBODY GETS HURT...

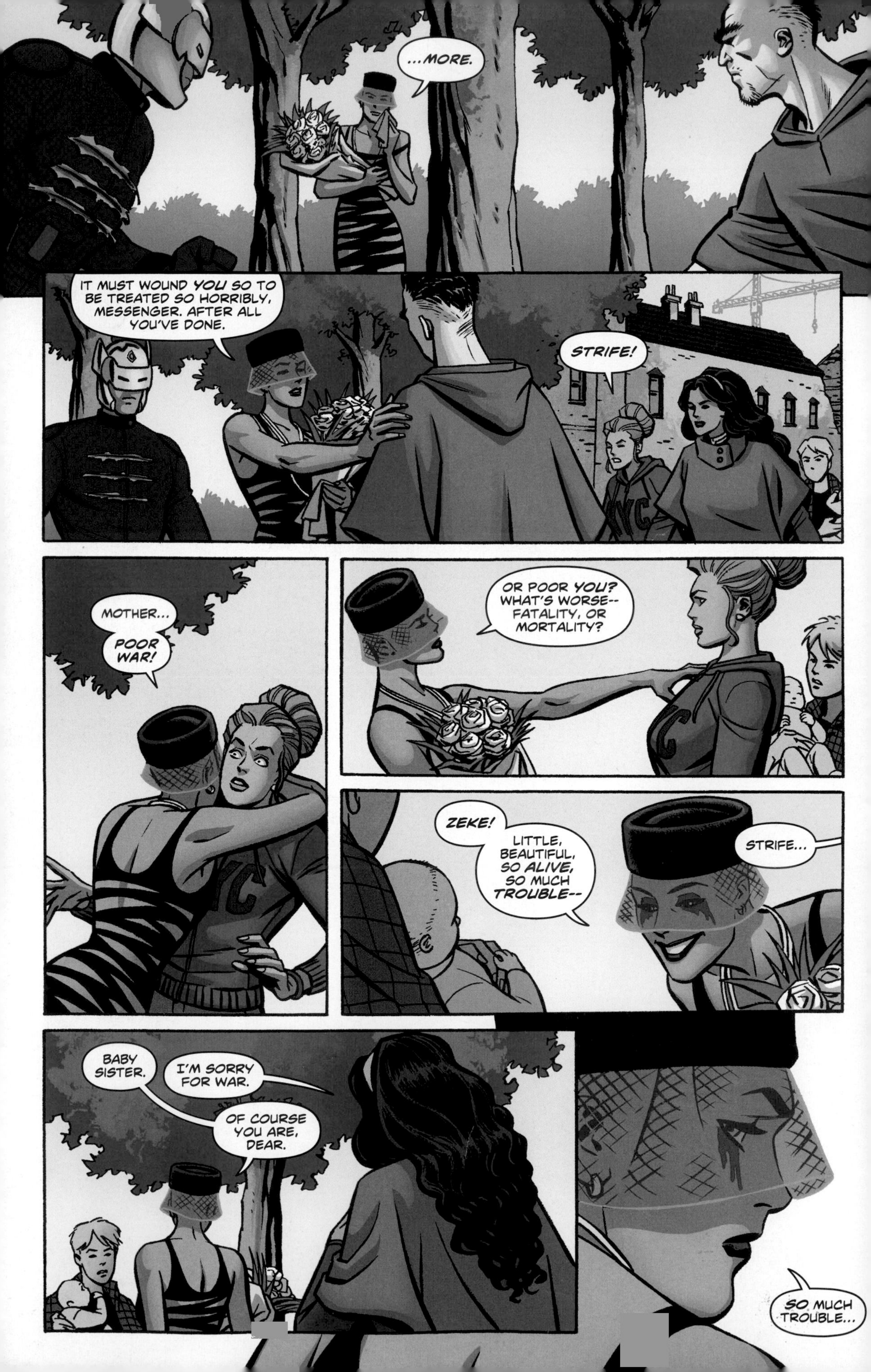
...MORE.
IT MUST WOUND YOU SO TO BE TREATED SO HORRIBLY, MESSENGER. AFTER ALL YOU'VE DONE.
STRIFE!
MOTHER...
POOR WAR!
OR POOR YOU? WHAT'S WORSE-- FATALITY, OR MORTALITY?
ZEKE!
LITTLE, BEAUTIFUL, SO ALIVE, SO MUCH TROUBLE--
STRIFE...
BABY SISTER.
I'M SORRY FOR WAR.
OF COURSE YOU ARE, DEAR.
SO MUCH TROUBLE...

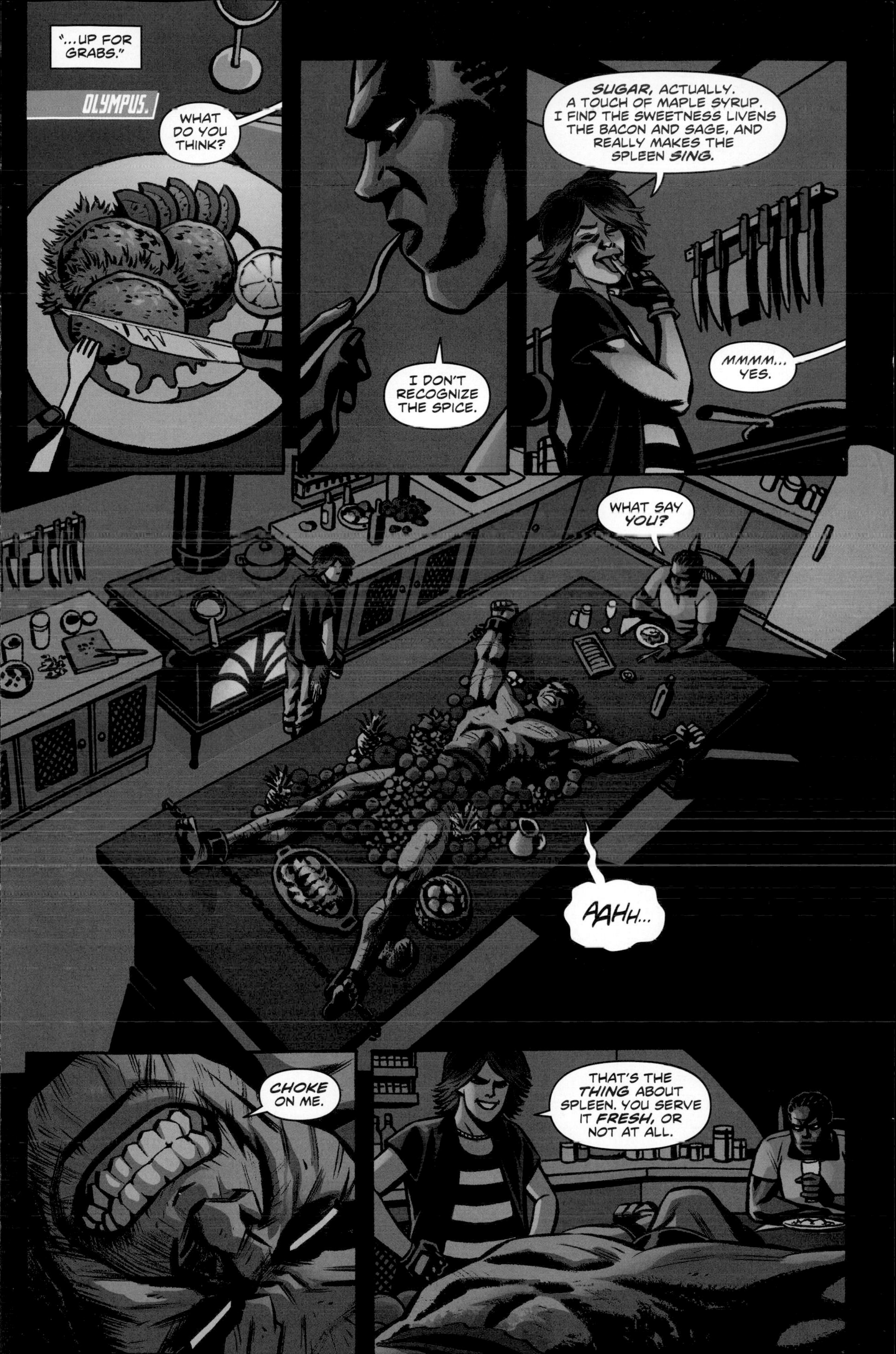
"...UP FOR GRABS."
OLYMPUS.
WHAT DO YOU THINK?
I DON'T RECOGNIZE THE SPICE.
SUGAR, ACTUALLY. A TOUCH OF MAPLE SYRUP. I FIND THE SWEETNESS LIVENS THE BACON AND SAGE, AND REALLY MAKES THE SPLEEN SING.
MMMM... YES.
WHAT SAY YOU?
AAHH...
CHOKE ON ME.
THAT'S THE THING ABOUT SPLEEN. YOU SERVE IT FRESH, OR NOT AT ALL.

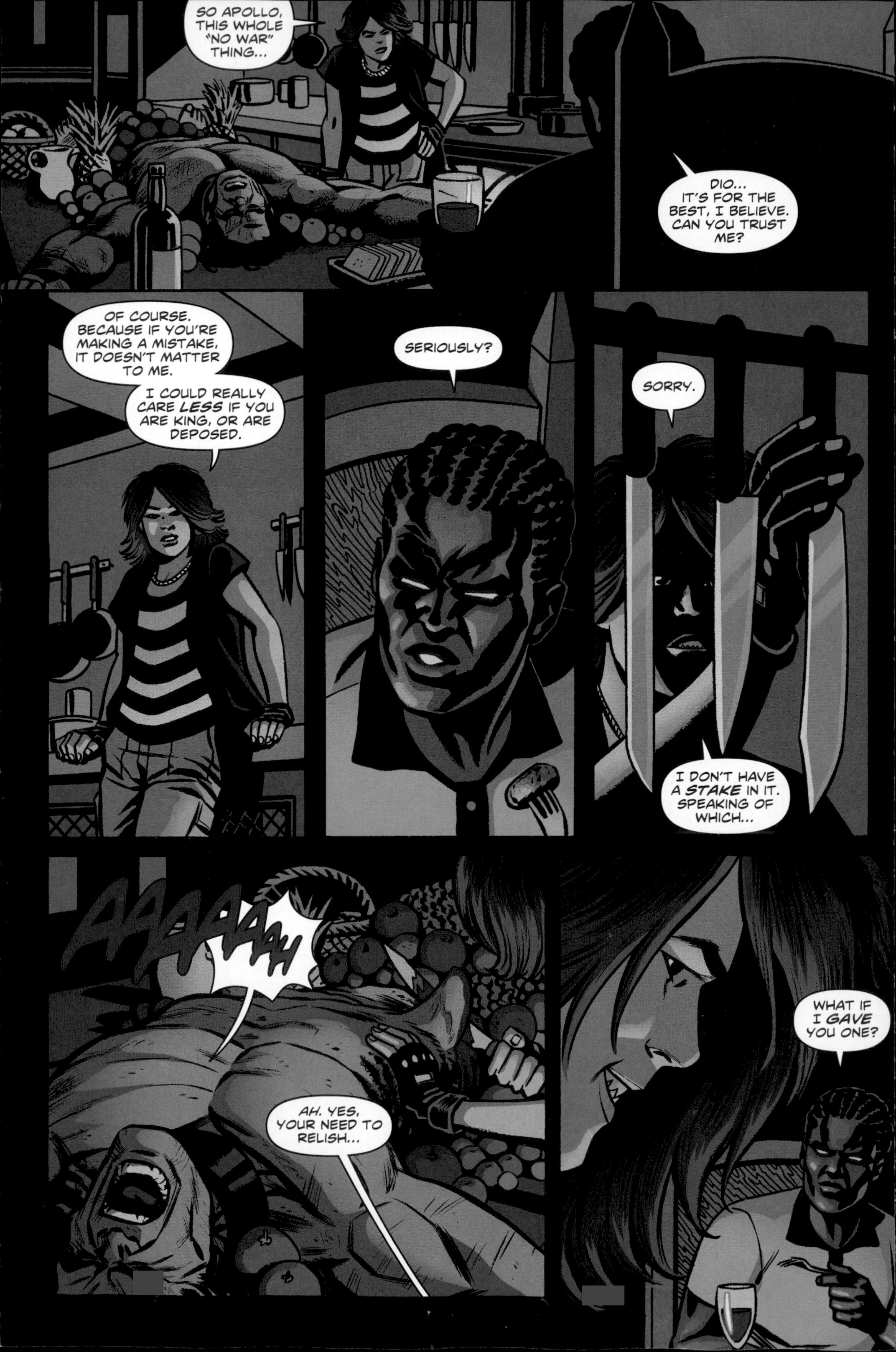
SO APOLLO, THIS WHOLE "NO WAR" THING...
DIO... IT'S FOR THE BEST, I BELIEVE. CAN YOU TRUST ME?
OF COURSE. BECAUSE IF YOU'RE MAKING A MISTAKE, IT DOESN'T MATTER TO ME.
I COULD REALLY CARE *LESS* IF YOU ARE KING, OR ARE DEPOSED.
SERIOUSLY?
SORRY.
I DON'T HAVE A *STAKE* IN IT. SPEAKING OF WHICH...
AAAAAAAH
AH. YES, YOUR NEED TO RELISH...
WHAT IF I *GAVE* YOU ONE?

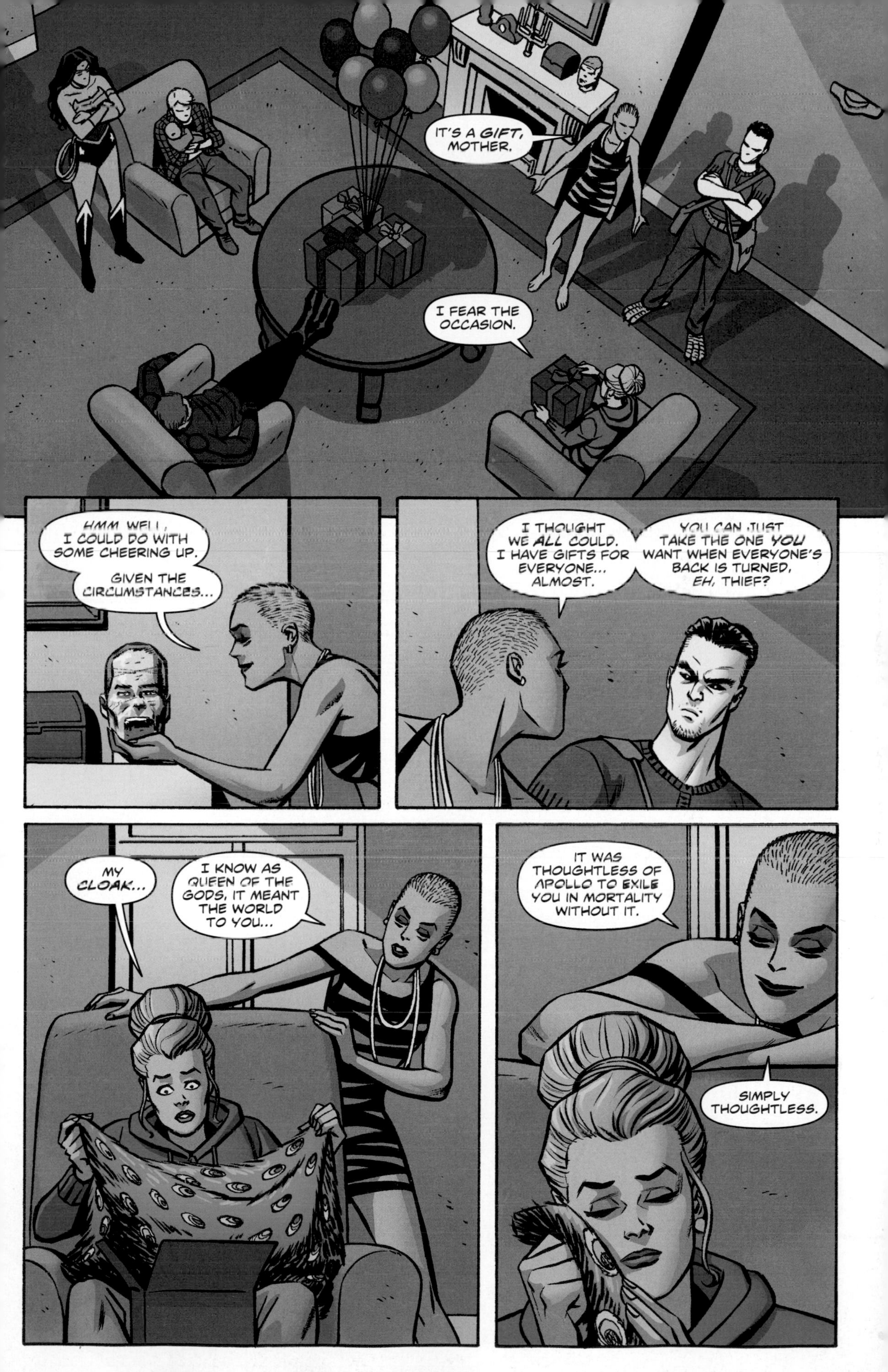
IT'S A GIFT, MOTHER.
I FEAR THE OCCASION.
HMM WELL, I COULD DO WITH SOME CHEERING UP.
GIVEN THE CIRCUMSTANCES...
I THOUGHT WE ALL COULD. I HAVE GIFTS FOR EVERYONE... ALMOST.
YOU CAN JUST TAKE THE ONE YOU WANT WHEN EVERYONE'S BACK IS TURNED, EH, THIEF?
MY CLOAK...
I KNOW AS QUEEN OF THE GODS, IT MEANT THE WORLD TO YOU...
IT WAS THOUGHTLESS OF APOLLO TO EXILE YOU IN MORTALITY WITHOUT IT.
SIMPLY THOUGHTLESS.

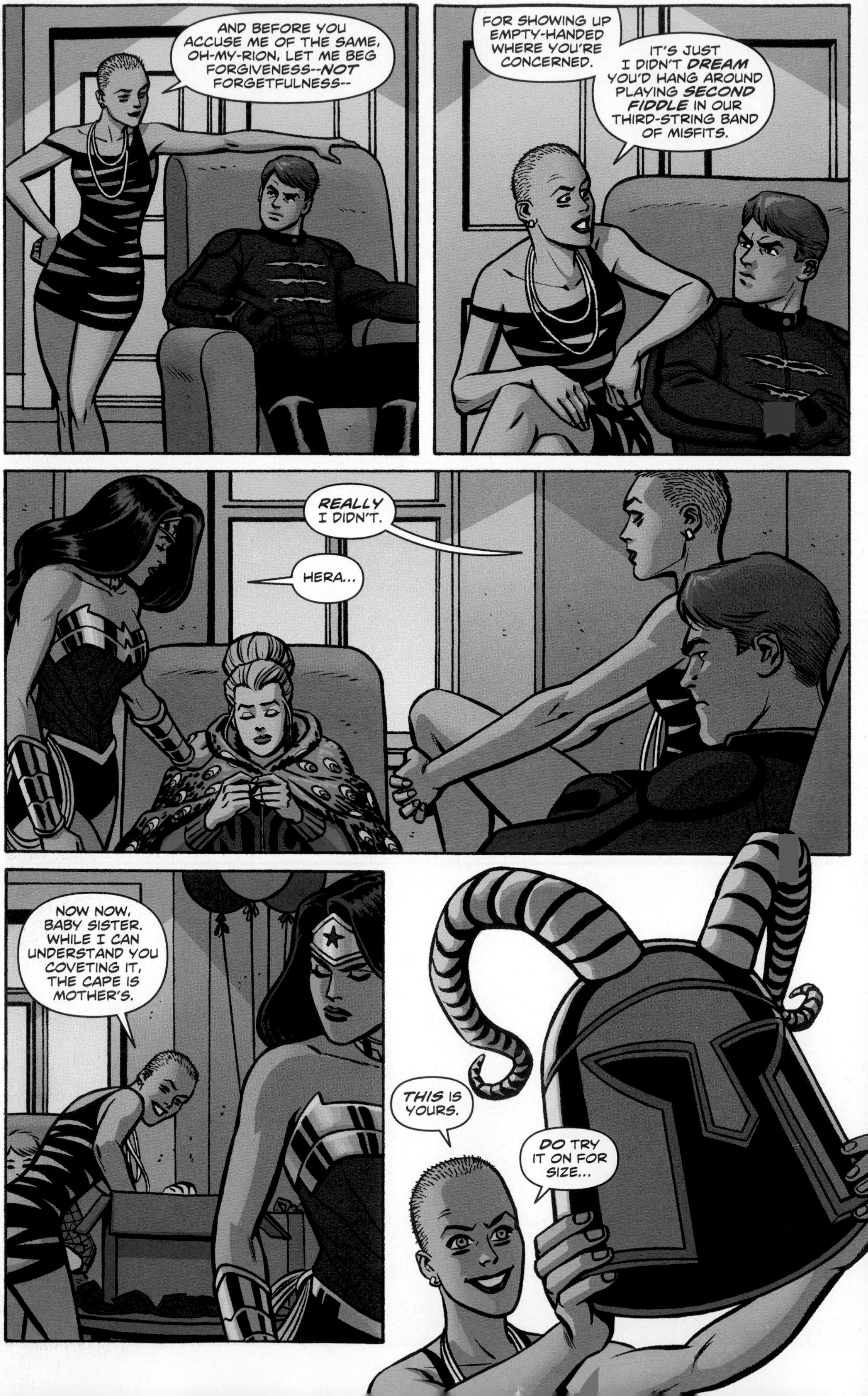
AND BEFORE YOU ACCUSE ME OF THE SAME, OH-MY-RION, LET ME BEG FORGIVENESS--NOT FORGETFULNESS--
FOR SHOWING UP EMPTY-HANDED WHERE YOU'RE CONCERNED.
IT'S JUST I DIDN'T DREAM YOU'D HANG AROUND PLAYING SECOND FIDDLE IN OUR THIRD-STRING BAND OF MISFITS.
REALLY I DIDN'T.
HERA...
NOW NOW, BABY SISTER. WHILE I CAN UNDERSTAND YOU COVETING IT, THE CAPE IS MOTHER'S.
THIS IS YOURS.
DO TRY IT ON FOR SIZE...

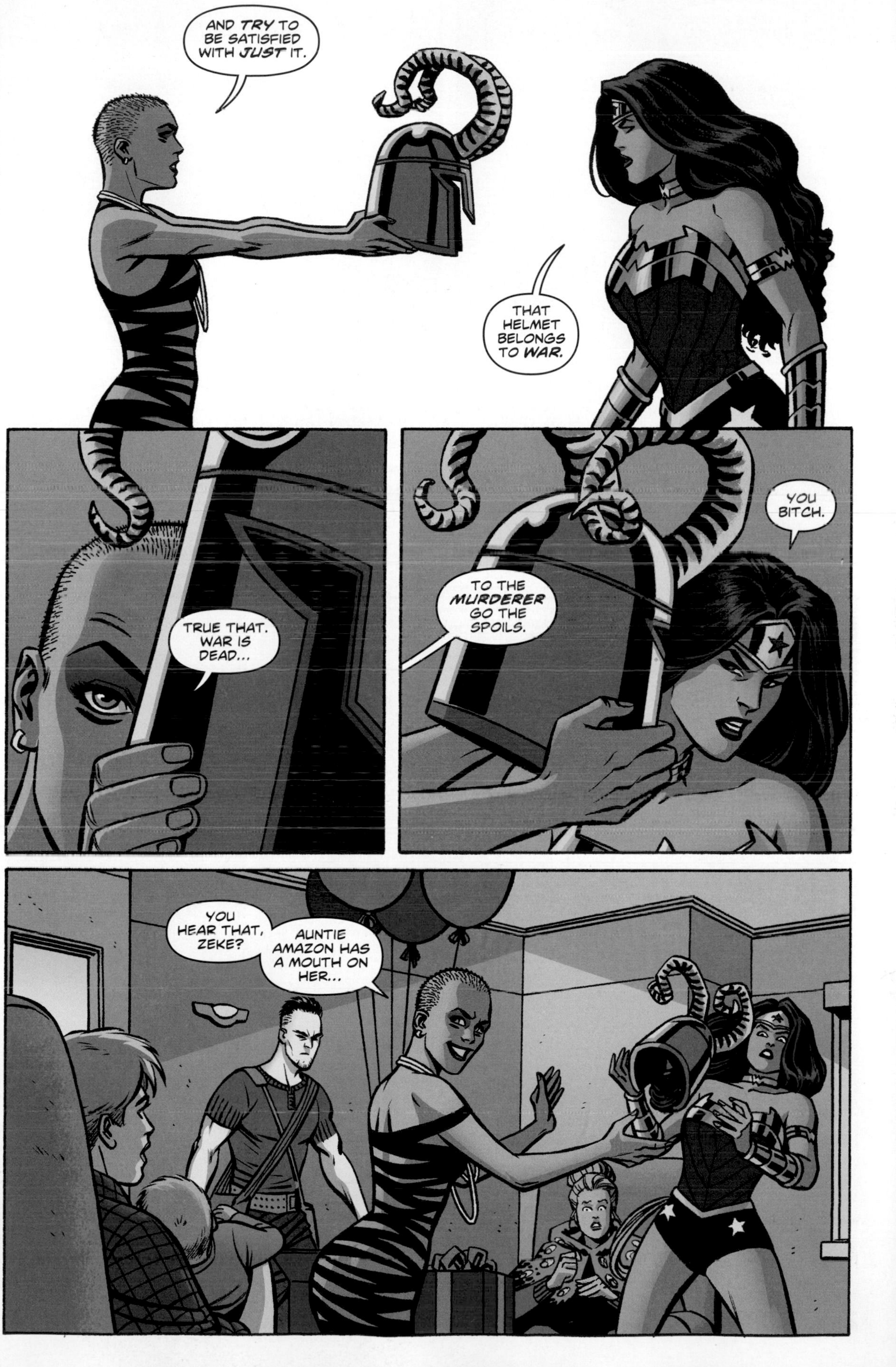
AND TRY TO BE SATISFIED WITH JUST IT.
THAT HELMET BELONGS TO WAR.
TRUE THAT. WAR IS DEAD...
TO THE MURDERER GO THE SPOILS.
YOU BITCH.
YOU HEAR THAT, ZEKE?
AUNTIE AMAZON HAS A MOUTH ON HER...

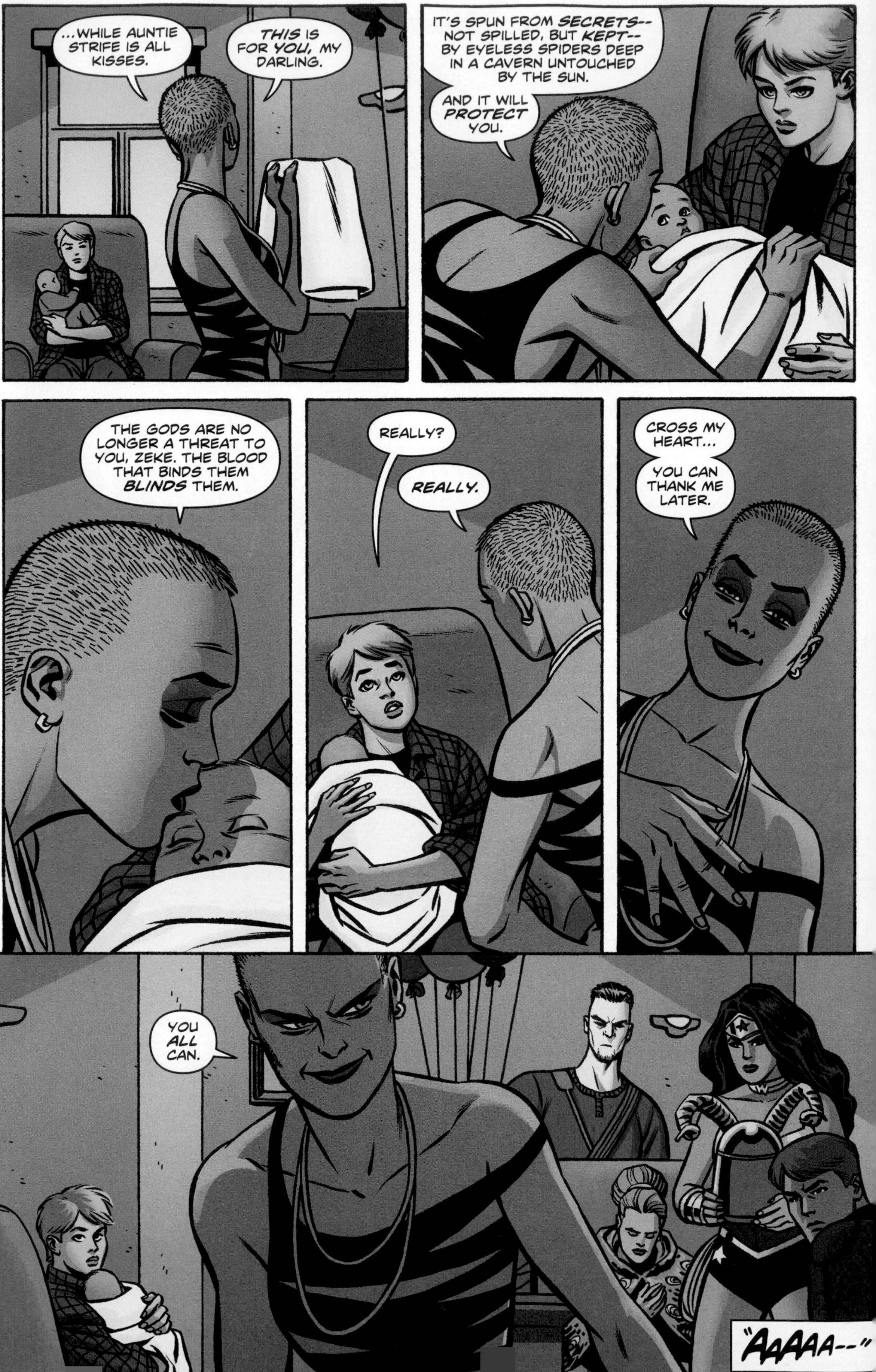
...WHILE AUNTIE STRIFE IS ALL KISSES.
THIS IS FOR YOU, MY DARLING.
IT'S SPUN FROM SECRETS-- NOT SPILLED, BUT KEPT-- BY EYELESS SPIDERS DEEP IN A CAVERN UNTOUCHED BY THE SUN.
AND IT WILL PROTECT YOU.
THE GODS ARE NO LONGER A THREAT TO YOU, ZEKE. THE BLOOD THAT BINDS THEM BLINDS THEM.
REALLY?
REALLY.
CROSS MY HEART...
YOU CAN THANK ME LATER.
YOU ALL CAN.
"AAAAA--"

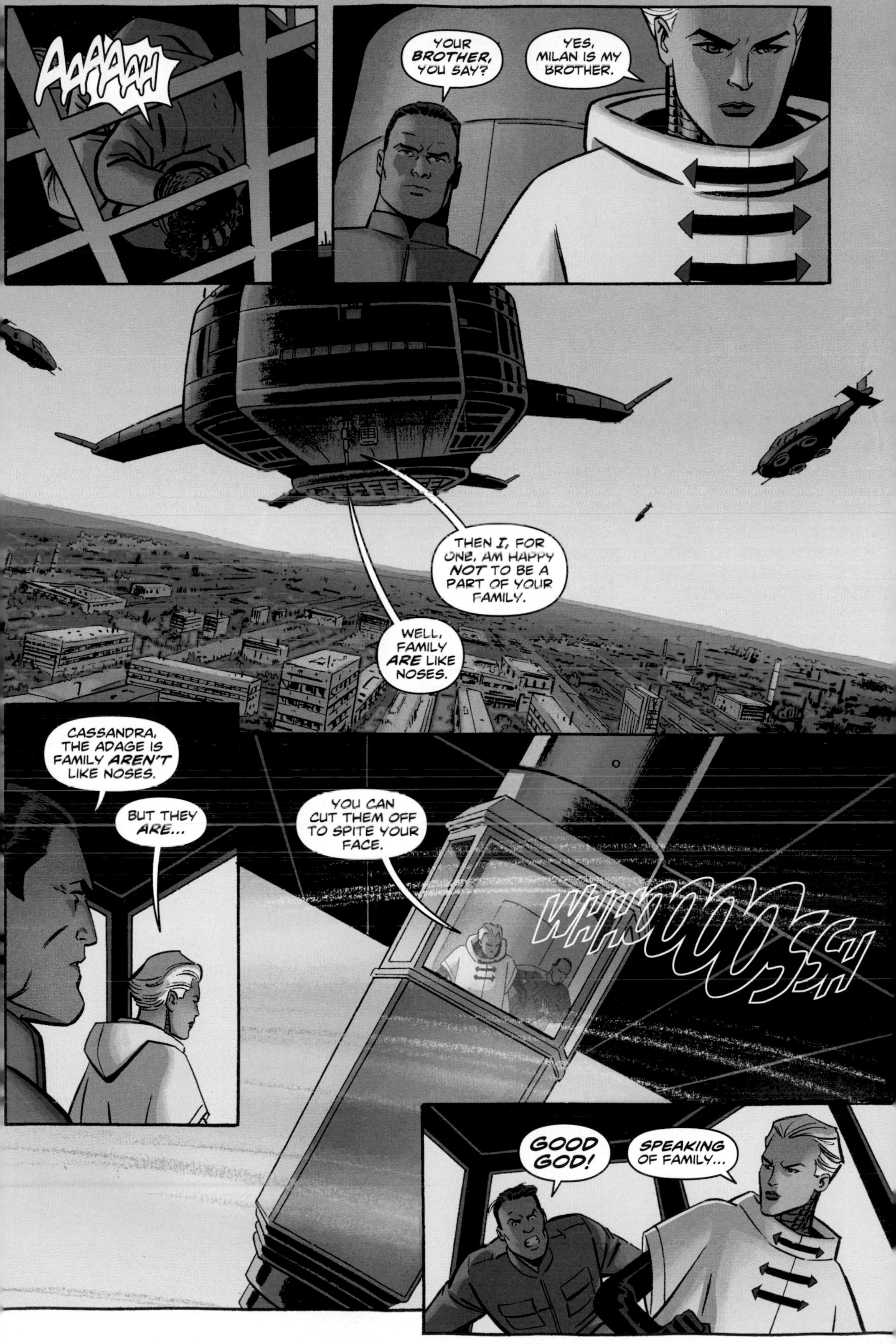
AAAAAAH
YOUR BROTHER, YOU SAY?
YES, MILAN IS MY BROTHER.
THEN I, FOR ONE, AM HAPPY NOT TO BE A PART OF YOUR FAMILY.
WELL, FAMILY ARE LIKE NOSES.
CASSANDRA, THE ADAGE IS FAMILY AREN'T LIKE NOSES.
BUT THEY ARE...
YOU CAN CUT THEM OFF TO SPITE YOUR FACE.
WHOOOOSH
GOOD GOD!
SPEAKING OF FAMILY...

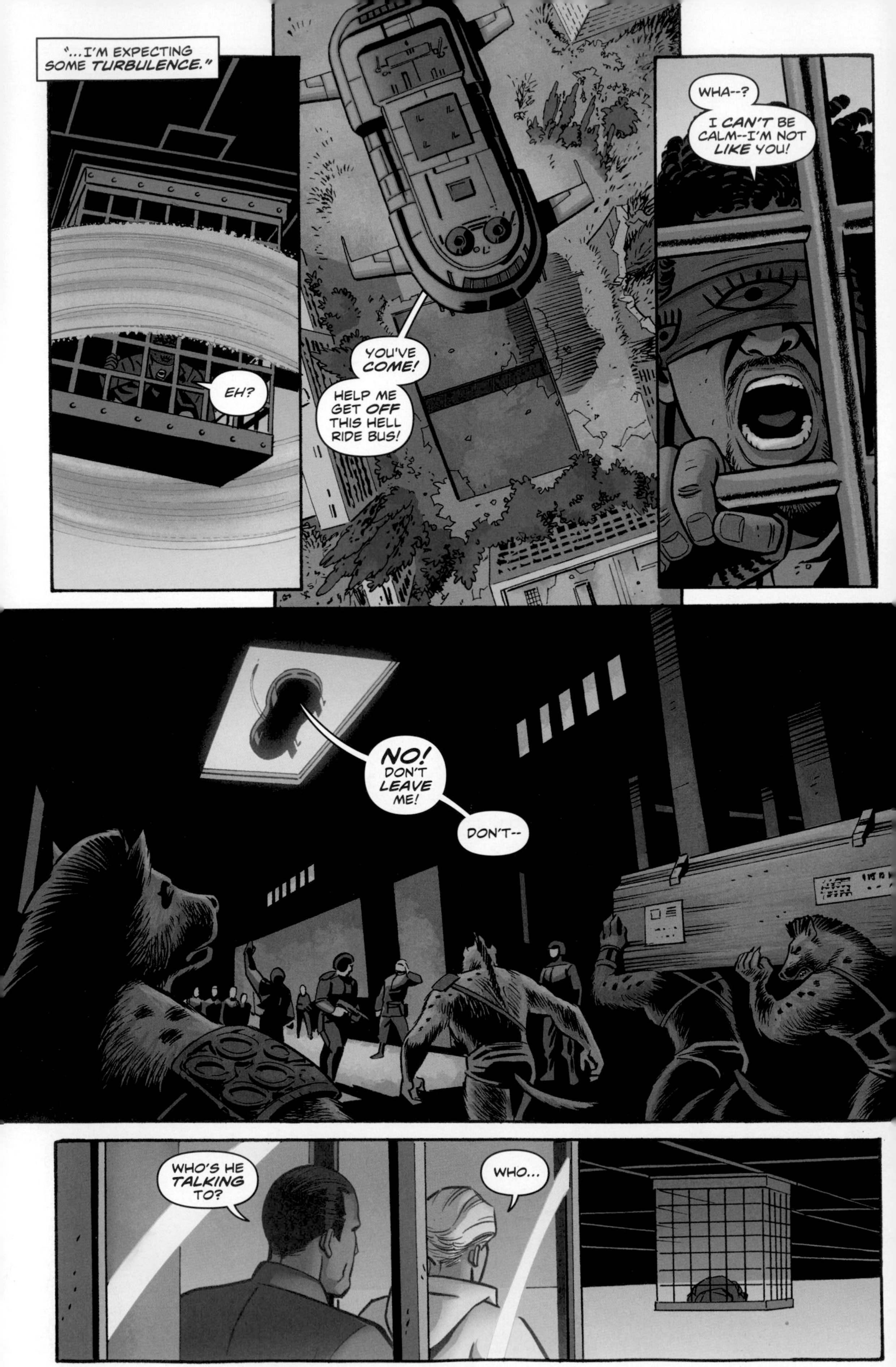
"...I'M EXPECTING SOME TURBULENCE."
EH?
YOU'VE COME!
HELP ME GET OFF THIS HELL RIDE BUS!
WHA--?
I CAN'T BE CALM--I'M NOT LIKE YOU!
NO! DON'T LEAVE ME!
DON'T--
WHO'S HE TALKING TO?
WHO...

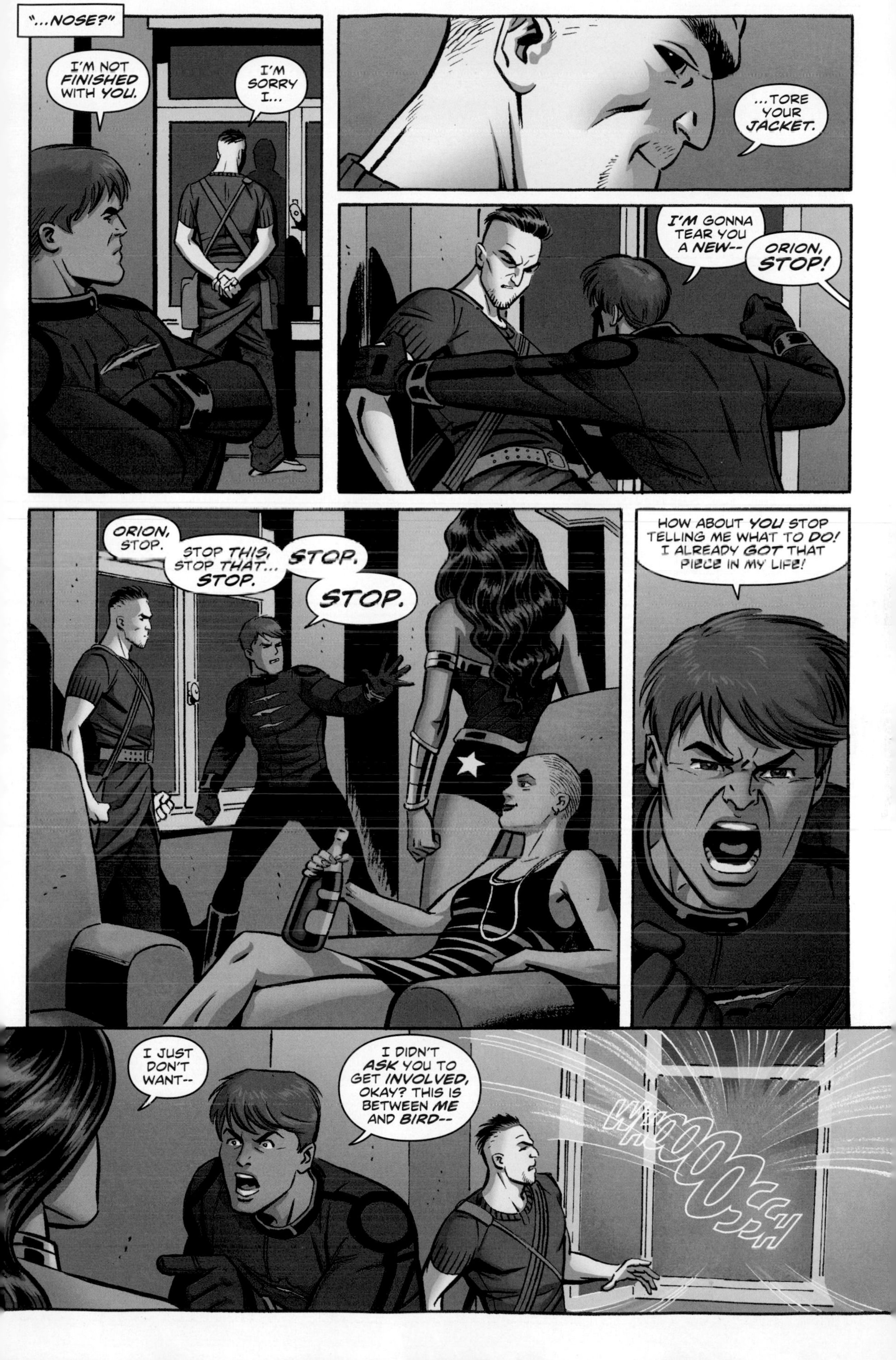
"...NOSE?"
I'M NOT FINISHED WITH YOU.
I'M SORRY I...
...TORE YOUR JACKET.
I'M GONNA TEAR YOU A NEW--
ORION, STOP!
ORION, STOP.
STOP THIS, STOP THAT... STOP.
STOP.
STOP.
HOW ABOUT YOU STOP TELLING ME WHAT TO DO! I ALREADY GOT THAT PIECE IN MY LIFE!
I JUST DON'T WANT--
I DIDN'T ASK YOU TO GET INVOLVED, OKAY? THIS IS BETWEEN ME AND BIRD--
WHOOOSH

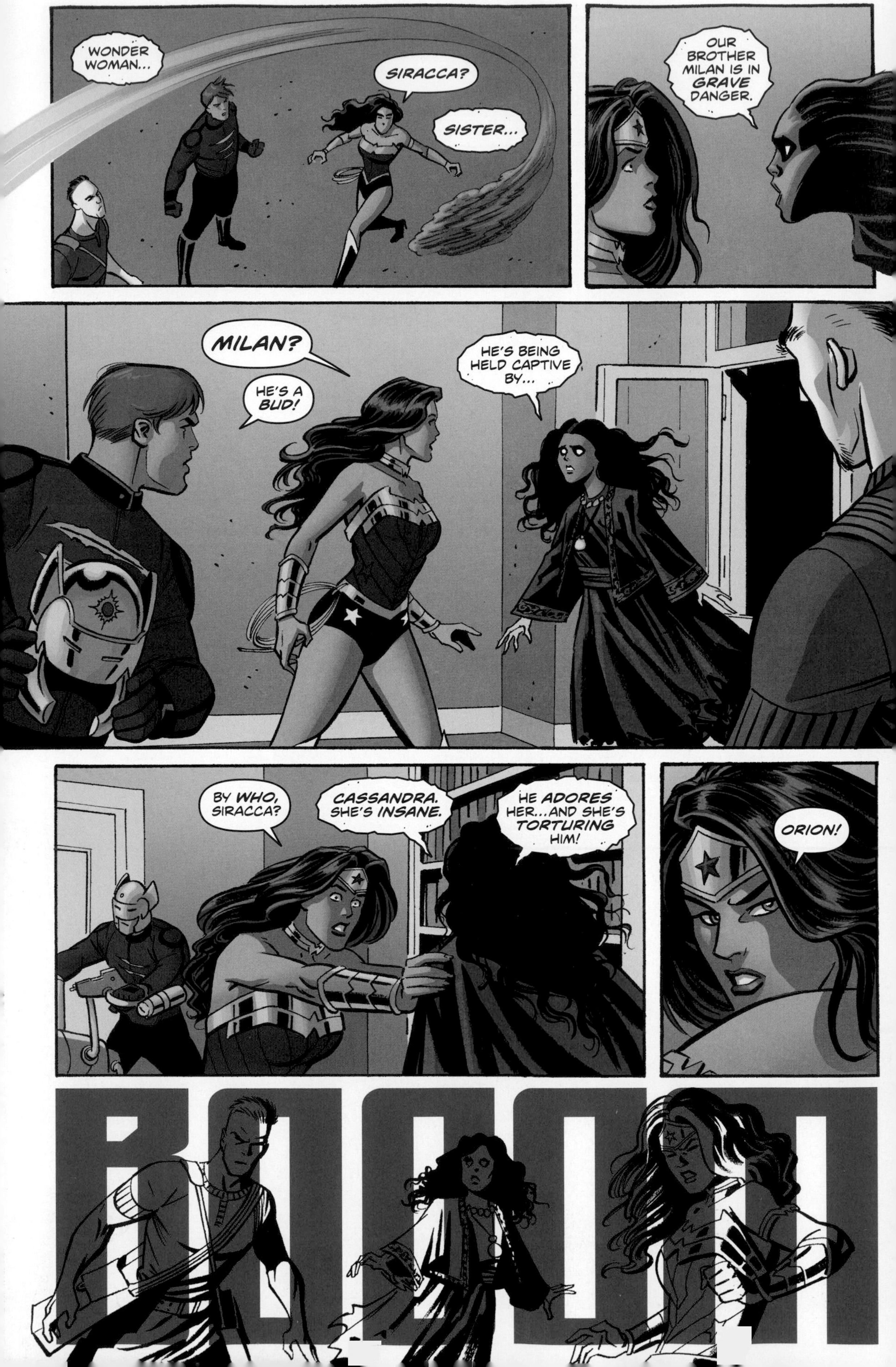
WONDER WOMAN...
SIRACCA?
SISTER...
OUR BROTHER MILAN IS IN GRAVE DANGER.
MILAN?
HE'S A BUD!
HE'S BEING HELD CAPTIVE BY...
BY WHO, SIRACCA?
CASSANDRA. SHE'S INSANE.
HE ADORES HER...AND SHE'S TORTURING HIM!
ORION!
BOOM

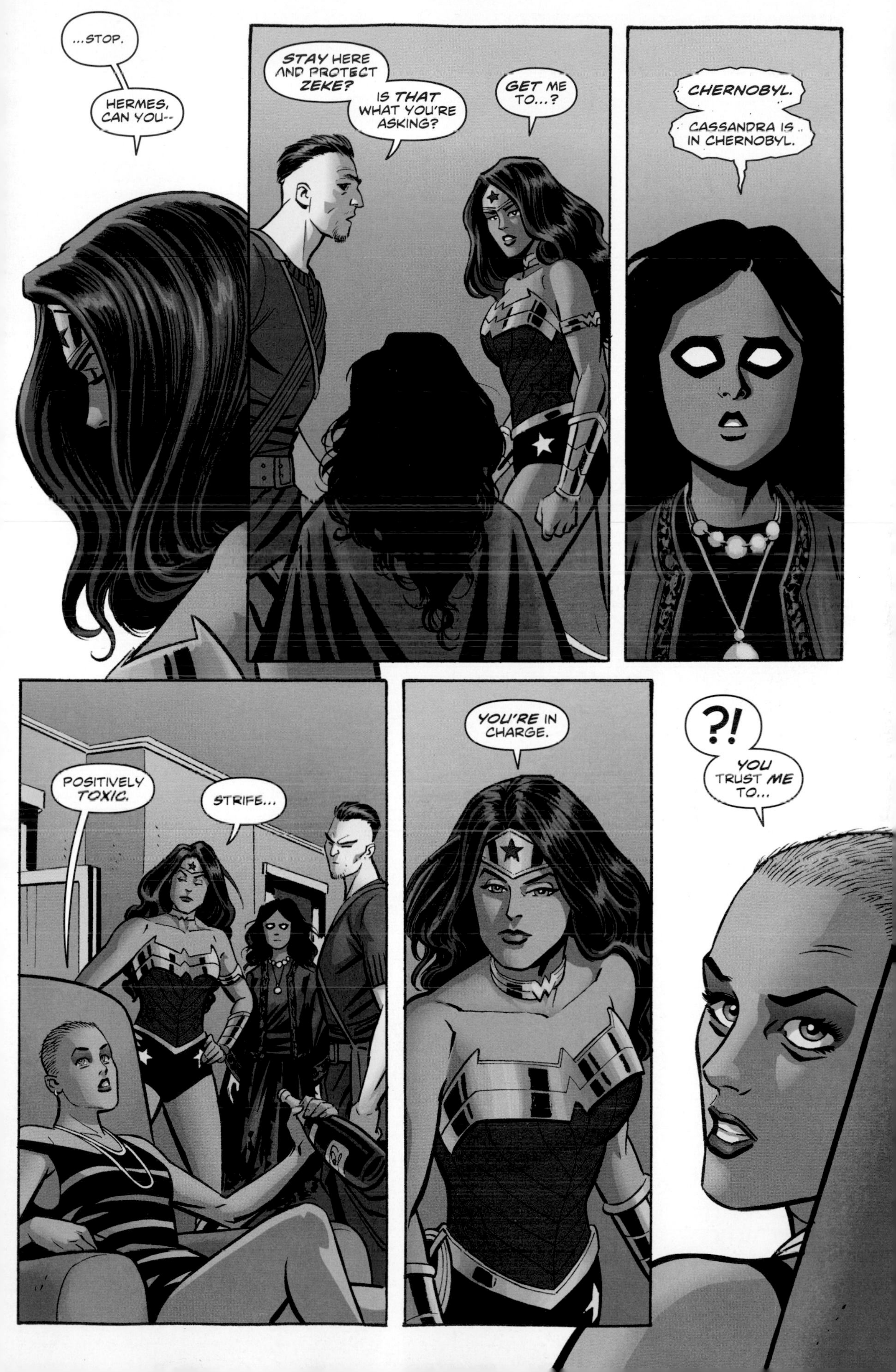
...STOP.
HERMES, CAN YOU--
STAY HERE AND PROTECT ZEKE?
IS THAT WHAT YOU'RE ASKING?
GET ME TO...?
CHERNOBYL.
CASSANDRA IS IN CHERNOBYL.
POSITIVELY TOXIC.
STRIFE...
YOU'RE IN CHARGE.
?!
YOU TRUST ME TO...

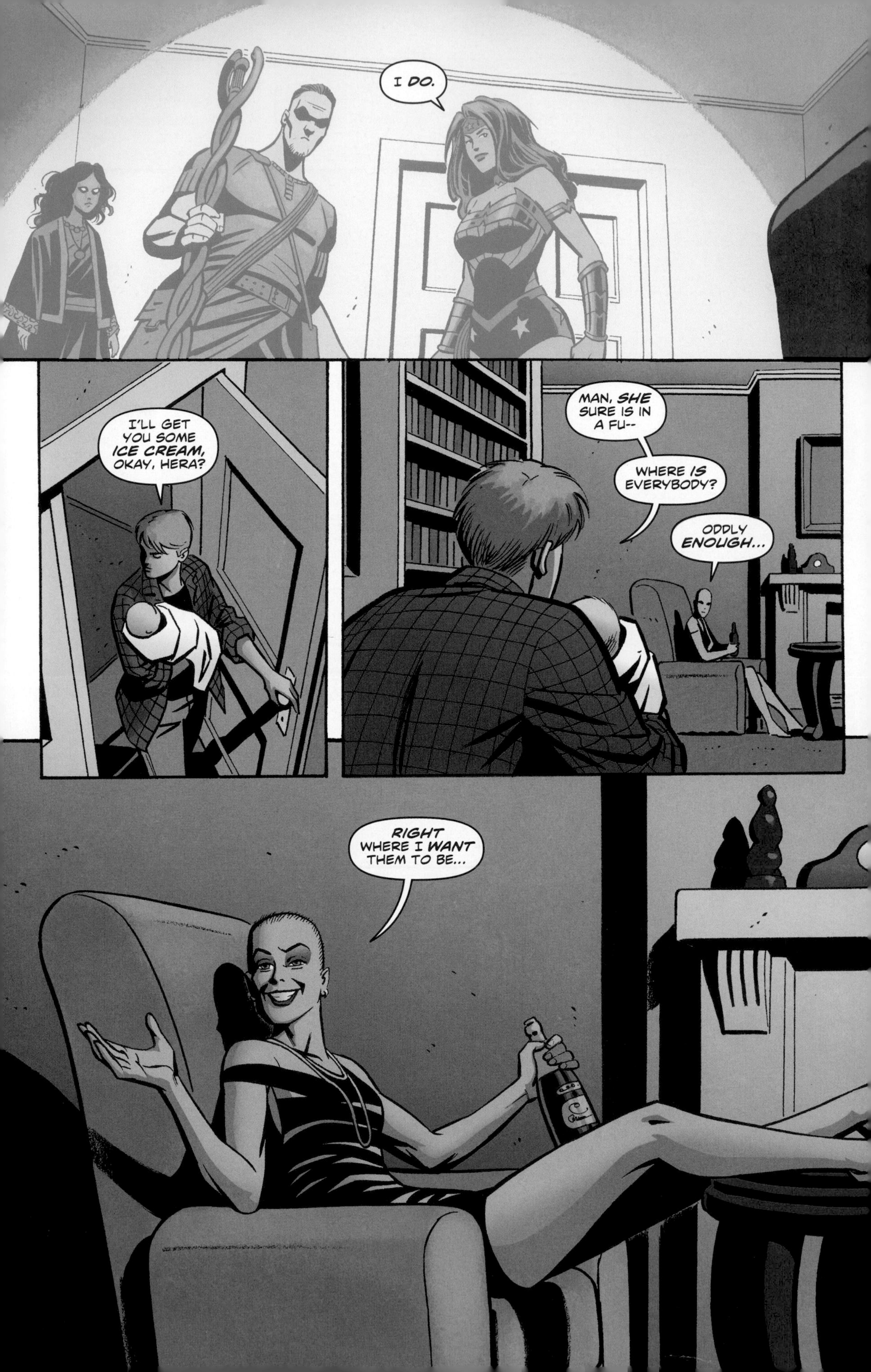
I DO.
I'LL GET YOU SOME ICE CREAM, OKAY, HERA?
MAN, SHE SURE IS IN A FU--
WHERE IS EVERYBODY?
ODDLY ENOUGH...
RIGHT WHERE I WANT THEM TO BE...

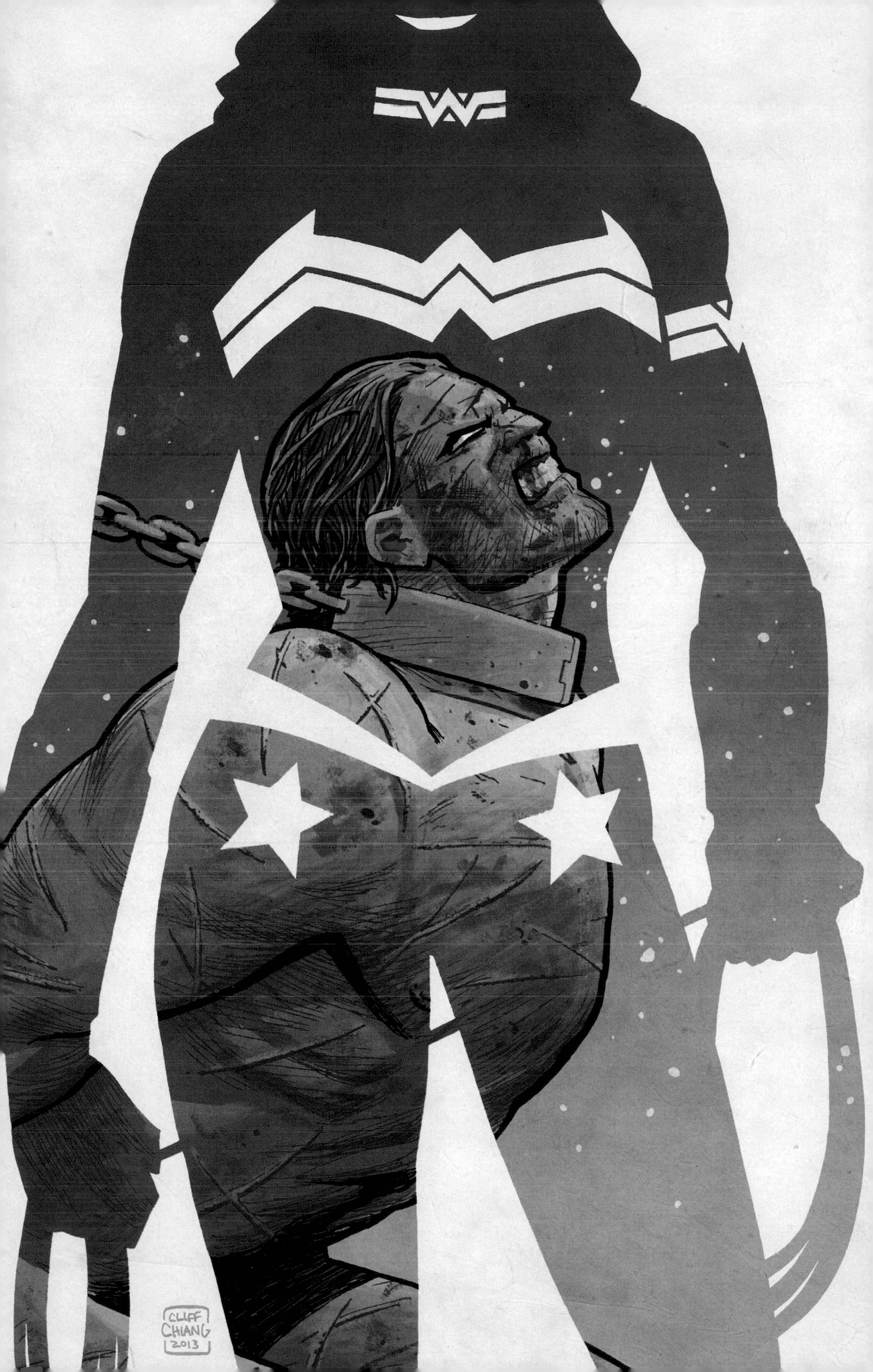
CLIFF
CHIANG
2013

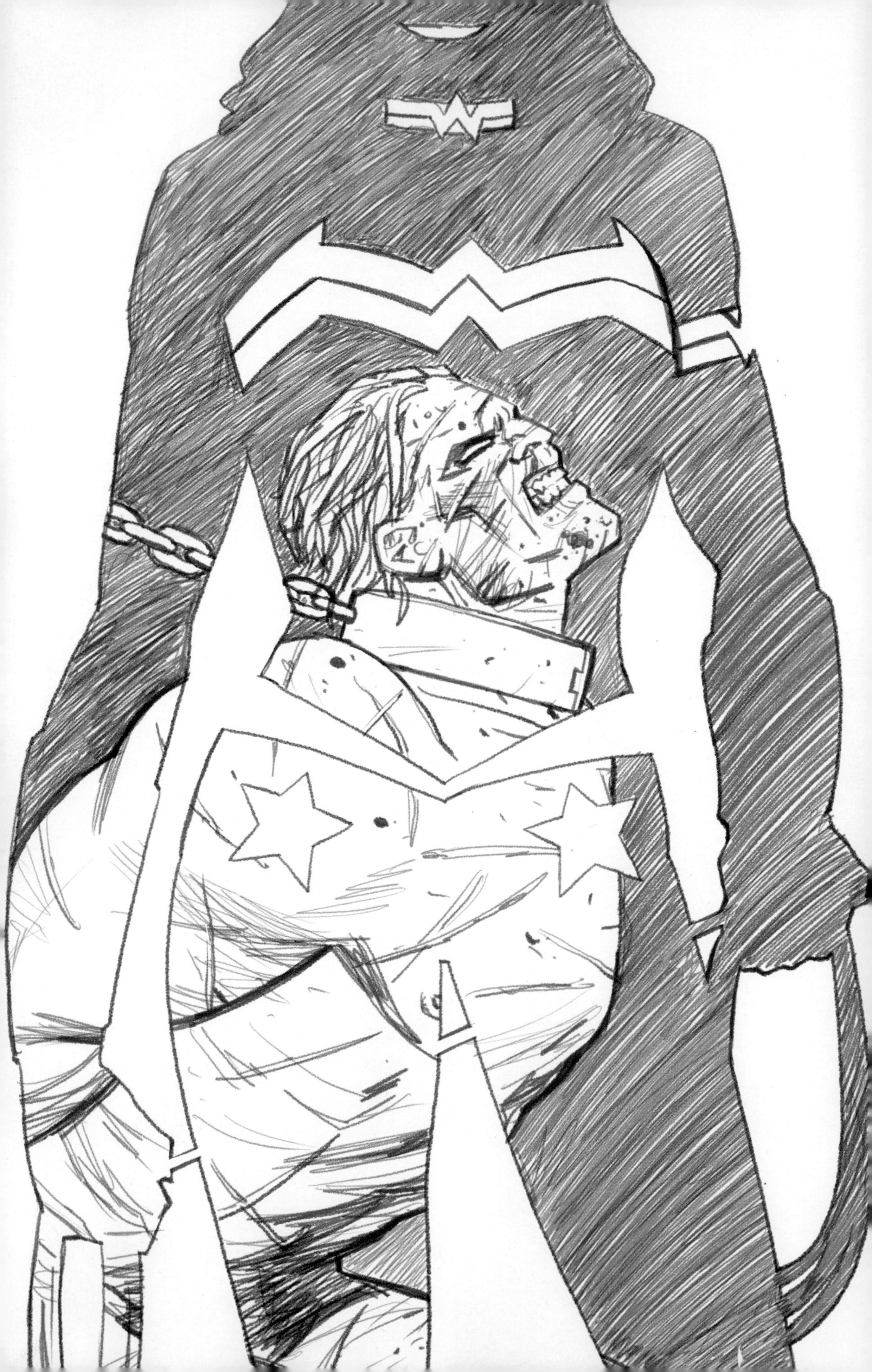

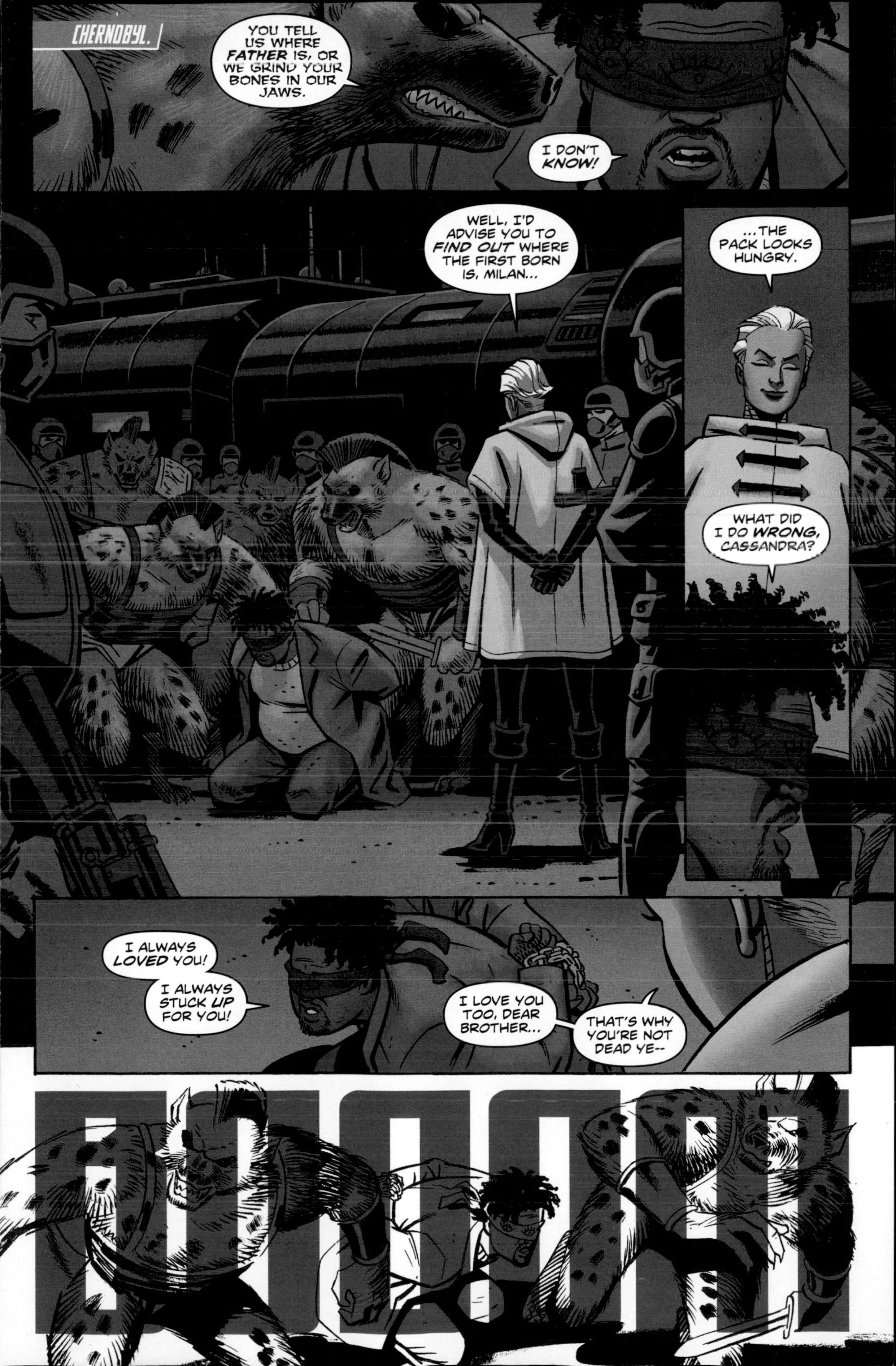
CHERNOBYL.
YOU TELL US WHERE FATHER IS, OR WE GRIND YOUR BONES IN OUR JAWS.
I DON'T KNOW!
WELL, I'D ADVISE YOU TO FIND OUT WHERE THE FIRST BORN IS, MILAN...
...THE PACK LOOKS HUNGRY.
WHAT DID I DO WRONG, CASSANDRA?
I ALWAYS LOVED YOU!
I ALWAYS STUCK UP FOR YOU!
I LOVE YOU TOO, DEAR BROTHER...
THAT'S WHY YOU'RE NOT DEAD YE--

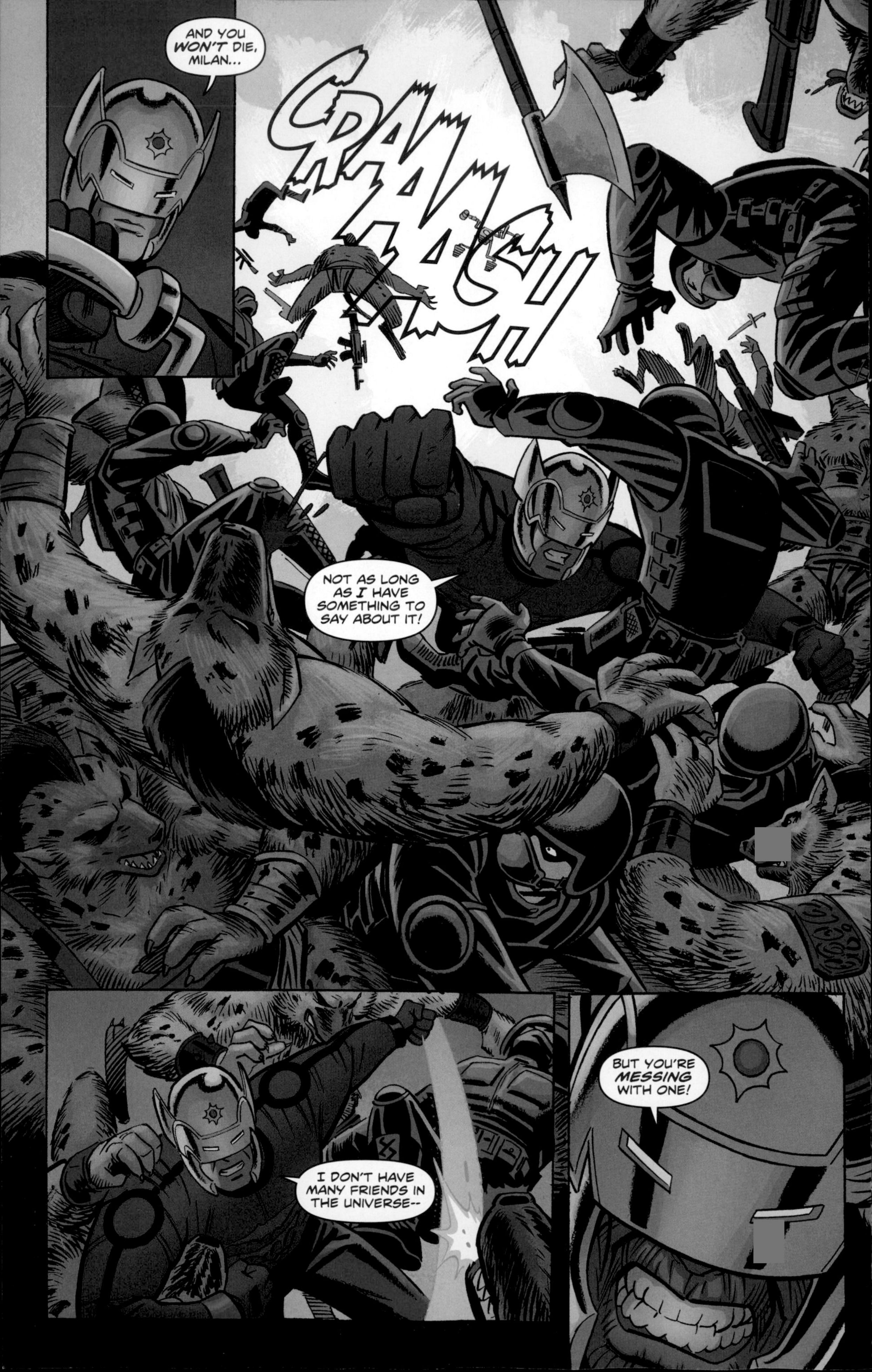
AND YOU WON'T DIE, MILAN...
CRAAACH
NOT AS LONG AS I HAVE SOMETHING TO SAY ABOUT IT!
I DON'T HAVE MANY FRIENDS IN THE UNIVERSE--
BUT YOU'RE MESSING WITH ONE!

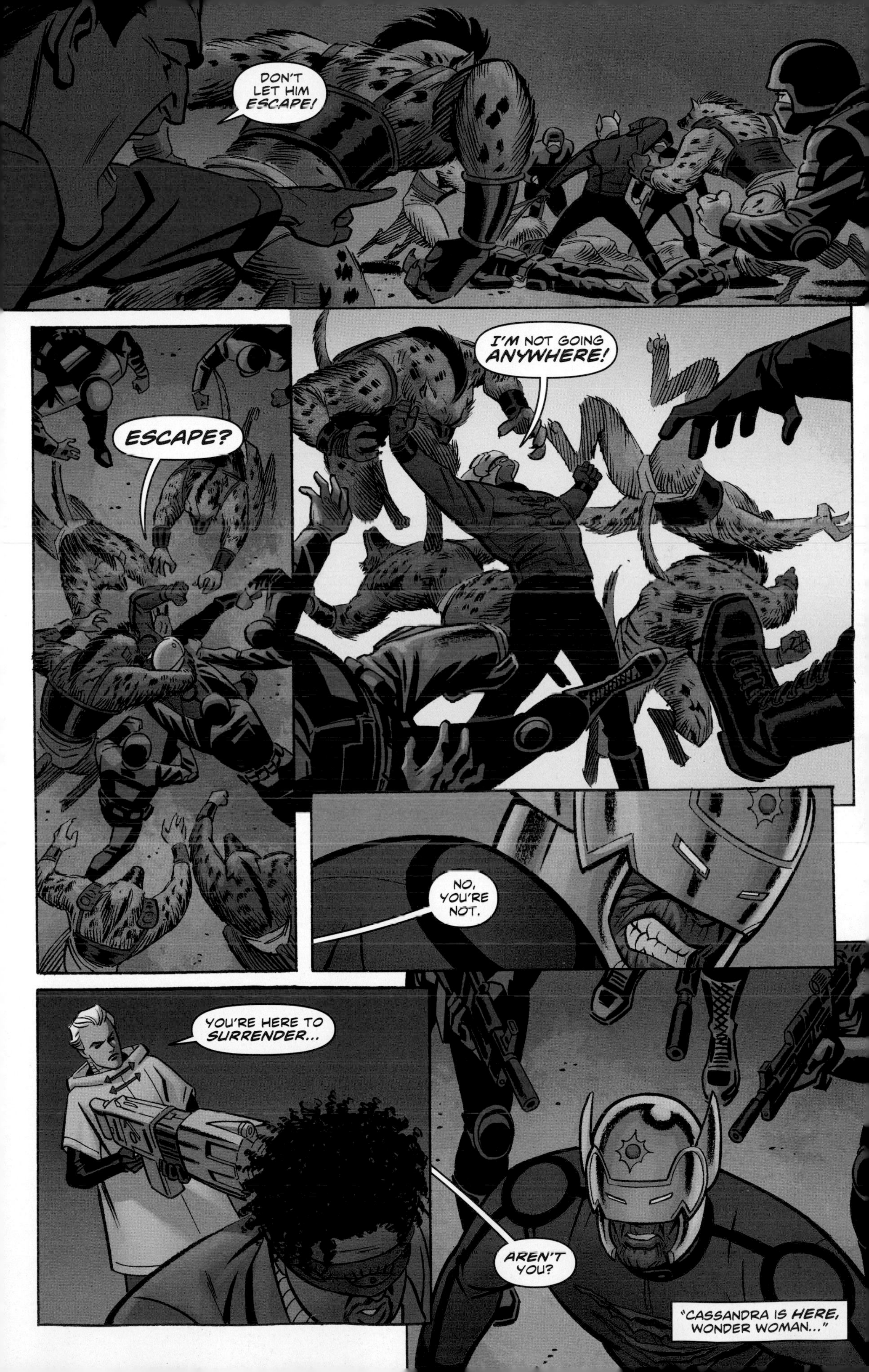
DON'T LET HIM ESCAPE!
ESCAPE?
I'M NOT GOING ANYWHERE!
NO, YOU'RE NOT.
YOU'RE HERE TO SURRENDER...
AREN'T YOU?
"CASSANDRA IS HERE, WONDER WOMAN..."

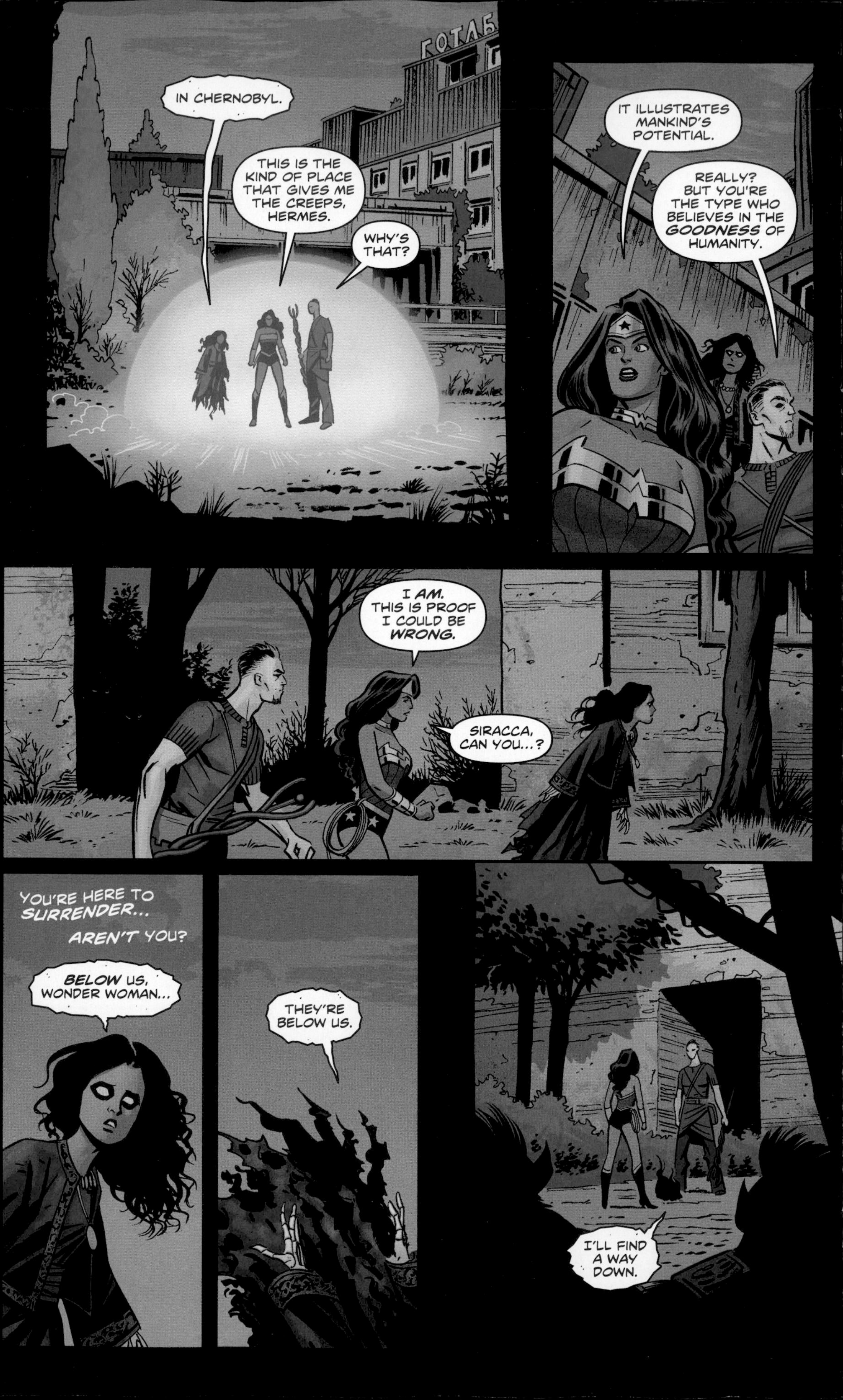
ГОТАБ
IN CHERNOBYL.
THIS IS THE KIND OF PLACE THAT GIVES ME THE CREEPS, HERMES.
WHY'S THAT?
IT ILLUSTRATES MANKIND'S POTENTIAL.
REALLY? BUT YOU'RE THE TYPE WHO BELIEVES IN THE *GOODNESS* OF HUMANITY.
I *AM.* THIS IS PROOF I COULD BE *WRONG.*
SIRACCA, CAN YOU...?
YOU'RE HERE TO *SURRENDER...*
*AREN'T* YOU?
*BELOW* US, WONDER WOMAN...
THEY'RE BELOW US.
I'LL FIND A WAY DOWN.

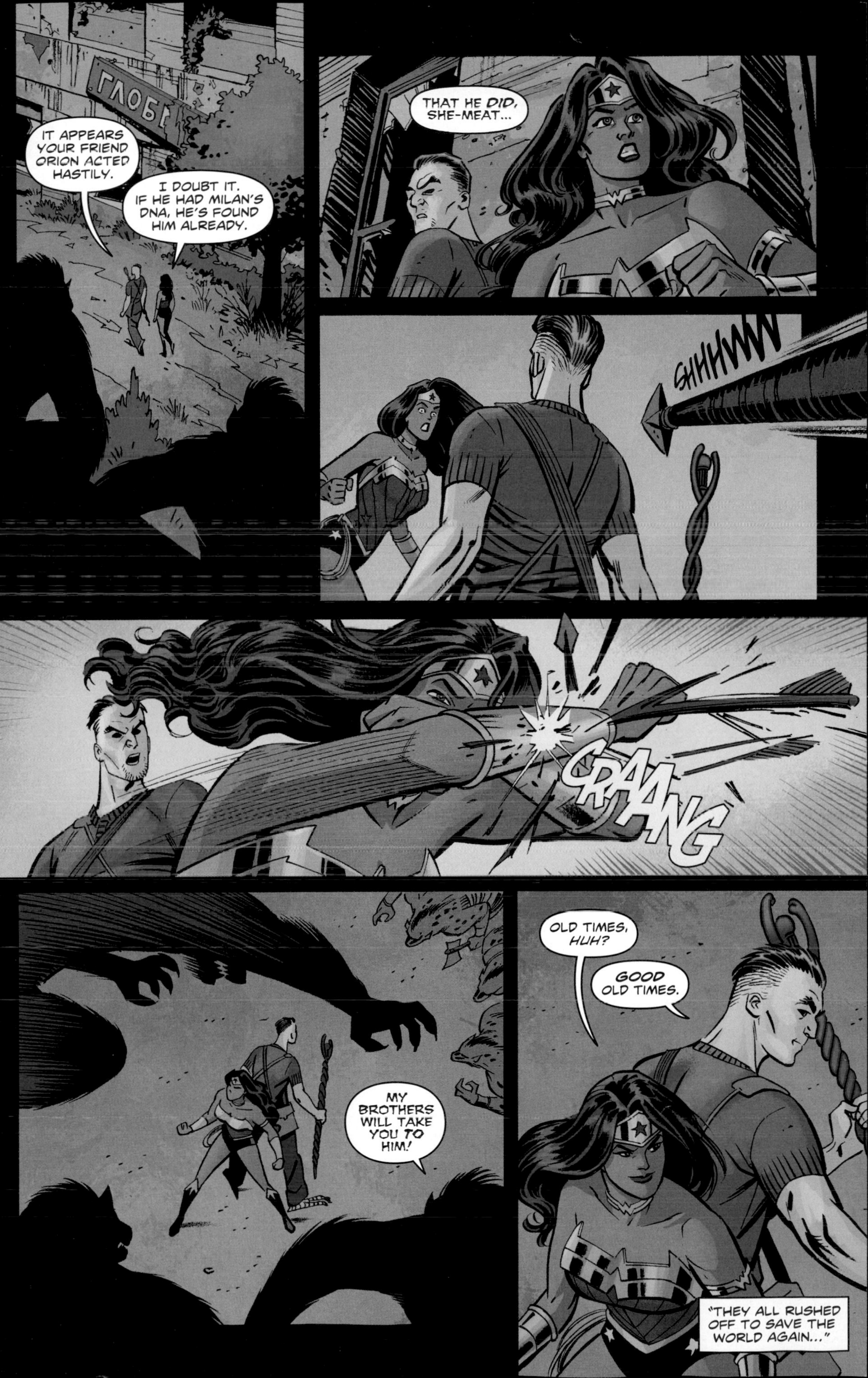
ГЛОБ[
IT APPEARS YOUR FRIEND ORION ACTED HASTILY.
I DOUBT IT. IF HE HAD MILAN'S DNA, HE'S FOUND HIM ALREADY.
THAT HE DID, SHE-MEAT...
SHHHWWW
CRAAANG
MY BROTHERS WILL TAKE YOU TO HIM!
OLD TIMES, HUH?
GOOD OLD TIMES.
"THEY ALL RUSHED OFF TO SAVE THE WORLD AGAIN..."

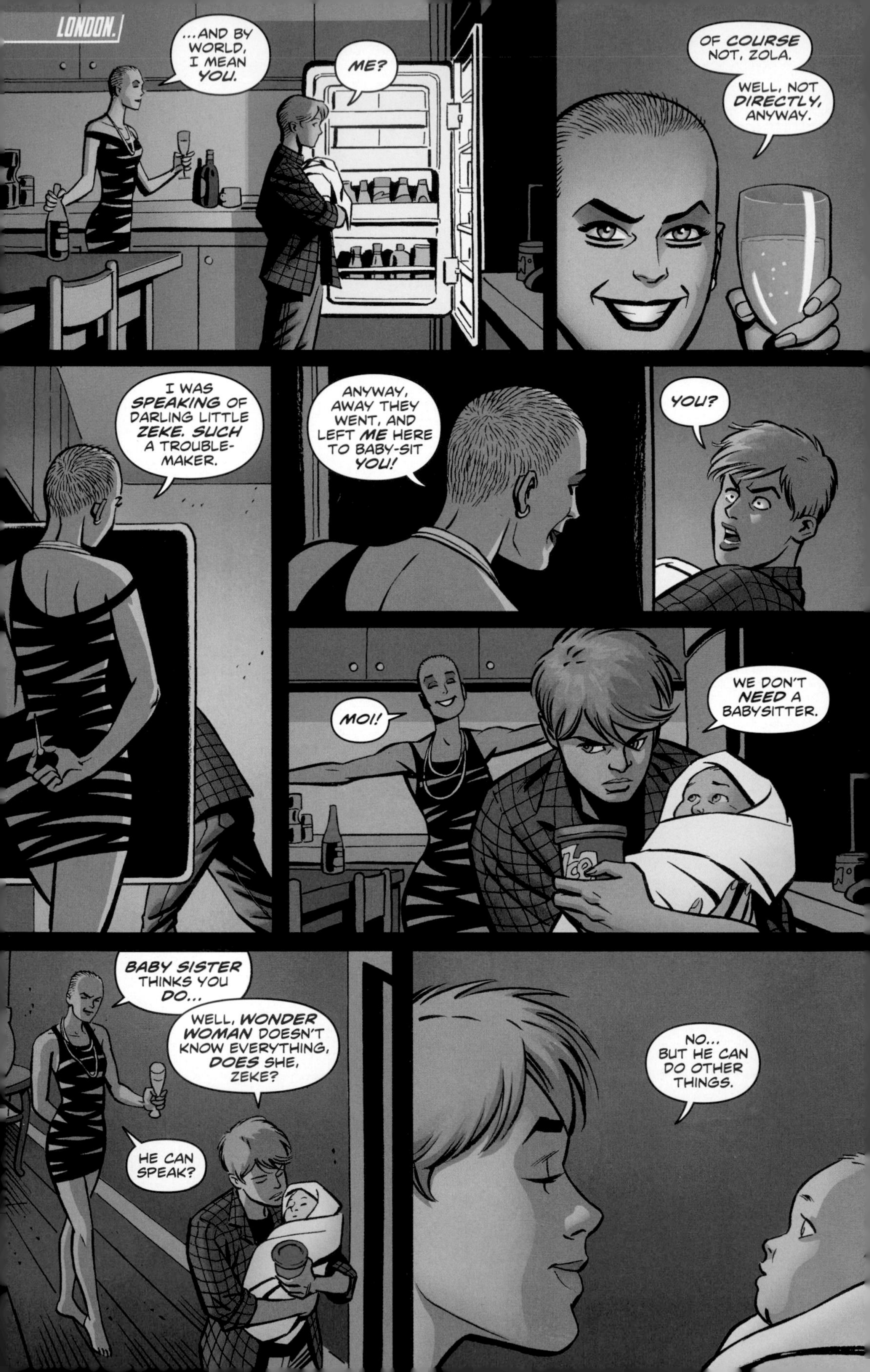
LONDON.
...AND BY WORLD, I MEAN YOU.
ME?
OF COURSE NOT, ZOLA.
WELL, NOT DIRECTLY, ANYWAY.
I WAS SPEAKING OF DARLING LITTLE ZEKE. SUCH A TROUBLE-MAKER.
ANYWAY, AWAY THEY WENT, AND LEFT ME HERE TO BABY-SIT YOU!
YOU?
MOI!
WE DON'T NEED A BABYSITTER.
BABY SISTER THINKS YOU DO...
WELL, WONDER WOMAN DOESN'T KNOW EVERYTHING, DOES SHE, ZEKE?
HE CAN SPEAK?
NO... BUT HE CAN DO OTHER THINGS.

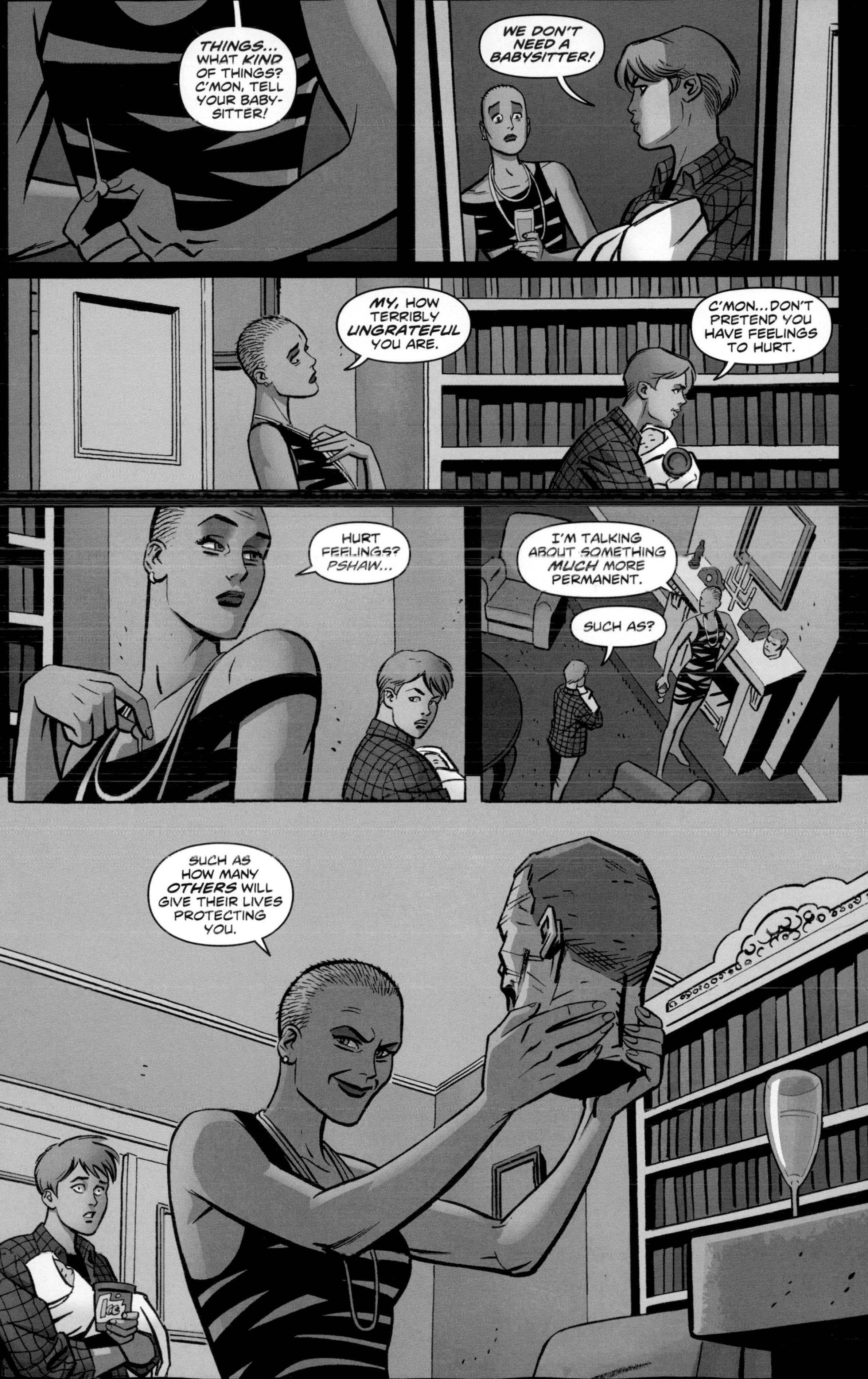
THINGS... WHAT KIND OF THINGS? C'MON, TELL YOUR BABY-SITTER!
WE DON'T NEED A BABYSITTER!
MY, HOW TERRIBLY UNGRATEFUL YOU ARE.
C'MON...DON'T PRETEND YOU HAVE FEELINGS TO HURT.
HURT FEELINGS? PSHAW...
I'M TALKING ABOUT SOMETHING MUCH MORE PERMANENT.
SUCH AS?
SUCH AS HOW MANY OTHERS WILL GIVE THEIR LIVES PROTECTING YOU.

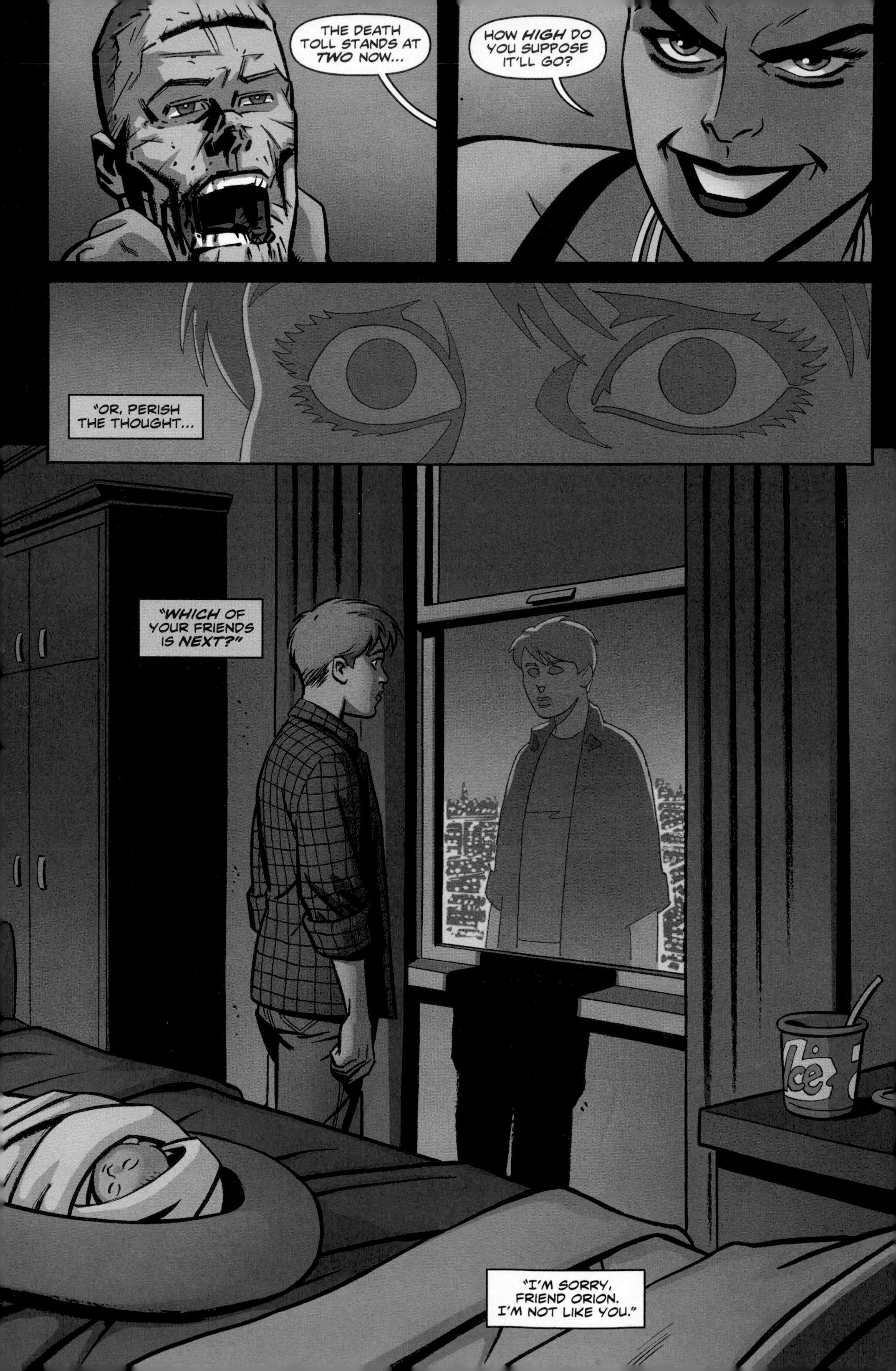
THE DEATH TOLL STANDS AT TWO NOW...
HOW HIGH DO YOU SUPPOSE IT'LL GO?
"OR, PERISH THE THOUGHT...
"WHICH OF YOUR FRIENDS IS NEXT?"
"I'M SORRY, FRIEND ORION. I'M NOT LIKE YOU."

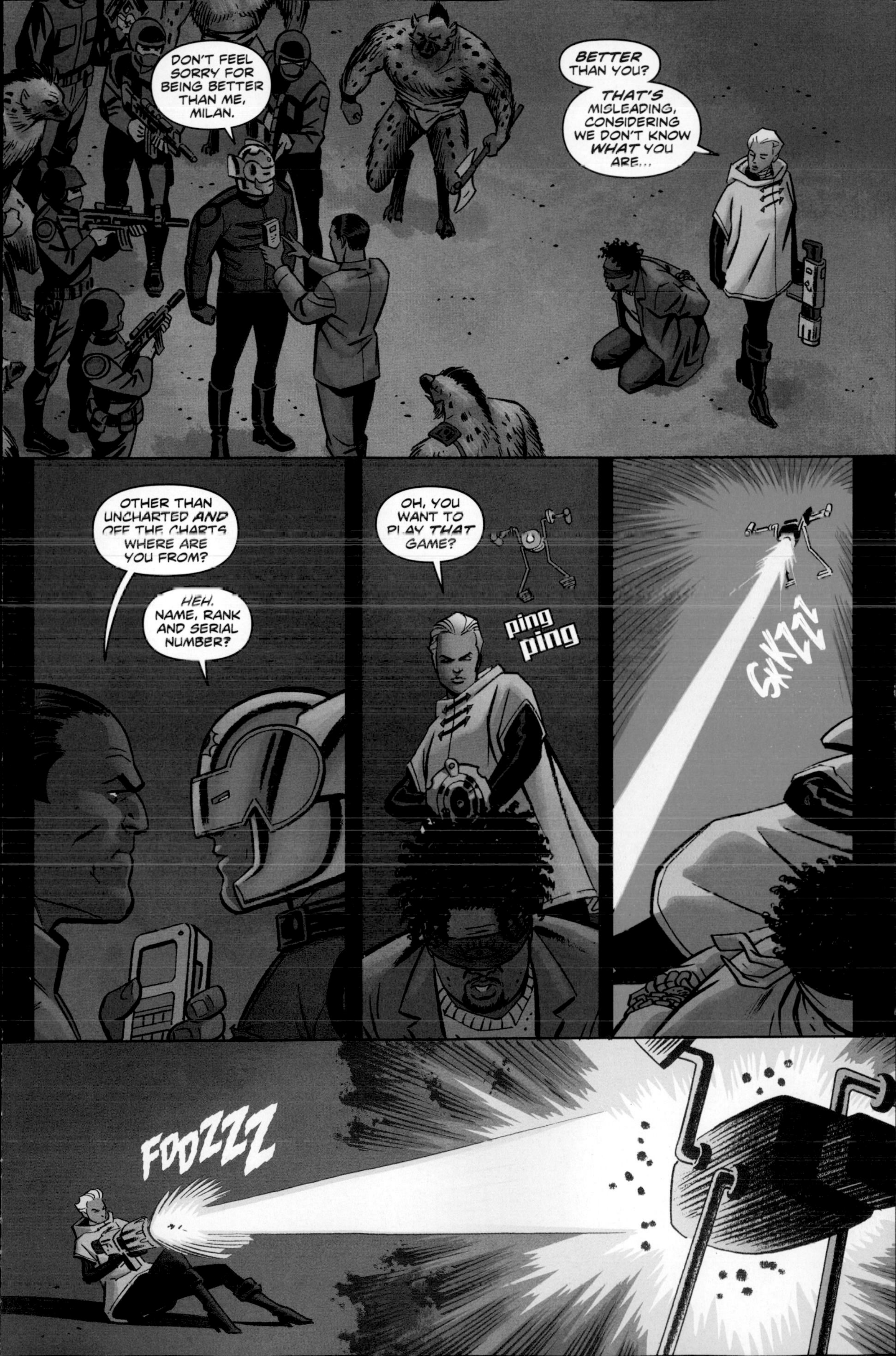
DON'T FEEL SORRY FOR BEING BETTER THAN ME, MILAN.
BETTER THAN YOU? THAT'S MISLEADING, CONSIDERING WE DON'T KNOW WHAT YOU ARE...
OTHER THAN UNCHARTED AND OFF THE CHARTS WHERE ARE YOU FROM?
HEH. NAME, RANK AND SERIAL NUMBER?
OH, YOU WANT TO PLAY THAT GAME?
ping ping
SKKZZZ
FOOZZZ

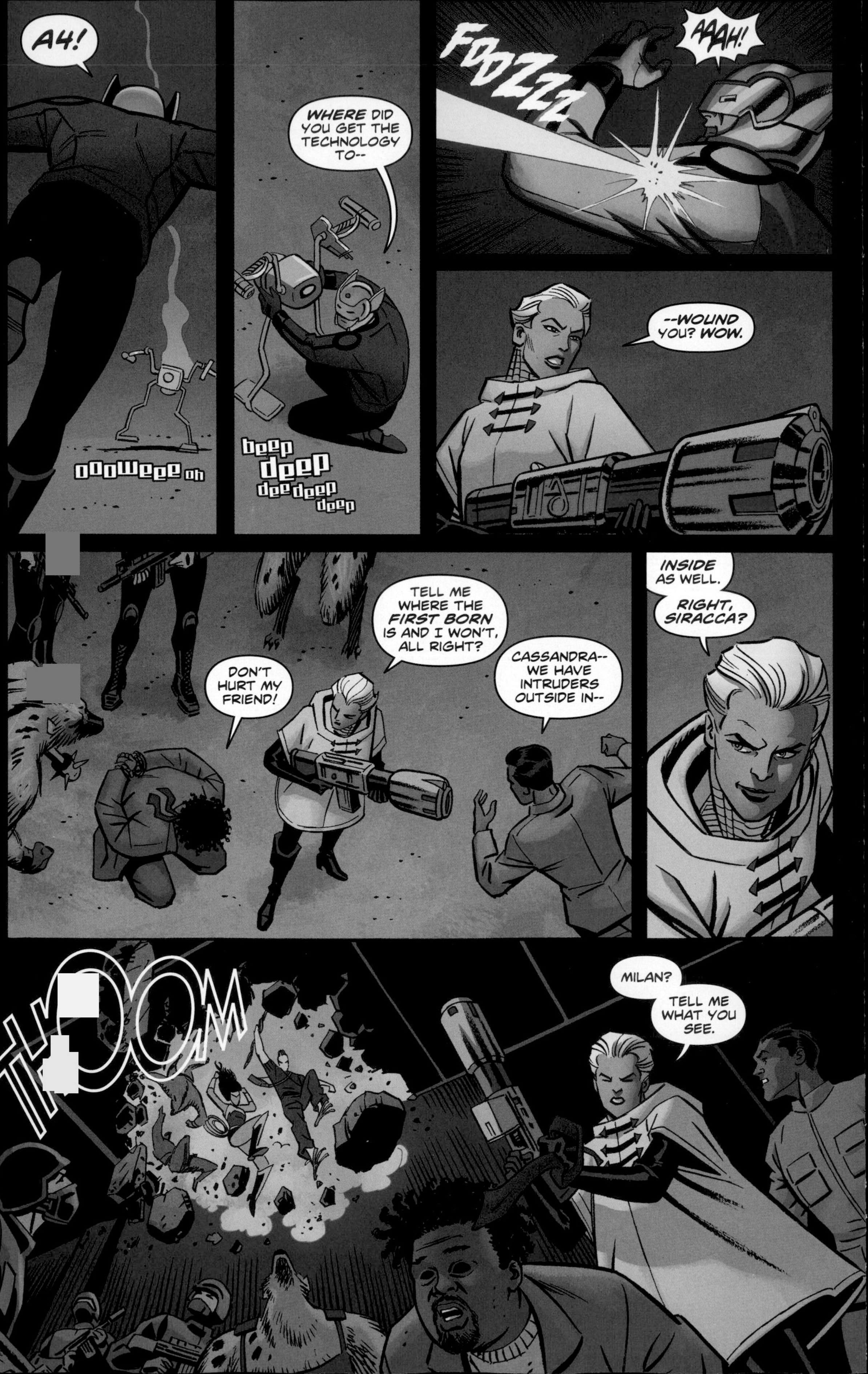
A4!
oooweee oh
WHERE DID YOU GET THE TECHNOLOGY TO--
beep deep deedeep deep
FOOZZZZ
AAAH!
--WOUND YOU? WOW.
DON'T HURT MY FRIEND!
TELL ME WHERE THE FIRST BORN IS AND I WON'T, ALL RIGHT?
CASSANDRA-- WE HAVE INTRUDERS OUTSIDE IN--
INSIDE AS WELL.
RIGHT, SIRACCA?
THOOM
MILAN?
TELL ME WHAT YOU SEE.

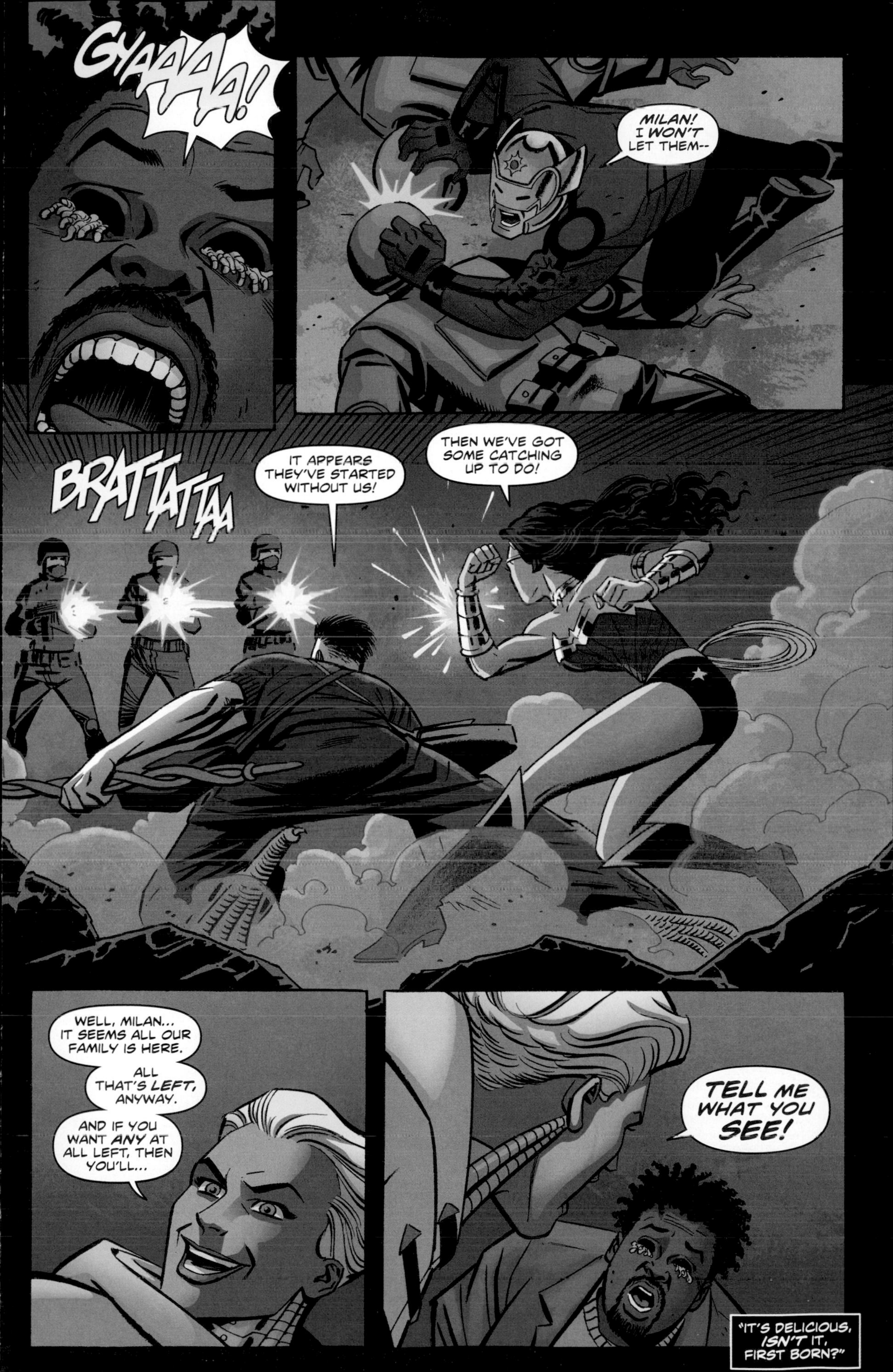
GYAAAA!
MILAN! I WON'T LET THEM--
BRATTATTAA
IT APPEARS THEY'VE STARTED WITHOUT US!
THEN WE'VE GOT SOME CATCHING UP TO DO!
WELL, MILAN... IT SEEMS ALL OUR FAMILY IS HERE.
ALL THAT'S LEFT, ANYWAY.
AND IF YOU WANT ANY AT ALL LEFT, THEN YOU'LL...
TELL ME WHAT YOU SEE!
"IT'S DELICIOUS, ISN'T IT, FIRST BORN?"

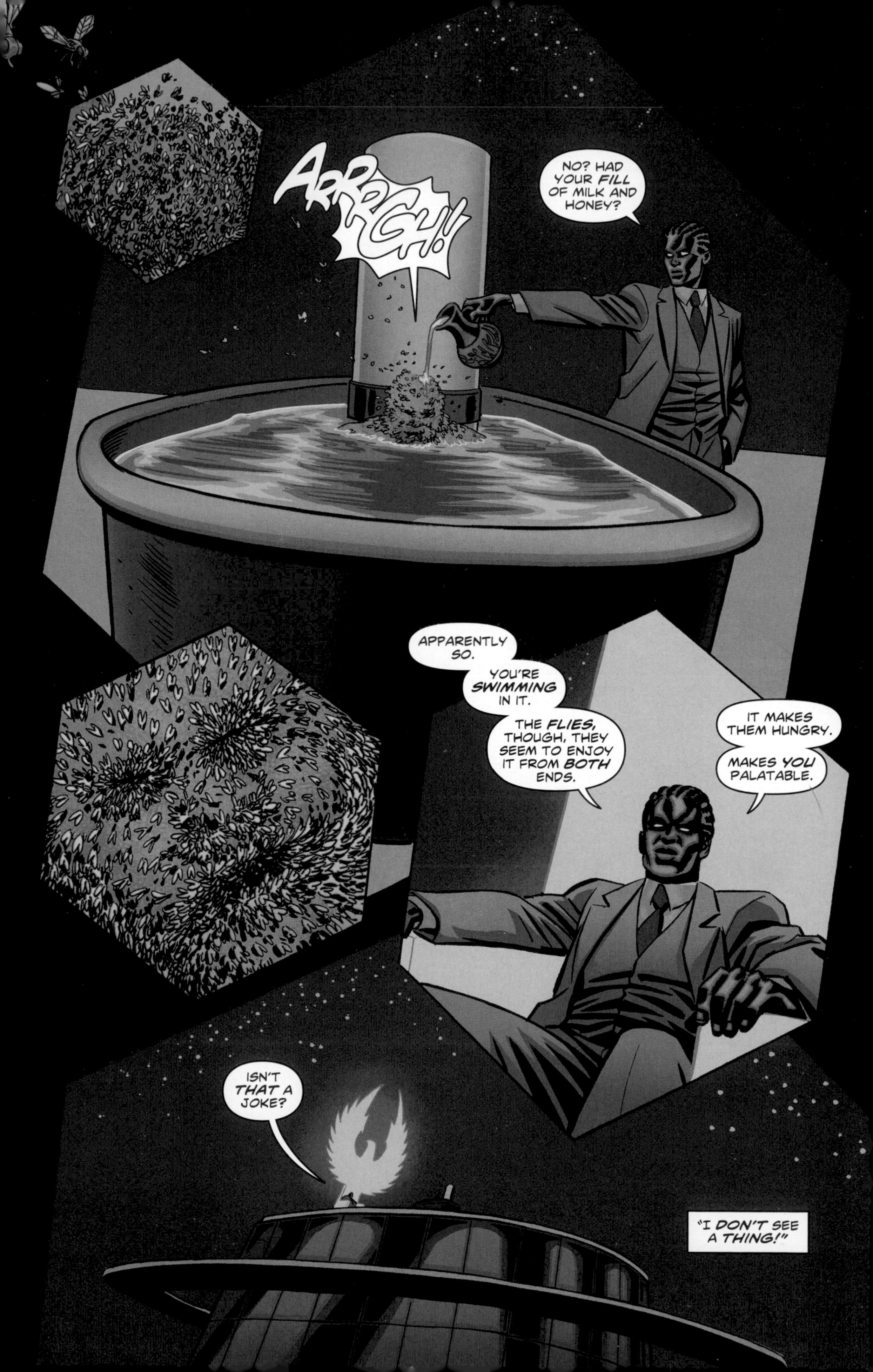
ARRRGH!!
NO? HAD YOUR FILL OF MILK AND HONEY?
APPARENTLY SO.
YOU'RE SWIMMING IN IT.
THE FLIES, THOUGH, THEY SEEM TO ENJOY IT FROM BOTH ENDS.
IT MAKES THEM HUNGRY.
MAKES YOU PALATABLE.
ISN'T THAT A JOKE?
"I DON'T SEE A THING!"

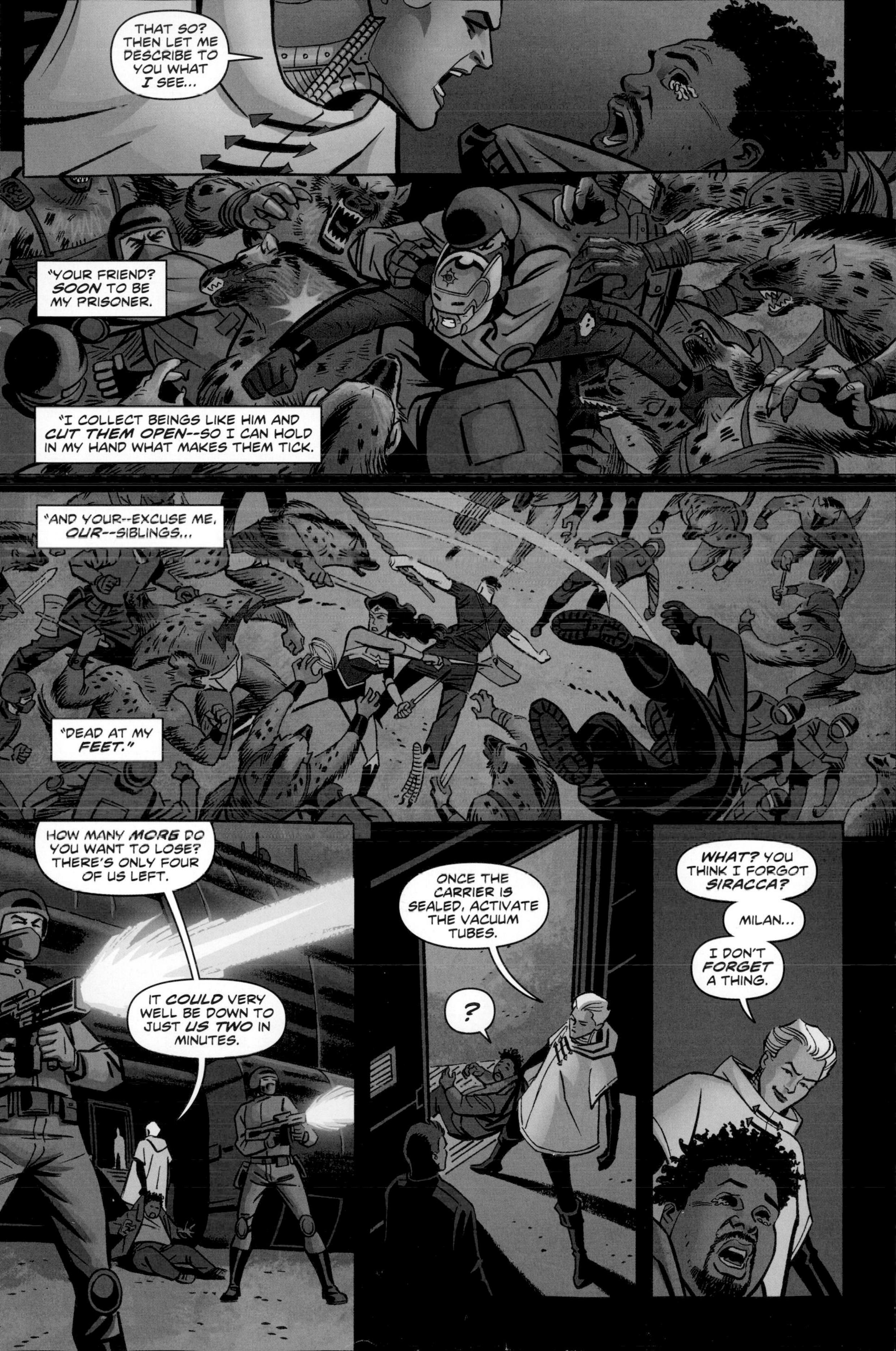
THAT SO? THEN LET ME DESCRIBE TO YOU WHAT I SEE...
"YOUR FRIEND? SOON TO BE MY PRISONER.
"I COLLECT BEINGS LIKE HIM AND CUT THEM OPEN--SO I CAN HOLD IN MY HAND WHAT MAKES THEM TICK.
"AND YOUR--EXCUSE ME, OUR--SIBLINGS...
"DEAD AT MY FEET."
HOW MANY MORE DO YOU WANT TO LOSE? THERE'S ONLY FOUR OF US LEFT.
IT COULD VERY WELL BE DOWN TO JUST US TWO IN MINUTES.
ONCE THE CARRIER IS SEALED, ACTIVATE THE VACUUM TUBES.
?
WHAT? YOU THINK I FORGOT SIRACCA?
MILAN...
I DON'T FORGET A THING.

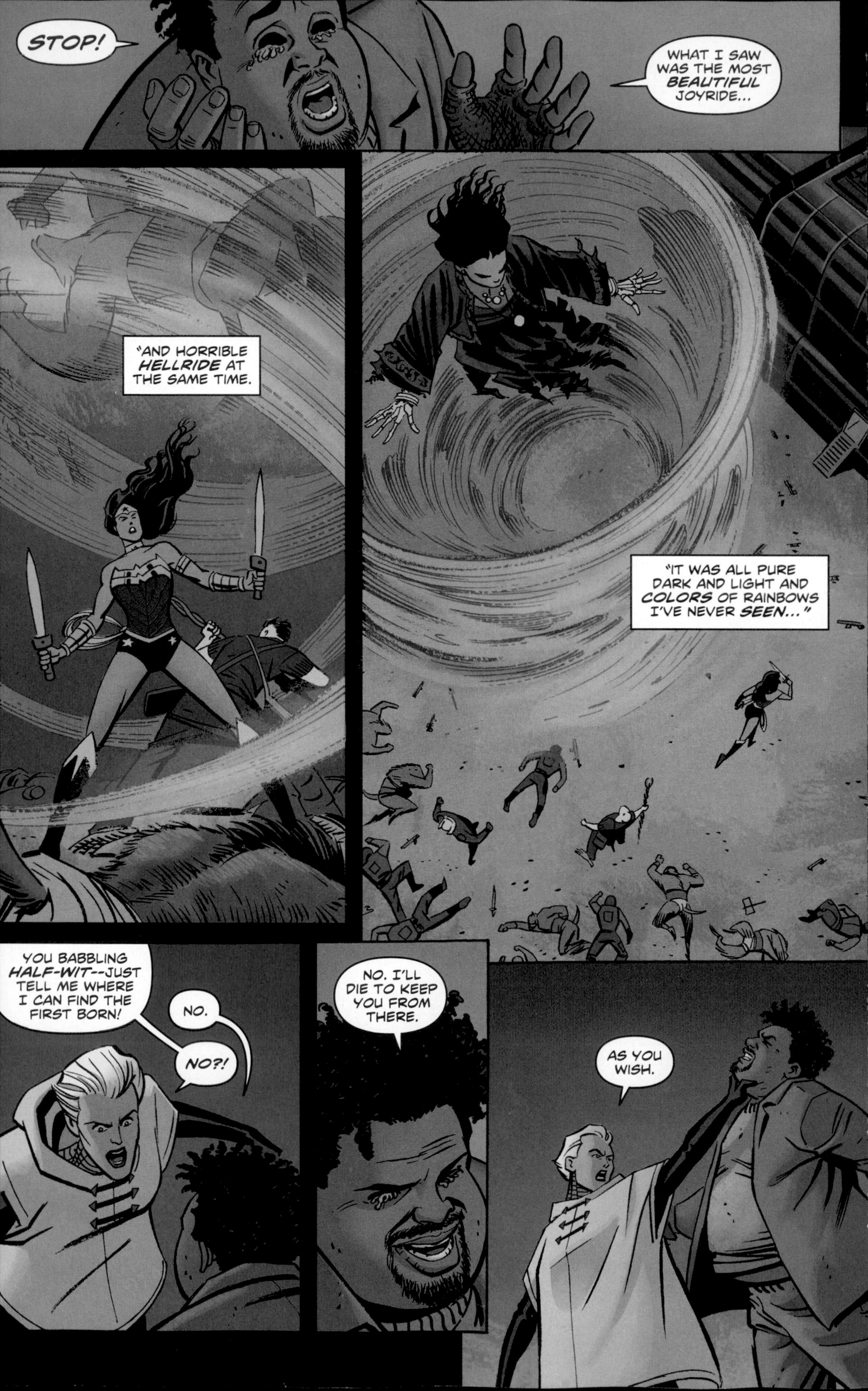
STOP!
WHAT I SAW WAS THE MOST BEAUTIFUL JOYRIDE...
"AND HORRIBLE HELLRIDE AT THE SAME TIME.
"IT WAS ALL PURE DARK AND LIGHT AND COLORS OF RAINBOWS I'VE NEVER SEEN..."
YOU BABBLING HALF-WIT--JUST TELL ME WHERE I CAN FIND THE FIRST BORN!
NO.
NO?!
NO. I'LL DIE TO KEEP YOU FROM THERE.
AS YOU WISH.

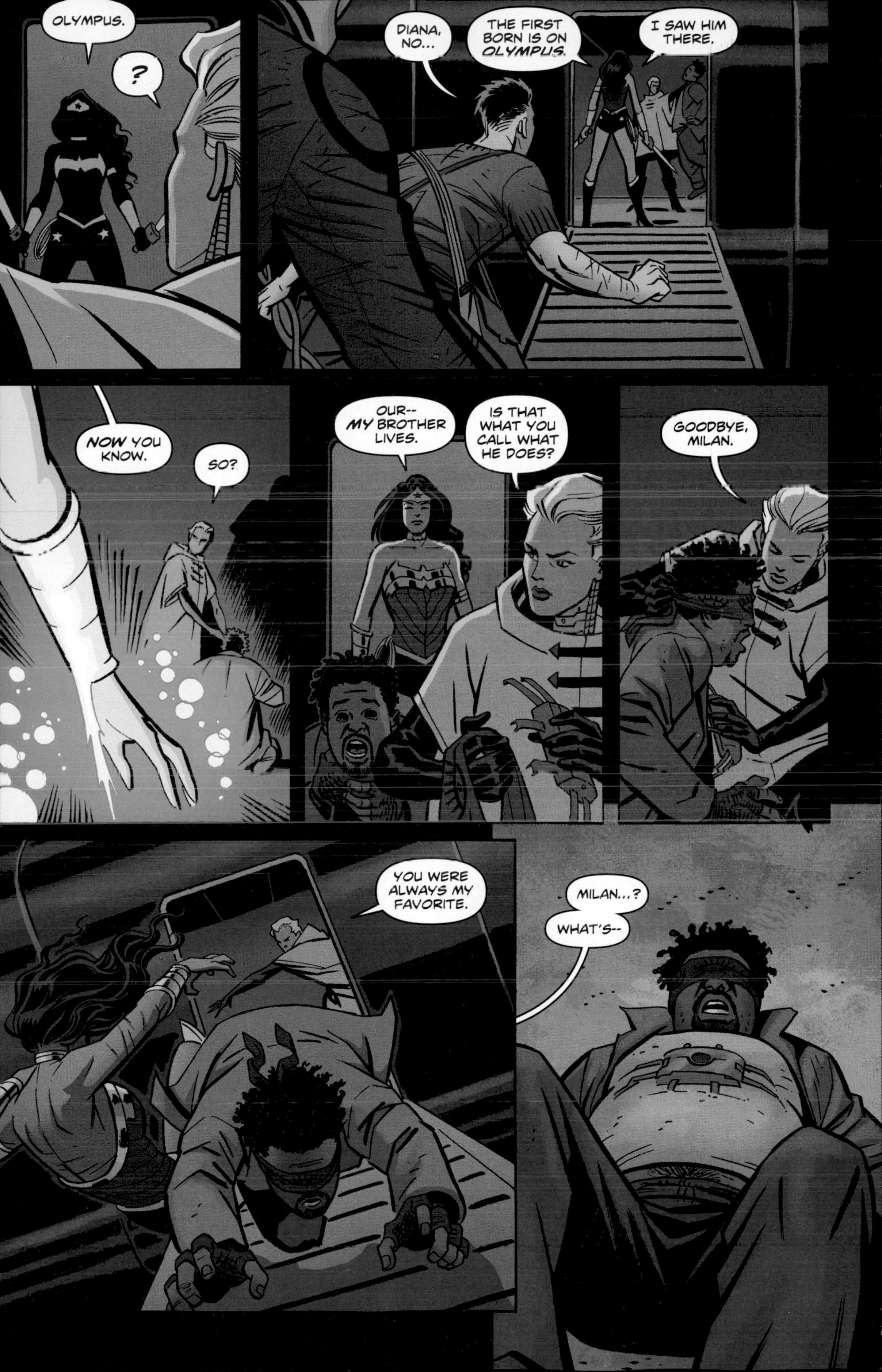
OLYMPUS.
?
DIANA, NO...
THE FIRST BORN IS ON OLYMPUS.
I SAW HIM THERE.
NOW YOU KNOW.
SO?
OUR-- MY BROTHER LIVES.
IS THAT WHAT YOU CALL WHAT HE DOES?
GOODBYE, MILAN.
YOU WERE ALWAYS MY FAVORITE.
MILAN...?
WHAT'S--

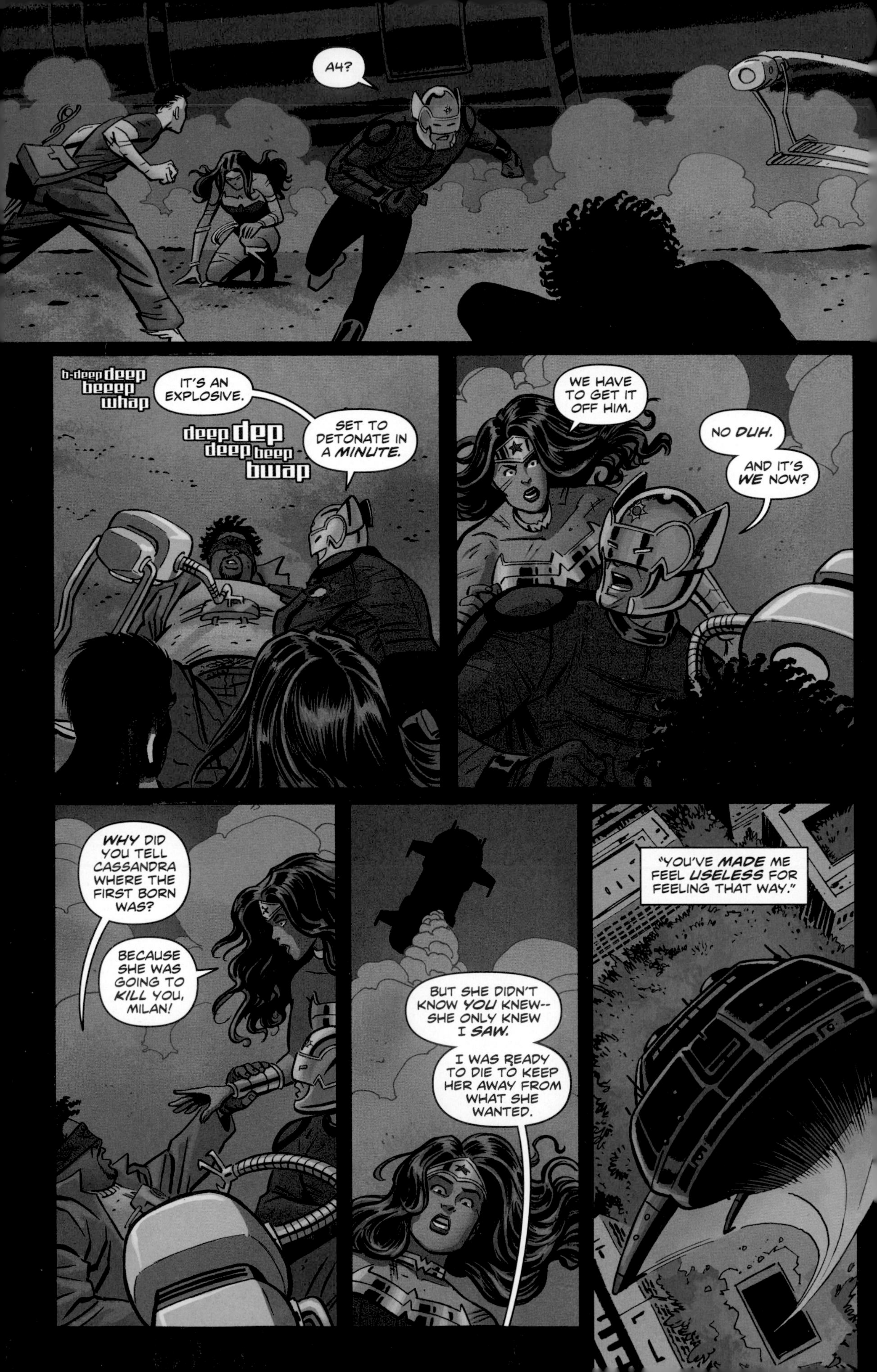
A4?
b-deep deep beeep whap
IT'S AN EXPLOSIVE.
deep dep deep beep bwap
SET TO DETONATE IN A MINUTE.
WE HAVE TO GET IT OFF HIM.
NO DUH.
AND IT'S WE NOW?
WHY DID YOU TELL CASSANDRA WHERE THE FIRST BORN WAS?
BECAUSE SHE WAS GOING TO KILL YOU, MILAN!
BUT SHE DIDN'T KNOW YOU KNEW-- SHE ONLY KNEW I SAW.
I WAS READY TO DIE TO KEEP HER AWAY FROM WHAT SHE WANTED.
"YOU'VE MADE ME FEEL USELESS FOR FEELING THAT WAY."

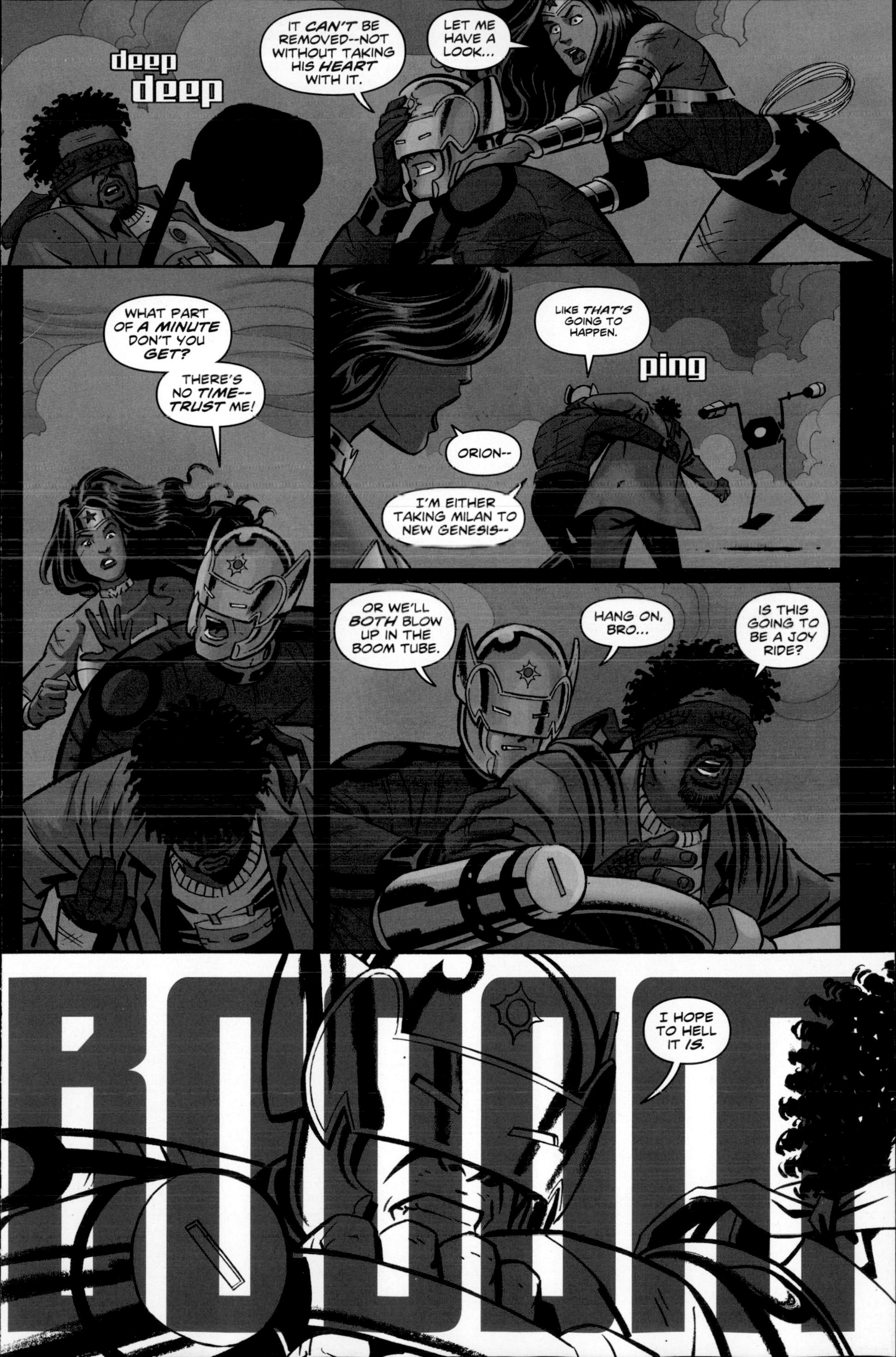
deep
deep
IT CAN'T BE REMOVED--NOT WITHOUT TAKING HIS HEART WITH IT.
LET ME HAVE A LOOK...
WHAT PART OF A MINUTE DON'T YOU GET?
THERE'S NO TIME--TRUST ME!
LIKE THAT'S GOING TO HAPPEN.
ping
ORION--
I'M EITHER TAKING MILAN TO NEW GENESIS--
OR WE'LL BOTH BLOW UP IN THE BOOM TUBE.
HANG ON, BRO...
IS THIS GOING TO BE A JOY RIDE?
I HOPE TO HELL IT IS.

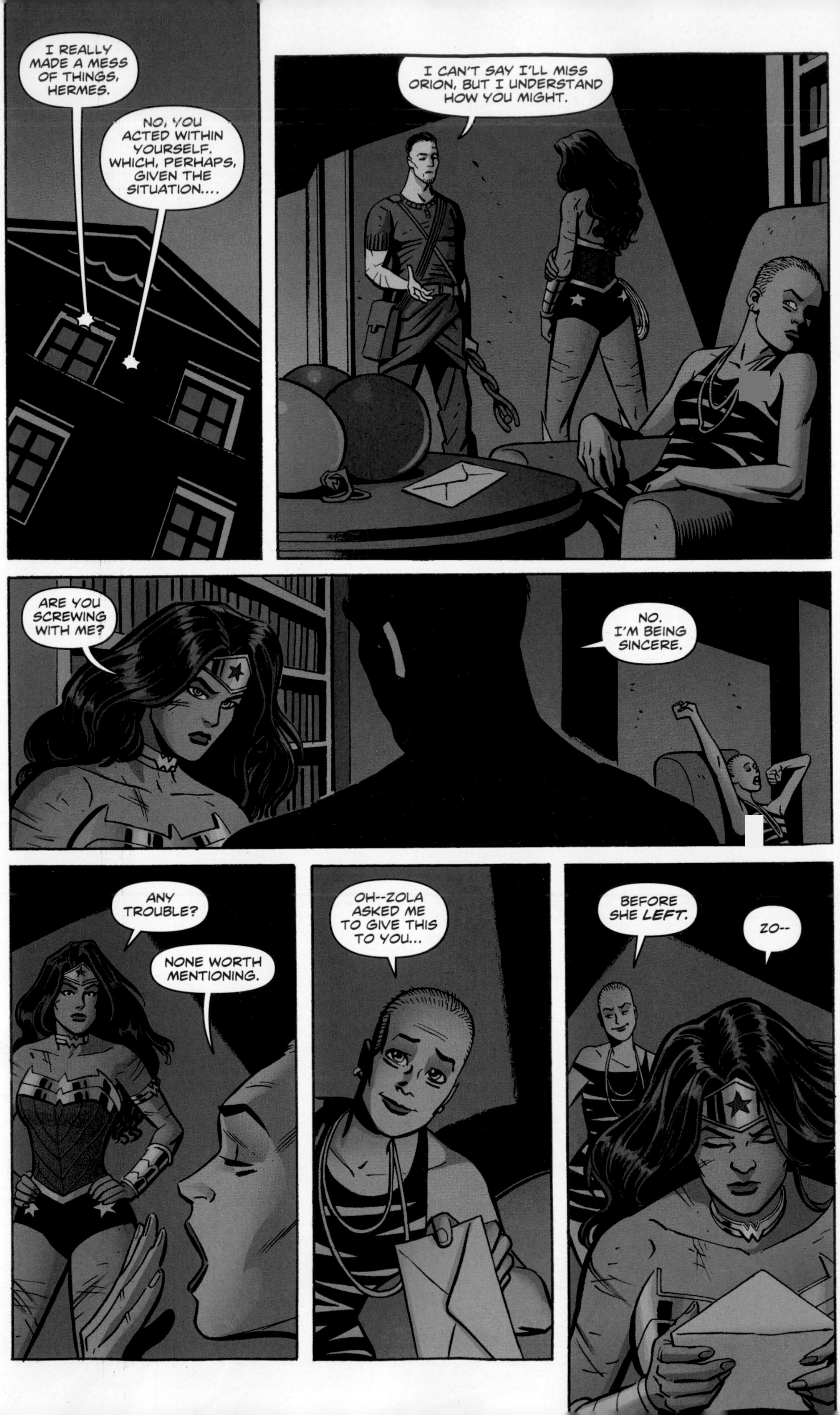
I REALLY MADE A MESS OF THINGS, HERMES.
NO, YOU ACTED WITHIN YOURSELF. WHICH, PERHAPS, GIVEN THE SITUATION....
I CAN'T SAY I'LL MISS ORION, BUT I UNDERSTAND HOW YOU MIGHT.
ARE YOU SCREWING WITH ME?
NO. I'M BEING SINCERE.
ANY TROUBLE?
NONE WORTH MENTIONING.
OH--ZOLA ASKED ME TO GIVE THIS TO YOU...
BEFORE SHE *LEFT*.
ZO--

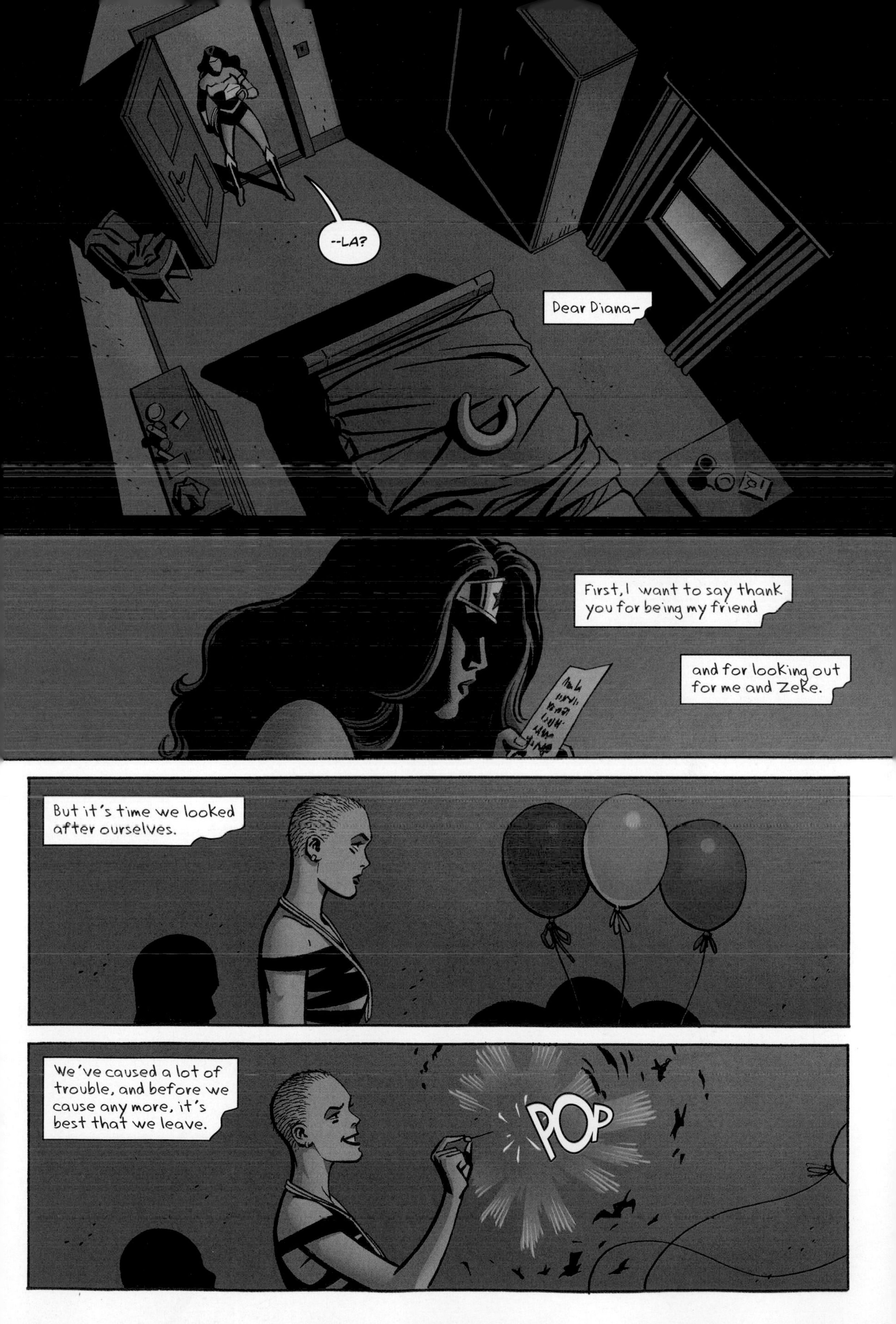
--LA?
Dear Diana-
First, I want to say thank you for being my friend
and for looking out for me and Zeke.
But it's time we looked after ourselves.
We've caused a lot of trouble, and before we cause any more, it's best that we leave.
POP

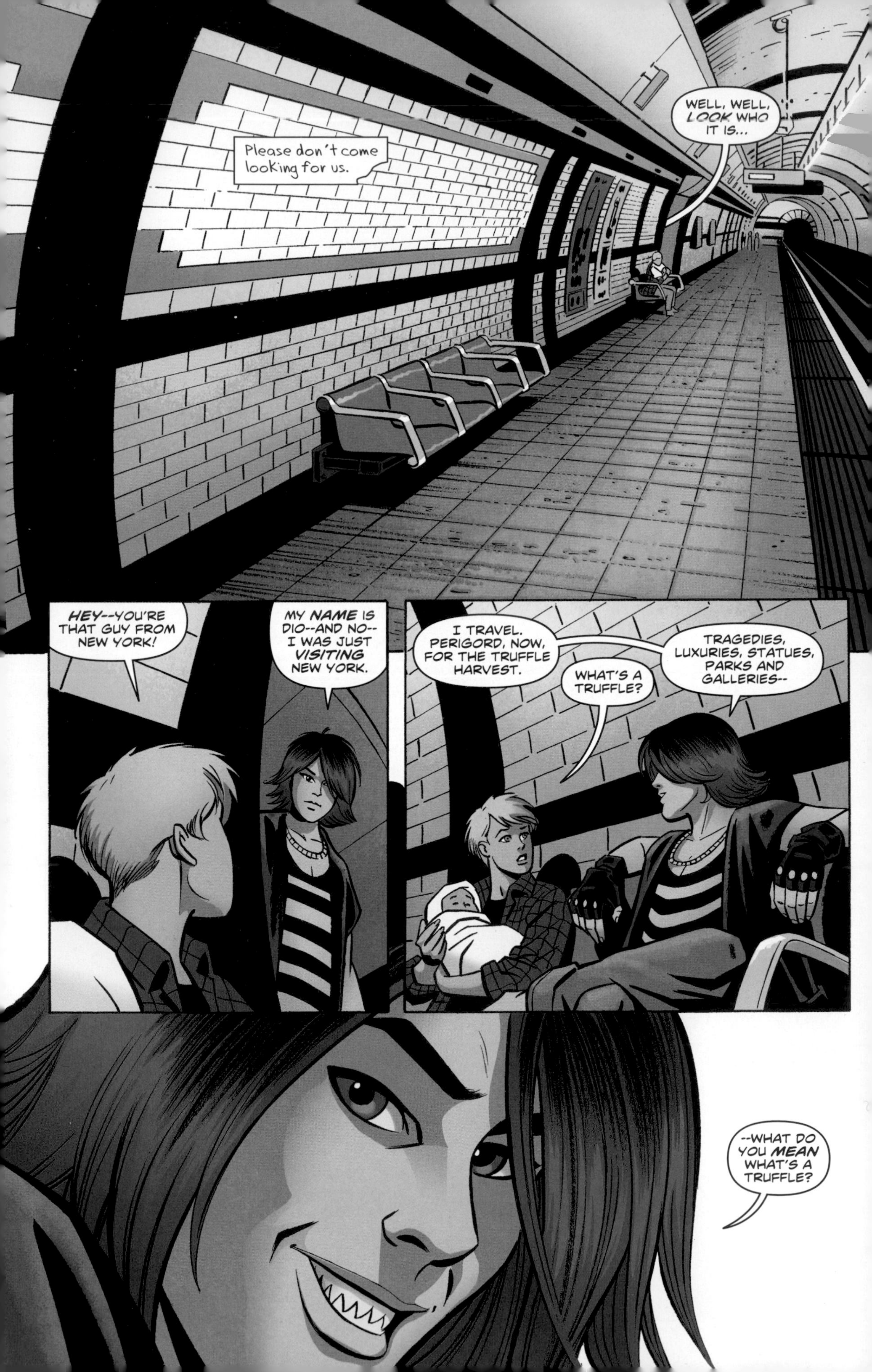
Please don't come looking for us.
WELL, WELL, LOOK WHO IT IS...
HEY--YOU'RE THAT GUY FROM NEW YORK!
MY NAME IS DIO--AND NO--I WAS JUST VISITING NEW YORK.
I TRAVEL. PERIGORD, NOW, FOR THE TRUFFLE HARVEST.
TRAGEDIES, LUXURIES, STATUES, PARKS AND GALLERIES--
WHAT'S A TRUFFLE?
--WHAT DO YOU MEAN WHAT'S A TRUFFLE?

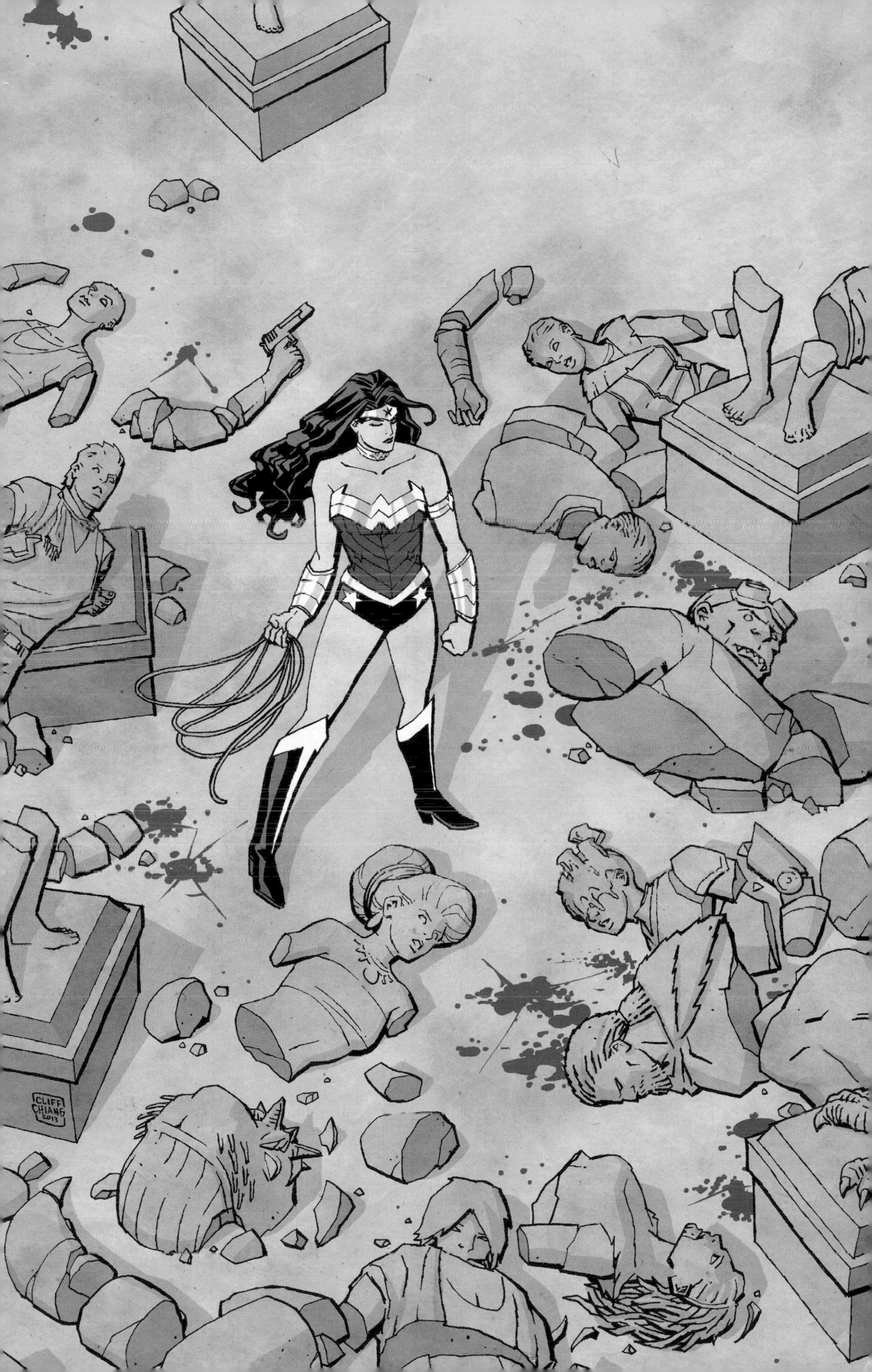
CLIFF CHIANG 2013

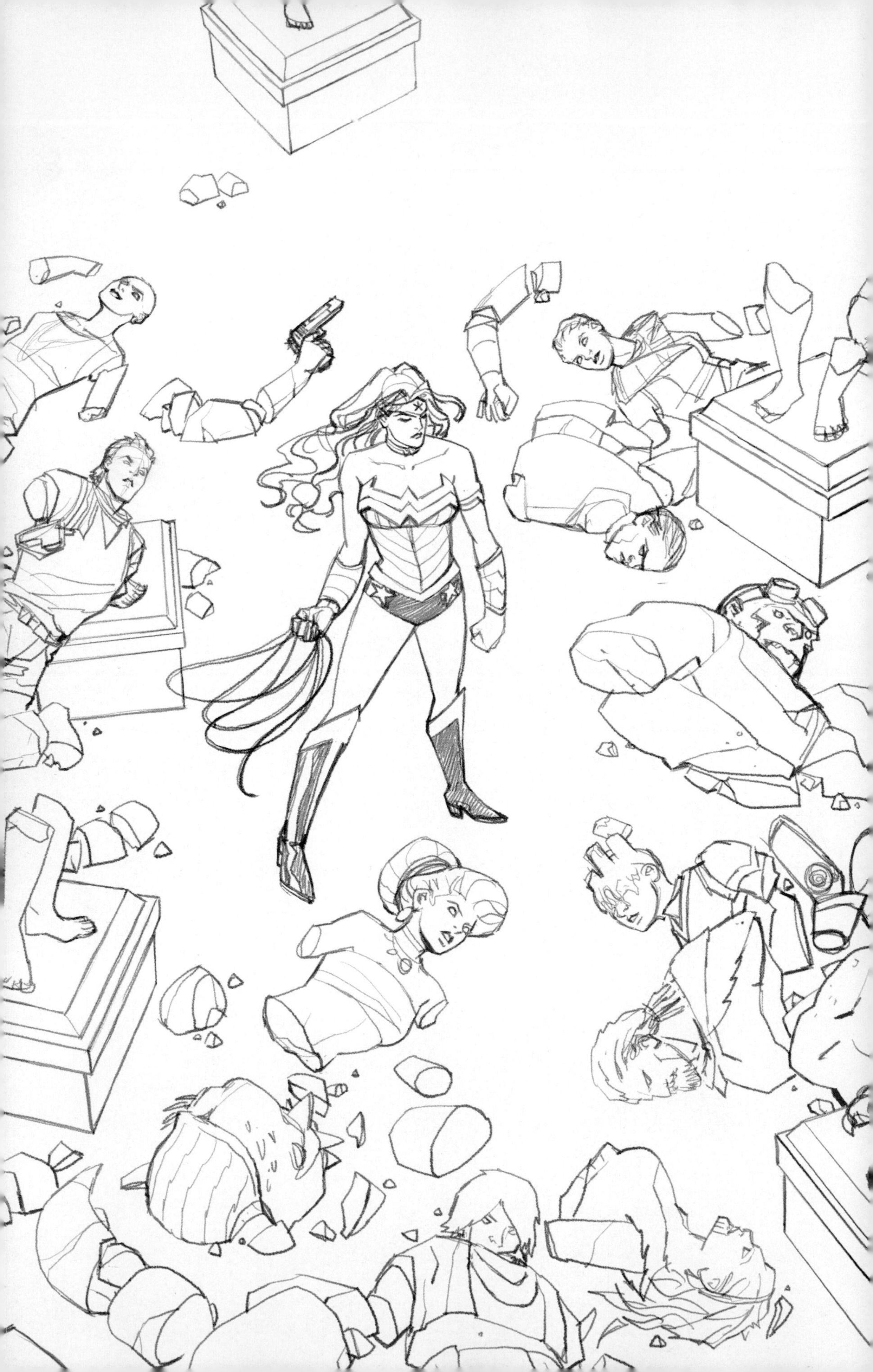

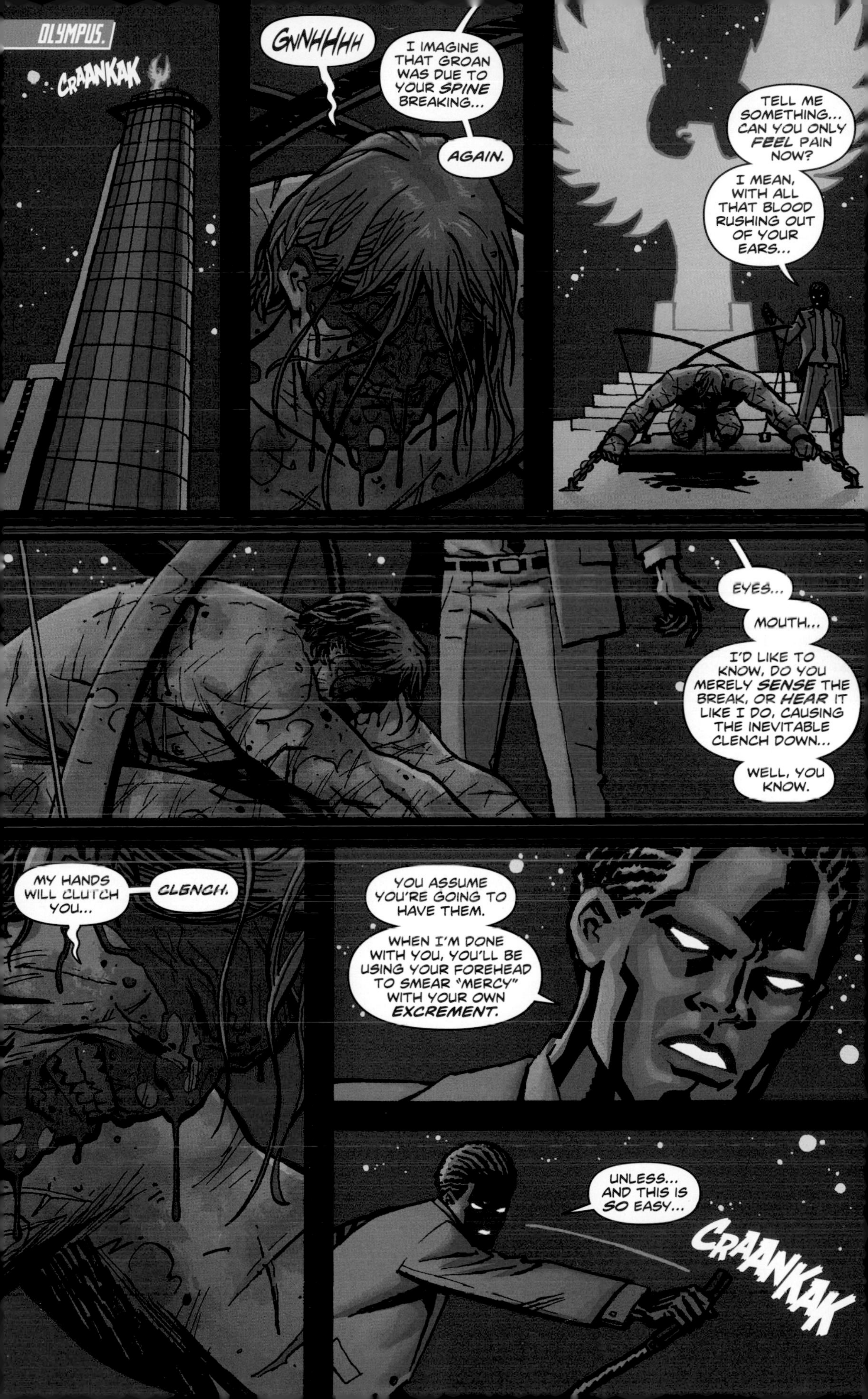
OLYMPUS.
CRAANKAK
GNNHHHH
I IMAGINE THAT GROAN WAS DUE TO YOUR SPINE BREAKING...
AGAIN.
TELL ME SOMETHING... CAN YOU ONLY FEEL PAIN NOW?
I MEAN, WITH ALL THAT BLOOD RUSHING OUT OF YOUR EARS...
EYES...
MOUTH...
I'D LIKE TO KNOW, DO YOU MERELY SENSE THE BREAK, OR HEAR IT LIKE I DO, CAUSING THE INEVITABLE CLENCH DOWN...
WELL, YOU KNOW.
MY HANDS WILL CLUTCH YOU...
CLENCH.
YOU ASSUME YOU'RE GOING TO HAVE THEM.
WHEN I'M DONE WITH YOU, YOU'LL BE USING YOUR FOREHEAD TO SMEAR "MERCY" WITH YOUR OWN EXCREMENT.
UNLESS... AND THIS IS SO EASY...
CRAANKAK

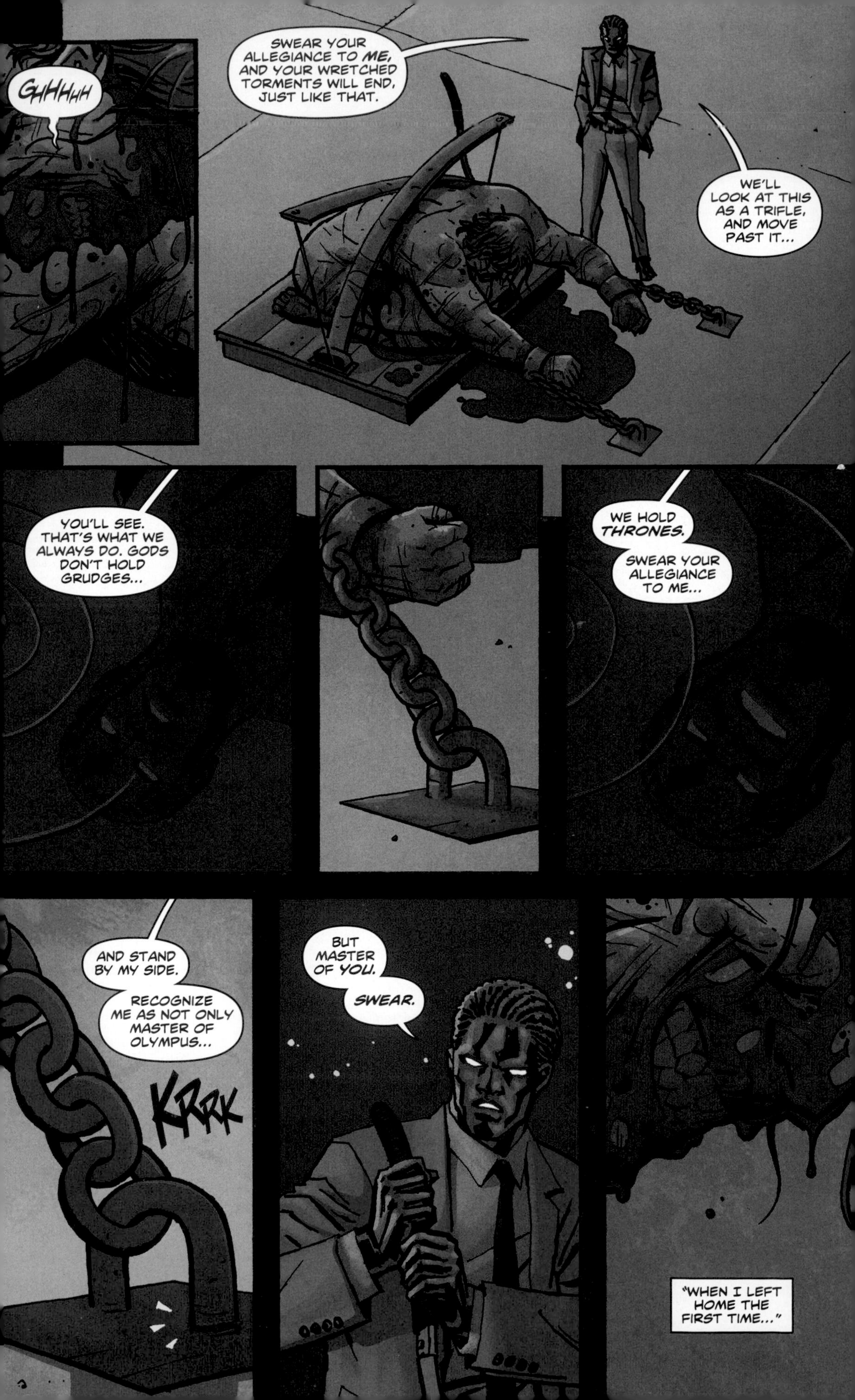
GHHHHH
SWEAR YOUR ALLEGIANCE TO ME, AND YOUR WRETCHED TORMENTS WILL END, JUST LIKE THAT.
WE'LL LOOK AT THIS AS A TRIFLE, AND MOVE PAST IT...
YOU'LL SEE. THAT'S WHAT WE ALWAYS DO. GODS DON'T HOLD GRUDGES...
WE HOLD THRONES.
SWEAR YOUR ALLEGIANCE TO ME...
AND STAND BY MY SIDE.
RECOGNIZE ME AS NOT ONLY MASTER OF OLYMPUS...
KRRK
BUT MASTER OF YOU.
SWEAR.
"WHEN I LEFT HOME THE FIRST TIME..."

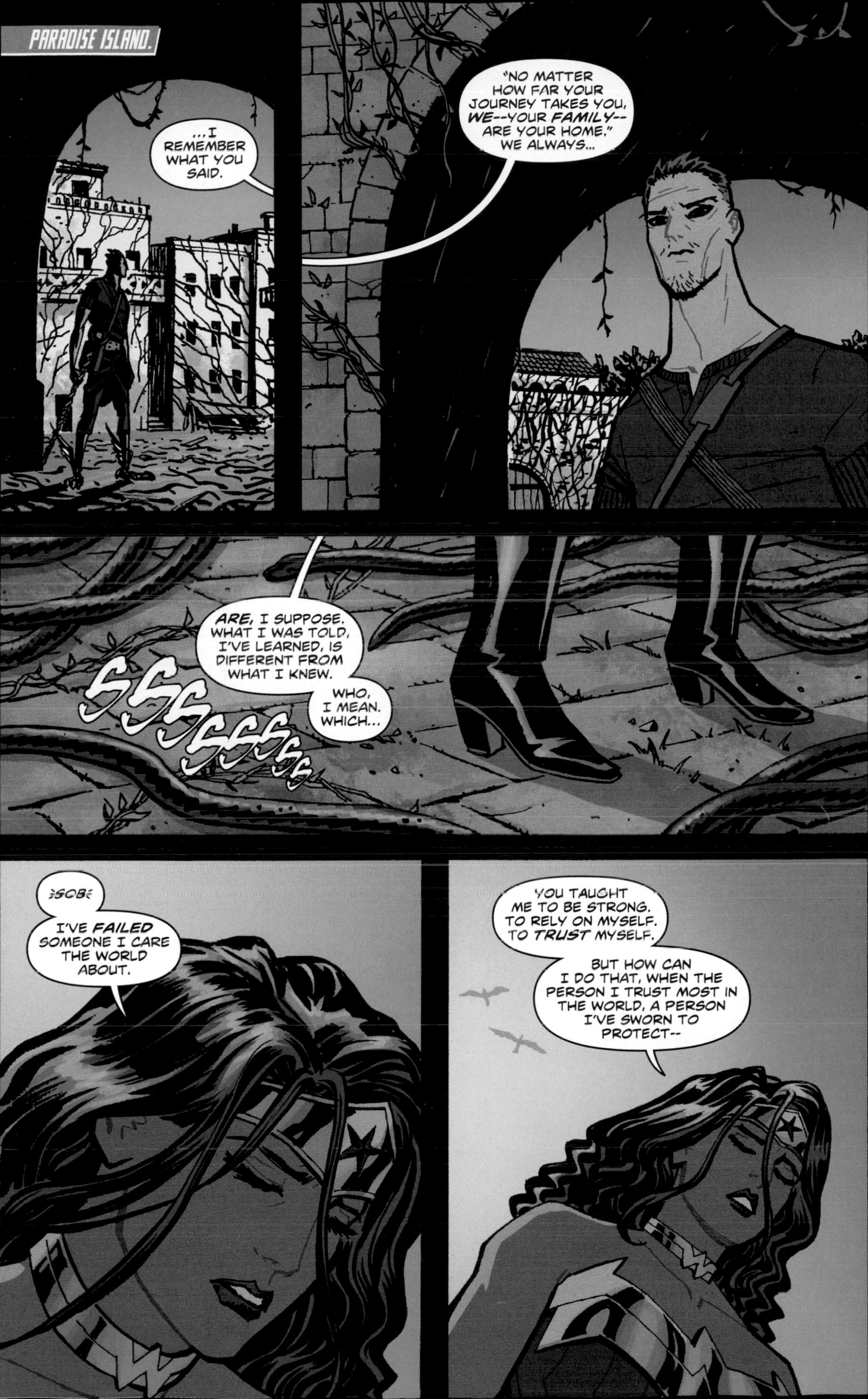
PARADISE ISLAND.
...I REMEMBER WHAT YOU SAID.
"NO MATTER HOW FAR YOUR JOURNEY TAKES YOU, WE--YOUR FAMILY--ARE YOUR HOME." WE ALWAYS...
ARE, I SUPPOSE. WHAT I WAS TOLD, I'VE LEARNED, IS DIFFERENT FROM WHAT I KNEW.
WHO, I MEAN. WHICH...
SSSSSSSSS
SOB
I'VE FAILED SOMEONE I CARE THE WORLD ABOUT.
YOU TAUGHT ME TO BE STRONG. TO RELY ON MYSELF. TO TRUST MYSELF.
BUT HOW CAN I DO THAT, WHEN THE PERSON I TRUST MOST IN THE WORLD, A PERSON I'VE SWORN TO PROTECT--

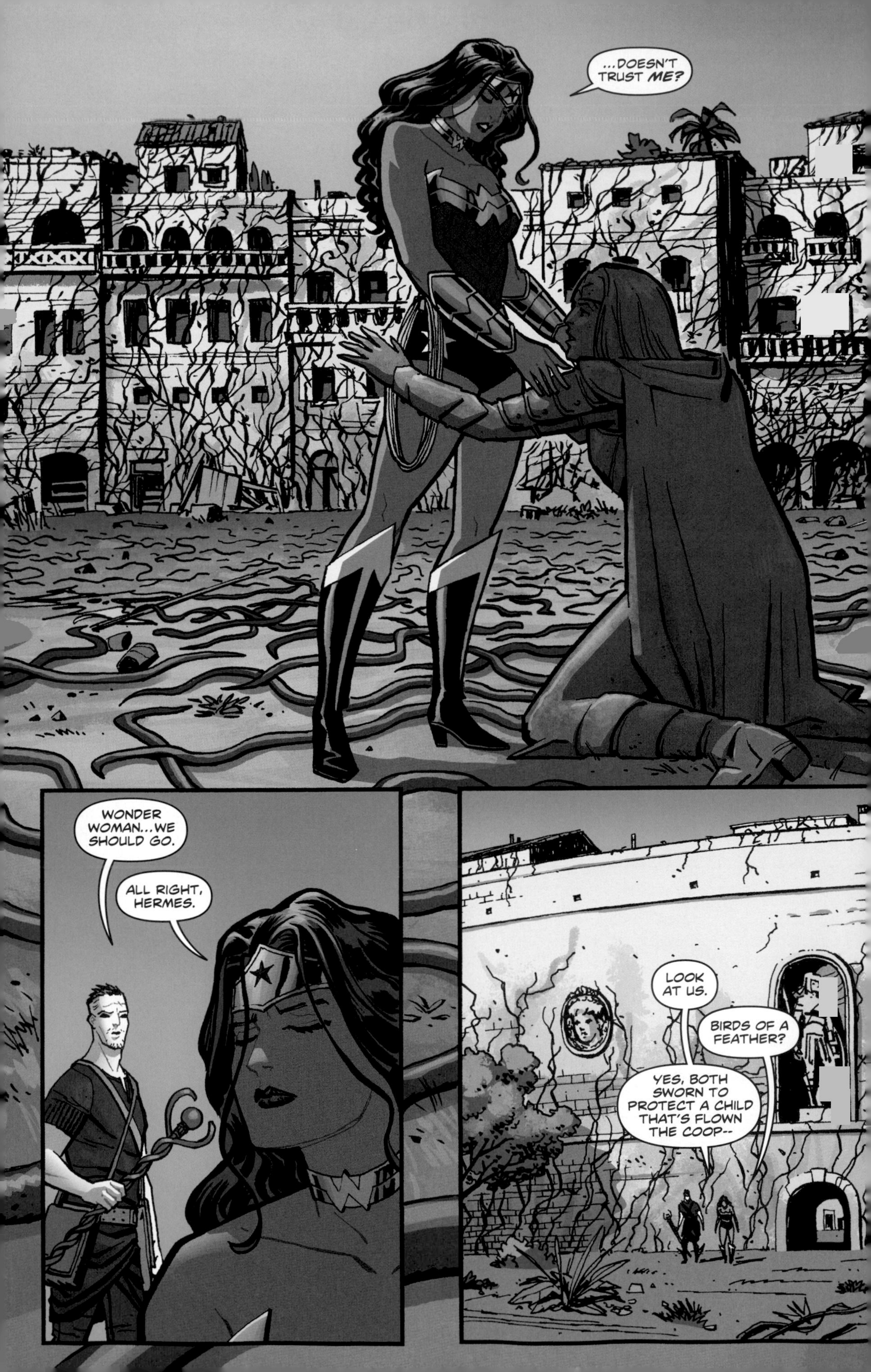
...DOESN'T TRUST *ME*?
WONDER WOMAN...WE SHOULD GO.
ALL RIGHT, HERMES.
LOOK AT US.
BIRDS OF A FEATHER?
YES, BOTH SWORN TO PROTECT A CHILD THAT'S FLOWN THE COOP--

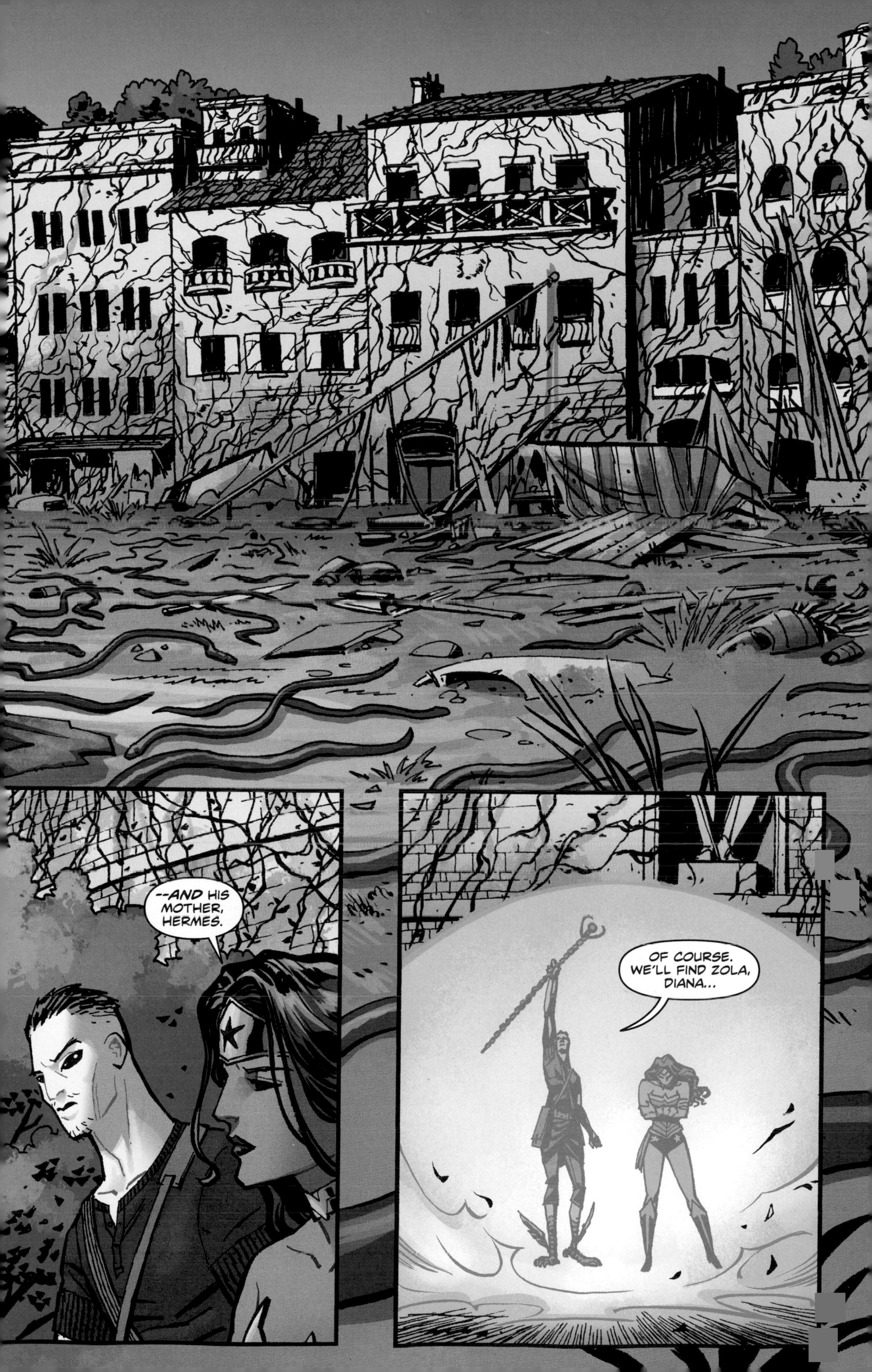
--AND HIS MOTHER, HERMES.
OF COURSE. WE'LL FIND ZOLA, DIANA...

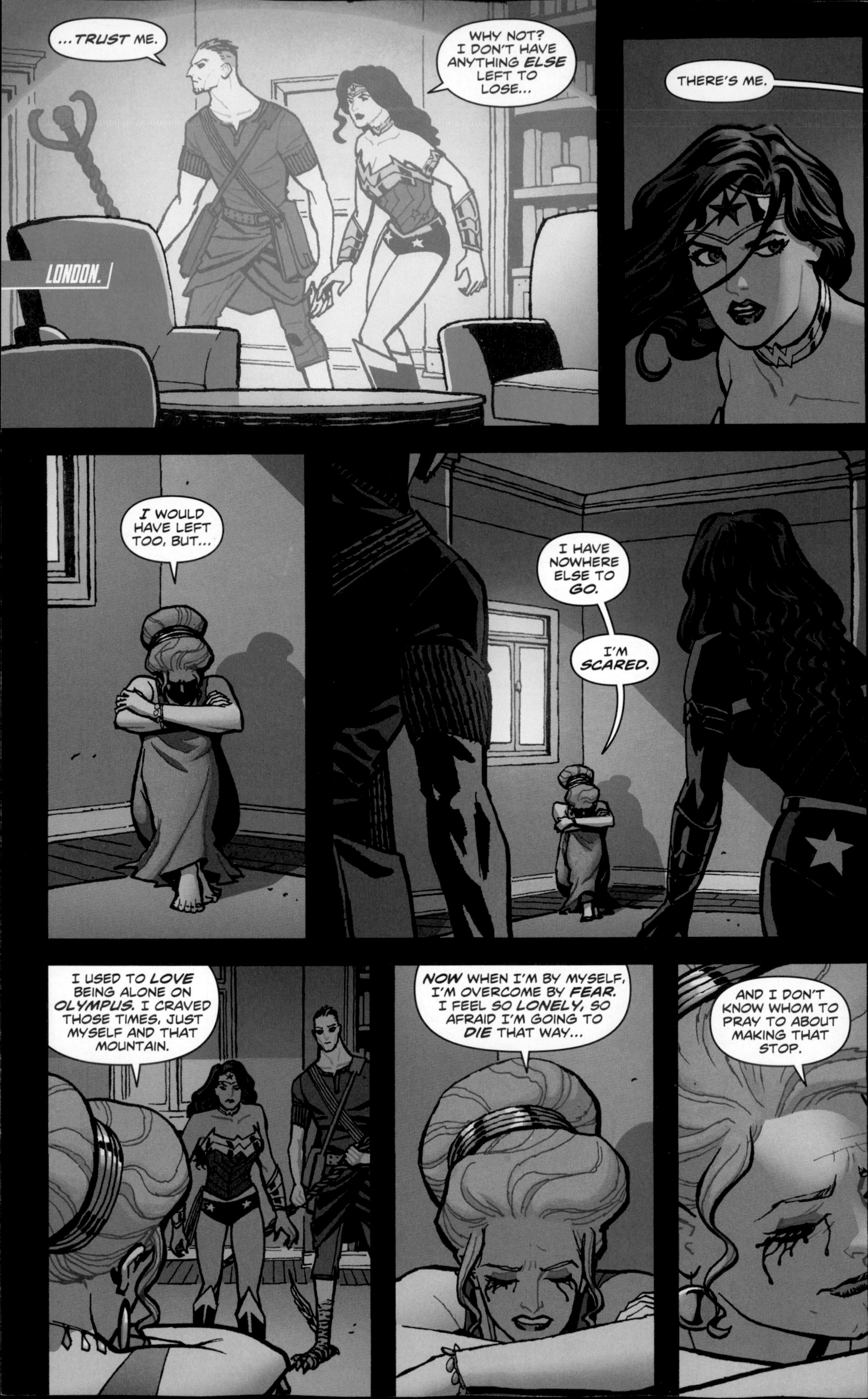

...TRUST ME.
WHY NOT? I DON'T HAVE ANYTHING ELSE LEFT TO LOSE...
LONDON.
THERE'S ME.
I WOULD HAVE LEFT TOO, BUT...
I HAVE NOWHERE ELSE TO GO.
I'M SCARED.
I USED TO LOVE BEING ALONE ON OLYMPUS. I CRAVED THOSE TIMES, JUST MYSELF AND THAT MOUNTAIN.
NOW WHEN I'M BY MYSELF, I'M OVERCOME BY FEAR. I FEEL SO LONELY, SO AFRAID I'M GOING TO DIE THAT WAY...
AND I DON'T KNOW WHOM TO PRAY TO ABOUT MAKING THAT STOP.

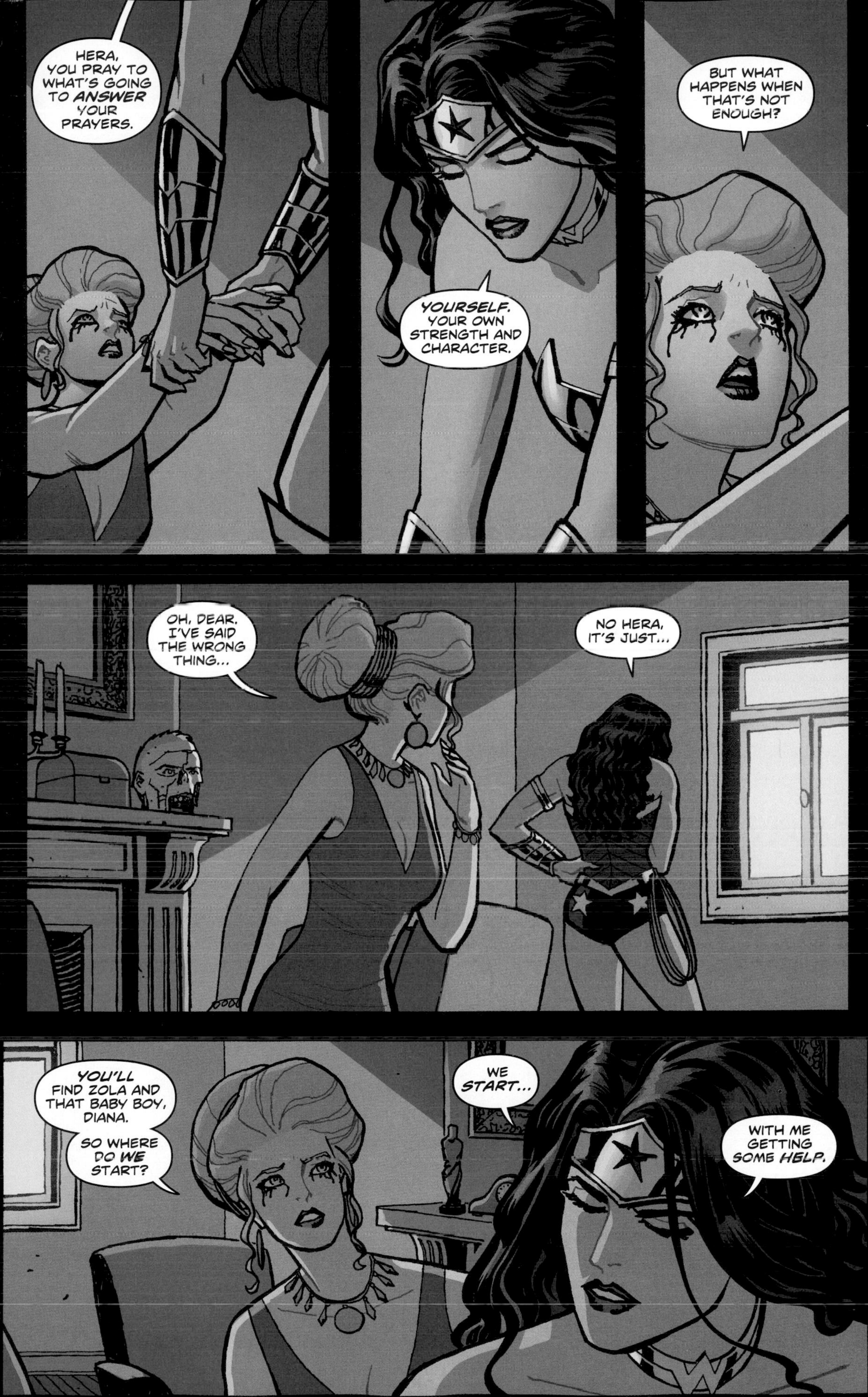
HERA, YOU PRAY TO WHAT'S GOING TO ANSWER YOUR PRAYERS.
YOURSELF. YOUR OWN STRENGTH AND CHARACTER.
BUT WHAT HAPPENS WHEN THAT'S NOT ENOUGH?
OH, DEAR. I'VE SAID THE WRONG THING...
NO HERA, IT'S JUST...
YOU'LL FIND ZOLA AND THAT BABY BOY, DIANA.
SO WHERE DO WE START?
WE START...
WITH ME GETTING SOME HELP.

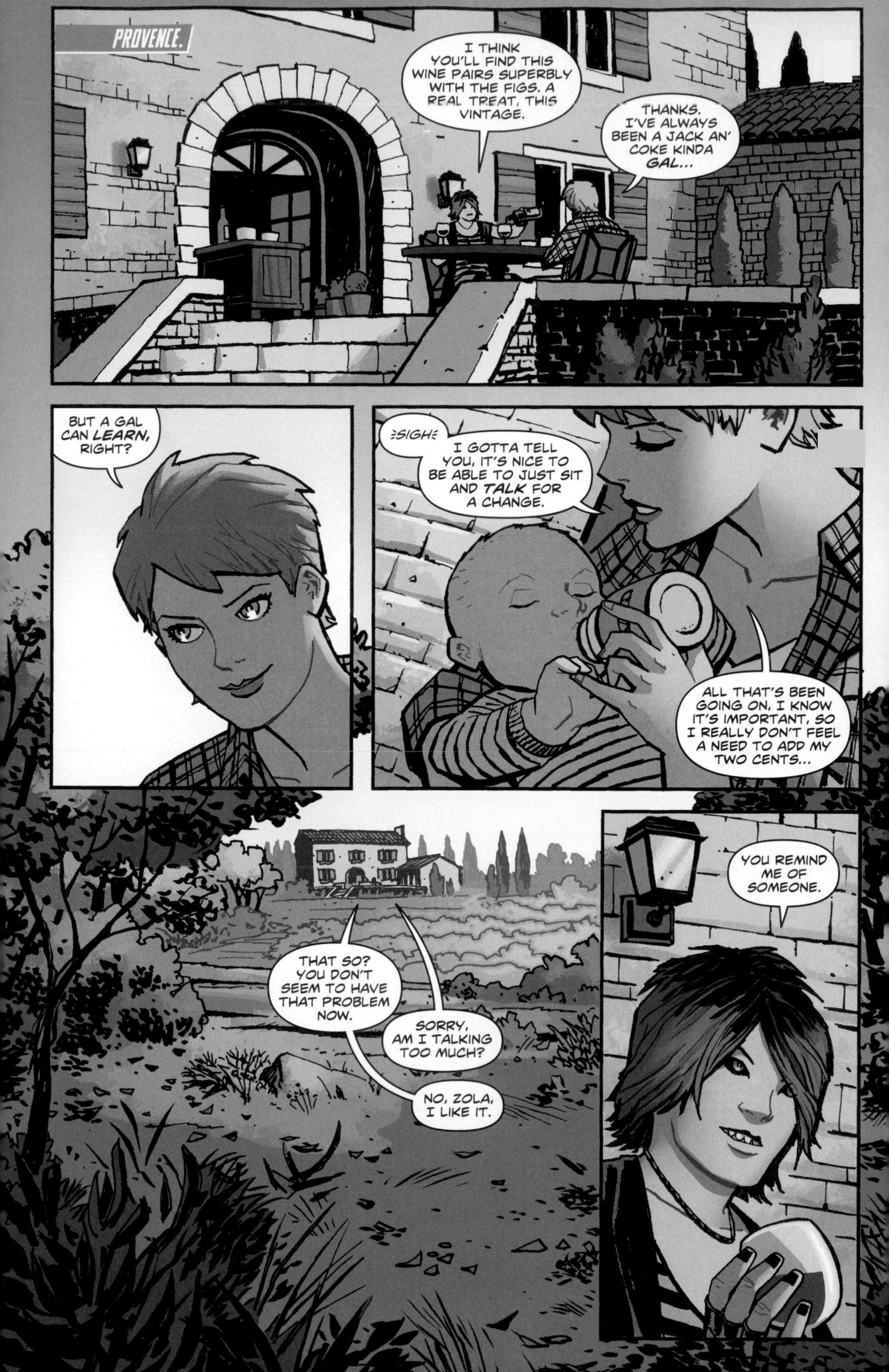
PROVENCE.
I THINK YOU'LL FIND THIS WINE PAIRS SUPERBLY WITH THE FIGS. A REAL TREAT, THIS VINTAGE.
THANKS. I'VE ALWAYS BEEN A JACK AN' COKE KINDA GAL...
BUT A GAL CAN LEARN, RIGHT?
SIGH
I GOTTA TELL YOU, IT'S NICE TO BE ABLE TO JUST SIT AND TALK FOR A CHANGE.
ALL THAT'S BEEN GOING ON, I KNOW IT'S IMPORTANT, SO I REALLY DON'T FEEL A NEED TO ADD MY TWO CENTS...
YOU REMIND ME OF SOMEONE.
THAT SO? YOU DON'T SEEM TO HAVE THAT PROBLEM NOW.
SORRY, AM I TALKING TOO MUCH?
NO, ZOLA, I LIKE IT.

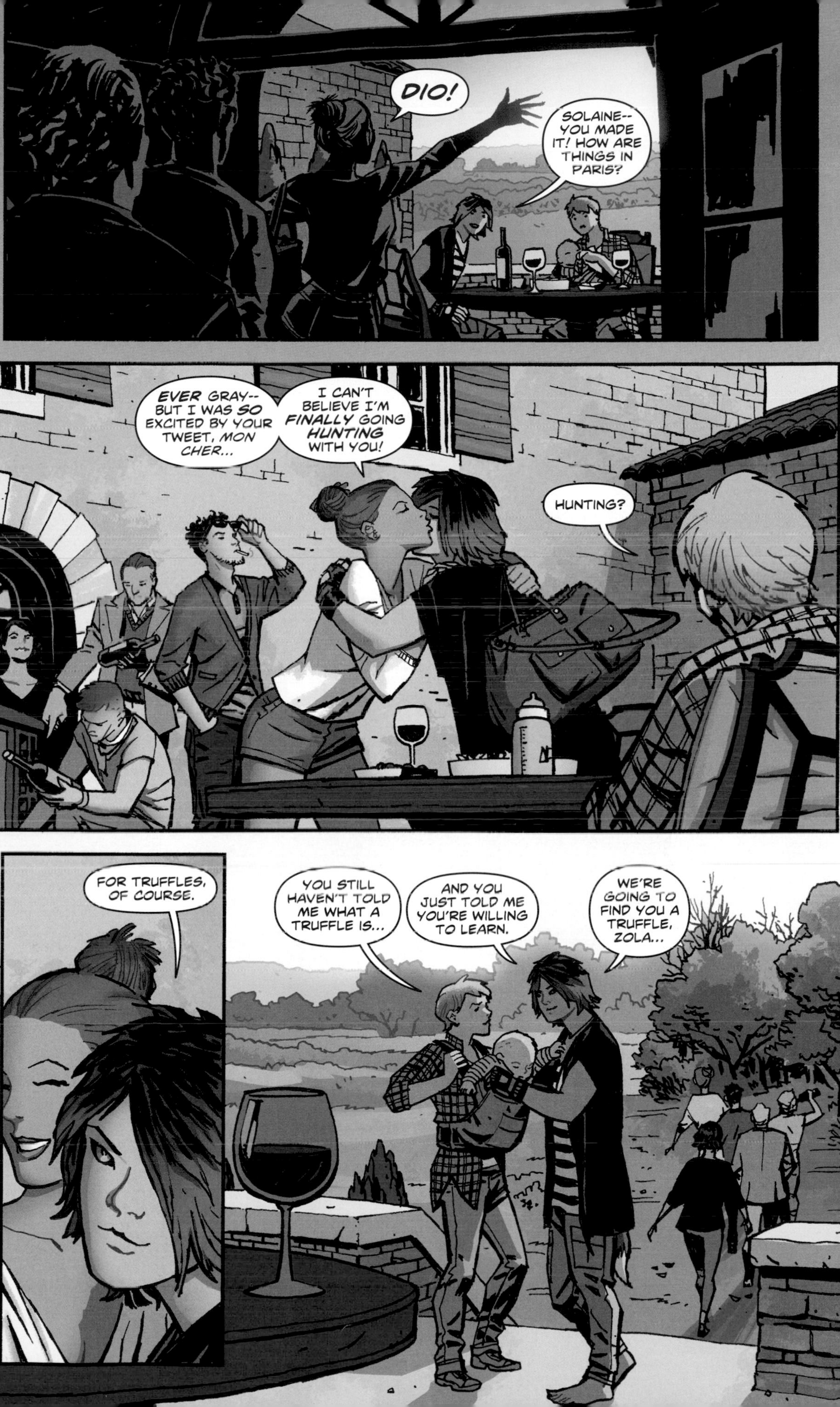
DIO!
SOLAINE-- YOU MADE IT! HOW ARE THINGS IN PARIS?
EVER GRAY-- BUT I WAS SO EXCITED BY YOUR TWEET, MON CHER...
I CAN'T BELIEVE I'M FINALLY GOING HUNTING WITH YOU!
HUNTING?
FOR TRUFFLES, OF COURSE.
YOU STILL HAVEN'T TOLD ME WHAT A TRUFFLE IS...
AND YOU JUST TOLD ME YOU'RE WILLING TO LEARN.
WE'RE GOING TO FIND YOU A TRUFFLE, ZOLA...

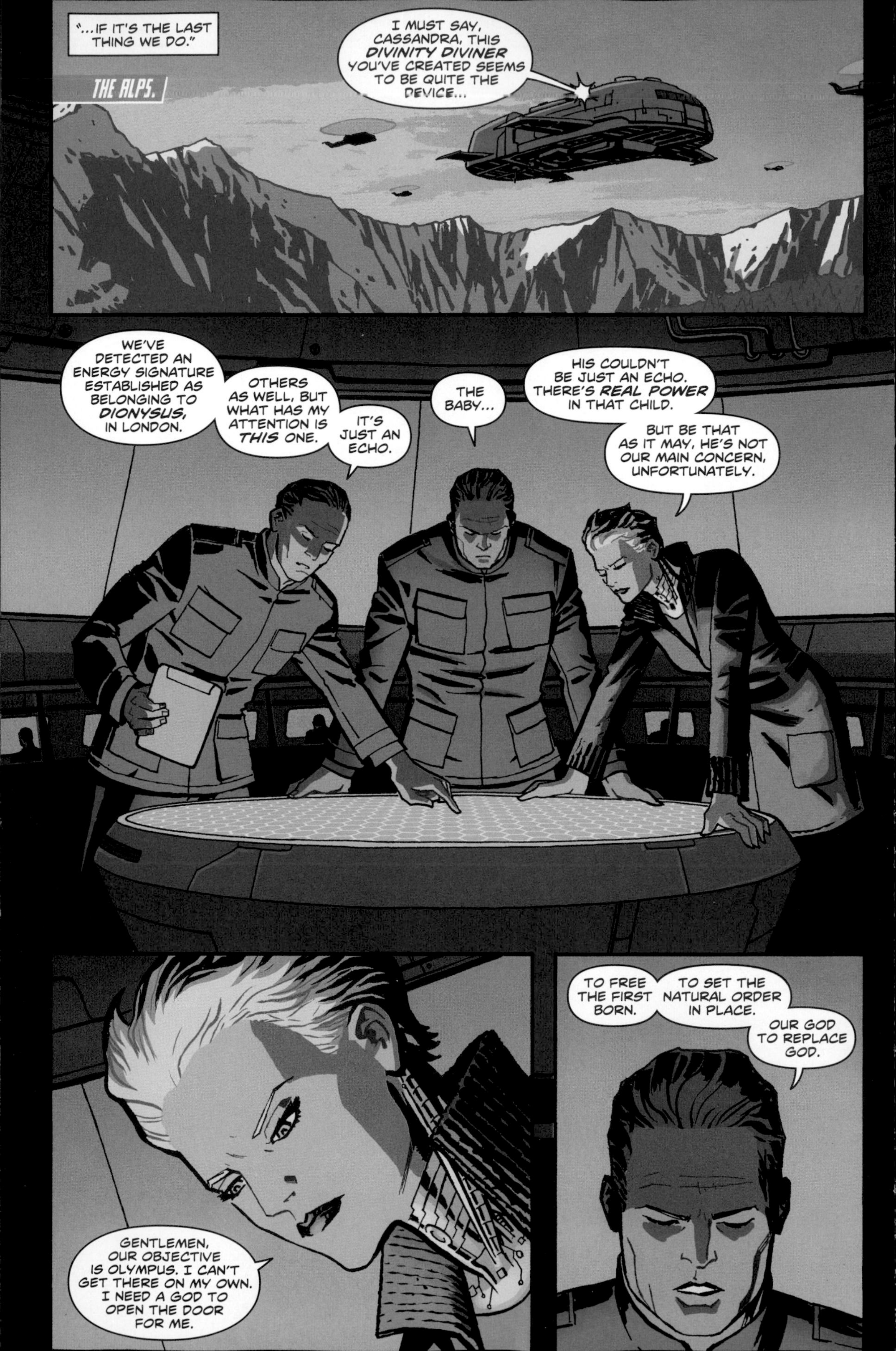

"...IF IT'S THE LAST THING WE DO."
THE ALPS.
I MUST SAY, CASSANDRA, THIS *DIVINITY DIVINER* YOU'VE CREATED SEEMS TO BE QUITE THE DEVICE...
WE'VE DETECTED AN ENERGY SIGNATURE ESTABLISHED AS BELONGING TO *DIONYSUS,* IN LONDON.
OTHERS AS WELL, BUT WHAT HAS MY ATTENTION IS *THIS* ONE.
IT'S JUST AN ECHO.
THE BABY...
HIS COULDN'T BE JUST AN ECHO. THERE'S *REAL POWER* IN THAT CHILD.
BUT BE THAT AS IT MAY, HE'S NOT OUR MAIN CONCERN, UNFORTUNATELY.
GENTLEMEN, OUR OBJECTIVE IS OLYMPUS. I CAN'T GET THERE ON MY OWN. I NEED A GOD TO OPEN THE DOOR FOR ME.
TO FREE THE FIRST BORN.
TO SET THE NATURAL ORDER IN PLACE.
OUR GOD TO REPLACE GOD.

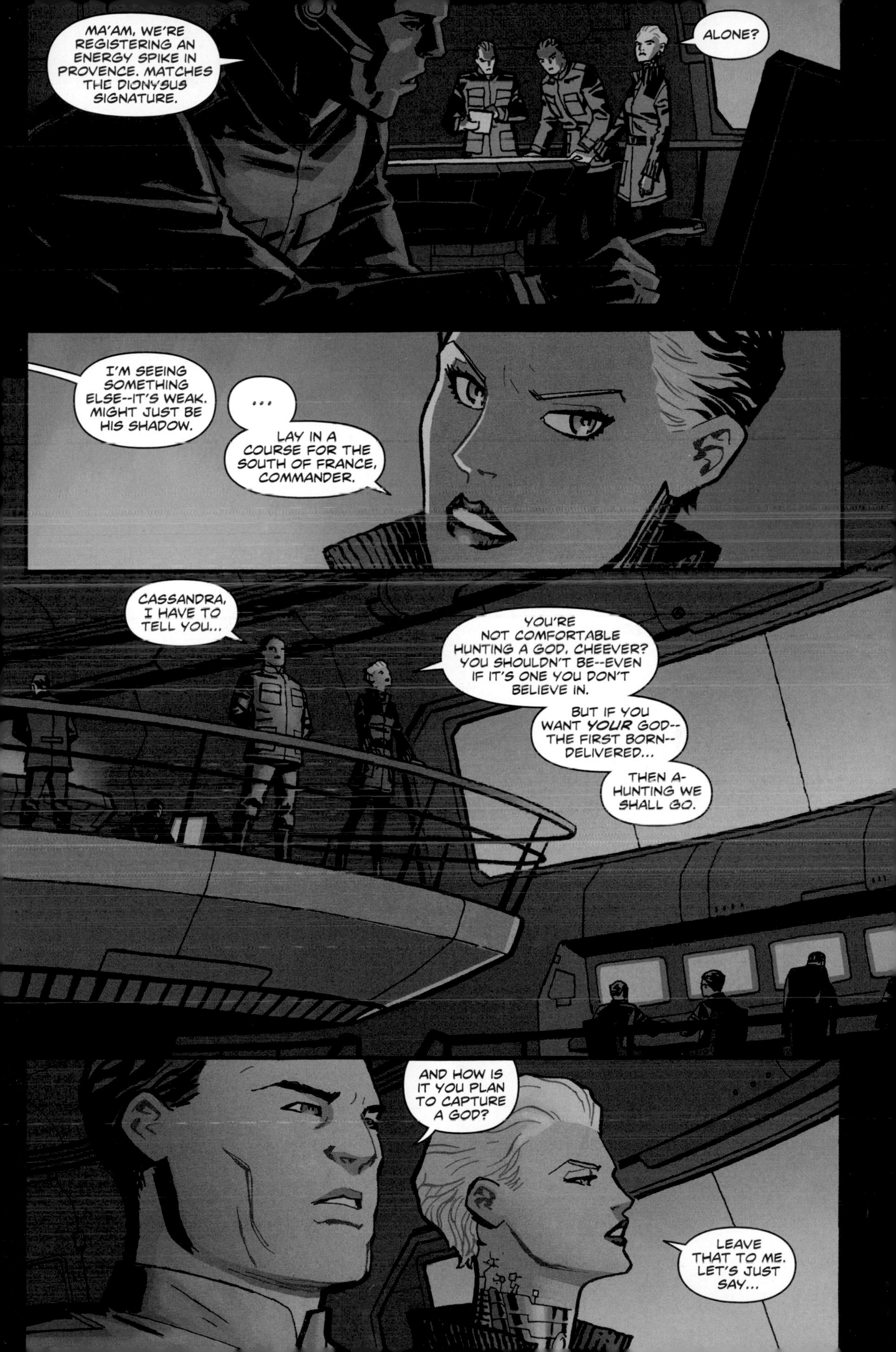
MA'AM, WE'RE REGISTERING AN ENERGY SPIKE IN PROVENCE. MATCHES THE DIONYSUS SIGNATURE.
ALONE?
I'M SEEING SOMETHING ELSE--IT'S WEAK. MIGHT JUST BE HIS SHADOW.
...
LAY IN A COURSE FOR THE SOUTH OF FRANCE, COMMANDER.
CASSANDRA, I HAVE TO TELL YOU...
YOU'RE NOT COMFORTABLE HUNTING A GOD, CHEEVER? YOU SHOULDN'T BE--EVEN IF IT'S ONE YOU DON'T BELIEVE IN.
BUT IF YOU WANT *YOUR* GOD-- THE FIRST BORN-- DELIVERED...
THEN A-HUNTING WE SHALL GO.
AND HOW IS IT YOU PLAN TO CAPTURE A GOD?
LEAVE THAT TO ME. LET'S JUST SAY...

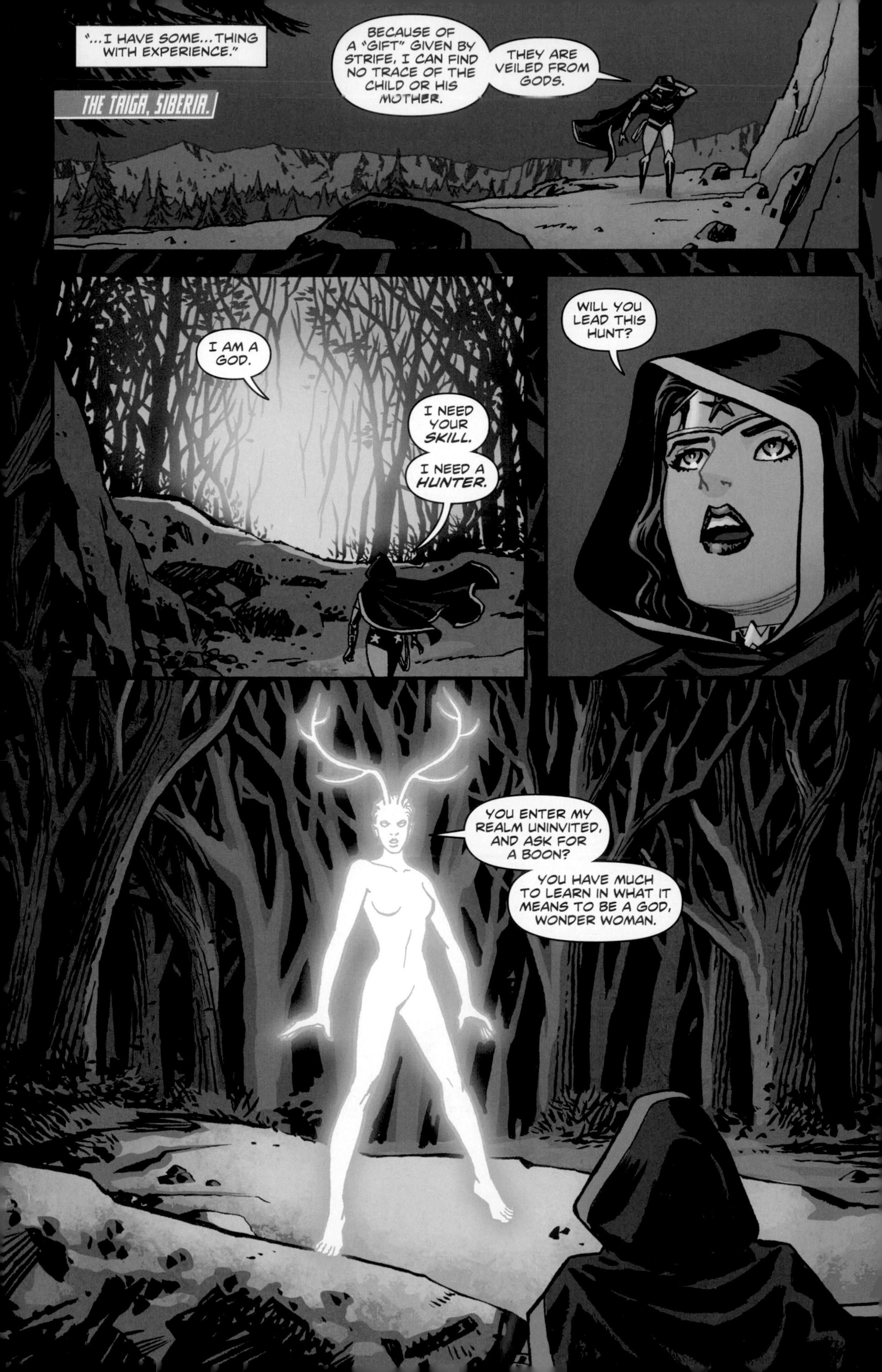
"...I HAVE SOME...THING WITH EXPERIENCE."
THE TAIGA, SIBERIA.
BECAUSE OF A "GIFT" GIVEN BY STRIFE, I CAN FIND NO TRACE OF THE CHILD OR HIS MOTHER.
THEY ARE VEILED FROM GODS.
I AM A GOD.
I NEED YOUR SKILL.
I NEED A HUNTER.
WILL YOU LEAD THIS HUNT?
YOU ENTER MY REALM UNINVITED, AND ASK FOR A BOON?
YOU HAVE MUCH TO LEARN IN WHAT IT MEANS TO BE A GOD, WONDER WOMAN.

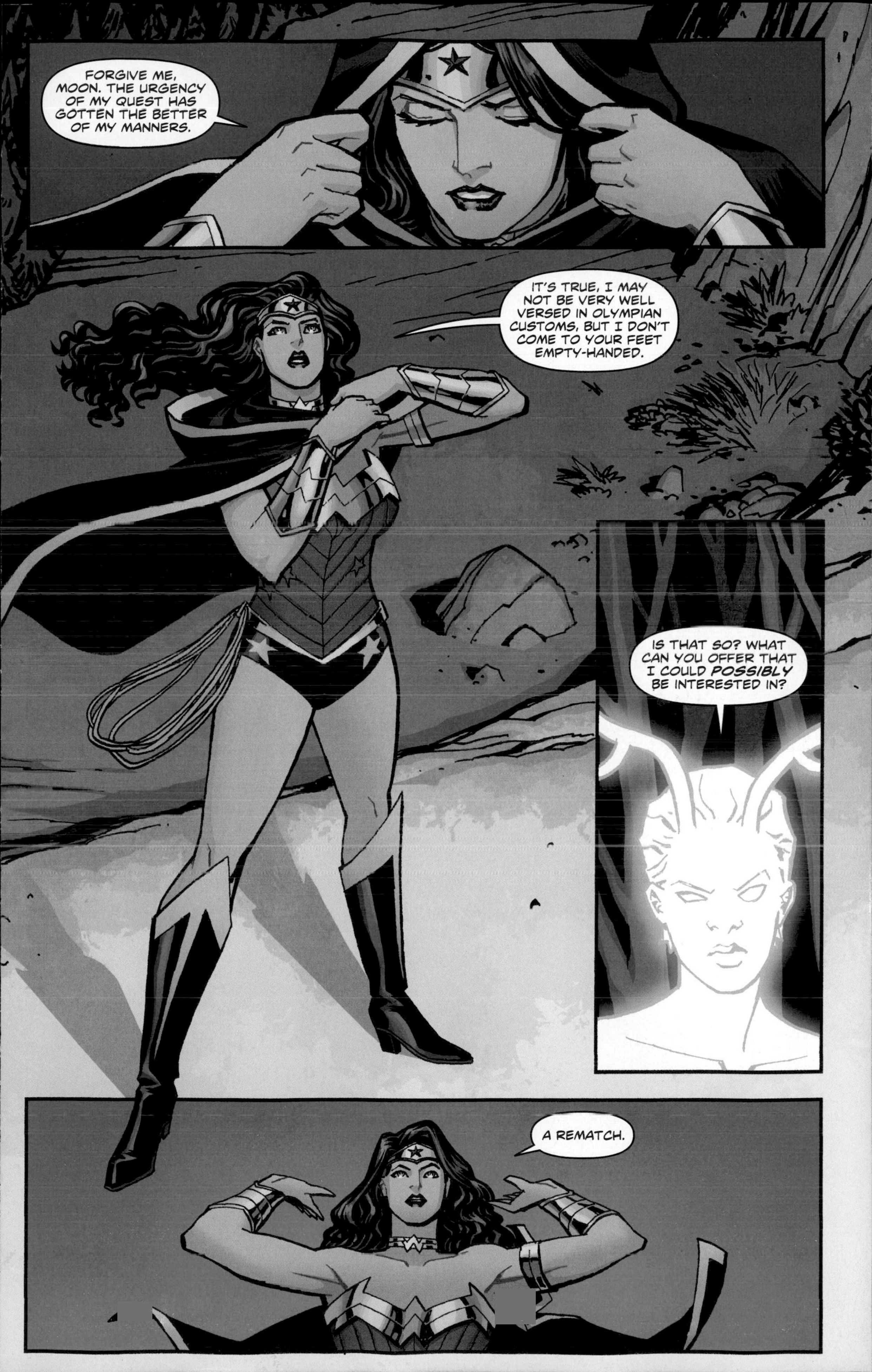
FORGIVE ME, MOON. THE URGENCY OF MY QUEST HAS GOTTEN THE BETTER OF MY MANNERS.
IT'S TRUE, I MAY NOT BE VERY WELL VERSED IN OLYMPIAN CUSTOMS, BUT I DON'T COME TO YOUR FEET EMPTY-HANDED.
IS THAT SO? WHAT CAN YOU OFFER THAT I COULD *POSSIBLY* BE INTERESTED IN?
A REMATCH.

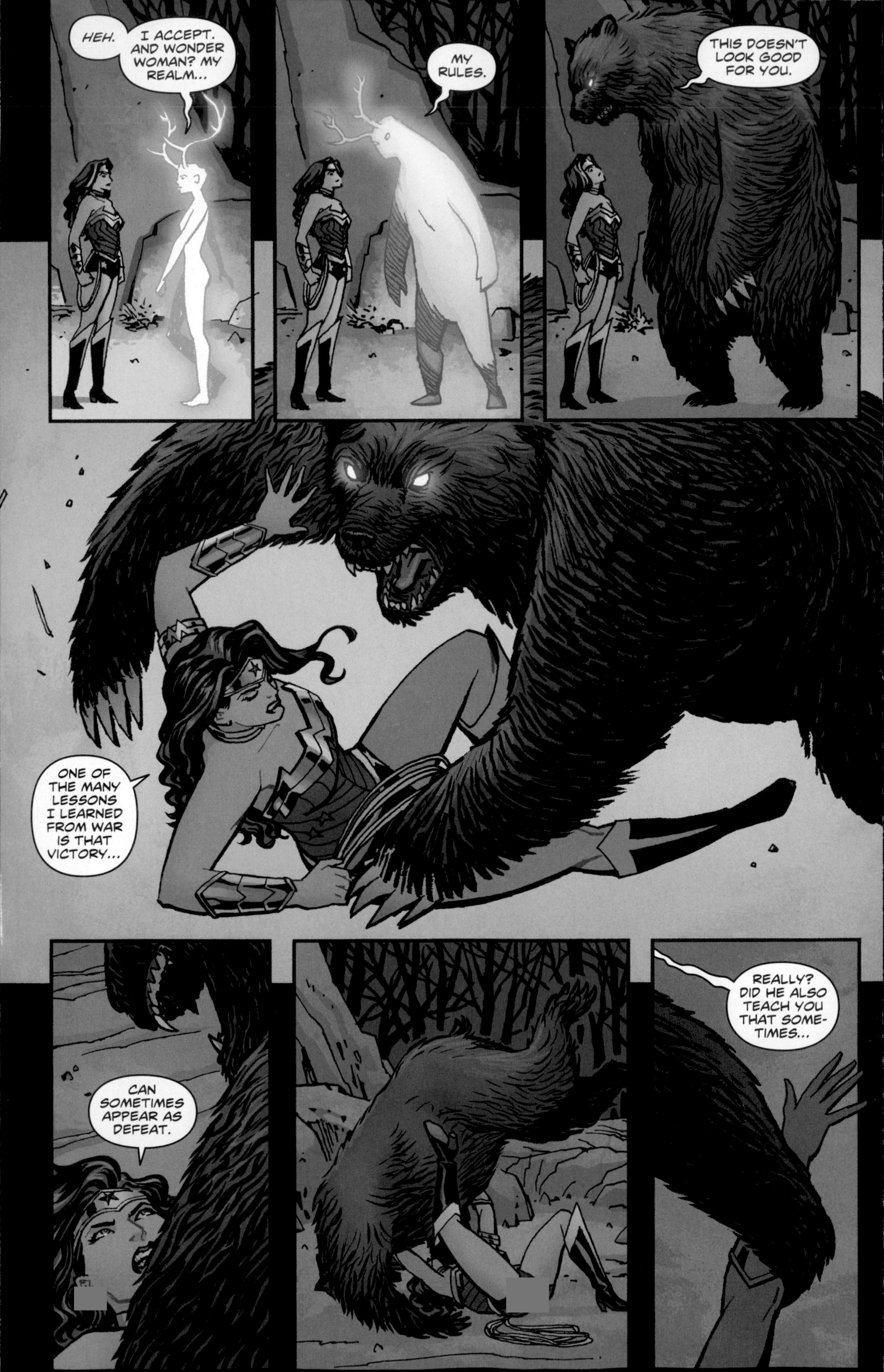
HEH.
I ACCEPT. AND WONDER WOMAN? MY REALM...
MY RULES.
THIS DOESN'T LOOK GOOD FOR YOU.
ONE OF THE MANY LESSONS I LEARNED FROM WAR IS THAT VICTORY...
CAN SOMETIMES APPEAR AS DEFEAT.
REALLY? DID HE ALSO TEACH YOU THAT SOME-TIMES...

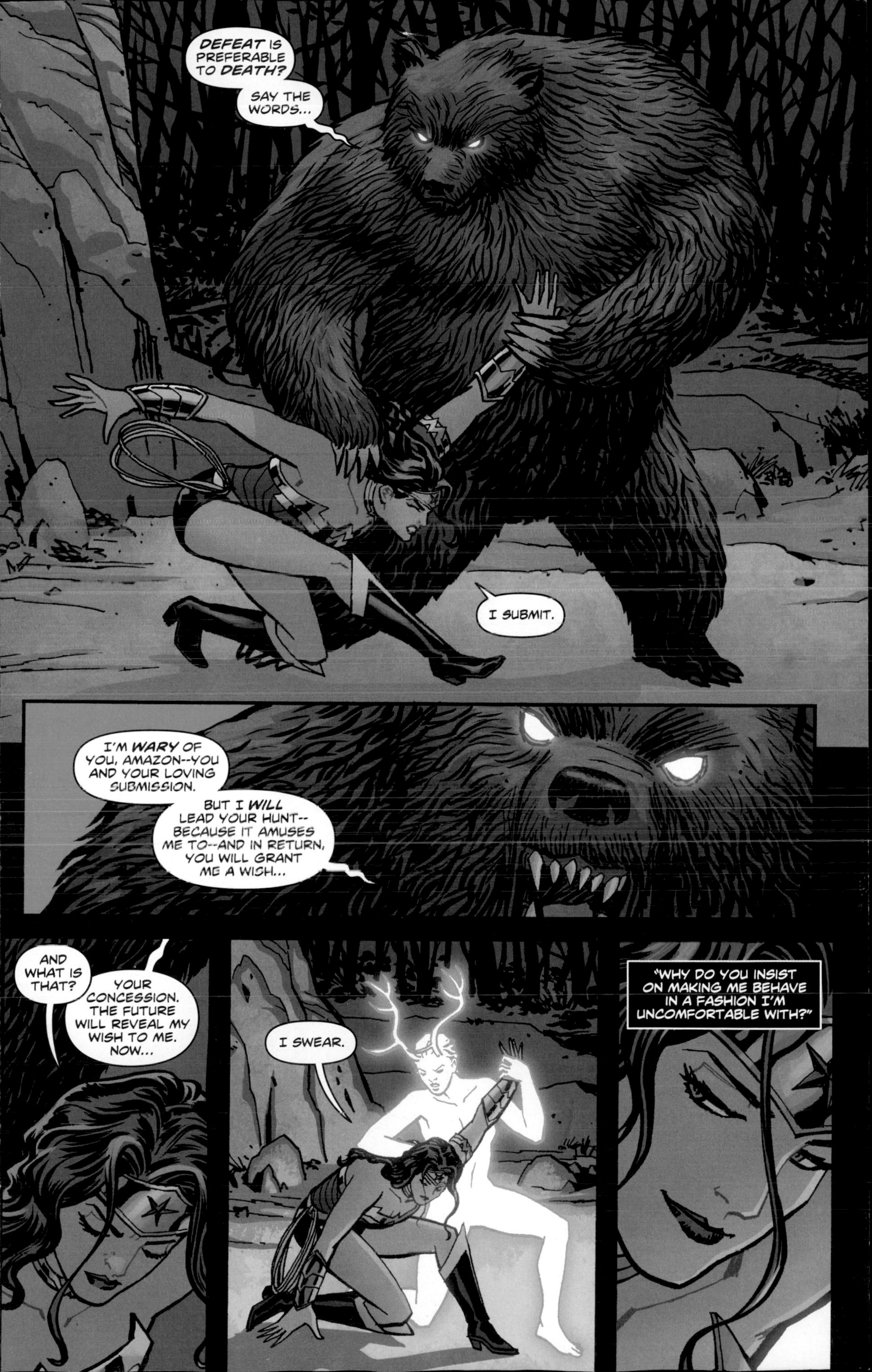
DEFEAT IS PREFERABLE TO DEATH?
SAY THE WORDS...
I SUBMIT.
I'M WARY OF YOU, AMAZON--YOU AND YOUR LOVING SUBMISSION.
BUT I WILL LEAD YOUR HUNT--BECAUSE IT AMUSES ME TO--AND IN RETURN, YOU WILL GRANT ME A WISH...
AND WHAT IS THAT?
YOUR CONCESSION. THE FUTURE WILL REVEAL MY WISH TO ME. NOW...
I SWEAR.
"WHY DO YOU INSIST ON MAKING ME BEHAVE IN A FASHION I'M UNCOMFORTABLE WITH?"

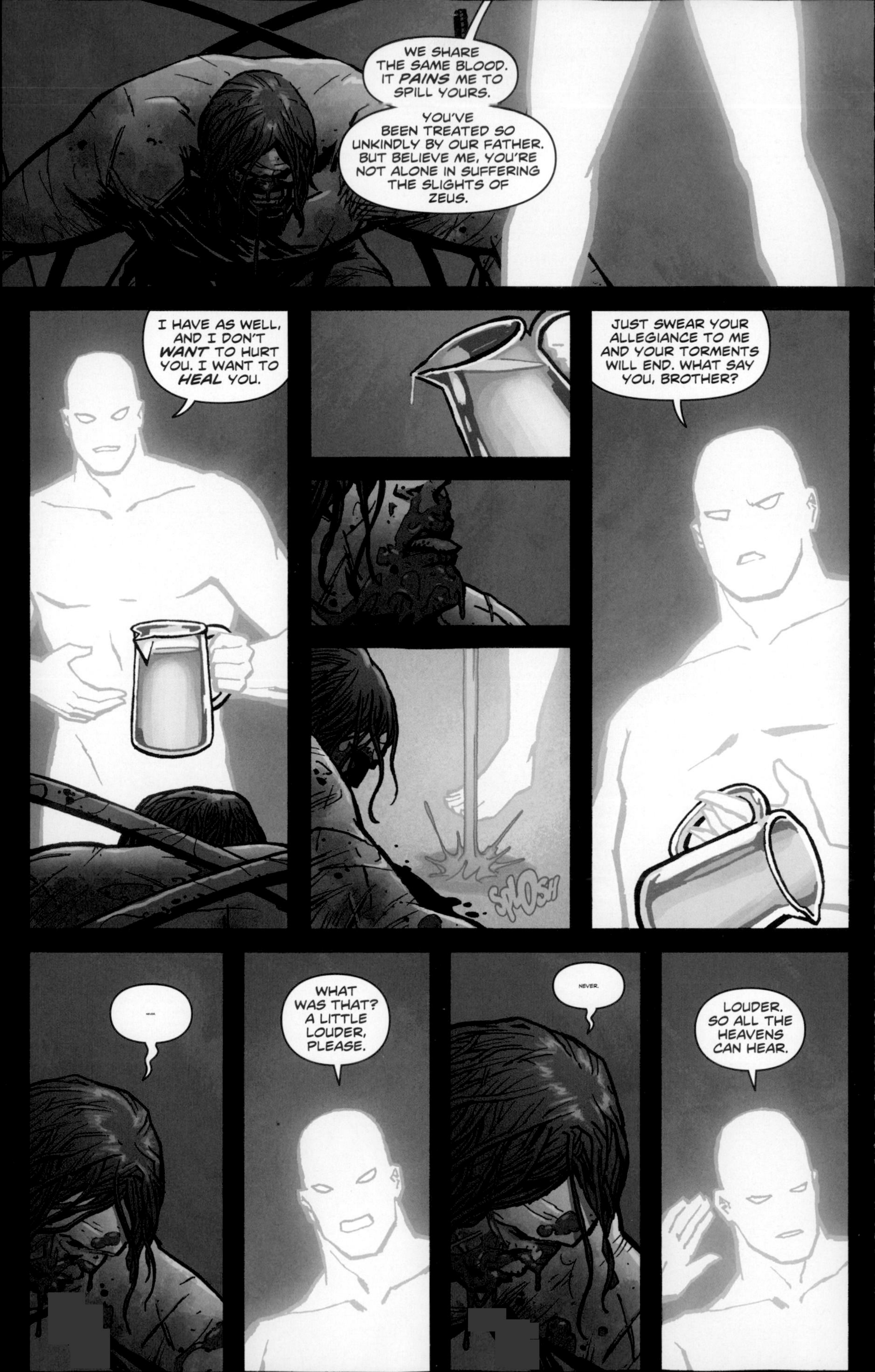
WE SHARE THE SAME BLOOD. IT PAINS ME TO SPILL YOURS.
YOU'VE BEEN TREATED SO UNKINDLY BY OUR FATHER. BUT BELIEVE ME, YOU'RE NOT ALONE IN SUFFERING THE SLIGHTS OF ZEUS.
I HAVE AS WELL, AND I DON'T WANT TO HURT YOU. I WANT TO HEAL YOU.
JUST SWEAR YOUR ALLEGIANCE TO ME AND YOUR TORMENTS WILL END. WHAT SAY YOU, BROTHER?
SPLOSH
NEVER.
WHAT WAS THAT? A LITTLE LOUDER, PLEASE.
NEVER.
LOUDER. SO ALL THE HEAVENS CAN HEAR.

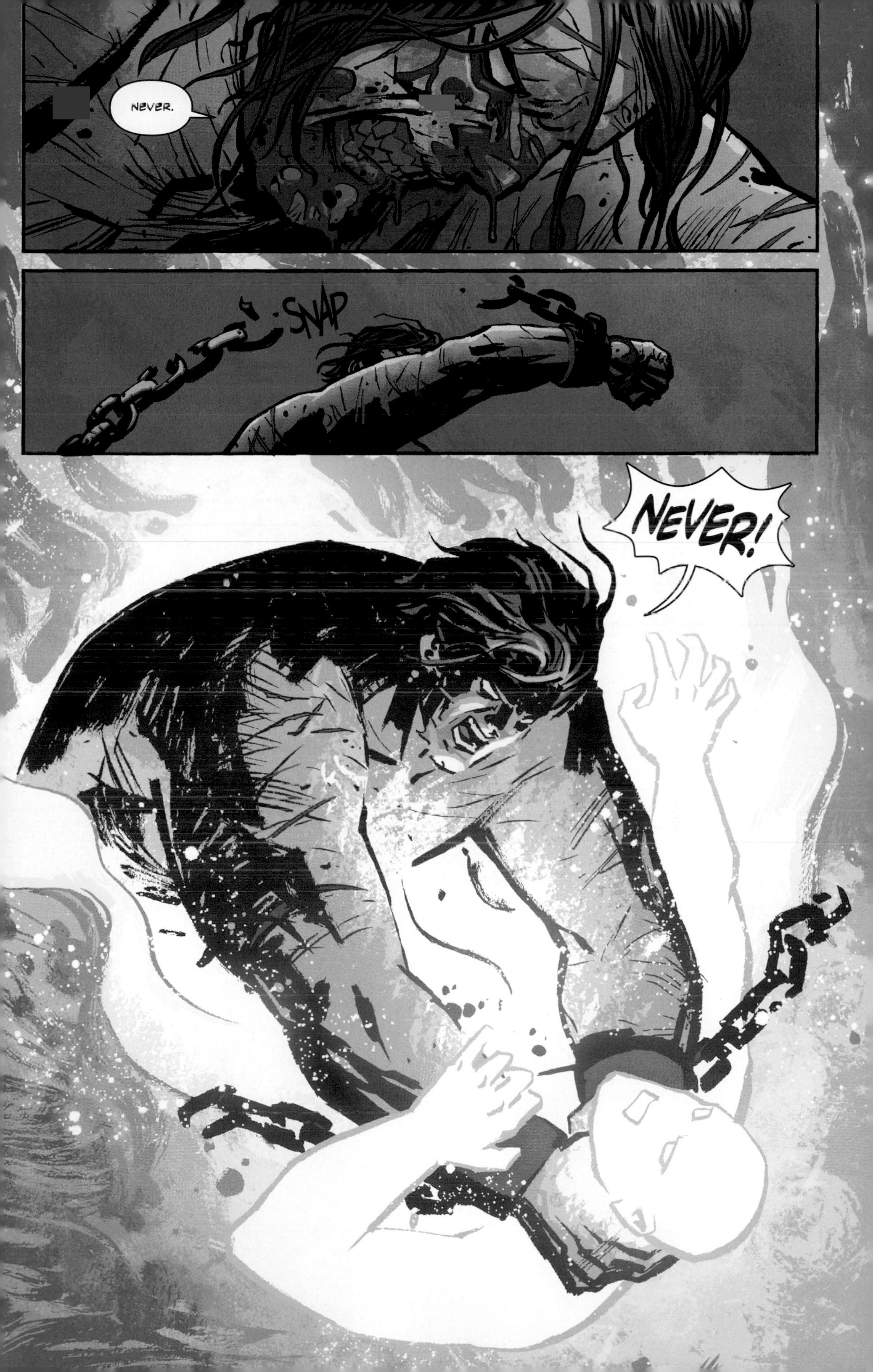
NEVER.
SNAP
NEVER!

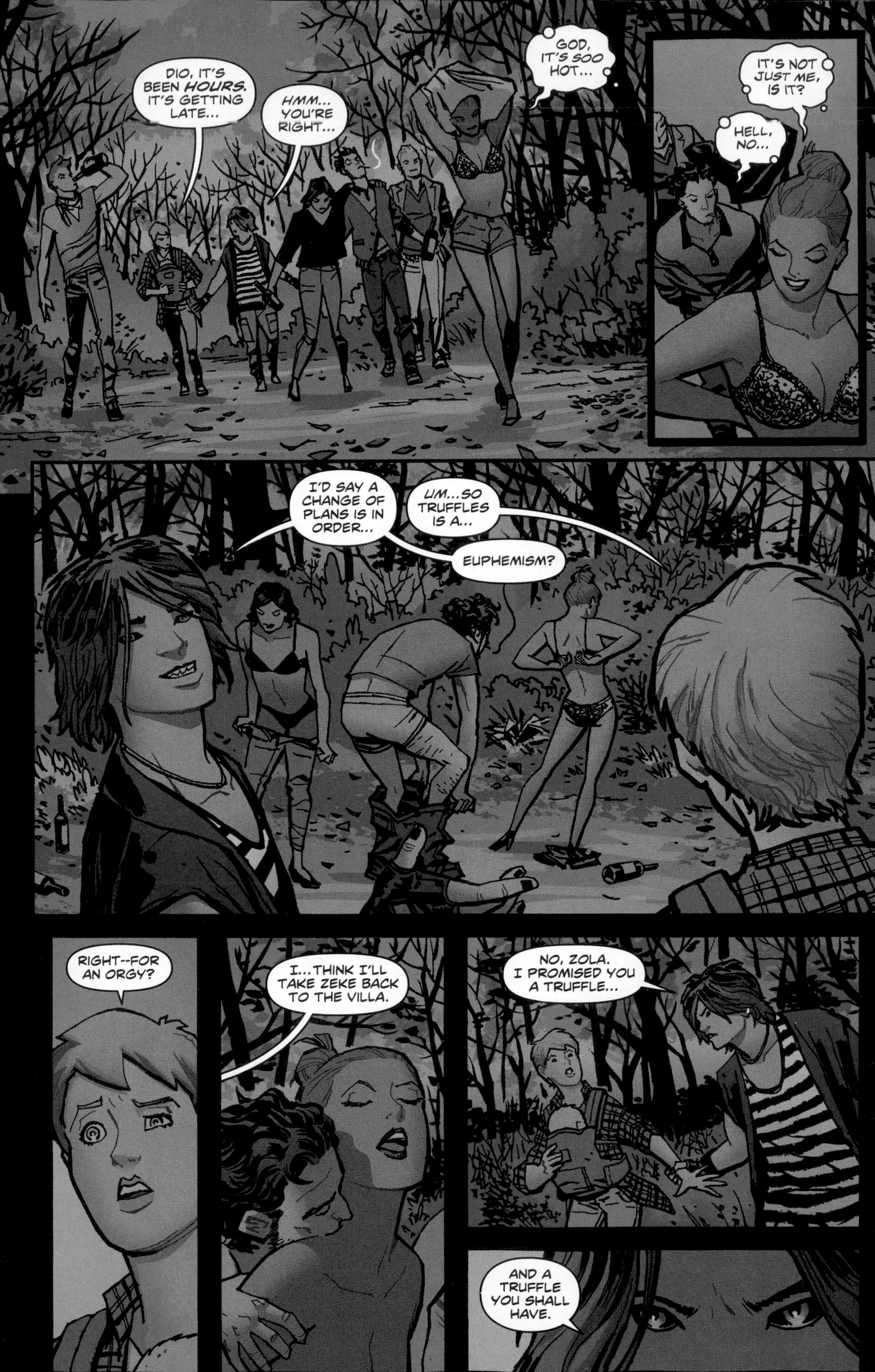
DIO, IT'S BEEN *HOURS.* IT'S GETTING LATE...
*HMM... YOU'RE RIGHT...*
GOD, IT'S SOO HOT...
IT'S NOT JUST ME, IS IT?
HELL, NO...
I'D SAY A CHANGE OF PLANS IS IN ORDER...
*UM*...SO TRUFFLES IS A...
EUPHEMISM?
RIGHT--FOR AN ORGY?
I...THINK I'LL TAKE ZEKE BACK TO THE VILLA.
NO, ZOLA. I PROMISED YOU A TRUFFLE...
AND A TRUFFLE YOU SHALL HAVE.

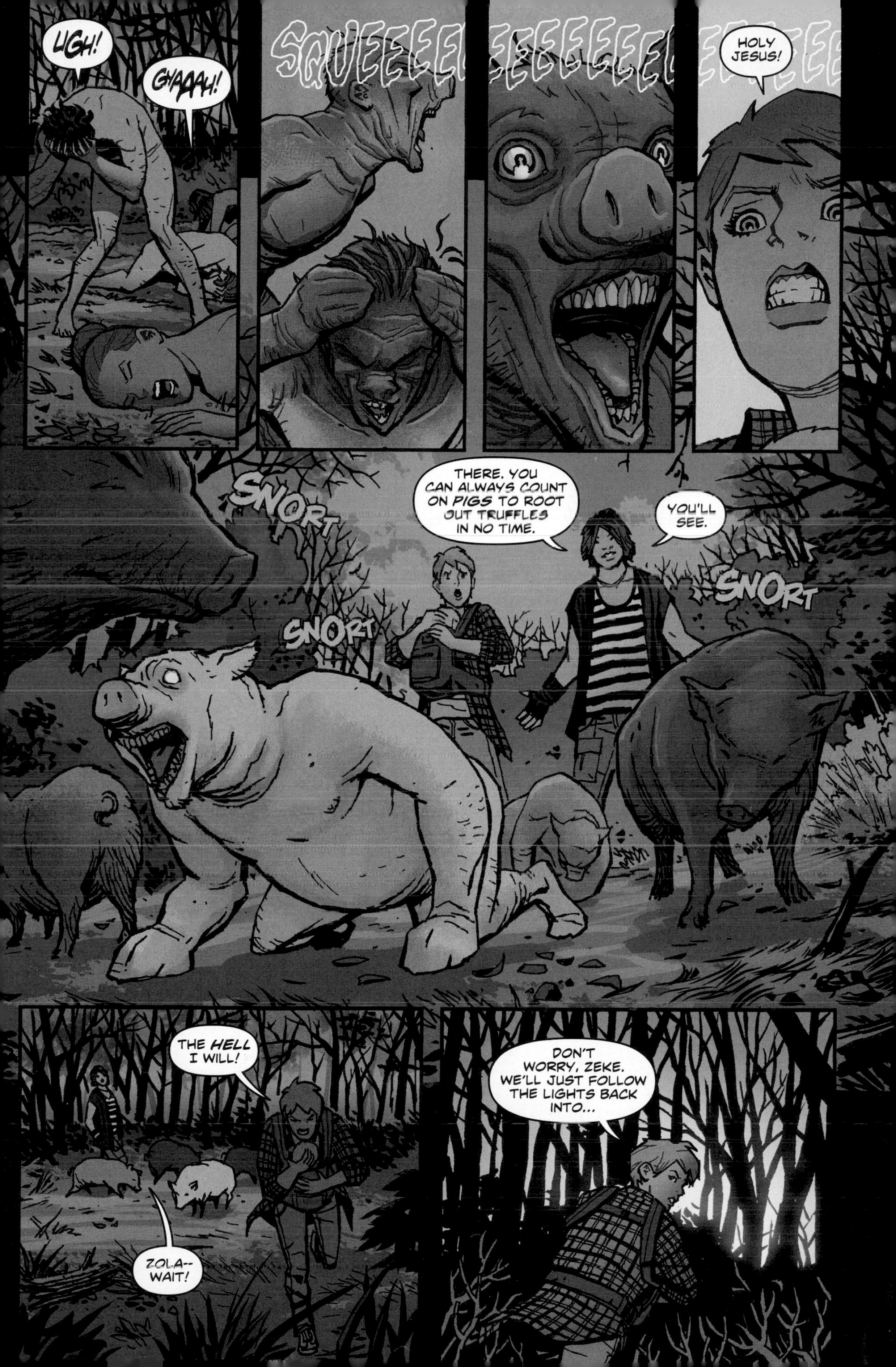
UGH!
GYAAAH!
SQUEEEEEEEEEEEEEEEEEE
HOLY JESUS!
SNORT
THERE. YOU CAN ALWAYS COUNT ON PIGS TO ROOT OUT TRUFFLES IN NO TIME.
YOU'LL SEE.
SNORT
SNORT
THE HELL I WILL!
ZOLA-- WAIT!
DON'T WORRY, ZEKE. WE'LL JUST FOLLOW THE LIGHTS BACK INTO...

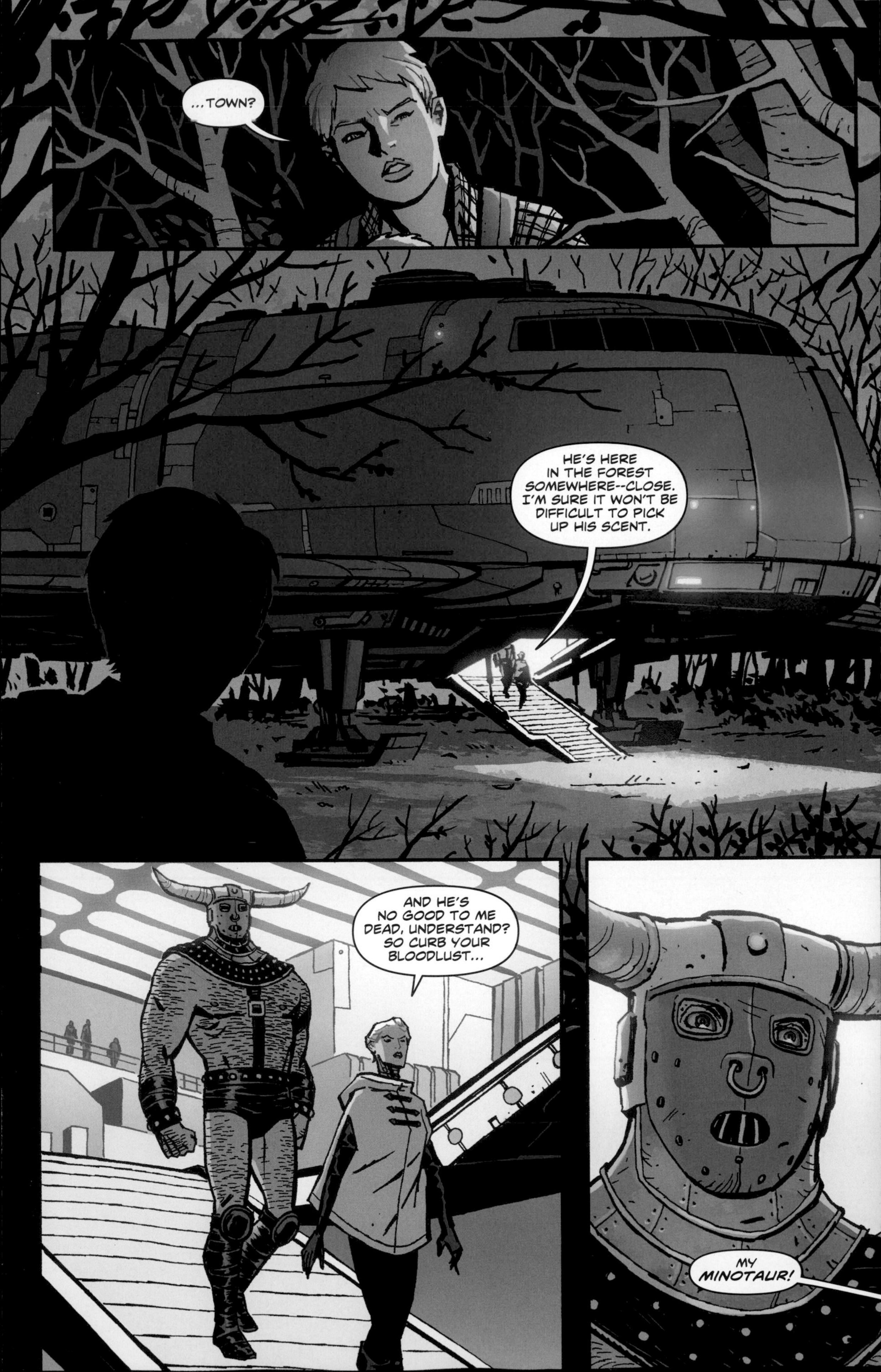
...TOWN?
HE'S HERE IN THE FOREST SOMEWHERE--CLOSE. I'M SURE IT WON'T BE DIFFICULT TO PICK UP HIS SCENT.
AND HE'S NO GOOD TO ME DEAD, UNDERSTAND? SO CURB YOUR BLOODLUST...
MY MINOTAUR!

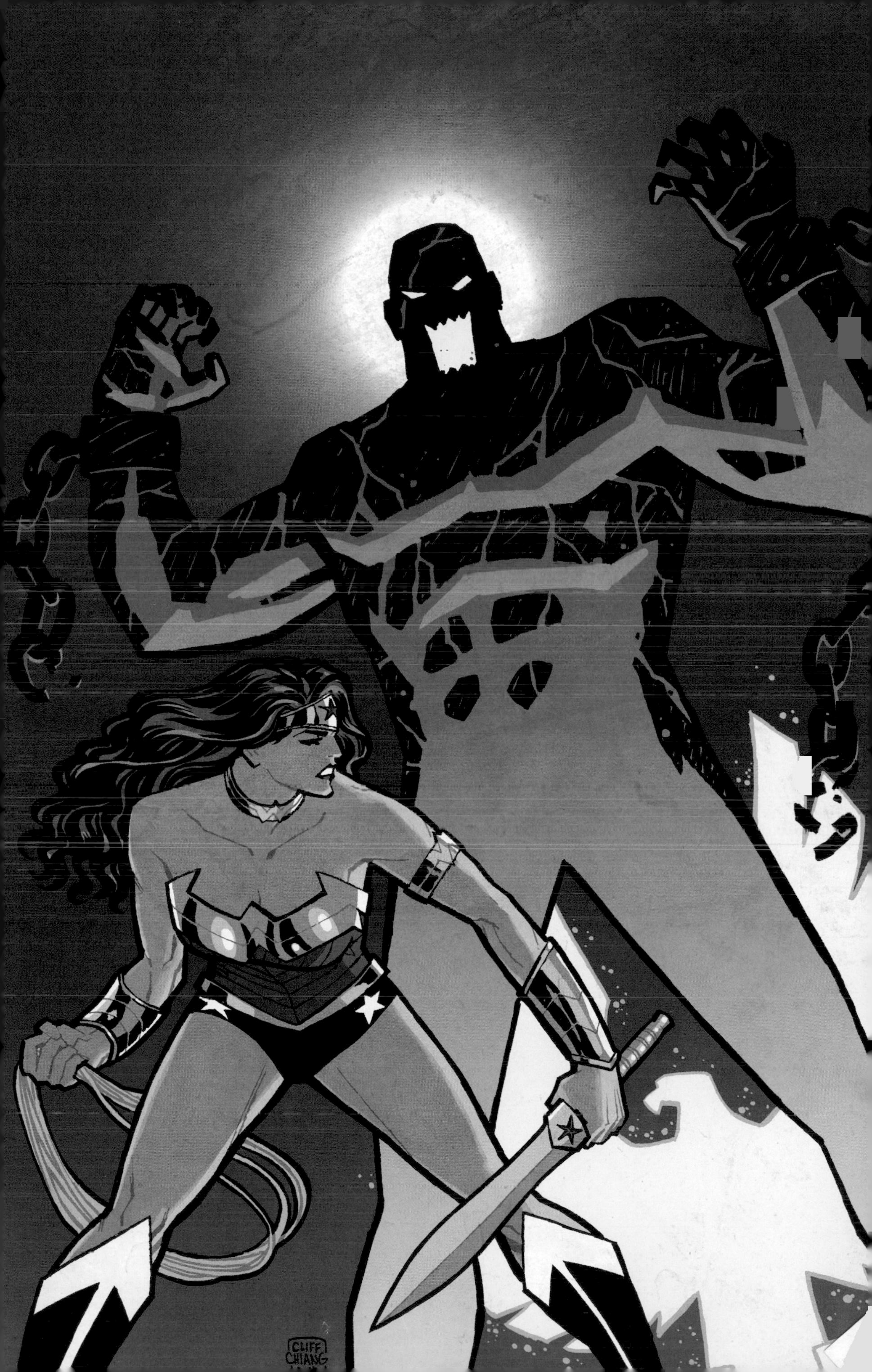
CLIFF CHIANG

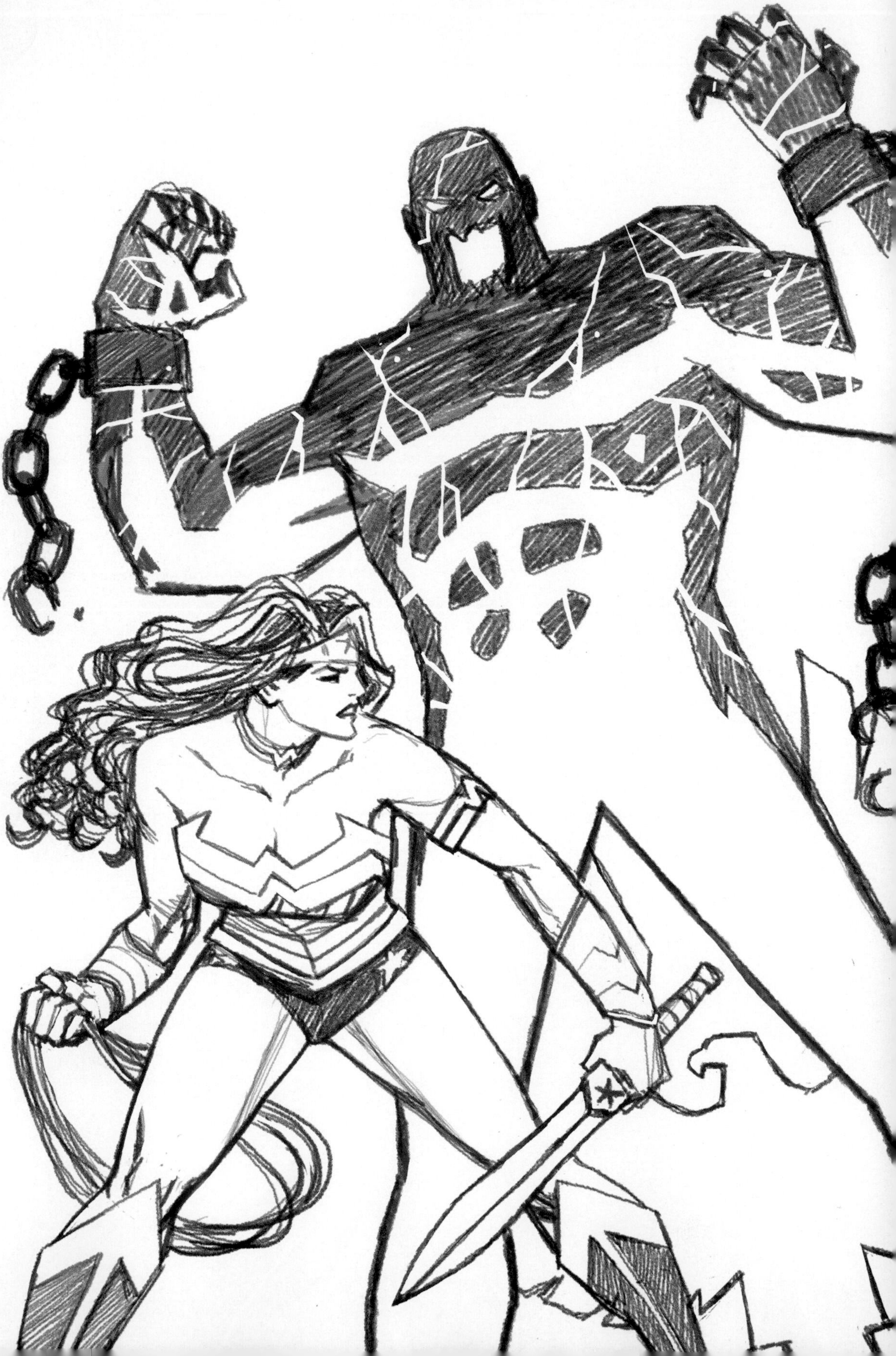

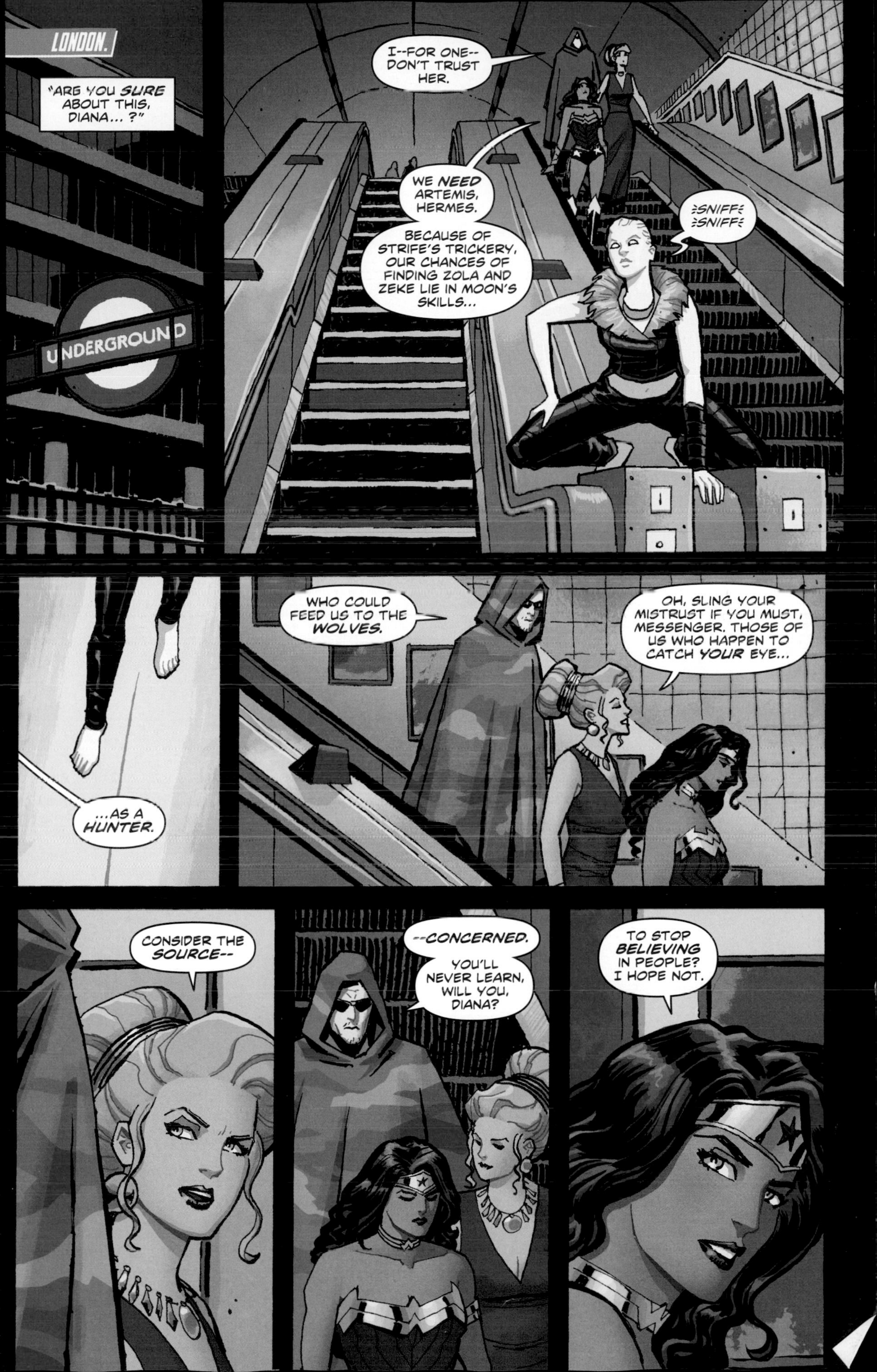
LONDON.
"ARE YOU SURE ABOUT THIS, DIANA... ?"
UNDERGROUND
I--FOR ONE--DON'T TRUST HER.
WE NEED ARTEMIS, HERMES.
BECAUSE OF STRIFE'S TRICKERY, OUR CHANCES OF FINDING ZOLA AND ZEKE LIE IN MOON'S SKILLS...
SNIFF SNIFF
...AS A HUNTER.
WHO COULD FEED US TO THE WOLVES.
OH, SLING YOUR MISTRUST IF YOU MUST, MESSENGER. THOSE OF US WHO HAPPEN TO CATCH YOUR EYE...
CONSIDER THE SOURCE--
--CONCERNED.
YOU'LL NEVER LEARN, WILL YOU, DIANA?
TO STOP BELIEVING IN PEOPLE? I HOPE NOT.

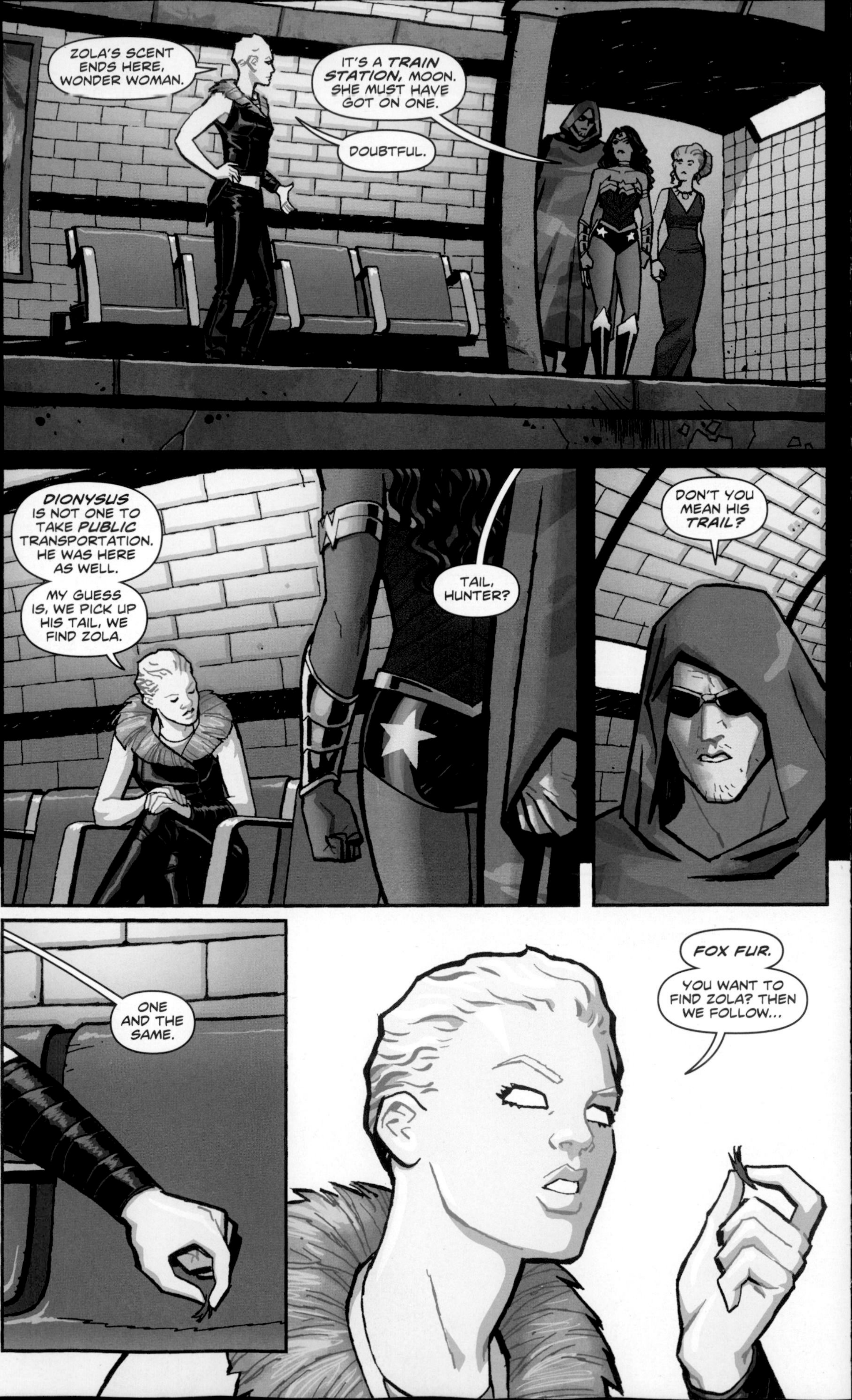
ZOLA'S SCENT ENDS HERE, WONDER WOMAN.
IT'S A TRAIN STATION, MOON. SHE MUST HAVE GOT ON ONE.
DOUBTFUL.
DIONYSUS IS NOT ONE TO TAKE PUBLIC TRANSPORTATION. HE WAS HERE AS WELL.
MY GUESS IS, WE PICK UP HIS TAIL, WE FIND ZOLA.
TAIL, HUNTER?
DON'T YOU MEAN HIS TRAIL?
ONE AND THE SAME.
FOX FUR.
YOU WANT TO FIND ZOLA? THEN WE FOLLOW...

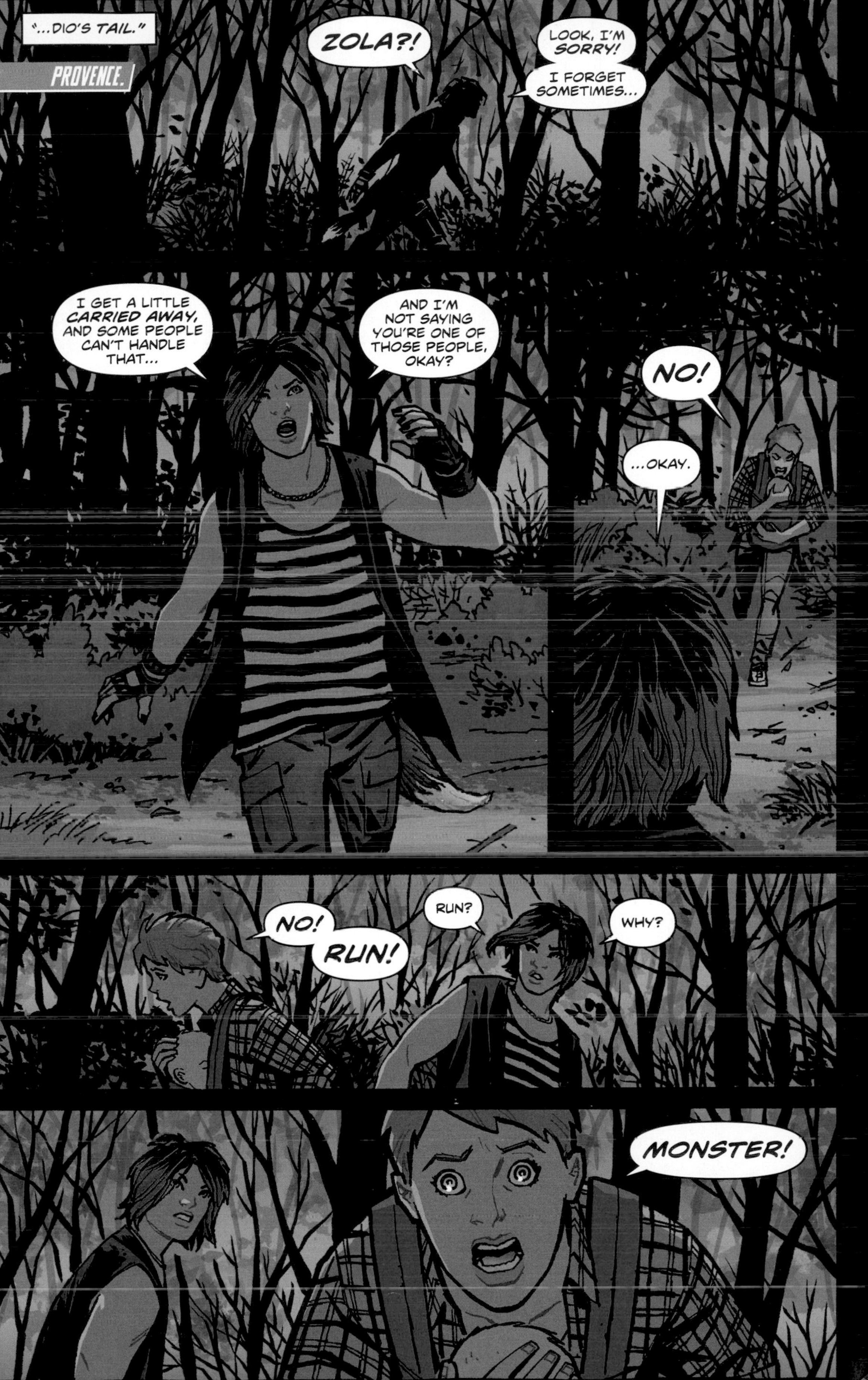
"...DIO'S TAIL."
PROVENCE.
ZOLA?!
LOOK, I'M SORRY!
I FORGET SOMETIMES...
I GET A LITTLE CARRIED AWAY, AND SOME PEOPLE CAN'T HANDLE THAT...
AND I'M NOT SAYING YOU'RE ONE OF THOSE PEOPLE, OKAY?
NO!
...OKAY.
NO! RUN!
RUN?
WHY?
MONSTER!

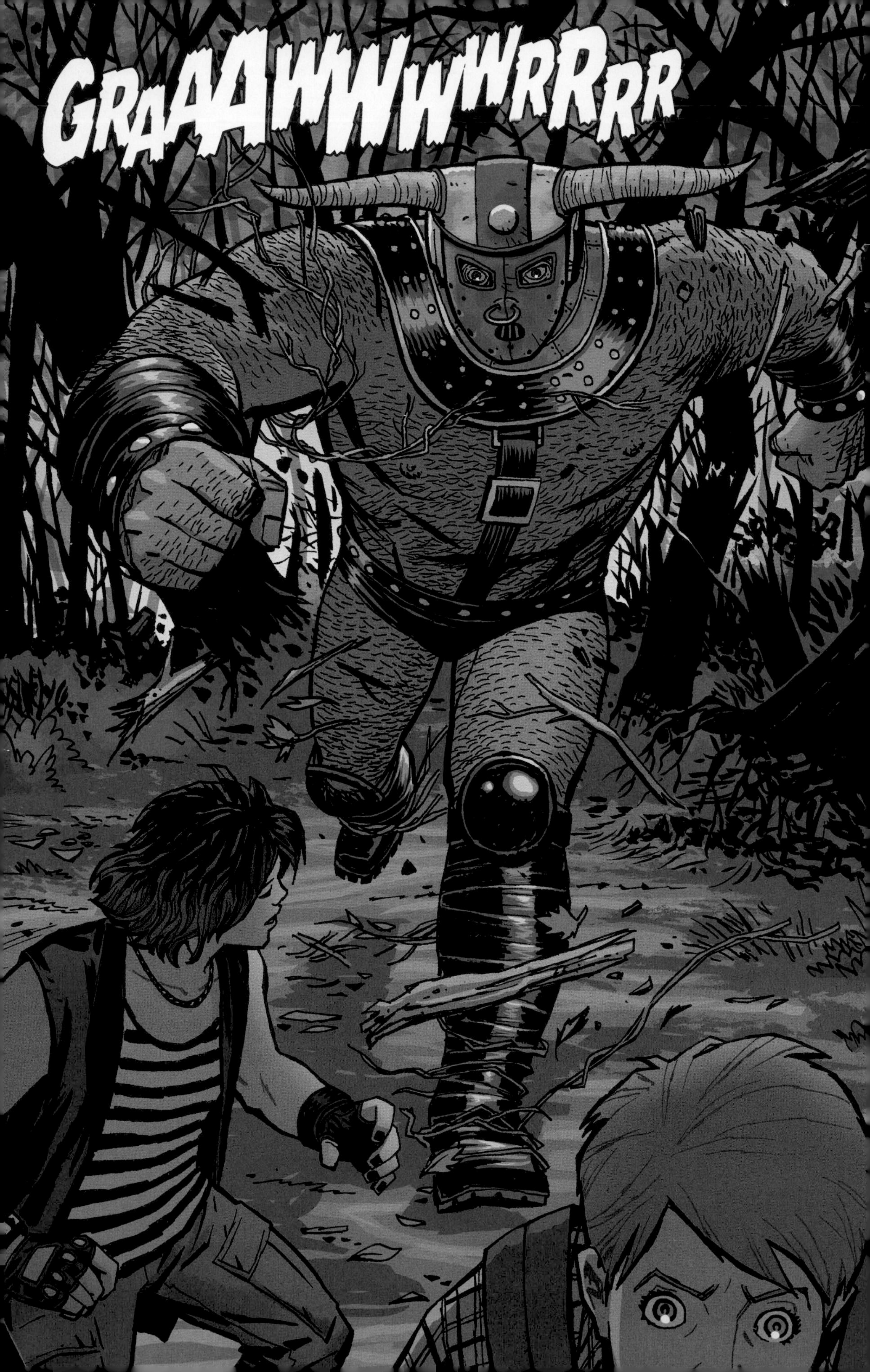
GRAAAWWWWRRRrr

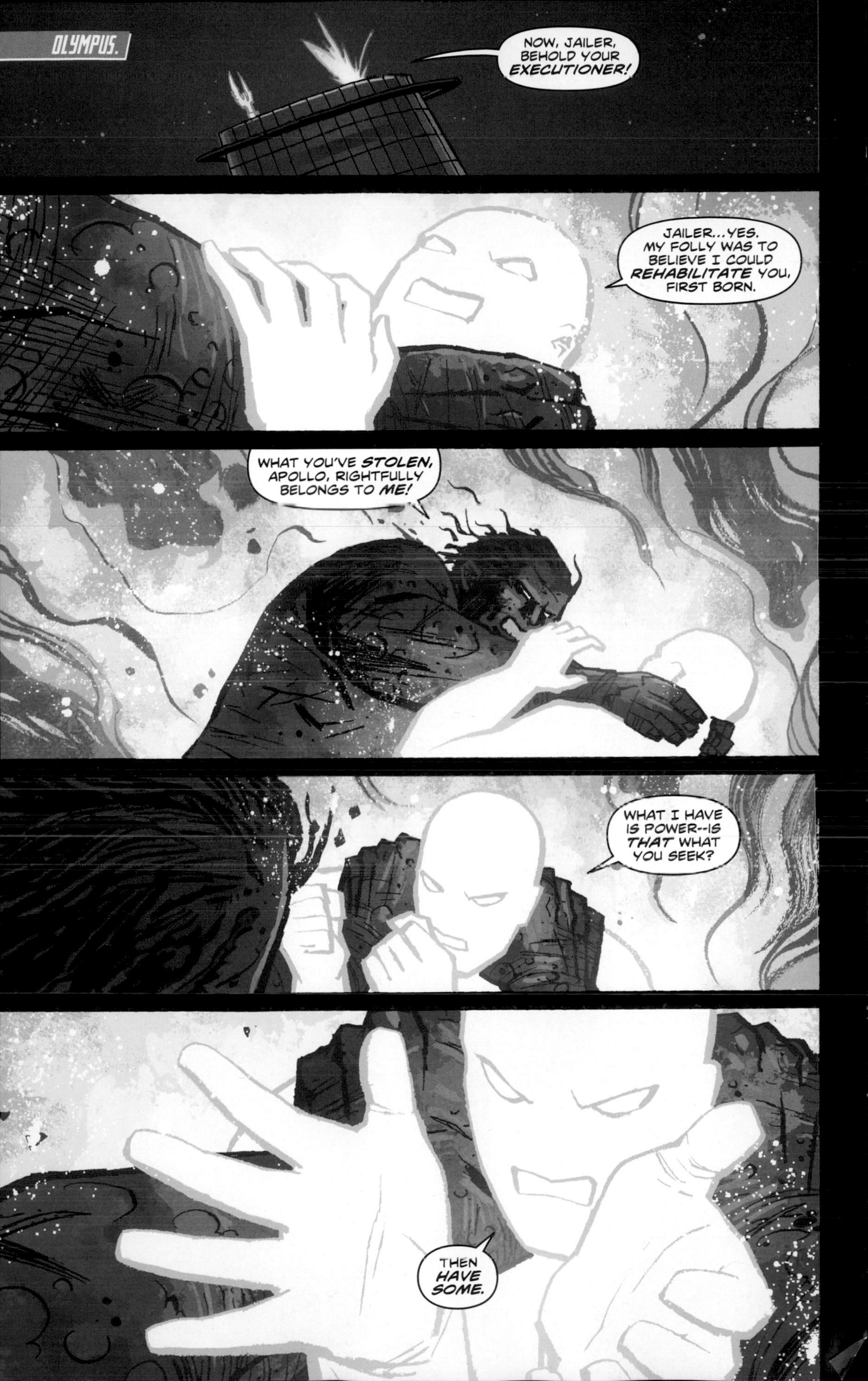
OLYMPUS.
NOW, JAILER, BEHOLD YOUR EXECUTIONER!
JAILER...YES. MY FOLLY WAS TO BELIEVE I COULD REHABILITATE YOU, FIRST BORN.
WHAT YOU'VE STOLEN, APOLLO, RIGHTFULLY BELONGS TO ME!
WHAT I HAVE IS POWER--IS THAT WHAT YOU SEEK?
THEN HAVE SOME.

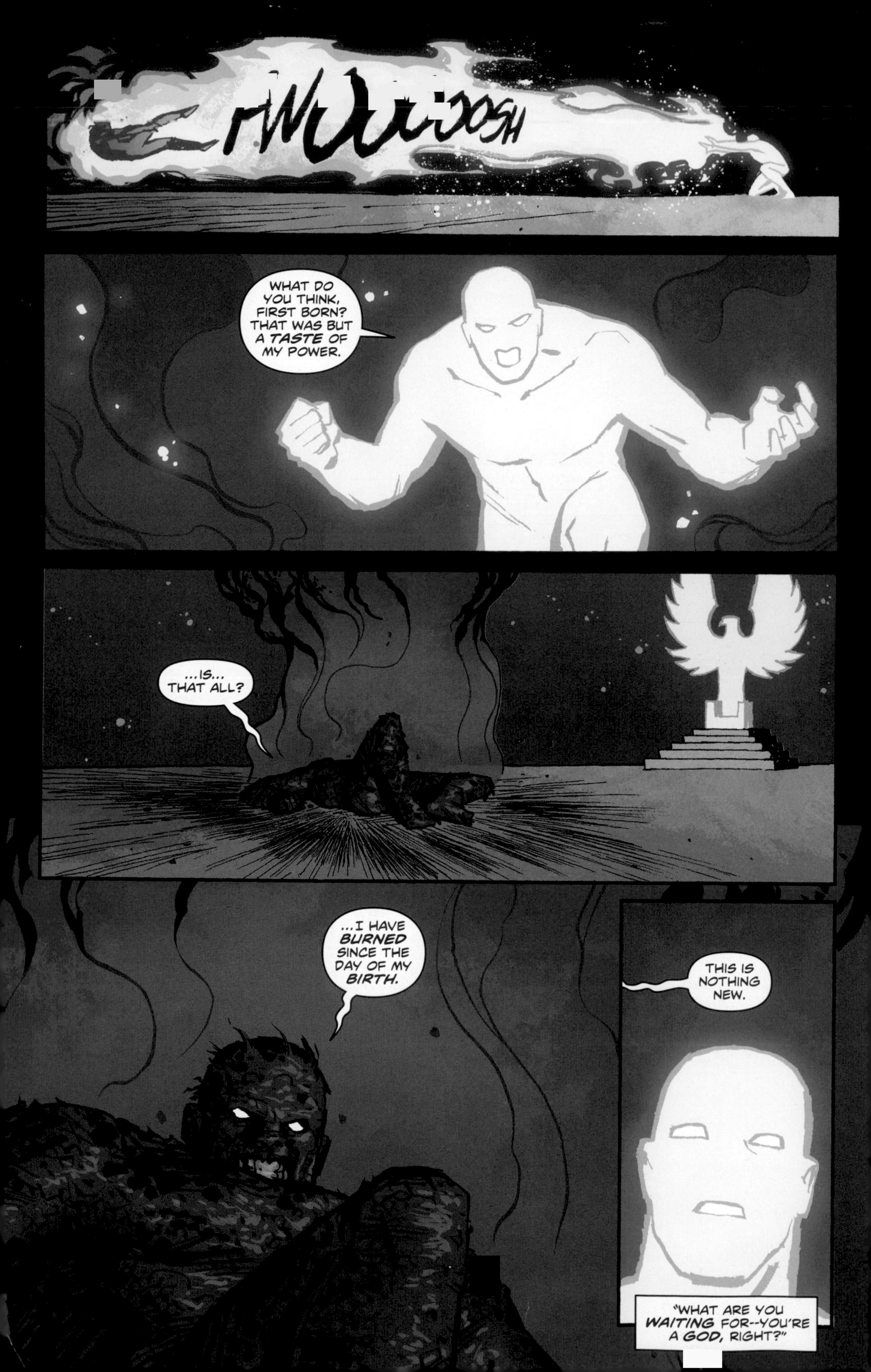
WHAT DO YOU THINK, FIRST BORN? THAT WAS BUT A TASTE OF MY POWER.
...IS... THAT ALL?
...I HAVE BURNED SINCE THE DAY OF MY BIRTH.
THIS IS NOTHING NEW.
"WHAT ARE YOU WAITING FOR--YOU'RE A GOD, RIGHT?"

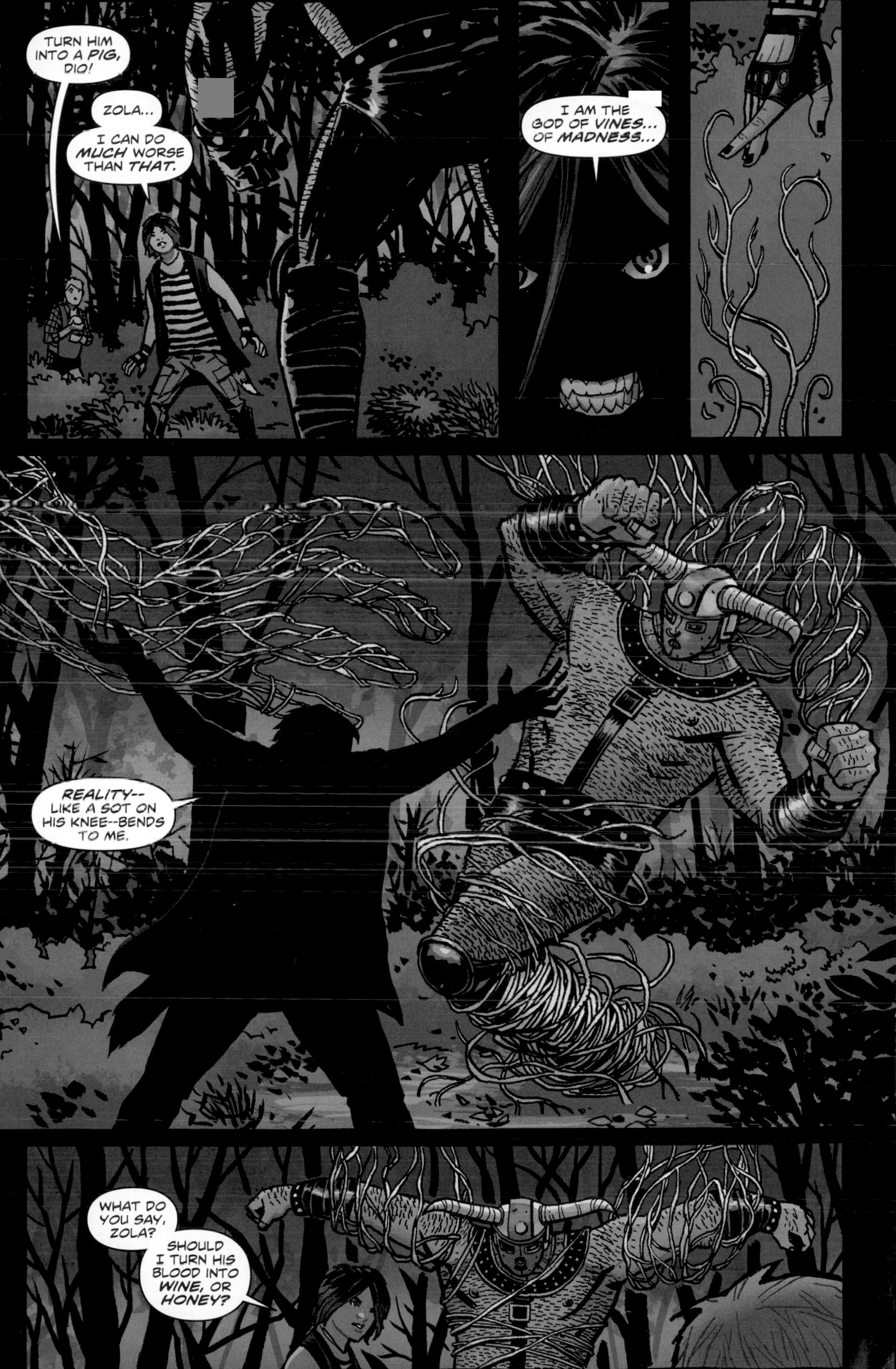
TURN HIM INTO A PIG, DIO!
ZOLA...
I CAN DO MUCH WORSE THAN THAT.
I AM THE GOD OF VINES... OF MADNESS...
REALITY-- LIKE A SOT ON HIS KNEE--BENDS TO ME.
WHAT DO YOU SAY, ZOLA?
SHOULD I TURN HIS BLOOD INTO WINE, OR HONEY?

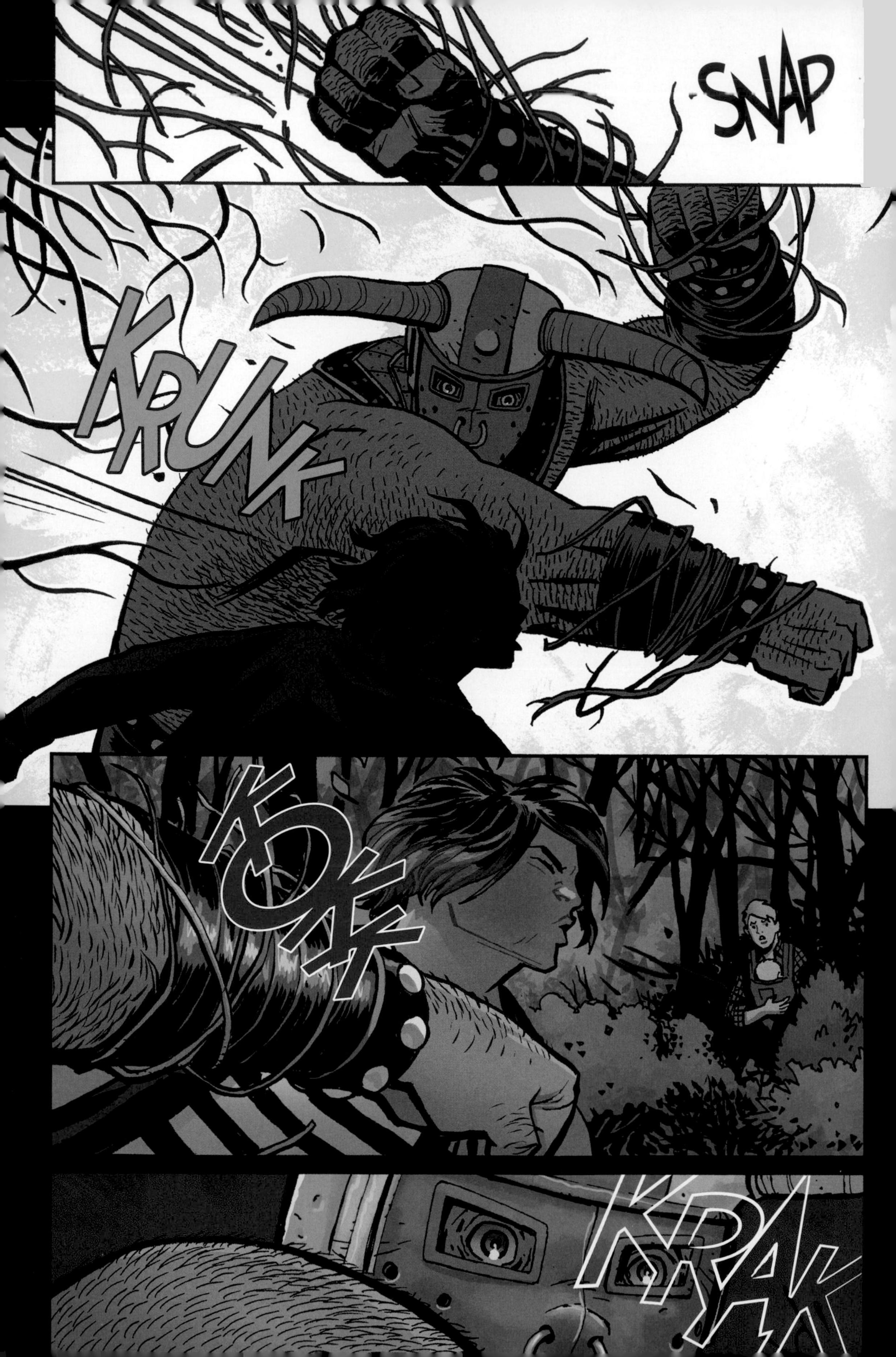
SNAP
KRUNK
KONK
KRAK

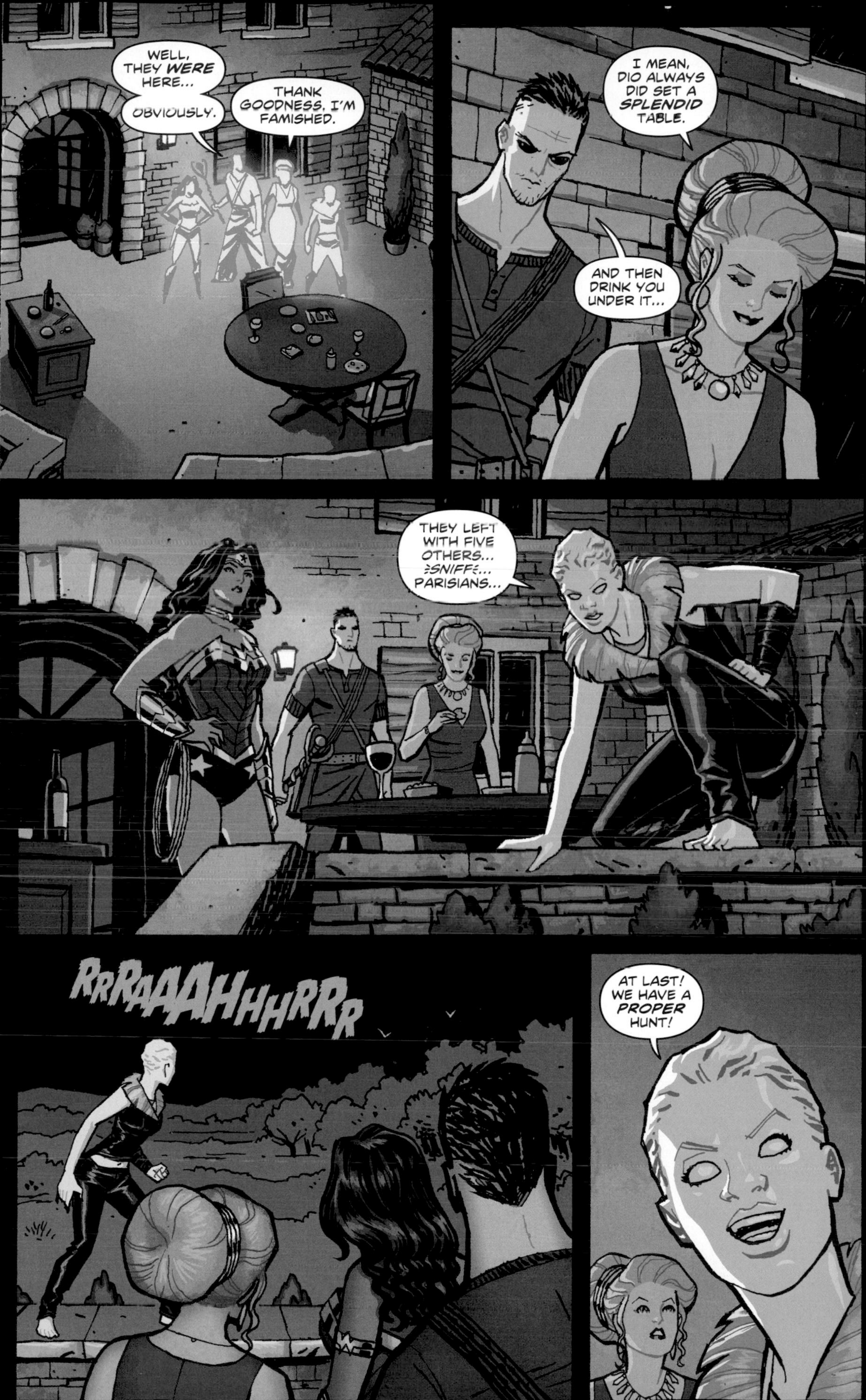
WELL, THEY WERE HERE...
OBVIOUSLY.
THANK GOODNESS. I'M FAMISHED.
I MEAN, DIO ALWAYS DID SET A SPLENDID TABLE.
AND THEN DRINK YOU UNDER IT...
THEY LEFT WITH FIVE OTHERS... SNIFF... PARISIANS...
RRRAAAHHHRRRR
AT LAST! WE HAVE A PROPER HUNT!

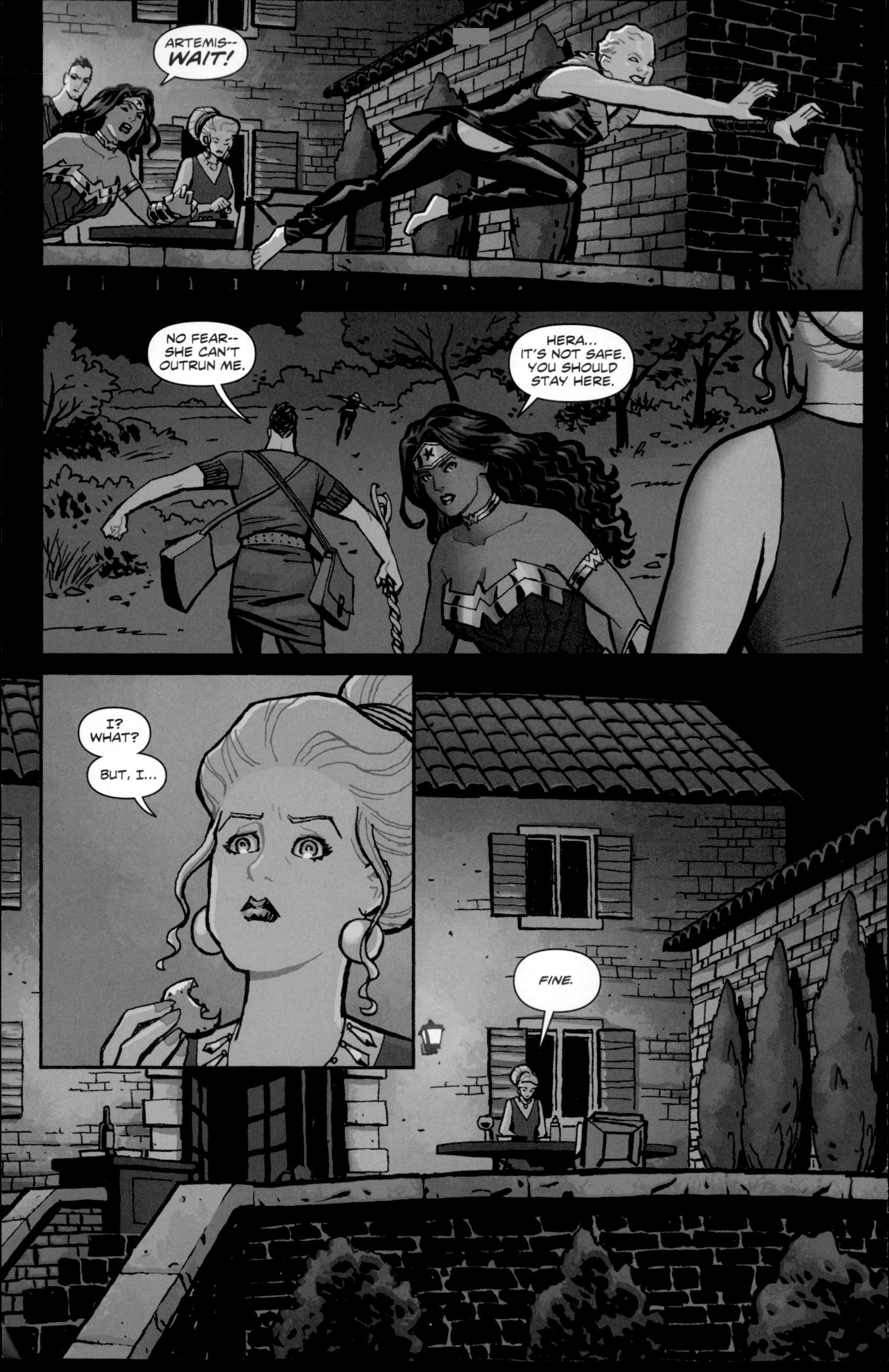
ARTEMIS--
WAIT!
NO FEAR--
SHE CAN'T
OUTRUN ME.
HERA...
IT'S NOT SAFE.
YOU SHOULD
STAY HERE.
I?
WHAT?
BUT, I...
FINE.

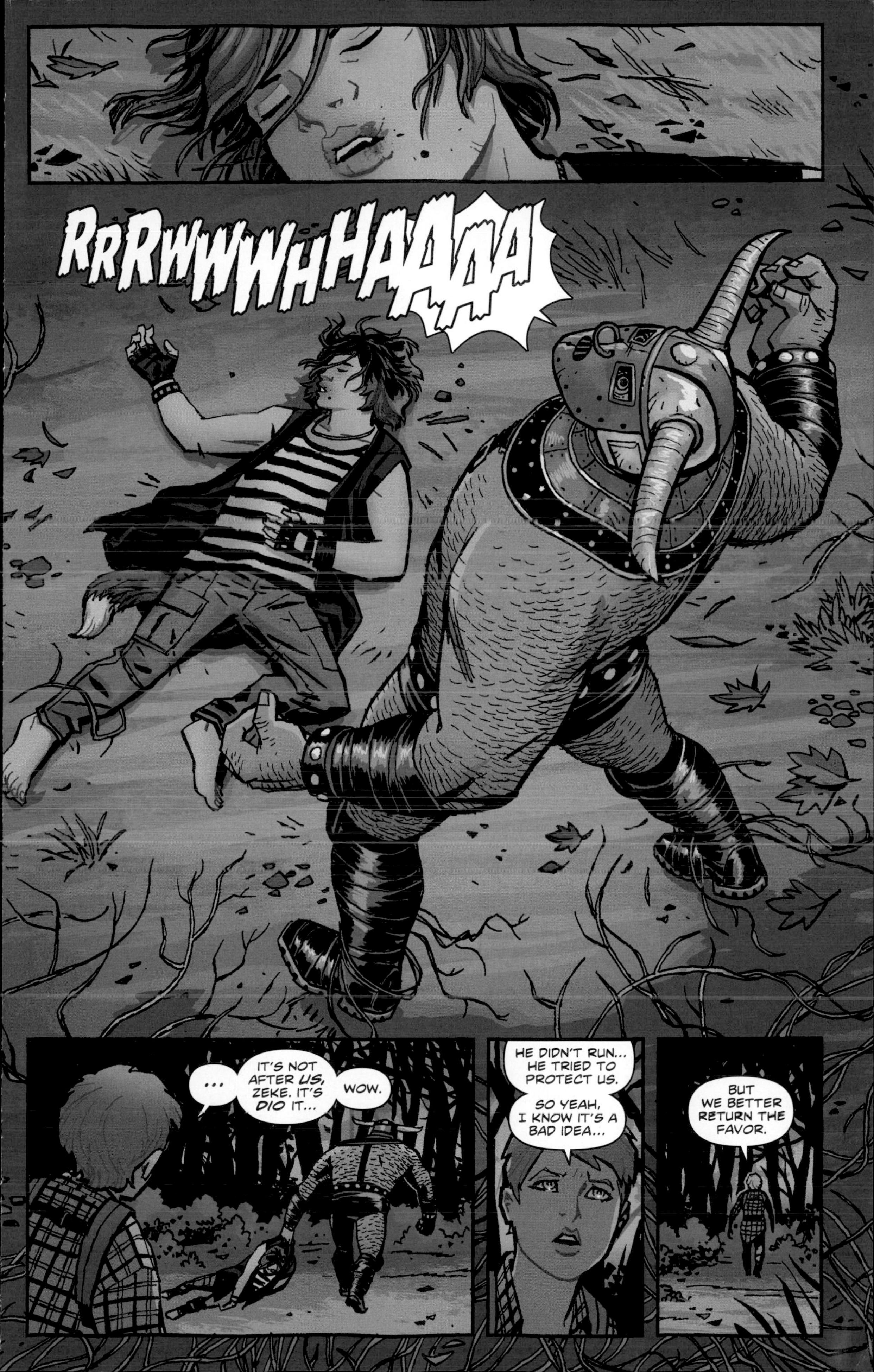

RRRWWWWHHAAAAA
...
IT'S NOT AFTER US, ZEKE. IT'S DIO IT...
WOW.
HE DIDN'T RUN... HE TRIED TO PROTECT US.
SO YEAH, I KNOW IT'S A BAD IDEA...
BUT WE BETTER RETURN THE FAVOR.

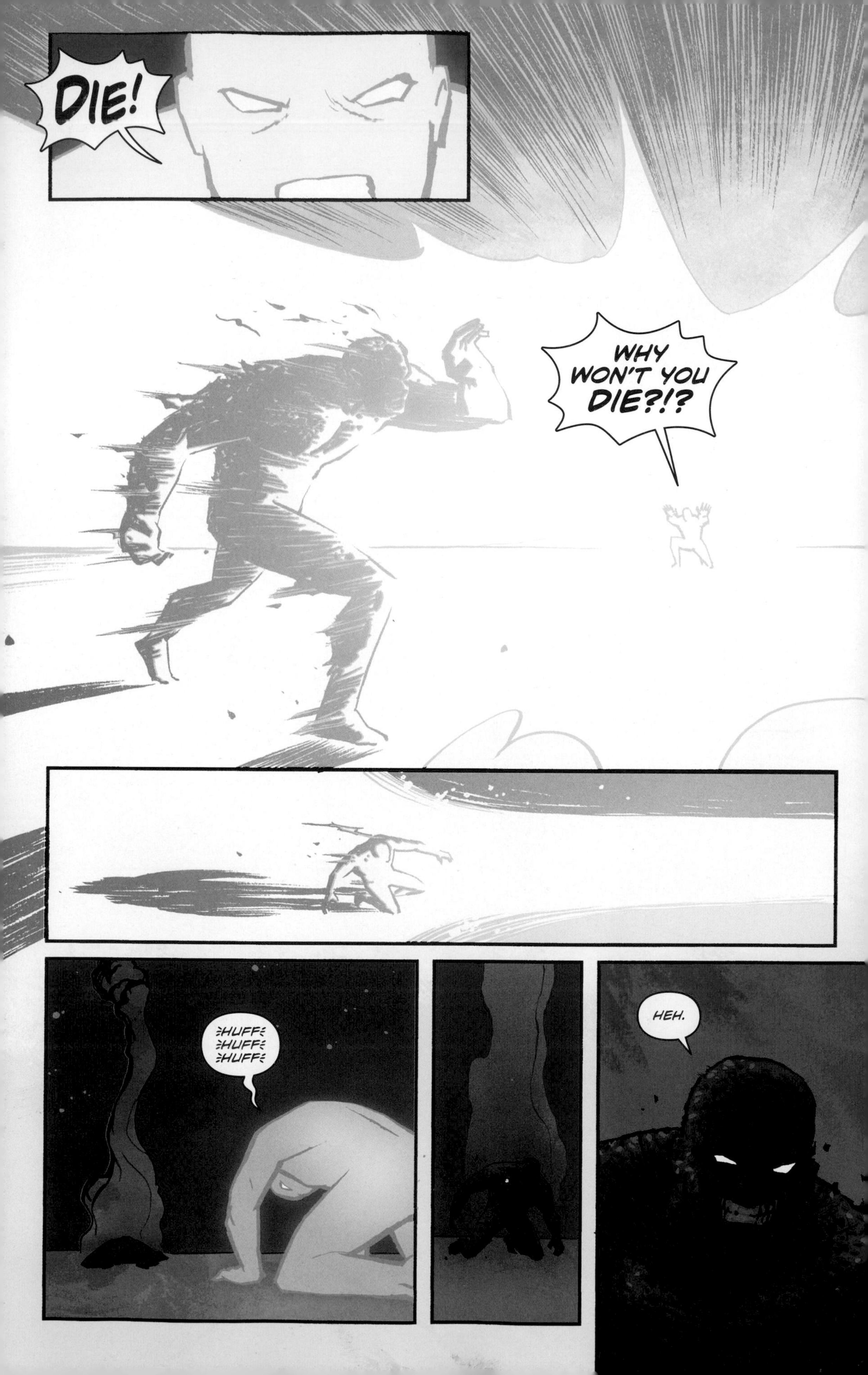
DIE!
WHY WON'T YOU DIE?!?
HUFF HUFF HUFF
HEH.

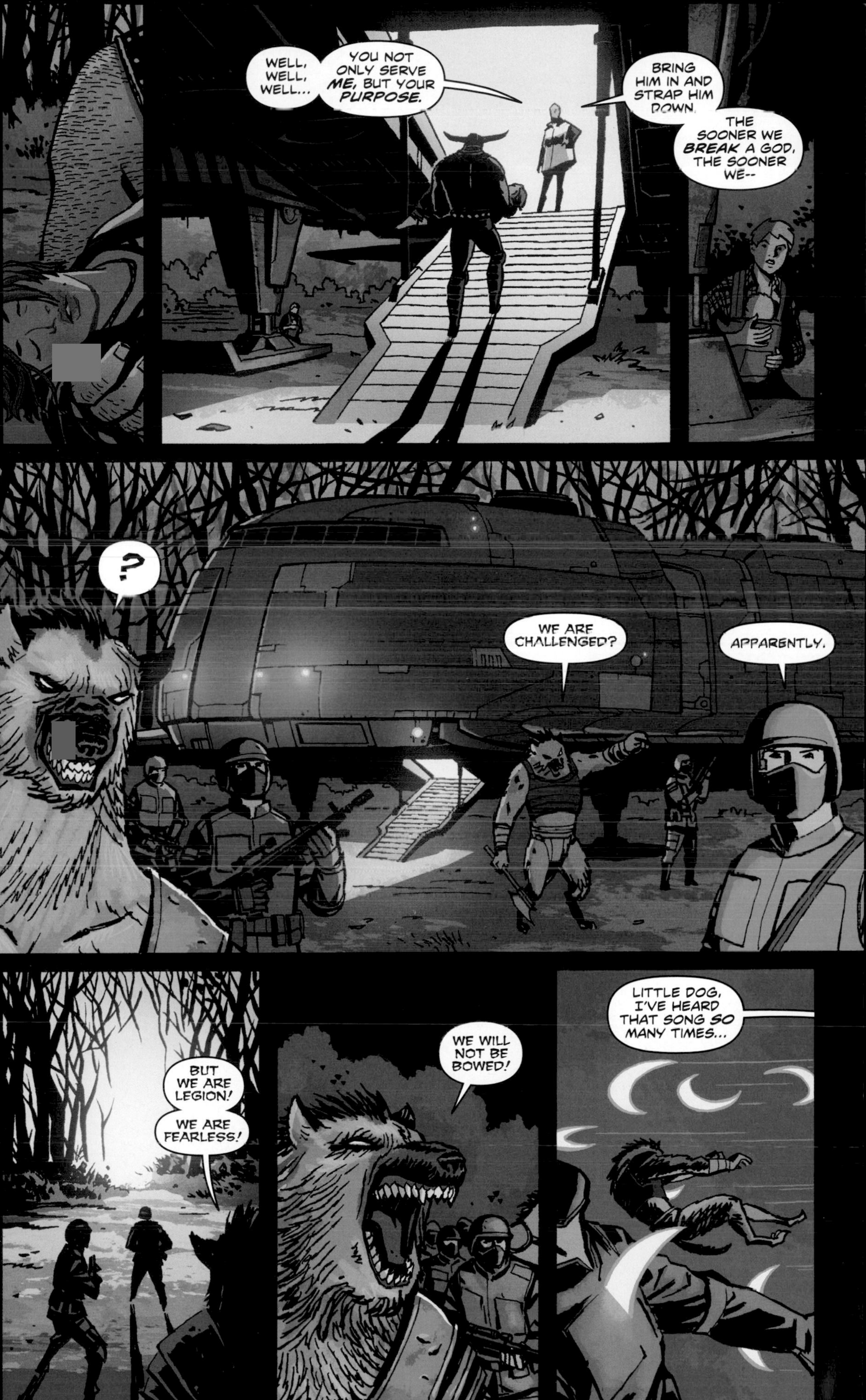
WELL, WELL, WELL...
YOU NOT ONLY SERVE *ME,* BUT YOUR *PURPOSE.*
BRING HIM IN AND STRAP HIM DOWN.
THE SOONER WE *BREAK* A GOD, THE SOONER WE--
?
WE ARE CHALLENGED?
APPARENTLY.
BUT WE ARE LEGION!
WE ARE FEARLESS!
WE WILL NOT BE BOWED!
LITTLE DOG, I'VE HEARD THAT SONG *SO* MANY TIMES...

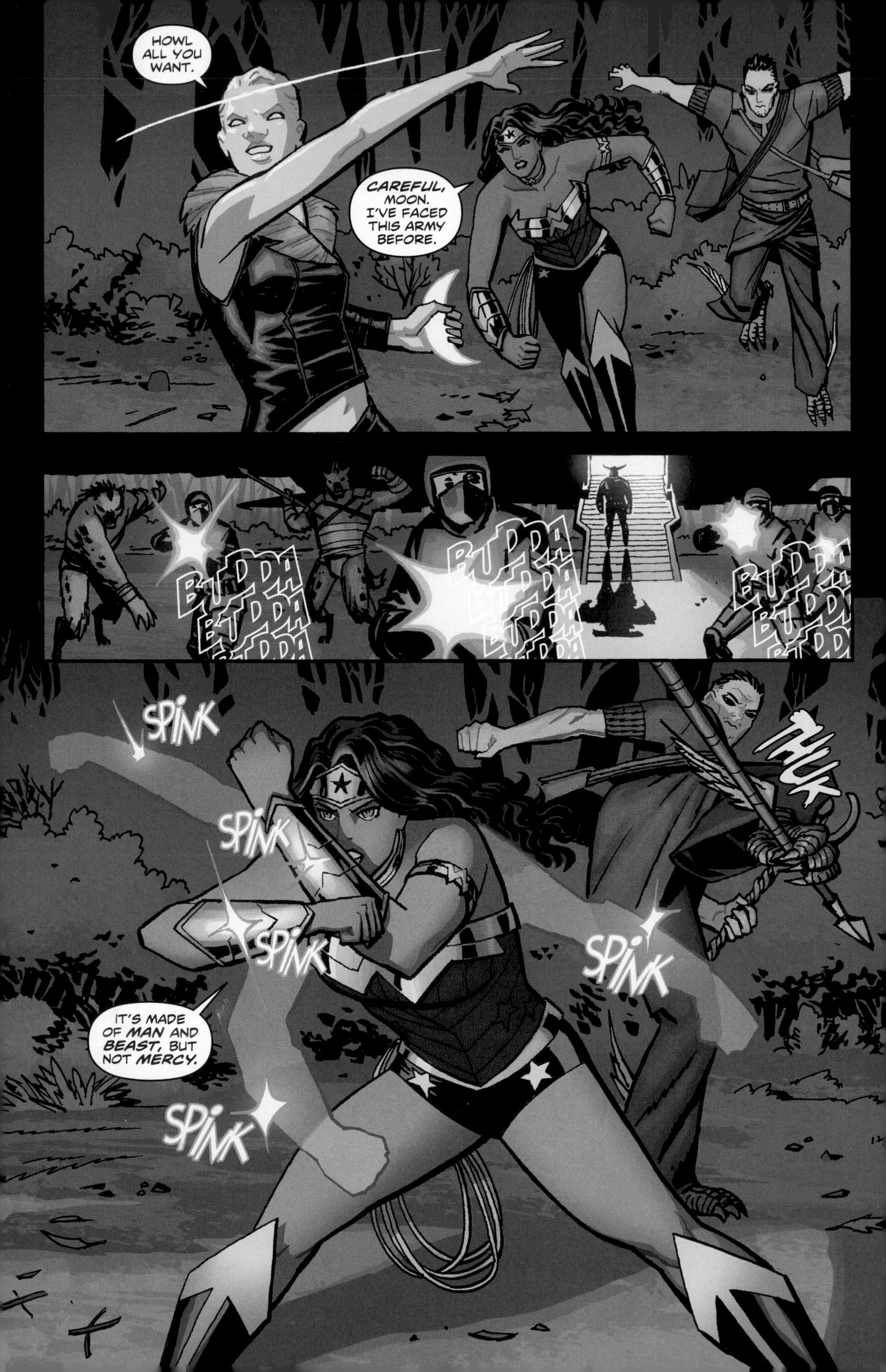
HOWL ALL YOU WANT.
CAREFUL, MOON. I'VE FACED THIS ARMY BEFORE.
BUDDA BUDDA BUDDA
BUDDA BUDDA BUDDA
BUDDA BUDDA BUDDA
SPINK
THUK
SPINK
SPINK
SPINK
IT'S MADE OF MAN AND BEAST, BUT NOT MERCY.
SPINK

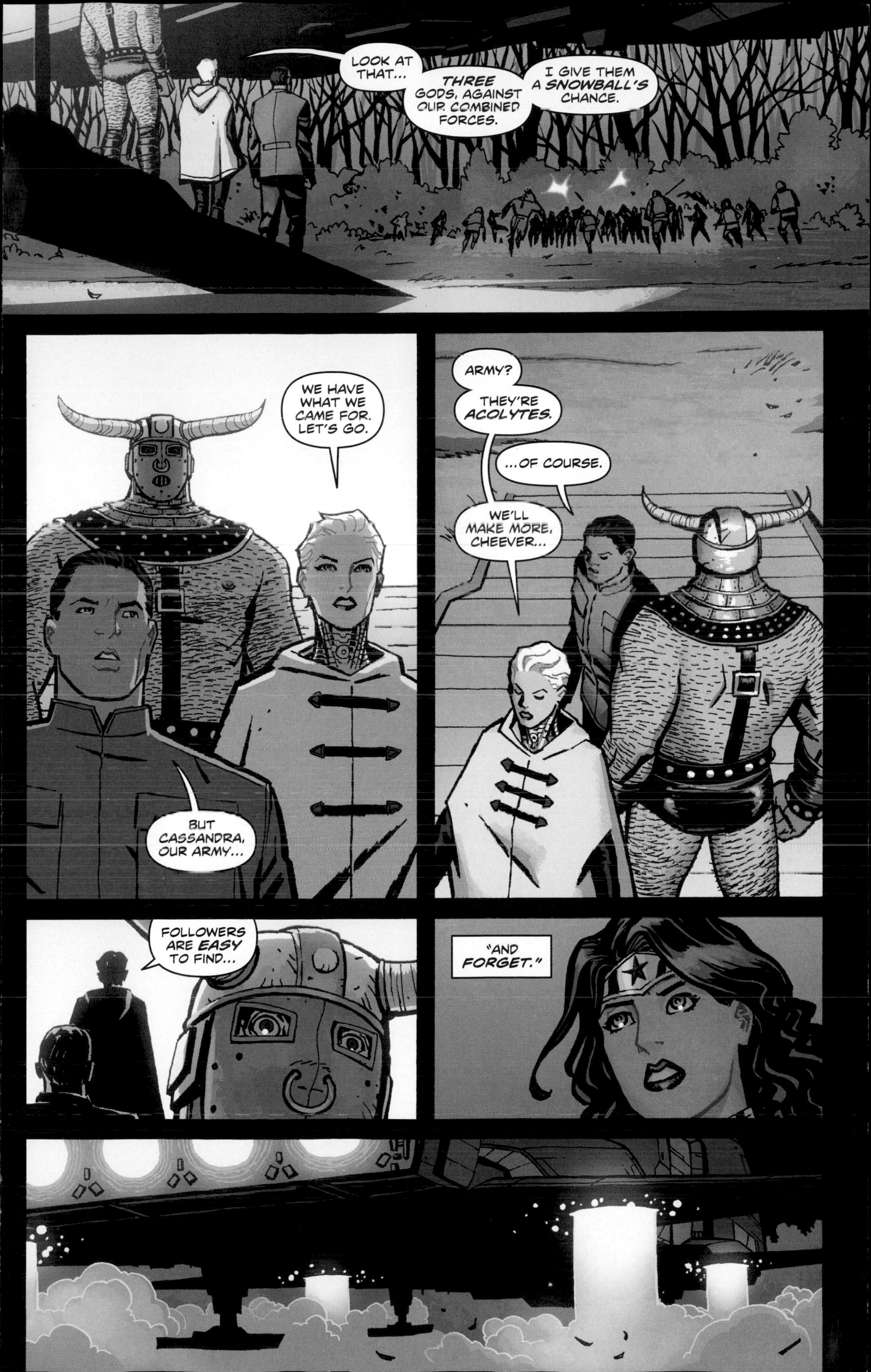
LOOK AT THAT...
THREE GODS, AGAINST OUR COMBINED FORCES.
I GIVE THEM A SNOWBALL'S CHANCE.
WE HAVE WHAT WE CAME FOR. LET'S GO.
BUT CASSANDRA, OUR ARMY...
ARMY?
THEY'RE ACOLYTES.
...OF COURSE.
WE'LL MAKE MORE, CHEEVER...
FOLLOWERS ARE EASY TO FIND...
"AND FORGET."

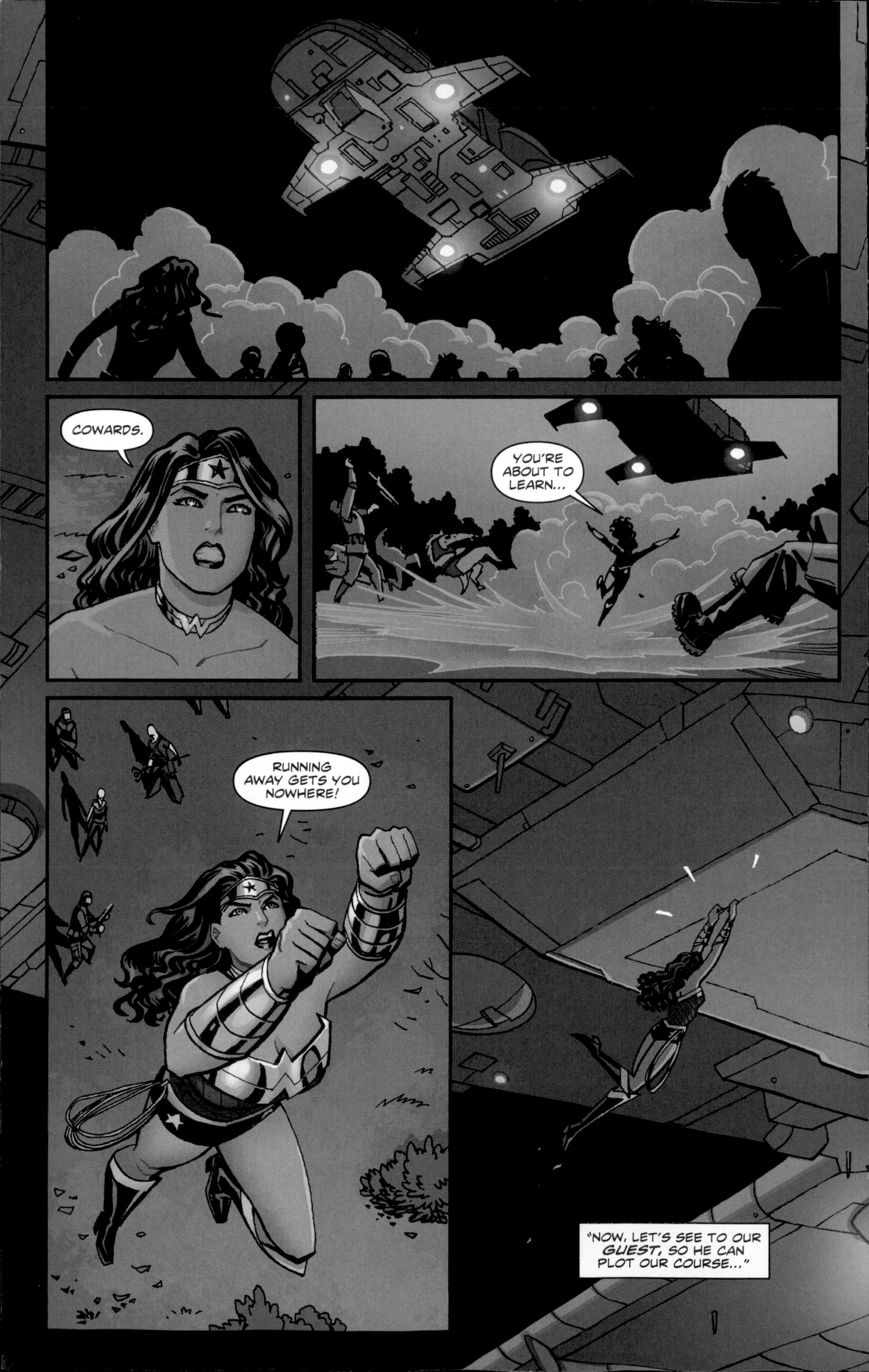
COWARDS.
YOU'RE ABOUT TO LEARN...
RUNNING AWAY GETS YOU NOWHERE!
"NOW, LET'S SEE TO OUR *GUEST,* SO HE CAN PLOT OUR COURSE..."

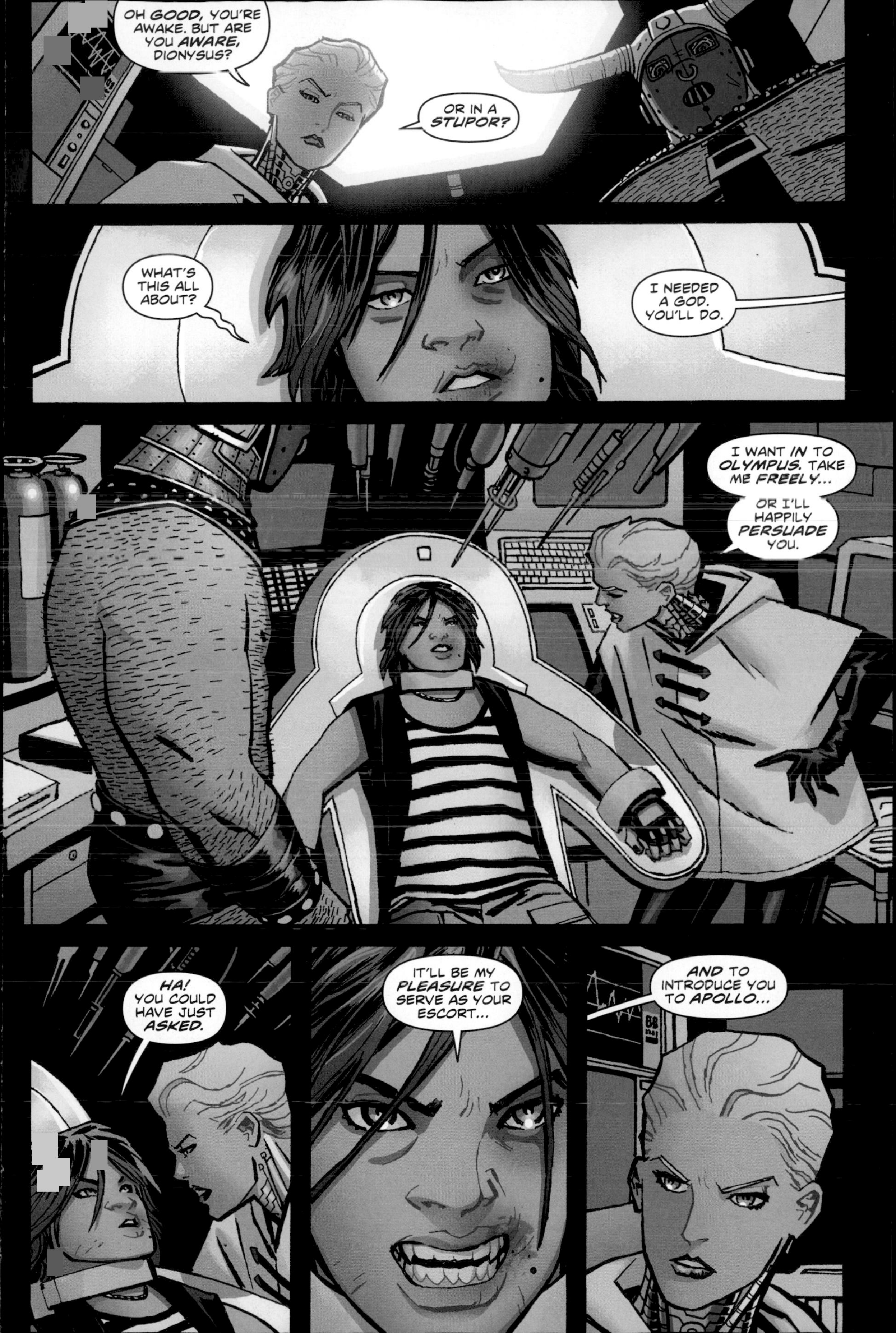
OH GOOD, YOU'RE AWAKE. BUT ARE YOU AWARE, DIONYSUS?
OR IN A STUPOR?
WHAT'S THIS ALL ABOUT?
I NEEDED A GOD. YOU'LL DO.
I WANT IN TO OLYMPUS. TAKE ME FREELY...
OR I'LL HAPPILY PERSUADE YOU.
HA! YOU COULD HAVE JUST ASKED.
IT'LL BE MY PLEASURE TO SERVE AS YOUR ESCORT...
AND TO INTRODUCE YOU TO APOLLO...

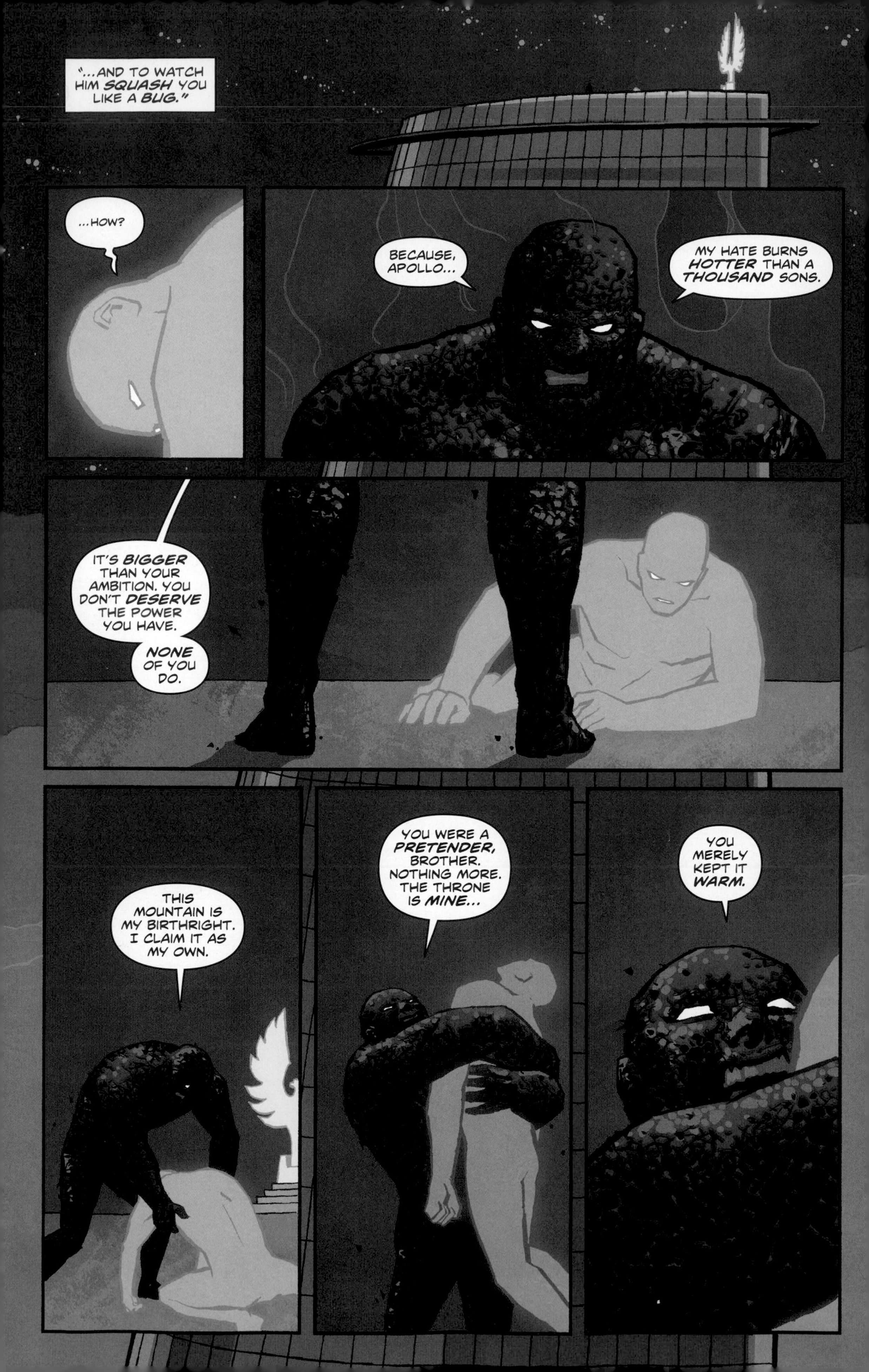
"...AND TO WATCH HIM SQUASH YOU LIKE A BUG."
...HOW?
BECAUSE, APOLLO...
MY HATE BURNS HOTTER THAN A THOUSAND SONS.
IT'S BIGGER THAN YOUR AMBITION. YOU DON'T DESERVE THE POWER YOU HAVE.
NONE OF YOU DO.
THIS MOUNTAIN IS MY BIRTHRIGHT. I CLAIM IT AS MY OWN.
YOU WERE A PRETENDER, BROTHER. NOTHING MORE. THE THRONE IS MINE...
YOU MERELY KEPT IT WARM.

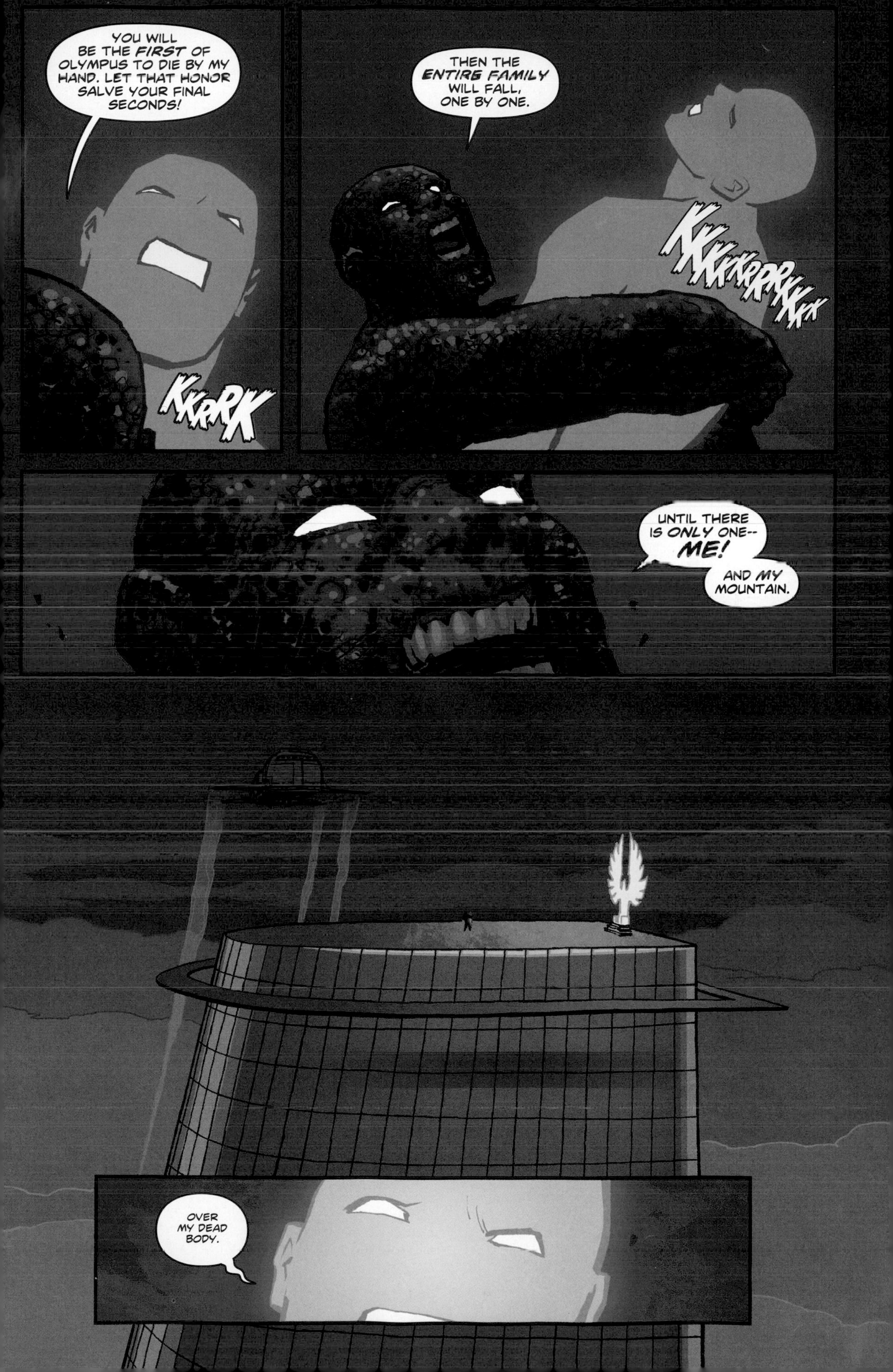
YOU WILL BE THE FIRST OF OLYMPUS TO DIE BY MY HAND. LET THAT HONOR SALVE YOUR FINAL SECONDS!
KKRRK
THEN THE ENTIRE FAMILY WILL FALL, ONE BY ONE.
KKKKKRRRKKKK
UNTIL THERE IS ONLY ONE-- ME!
AND MY MOUNTAIN.
OVER MY DEAD BODY.

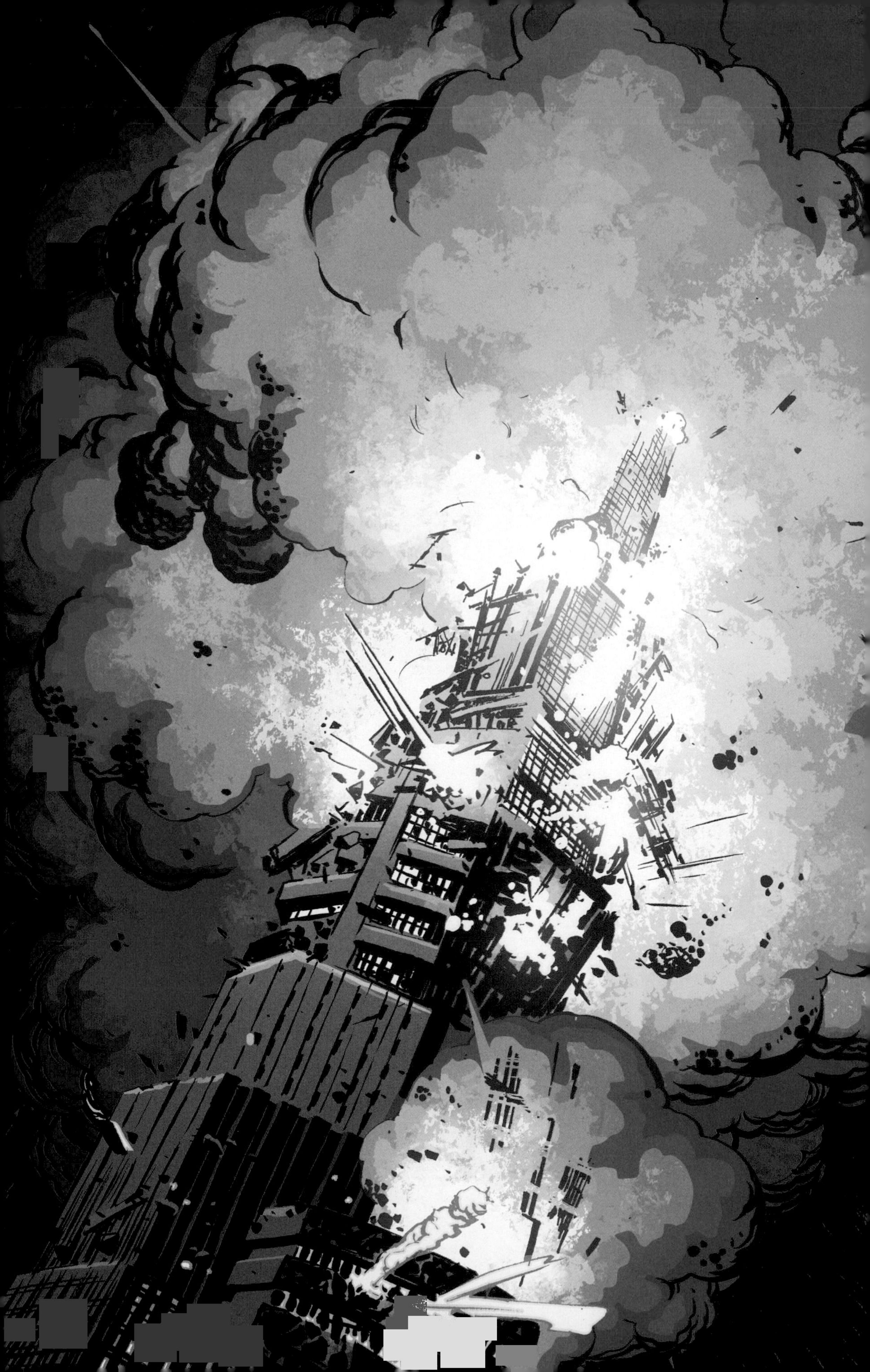

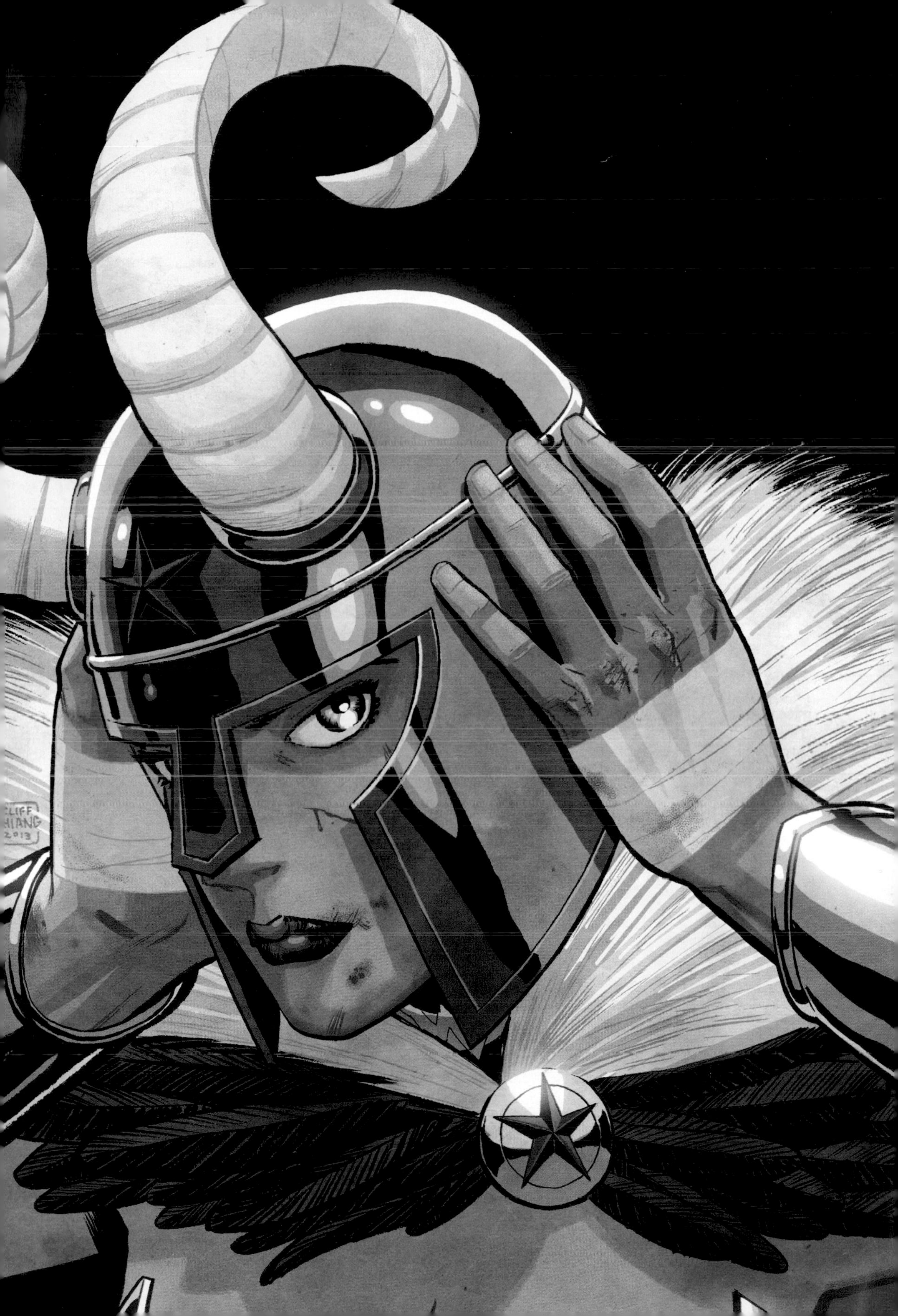
CLIFF CHIANG 2013

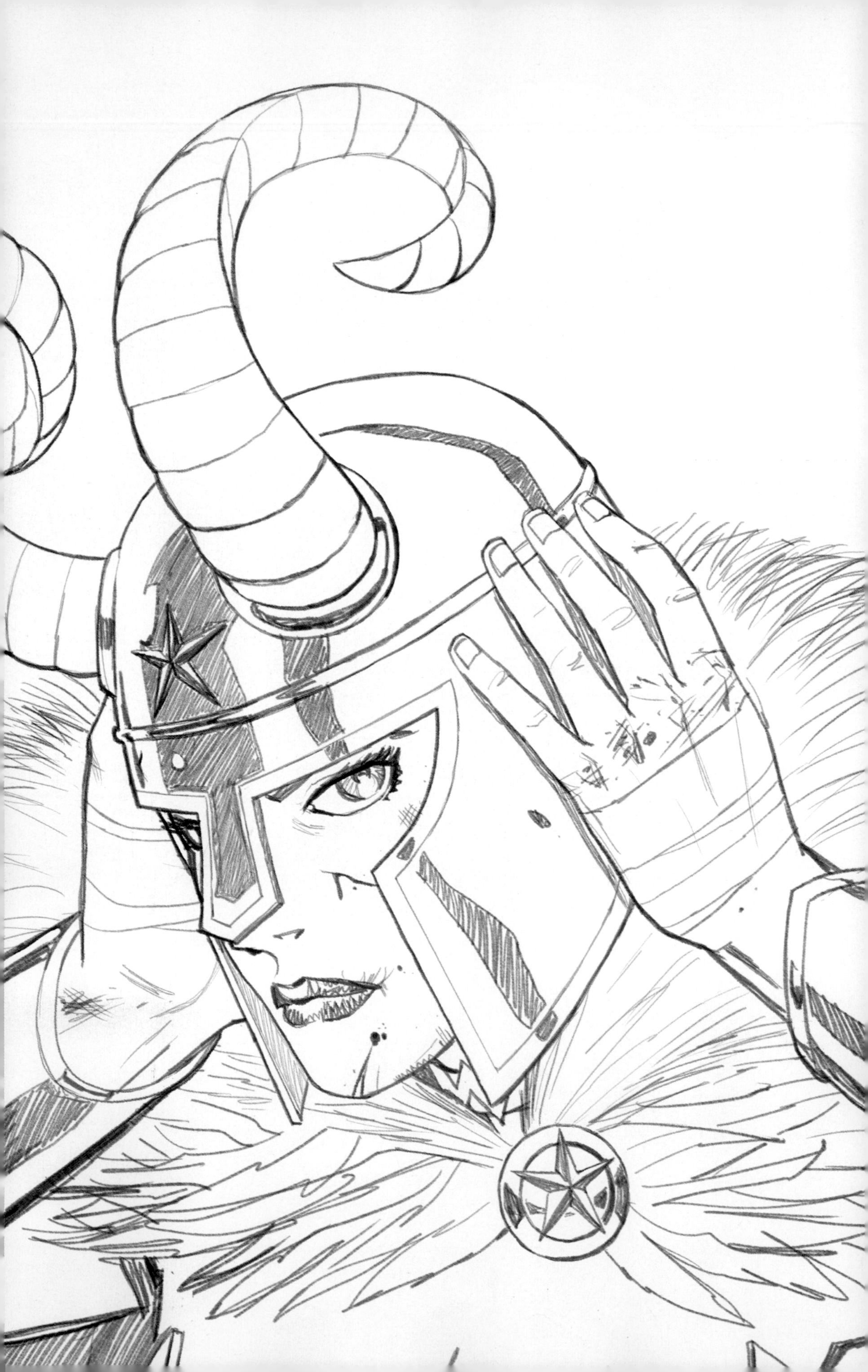

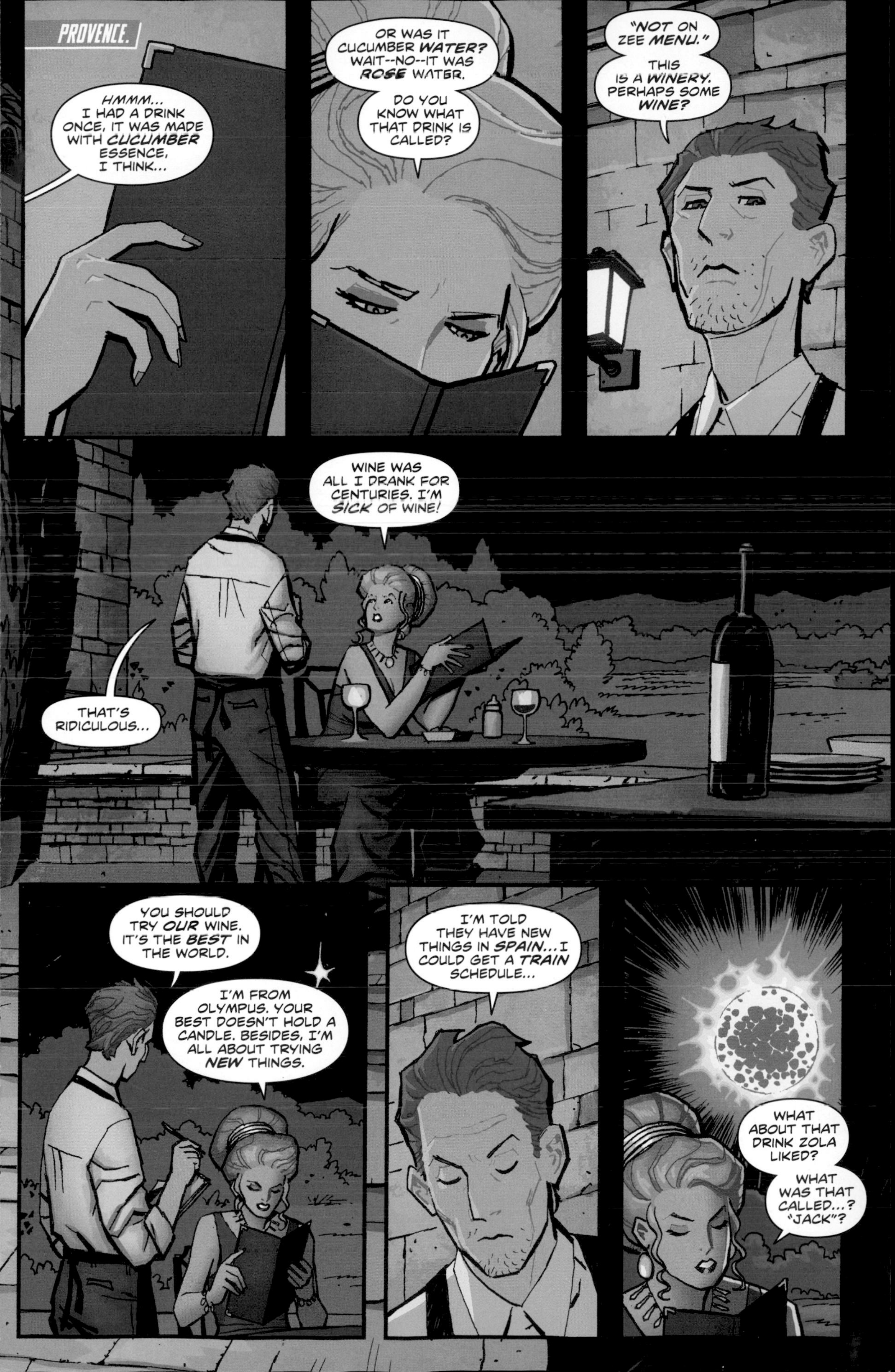
PROVENCE.
HMMM... I HAD A DRINK ONCE, IT WAS MADE WITH CUCUMBER ESSENCE, I THINK...
OR WAS IT CUCUMBER WATER? WAIT--NO--IT WAS ROSE WATER.
DO YOU KNOW WHAT THAT DRINK IS CALLED?
"NOT ON ZEE MENU."
THIS IS A WINERY. PERHAPS SOME WINE?
WINE WAS ALL I DRANK FOR CENTURIES. I'M SICK OF WINE!
THAT'S RIDICULOUS...
YOU SHOULD TRY OUR WINE. IT'S THE BEST IN THE WORLD.
I'M FROM OLYMPUS. YOUR BEST DOESN'T HOLD A CANDLE. BESIDES, I'M ALL ABOUT TRYING NEW THINGS.
I'M TOLD THEY HAVE NEW THINGS IN SPAIN... I COULD GET A TRAIN SCHEDULE...
WHAT ABOUT THAT DRINK ZOLA LIKED?
WHAT WAS THAT CALLED...? "JACK"?

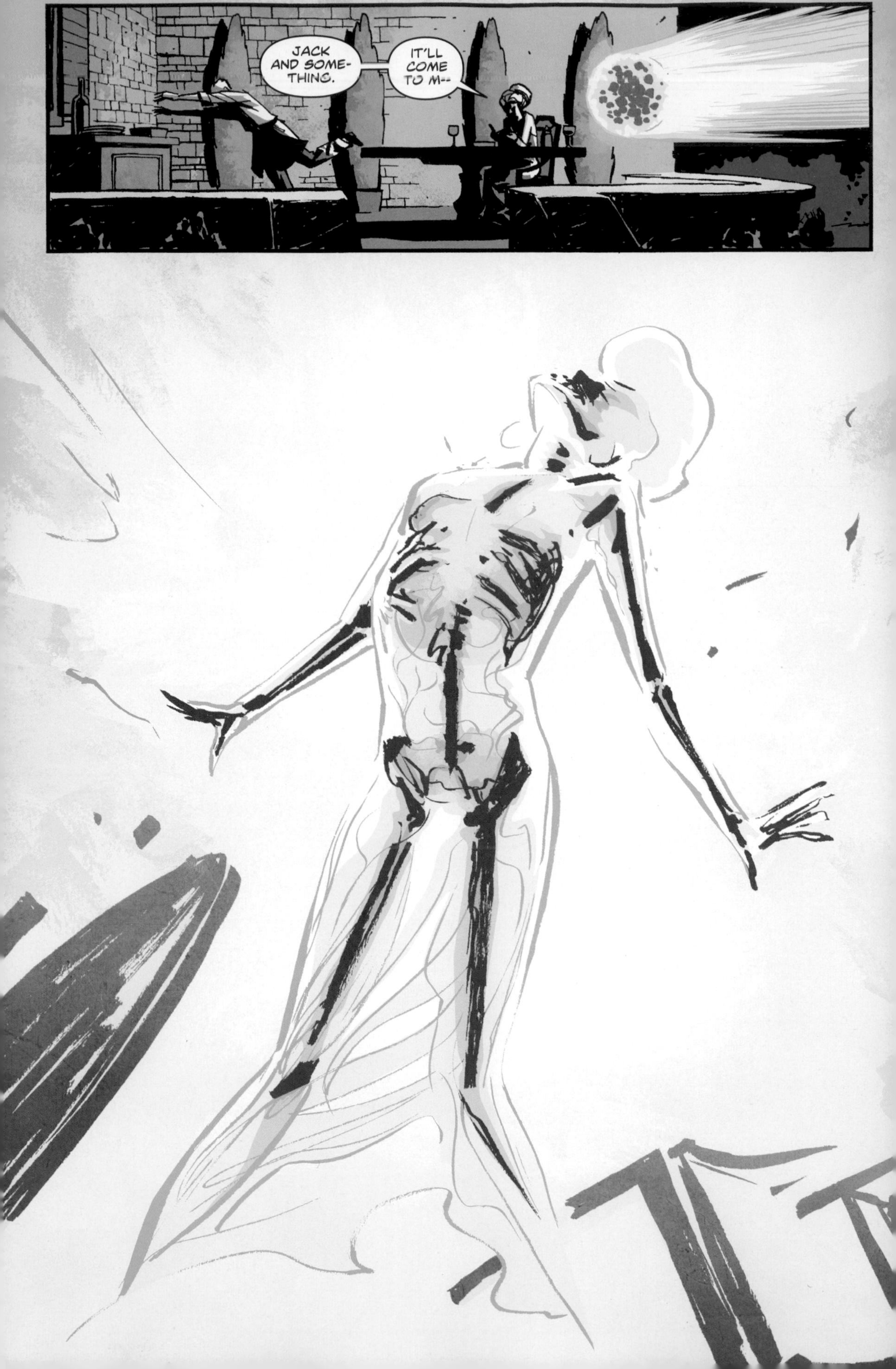
JACK AND SOME-THING.
IT'LL COME TO M--

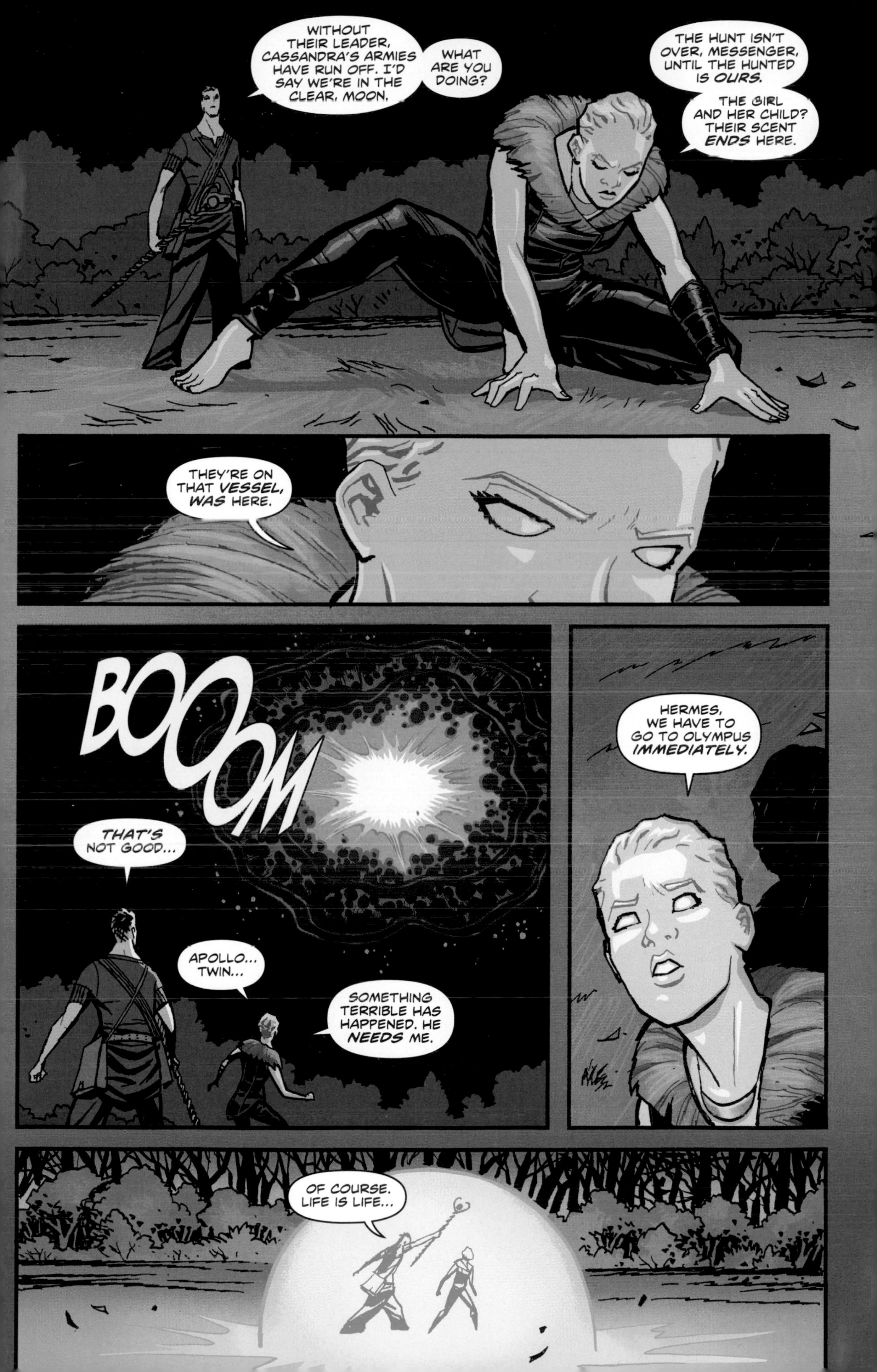
WITHOUT THEIR LEADER, CASSANDRA'S ARMIES HAVE RUN OFF. I'D SAY WE'RE IN THE CLEAR, MOON.
WHAT ARE YOU DOING?
THE HUNT ISN'T OVER, MESSENGER, UNTIL THE HUNTED IS OURS.
THE GIRL AND HER CHILD? THEIR SCENT ENDS HERE.
THEY'RE ON THAT VESSEL, WAS HERE.
BOOOM
THAT'S NOT GOOD...
APOLLO... TWIN...
SOMETHING TERRIBLE HAS HAPPENED. HE NEEDS ME.
HERMES, WE HAVE TO GO TO OLYMPUS IMMEDIATELY.
OF COURSE. LIFE IS LIFE...

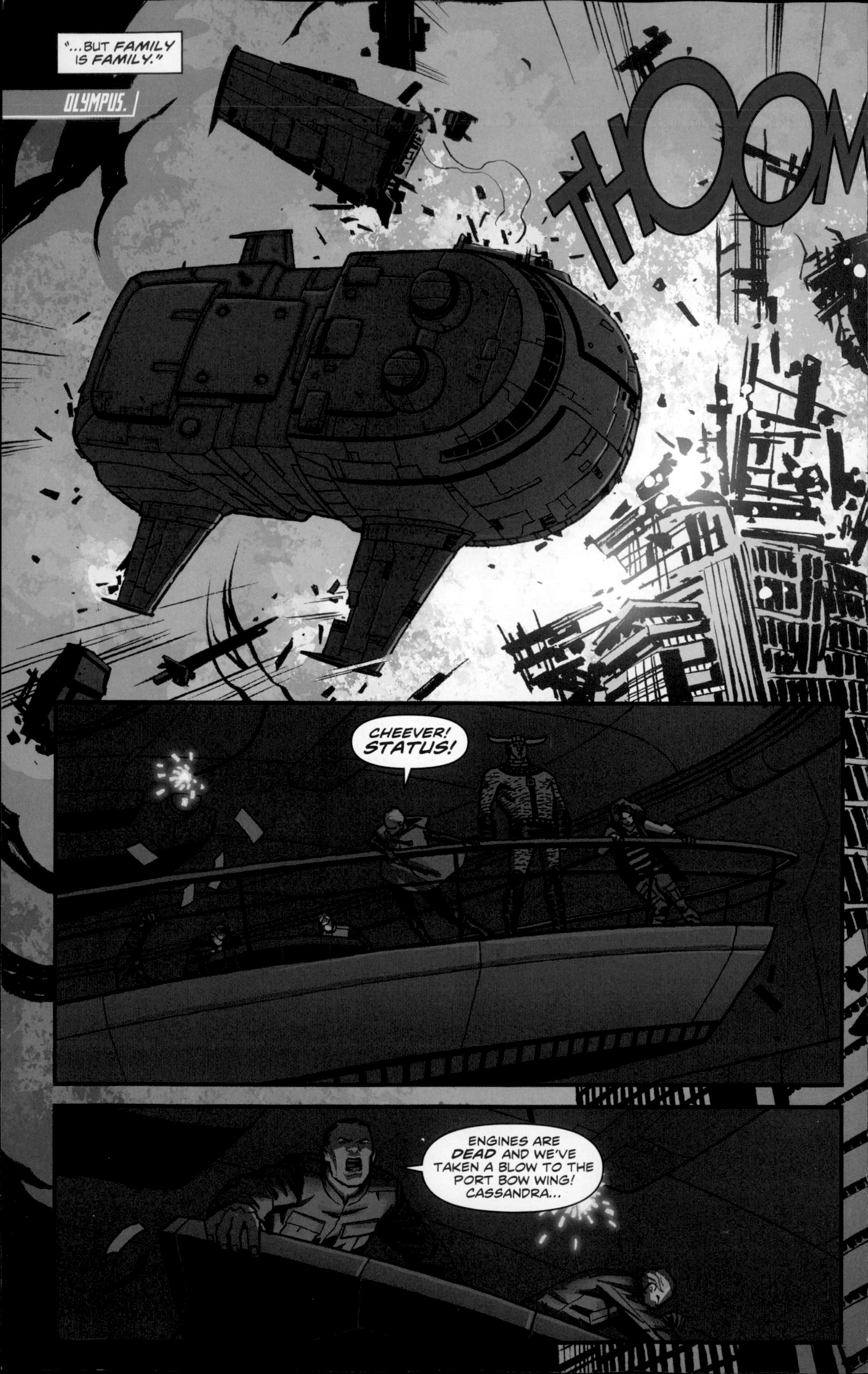
"...BUT FAMILY IS FAMILY."
OLYMPUS.
THOOM
CHEEVER! STATUS!
ENGINES ARE DEAD AND WE'VE TAKEN A BLOW TO THE PORT BOW WING! CASSANDRA...

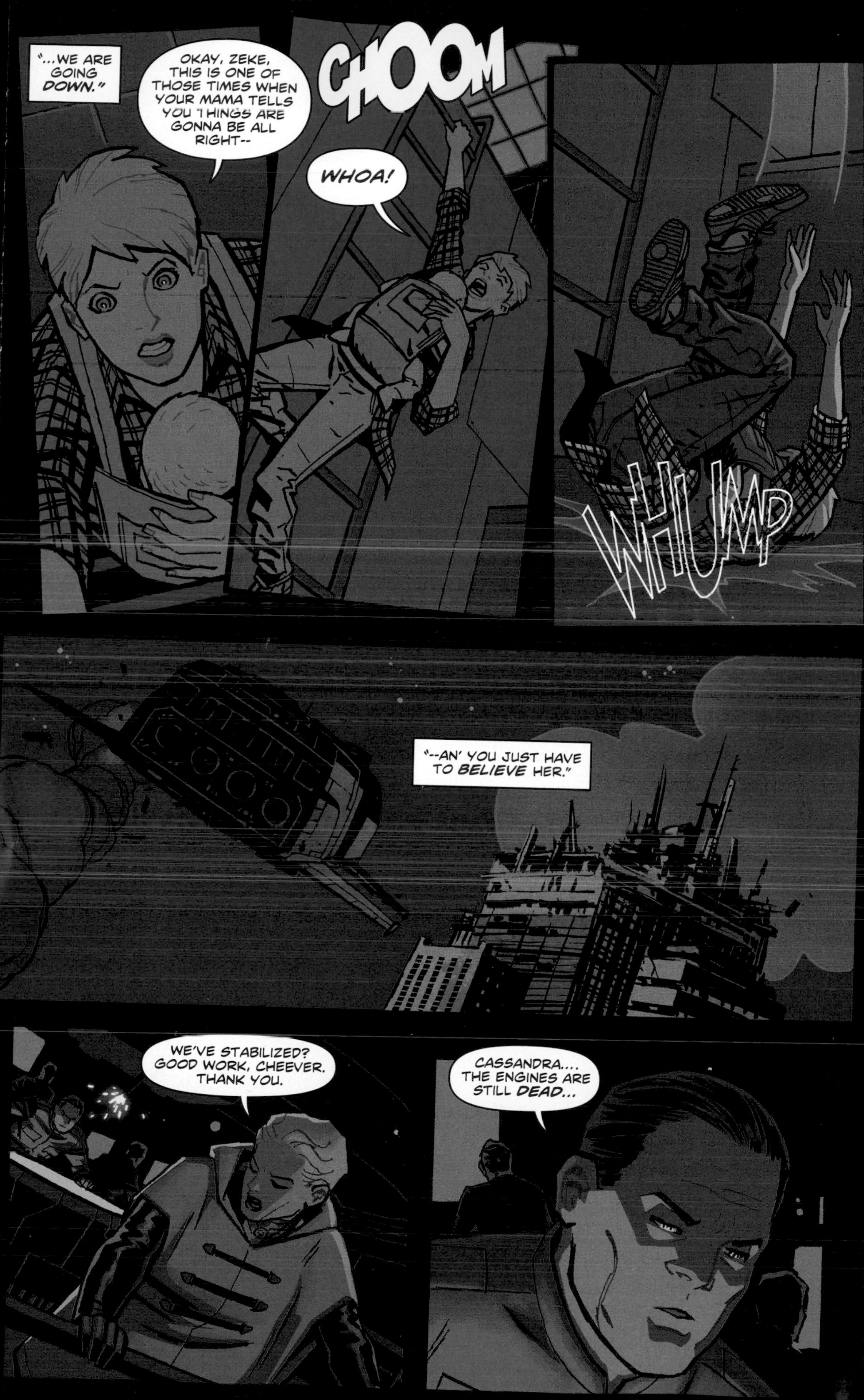
"...WE ARE GOING DOWN."
OKAY, ZEKE, THIS IS ONE OF THOSE TIMES WHEN YOUR MAMA TELLS YOU THINGS ARE GONNA BE ALL RIGHT--
CHOOM
WHOA!
WHUMP
"--AN' YOU JUST HAVE TO BELIEVE HER."
WE'VE STABILIZED? GOOD WORK, CHEEVER. THANK YOU.
CASSANDRA.... THE ENGINES ARE STILL DEAD...

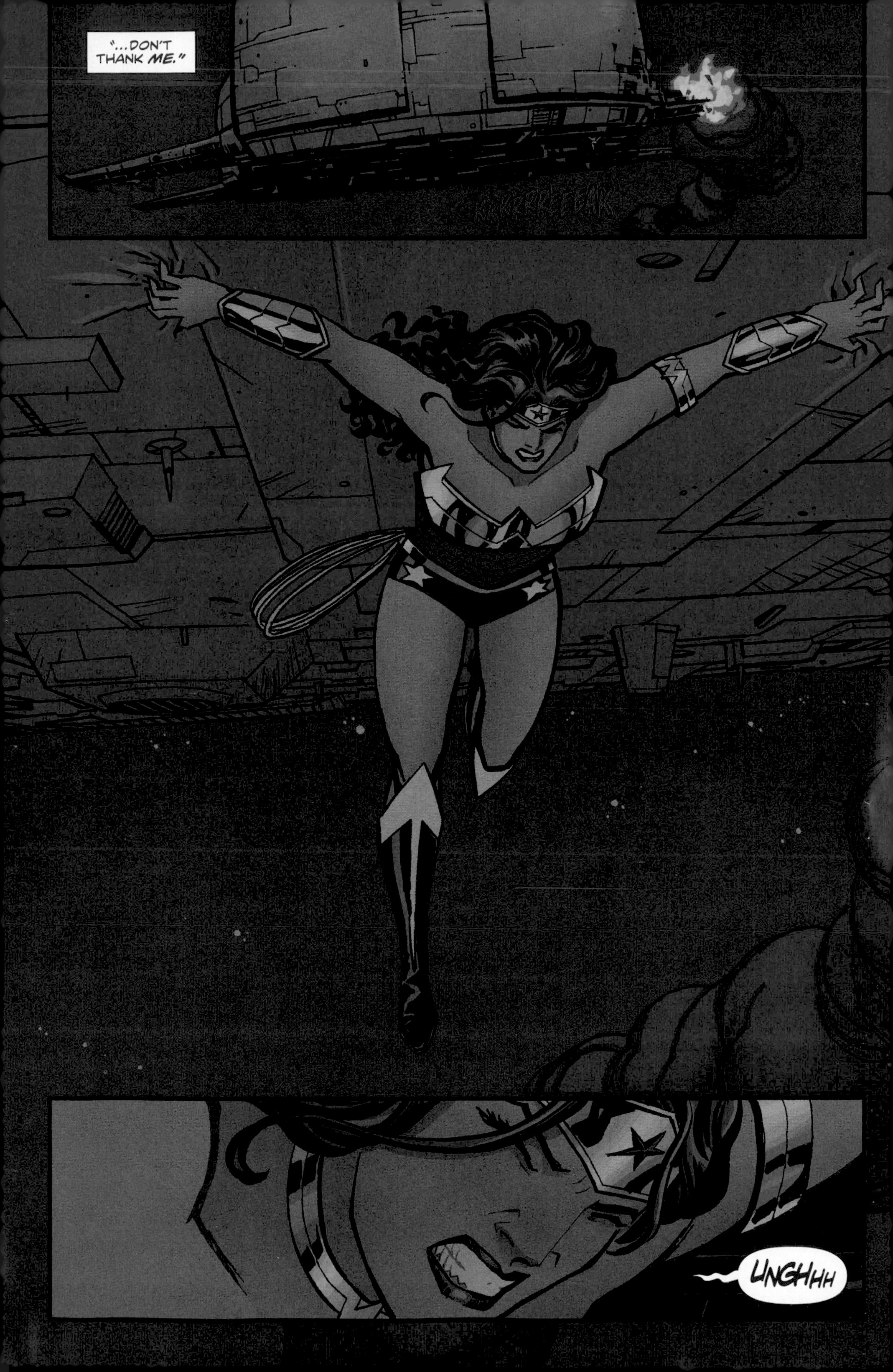
"...DON'T THANK *ME.*"
UNGHHH

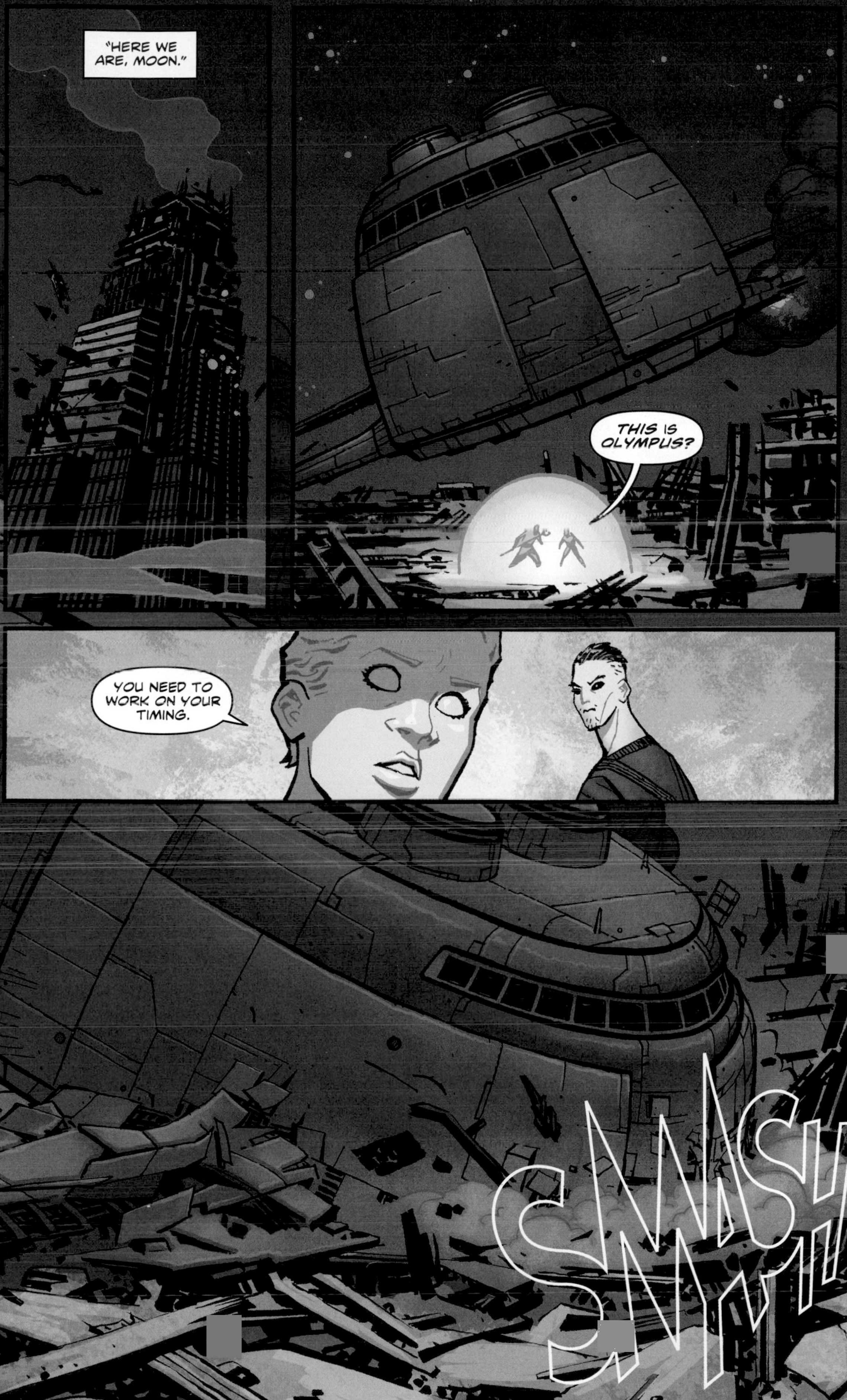
"HERE WE ARE, MOON."
THIS IS OLYMPUS?
YOU NEED TO WORK ON YOUR TIMING.
SMASH

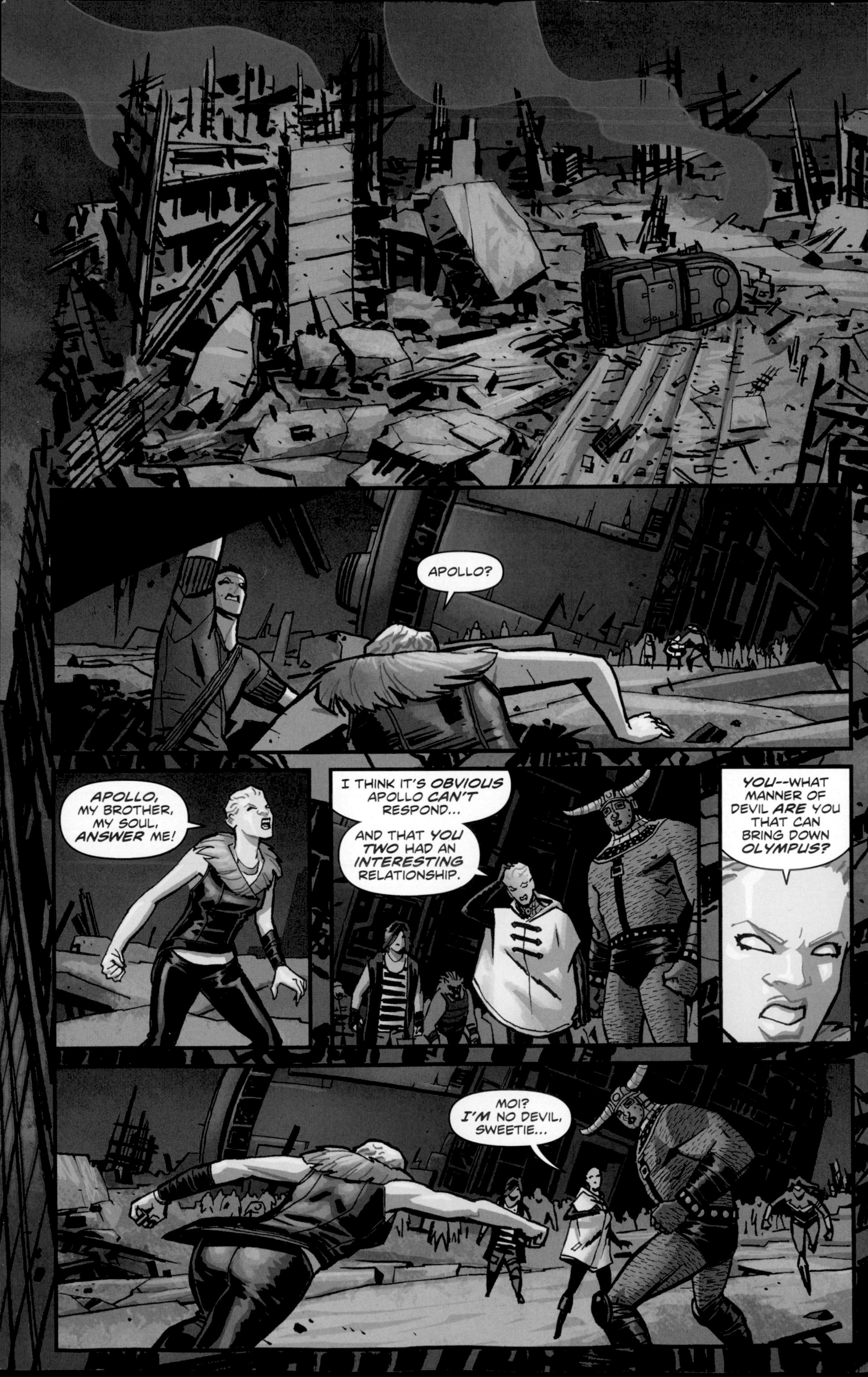
APOLLO?
APOLLO, MY BROTHER, MY SOUL, ANSWER ME!
I THINK IT'S OBVIOUS APOLLO CAN'T RESPOND...
AND THAT YOU TWO HAD AN INTERESTING RELATIONSHIP.
YOU--WHAT MANNER OF DEVIL ARE YOU THAT CAN BRING DOWN OLYMPUS?
MOI? I'M NO DEVIL, SWEETIE...

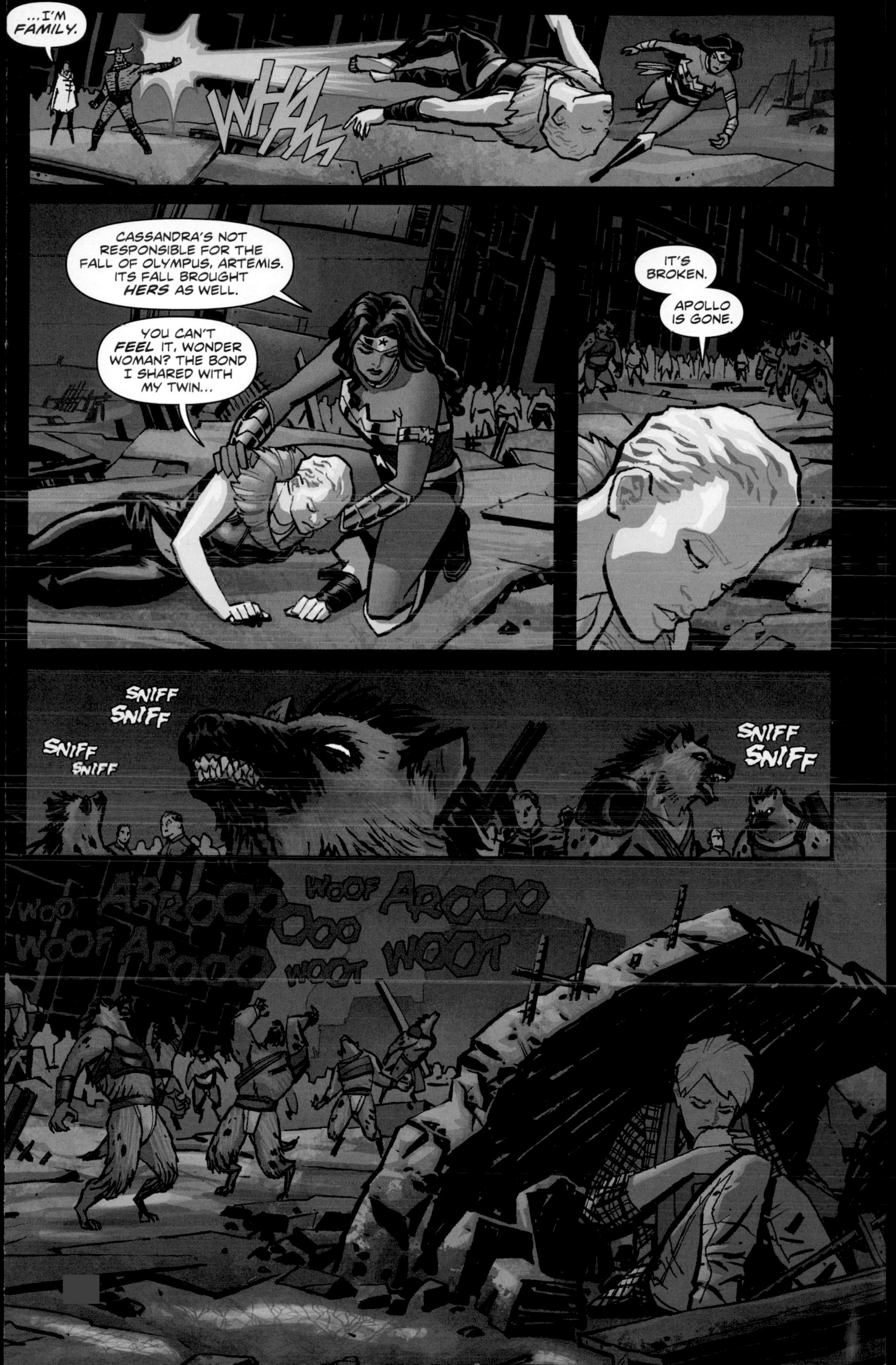

...I'M FAMILY.
WHAM
CASSANDRA'S NOT RESPONSIBLE FOR THE FALL OF OLYMPUS, ARTEMIS. ITS FALL BROUGHT HERS AS WELL.
YOU CAN'T FEEL IT, WONDER WOMAN? THE BOND I SHARED WITH MY TWIN...
IT'S BROKEN.
APOLLO IS GONE.
SNIFF SNIFF
SNIFF SNIFF
SNIFF SNIFF
WOOF AROOOOOOO
WOOF AROOO
WOOF AROOO
WOOT WOOT

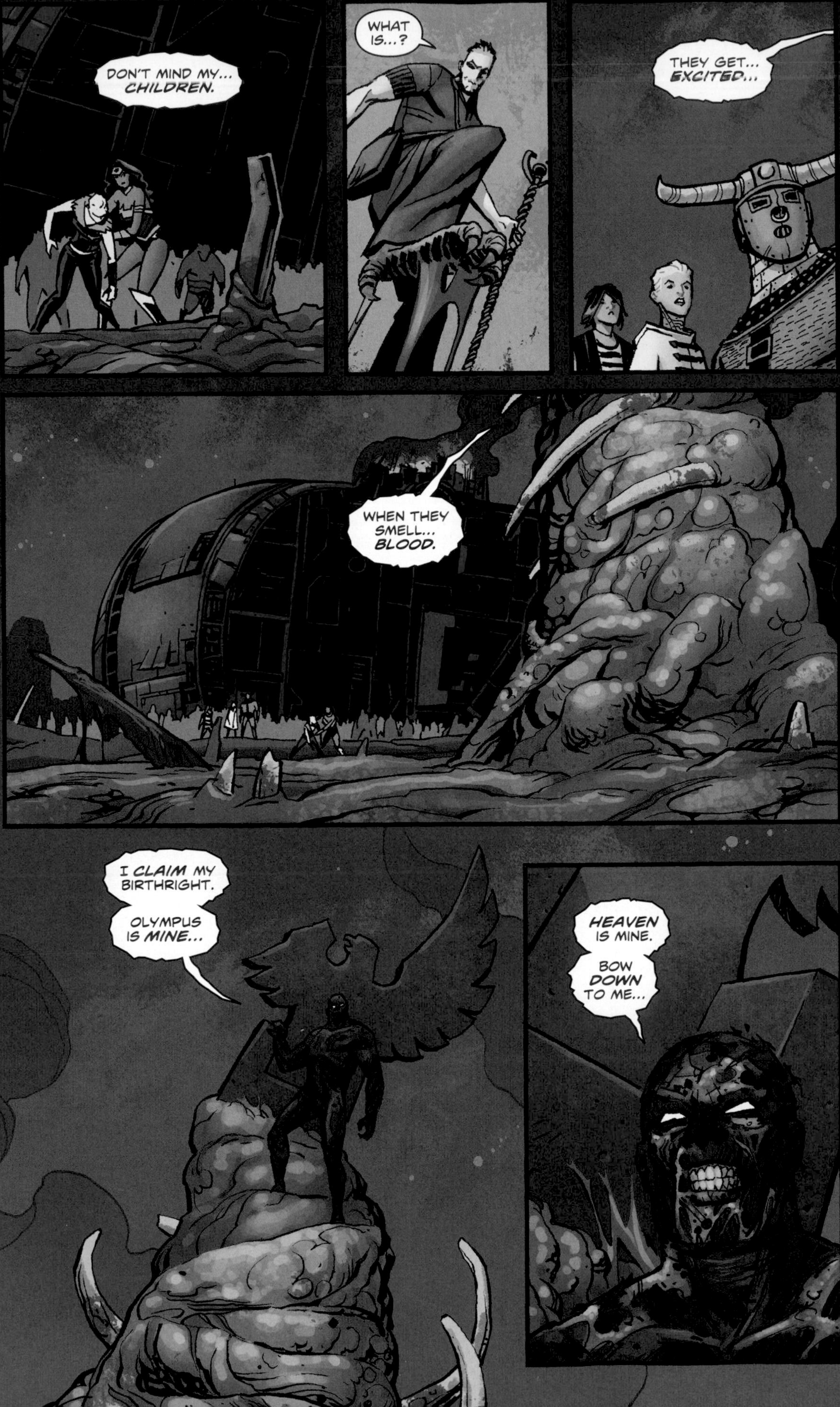
DON'T MIND MY... CHILDREN.
WHAT IS...?
THEY GET... EXCITED...
WHEN THEY SMELL... BLOOD.
I CLAIM MY BIRTHRIGHT.
OLYMPUS IS MINE...
HEAVEN IS MINE.
BOW DOWN TO ME...

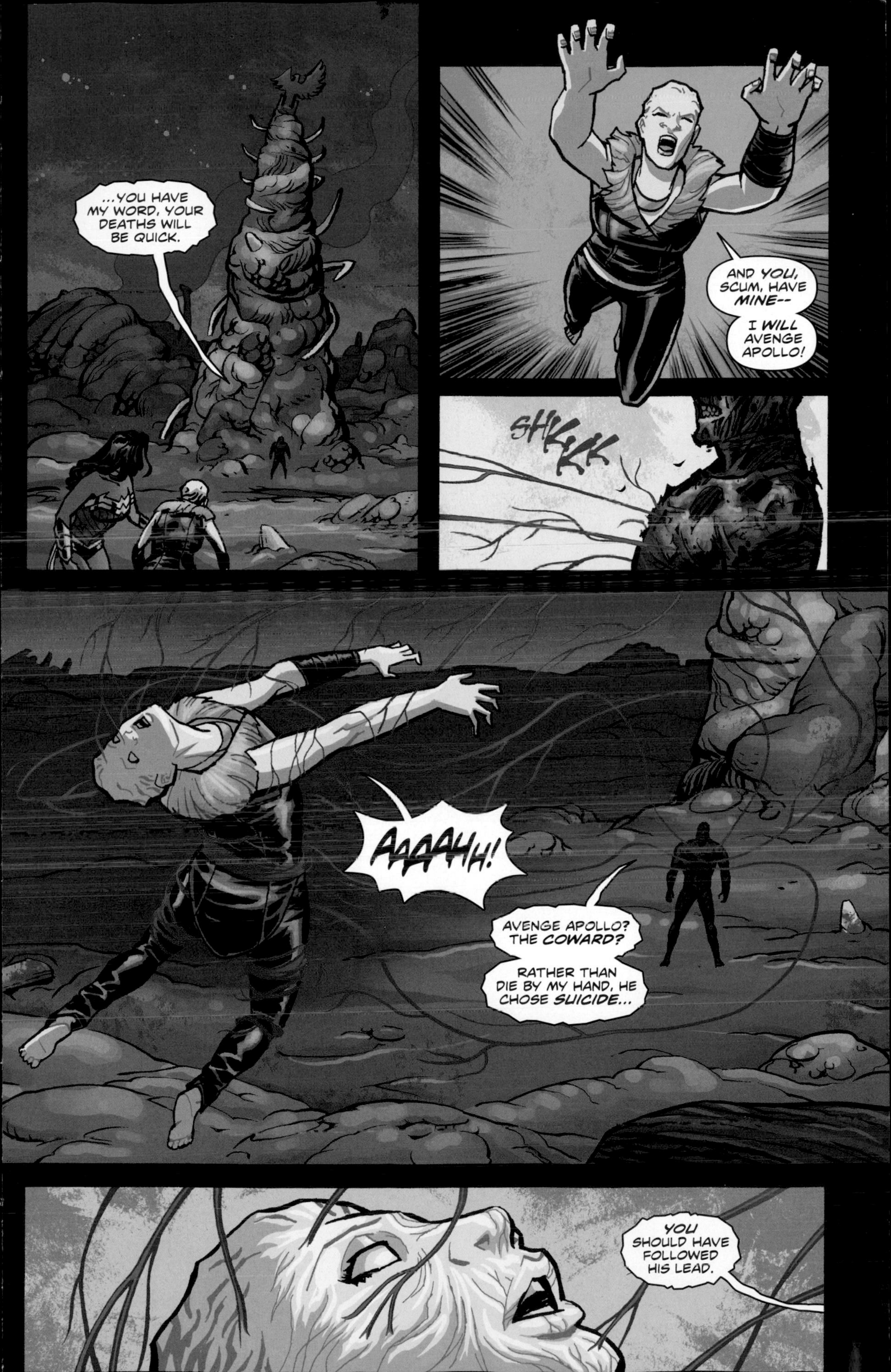
...YOU HAVE MY WORD, YOUR DEATHS WILL BE QUICK.
AND YOU, SCUM, HAVE MINE--
I WILL AVENGE APOLLO!
SHKKKK
AAAAHH!
AVENGE APOLLO? THE COWARD?
RATHER THAN DIE BY MY HAND, HE CHOSE SUICIDE...
YOU SHOULD HAVE FOLLOWED HIS LEAD.

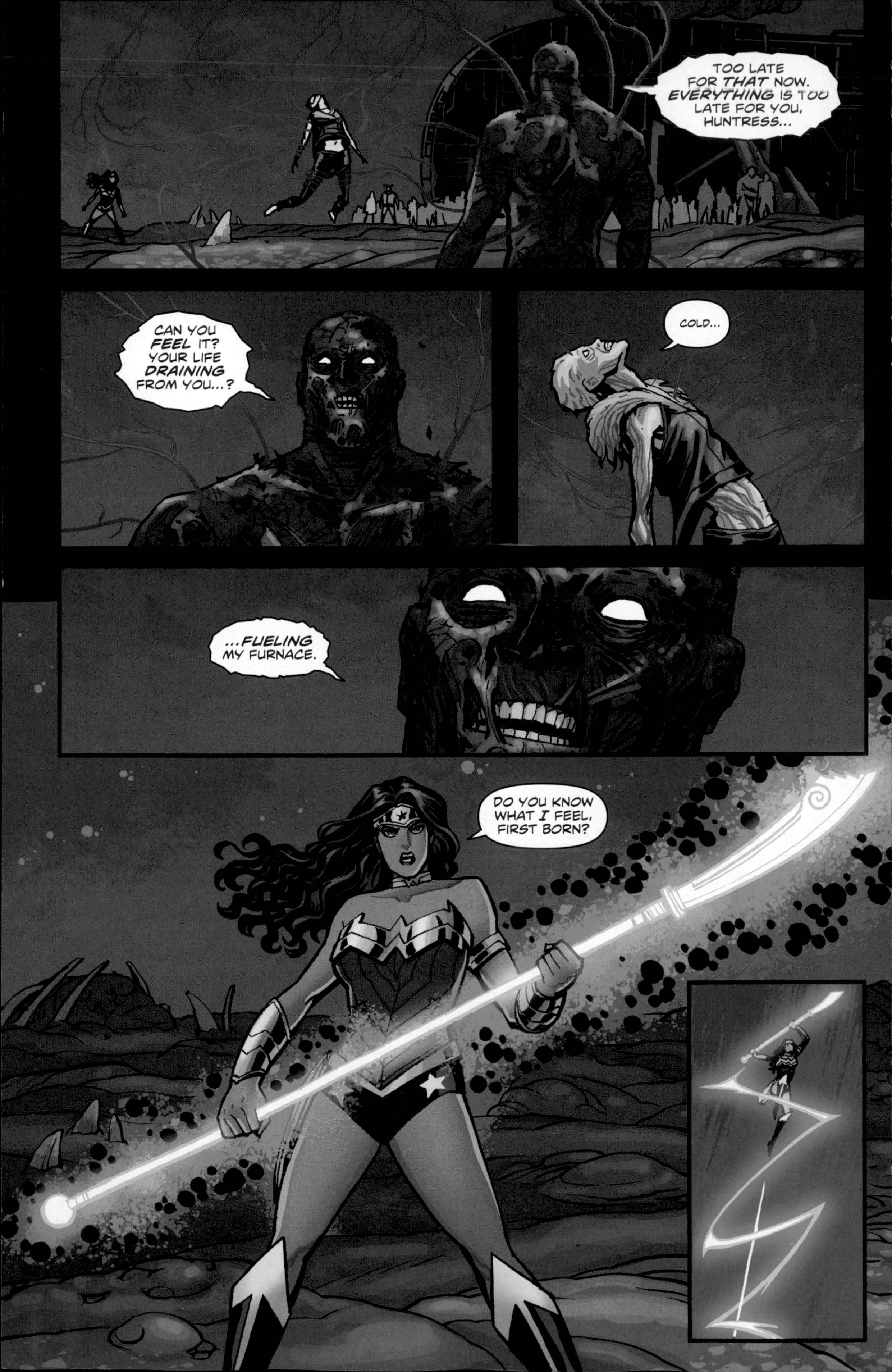
TOO LATE FOR THAT NOW. EVERYTHING IS TOO LATE FOR YOU, HUNTRESS...
CAN YOU FEEL IT? YOUR LIFE DRAINING FROM YOU...?
COLD...
...FUELING MY FURNACE.
DO YOU KNOW WHAT I FEEL, FIRST BORN?

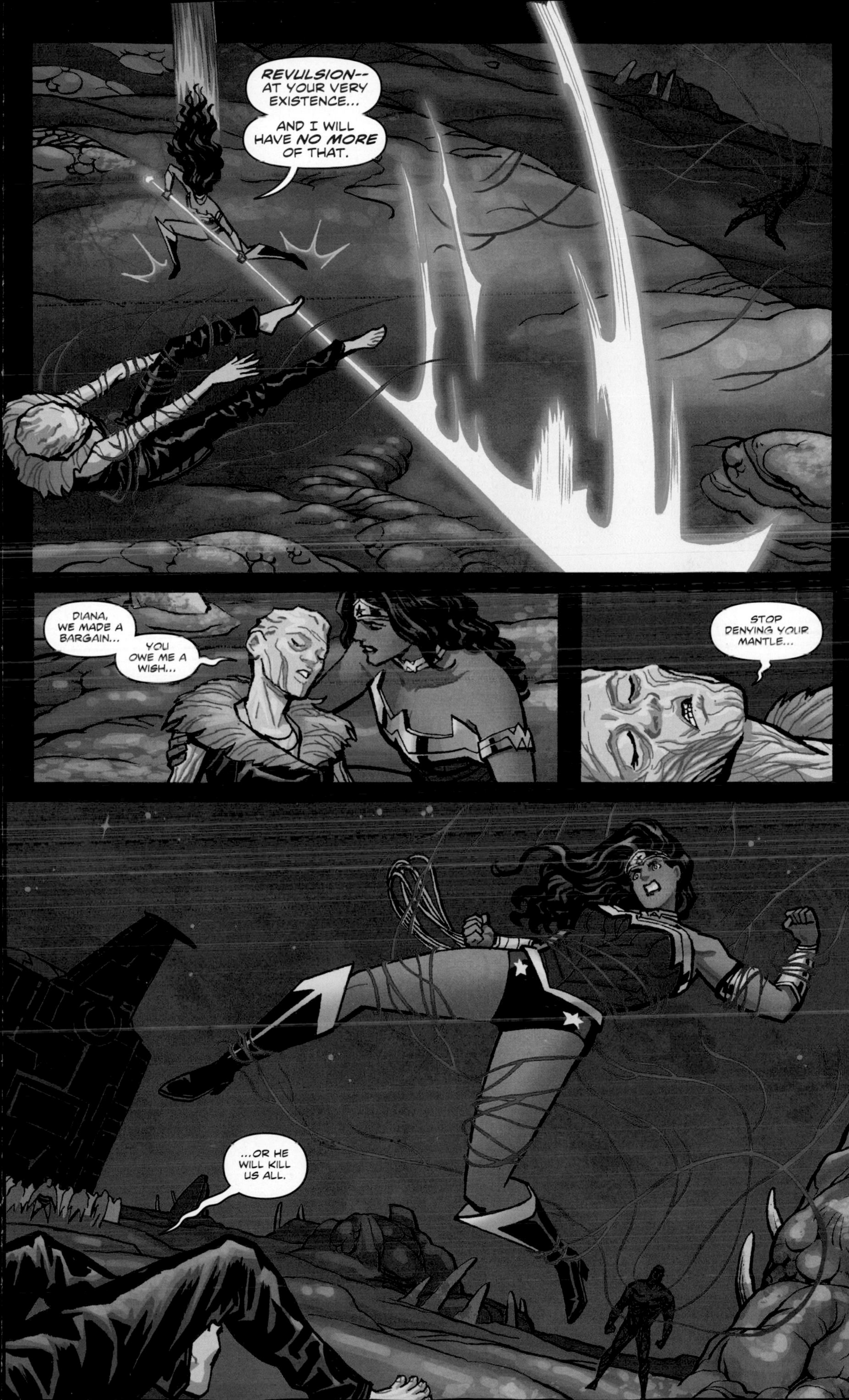
REVULSION-- AT YOUR VERY EXISTENCE...
AND I WILL HAVE NO MORE OF THAT.
DIANA, WE MADE A BARGAIN...
YOU OWE ME A WISH...
STOP DENYING YOUR MANTLE...
...OR HE WILL KILL US ALL.

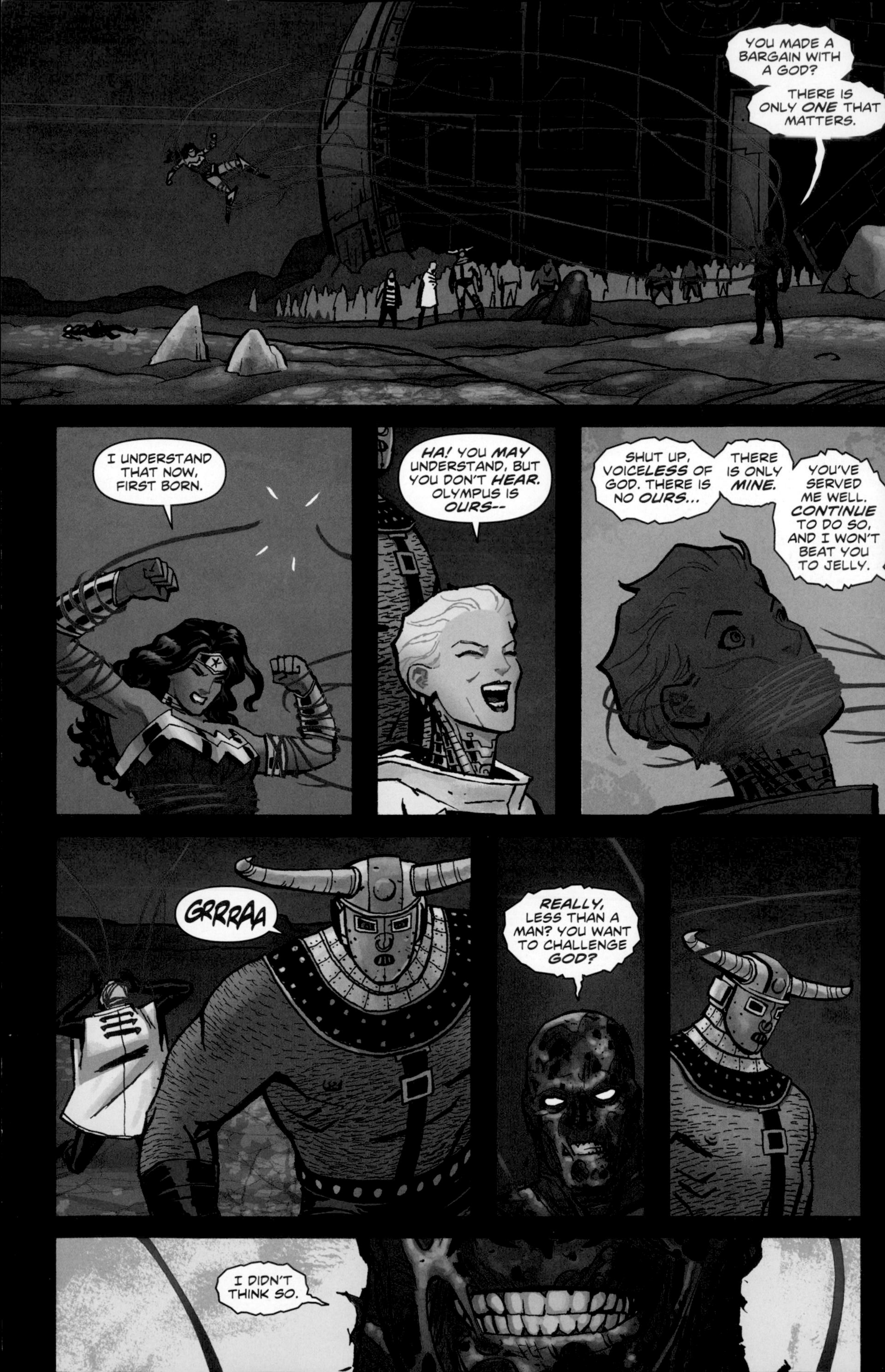
YOU MADE A BARGAIN WITH A GOD?
THERE IS ONLY ONE THAT MATTERS.
I UNDERSTAND THAT NOW, FIRST BORN.
HA! YOU MAY UNDERSTAND, BUT YOU DON'T HEAR. OLYMPUS IS OURS--
SHUT UP, VOICELESS OF GOD. THERE IS NO OURS...
THERE IS ONLY MINE.
YOU'VE SERVED ME WELL. CONTINUE TO DO SO, AND I WON'T BEAT YOU TO JELLY.
GRRRAA
REALLY, LESS THAN A MAN? YOU WANT TO CHALLENGE GOD?
I DIDN'T THINK SO.

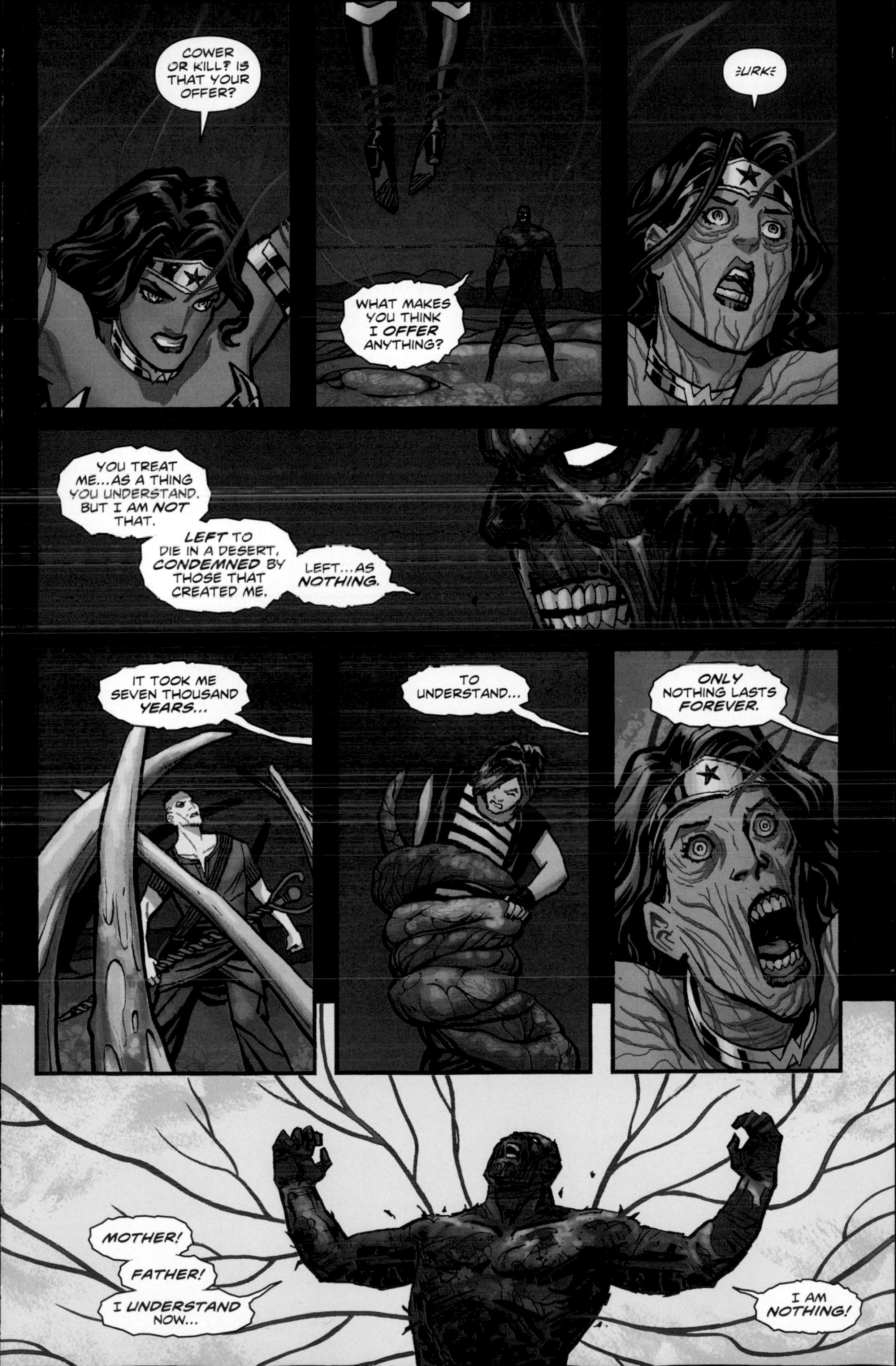
COWER OR KILL? IS THAT YOUR OFFER?
WHAT MAKES YOU THINK I OFFER ANYTHING?
ƐURKƐ
YOU TREAT ME...AS A THING YOU UNDERSTAND. BUT I AM NOT THAT.
LEFT TO DIE IN A DESERT, CONDEMNED BY THOSE THAT CREATED ME.
LEFT...AS NOTHING.
IT TOOK ME SEVEN THOUSAND YEARS...
TO UNDERSTAND...
ONLY NOTHING LASTS FOREVER.
MOTHER!
FATHER!
I UNDERSTAND NOW...
I AM NOTHING!

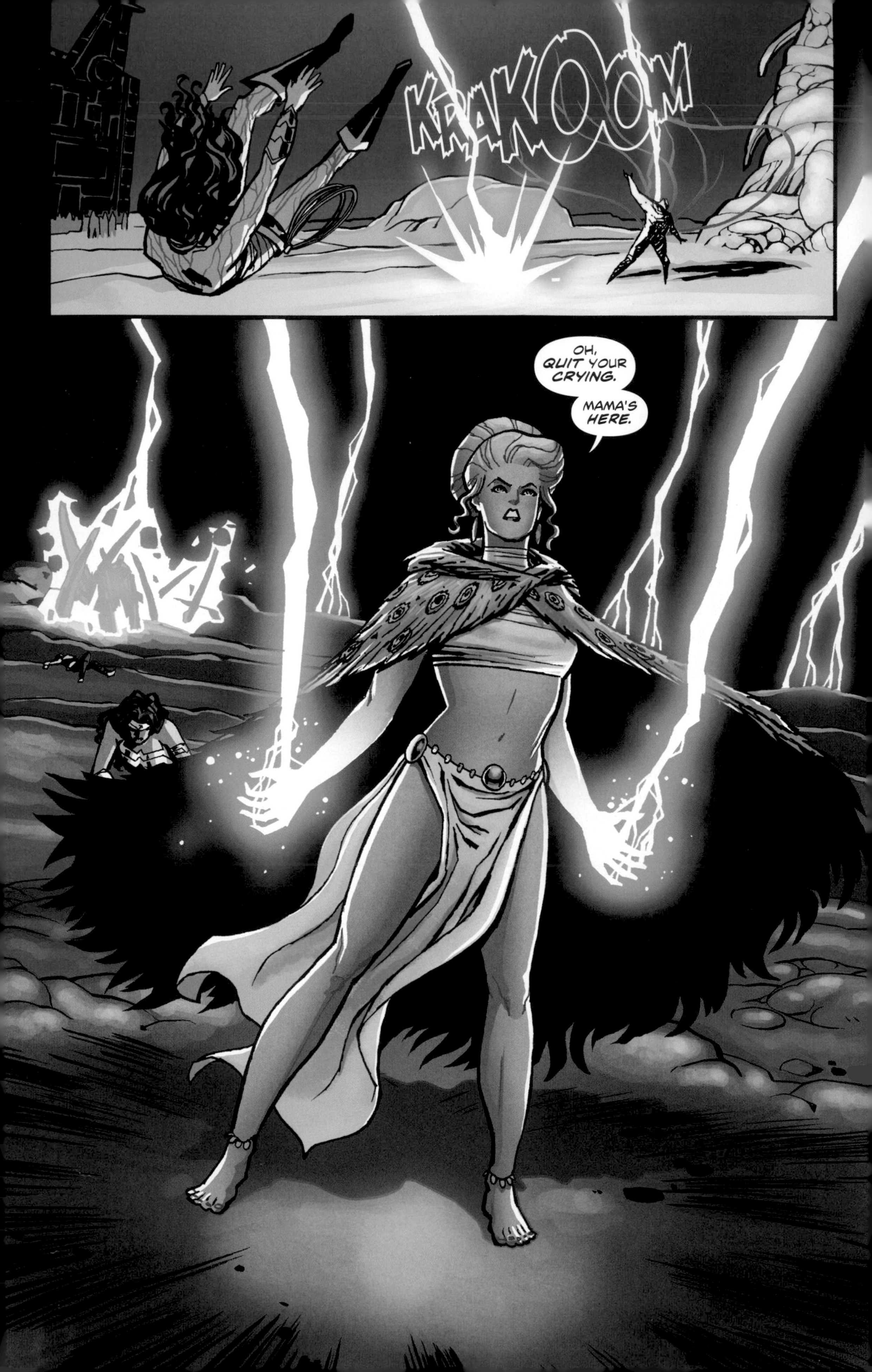
KRAKOOOM
OH, QUIT YOUR CRYING.
MAMA'S HERE.

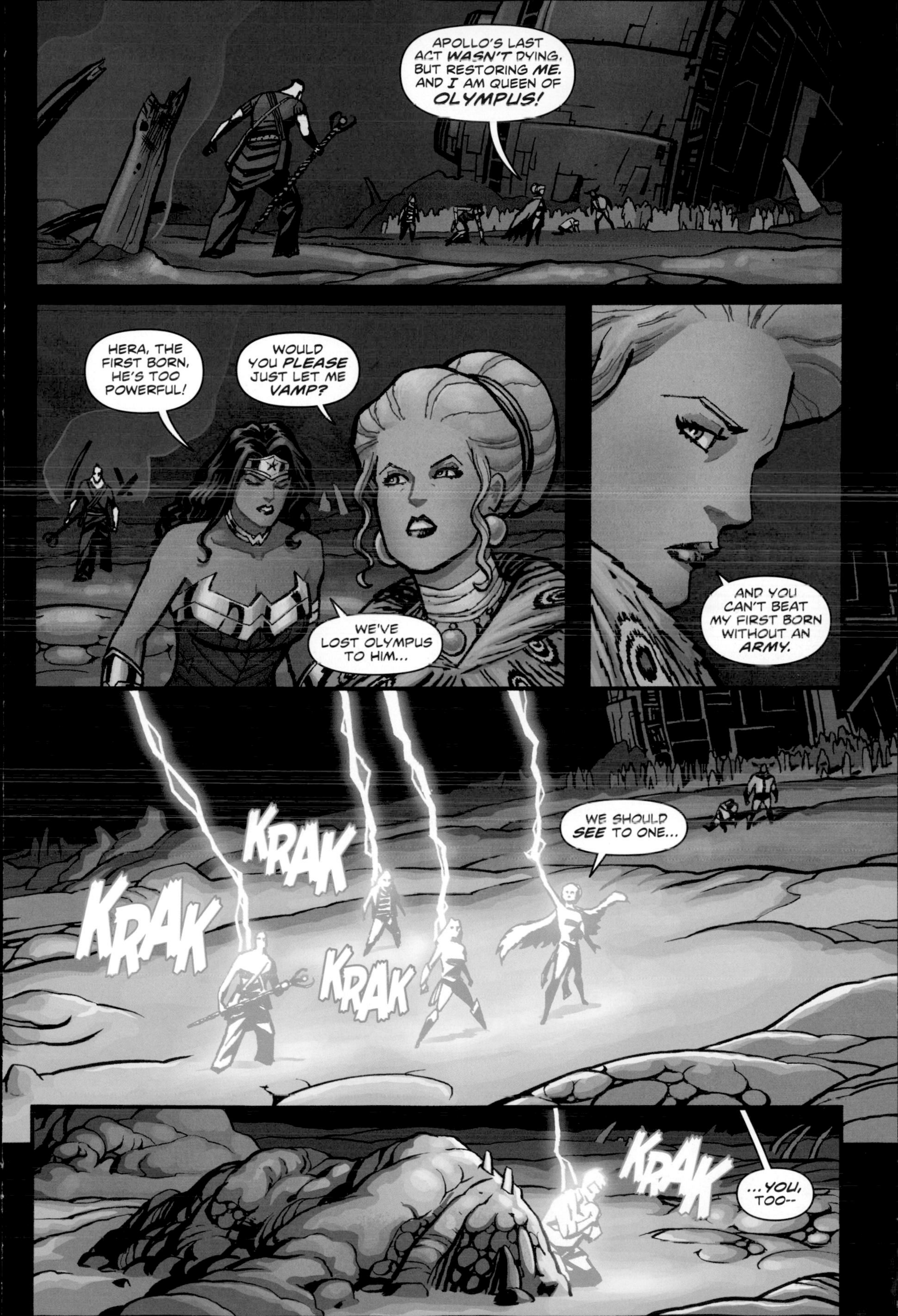
APOLLO'S LAST ACT WASN'T DYING, BUT RESTORING ME. AND I AM QUEEN OF OLYMPUS!
HERA, THE FIRST BORN, HE'S TOO POWERFUL!
WOULD YOU PLEASE JUST LET ME VAMP?
WE'VE LOST OLYMPUS TO HIM...
AND YOU CAN'T BEAT MY FIRST BORN WITHOUT AN ARMY.
KRAK
KRAK
KRAK
WE SHOULD SEE TO ONE...
KRAK
...YOU, TOO--

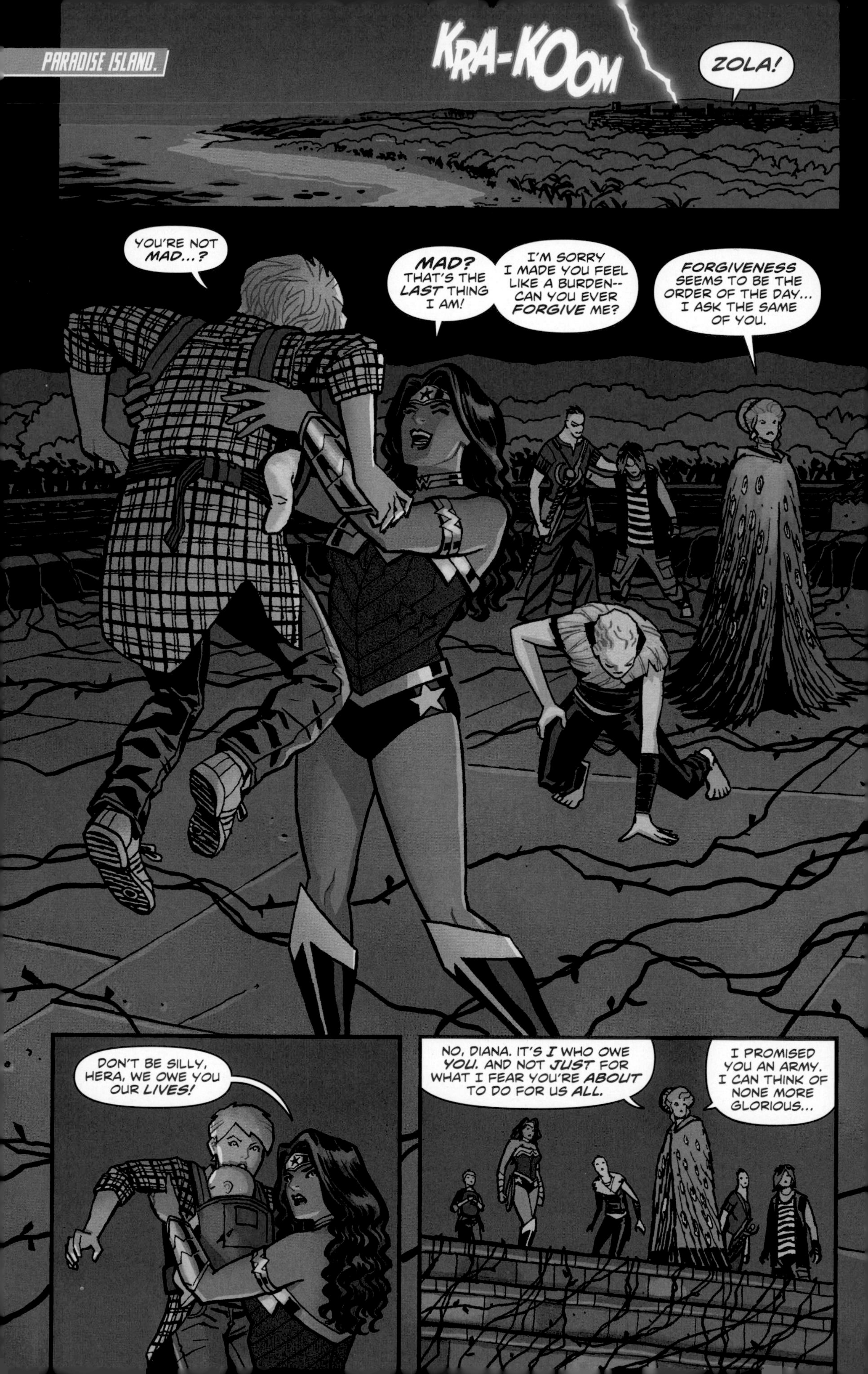
PARADISE ISLAND.
KRA-KOOM
ZOLA!
YOU'RE NOT MAD...?
MAD? THAT'S THE LAST THING I AM!
I'M SORRY I MADE YOU FEEL LIKE A BURDEN-- CAN YOU EVER FORGIVE ME?
FORGIVENESS SEEMS TO BE THE ORDER OF THE DAY... I ASK THE SAME OF YOU.
DON'T BE SILLY, HERA, WE OWE YOU OUR LIVES!
NO, DIANA. IT'S I WHO OWE YOU. AND NOT JUST FOR WHAT I FEAR YOU'RE ABOUT TO DO FOR US ALL.
I PROMISED YOU AN ARMY. I CAN THINK OF NONE MORE GLORIOUS...

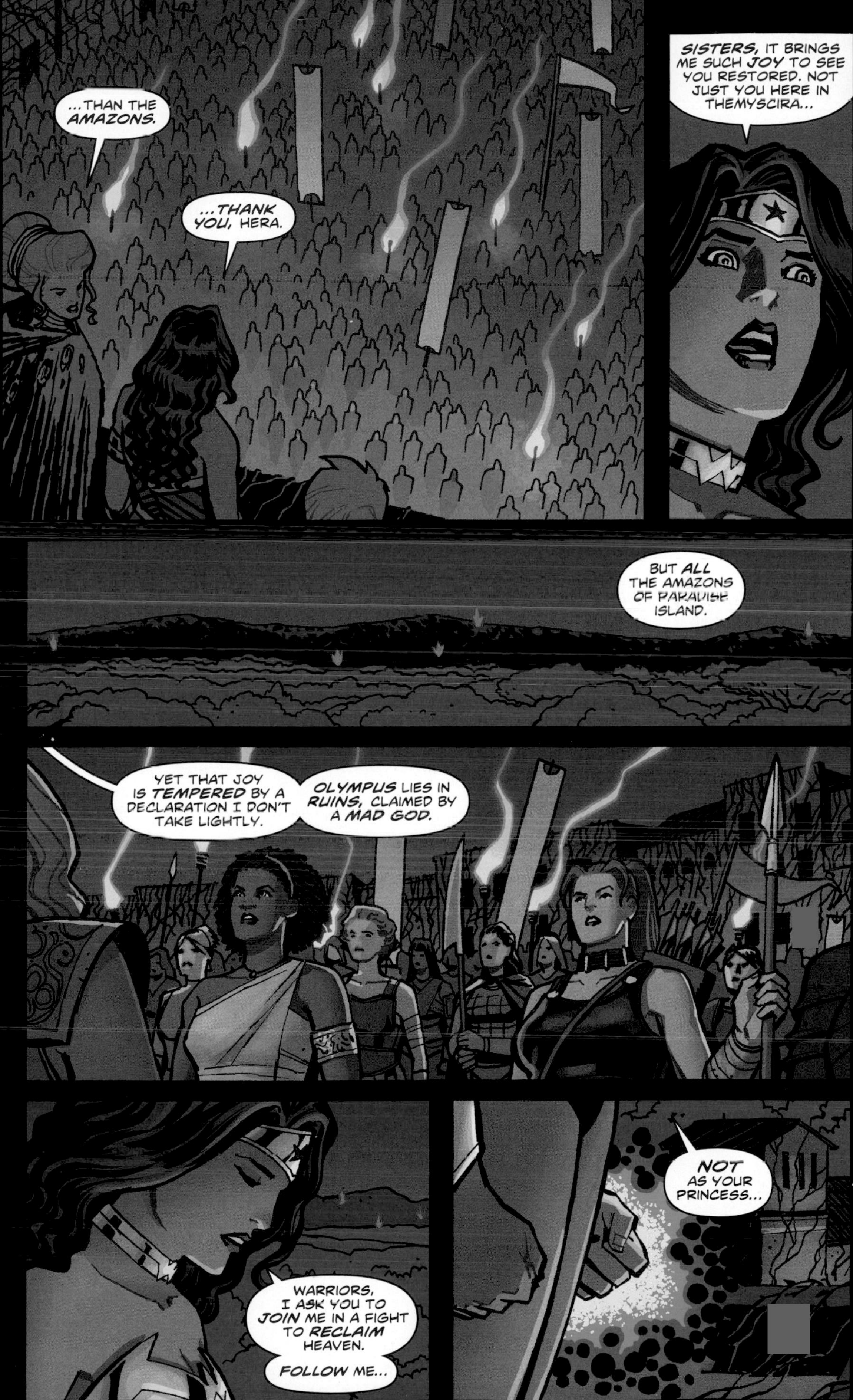
...THAN THE AMAZONS.
...THANK YOU, HERA.
SISTERS, IT BRINGS ME SUCH JOY TO SEE YOU RESTORED. NOT JUST YOU HERE IN THEMYSCIRA...
BUT ALL THE AMAZONS OF PARADISE ISLAND.
YET THAT JOY IS TEMPERED BY A DECLARATION I DON'T TAKE LIGHTLY.
OLYMPUS LIES IN RUINS, CLAIMED BY A MAD GOD.
WARRIORS, I ASK YOU TO JOIN ME IN A FIGHT TO RECLAIM HEAVEN.
FOLLOW ME...
NOT AS YOUR PRINCESS...

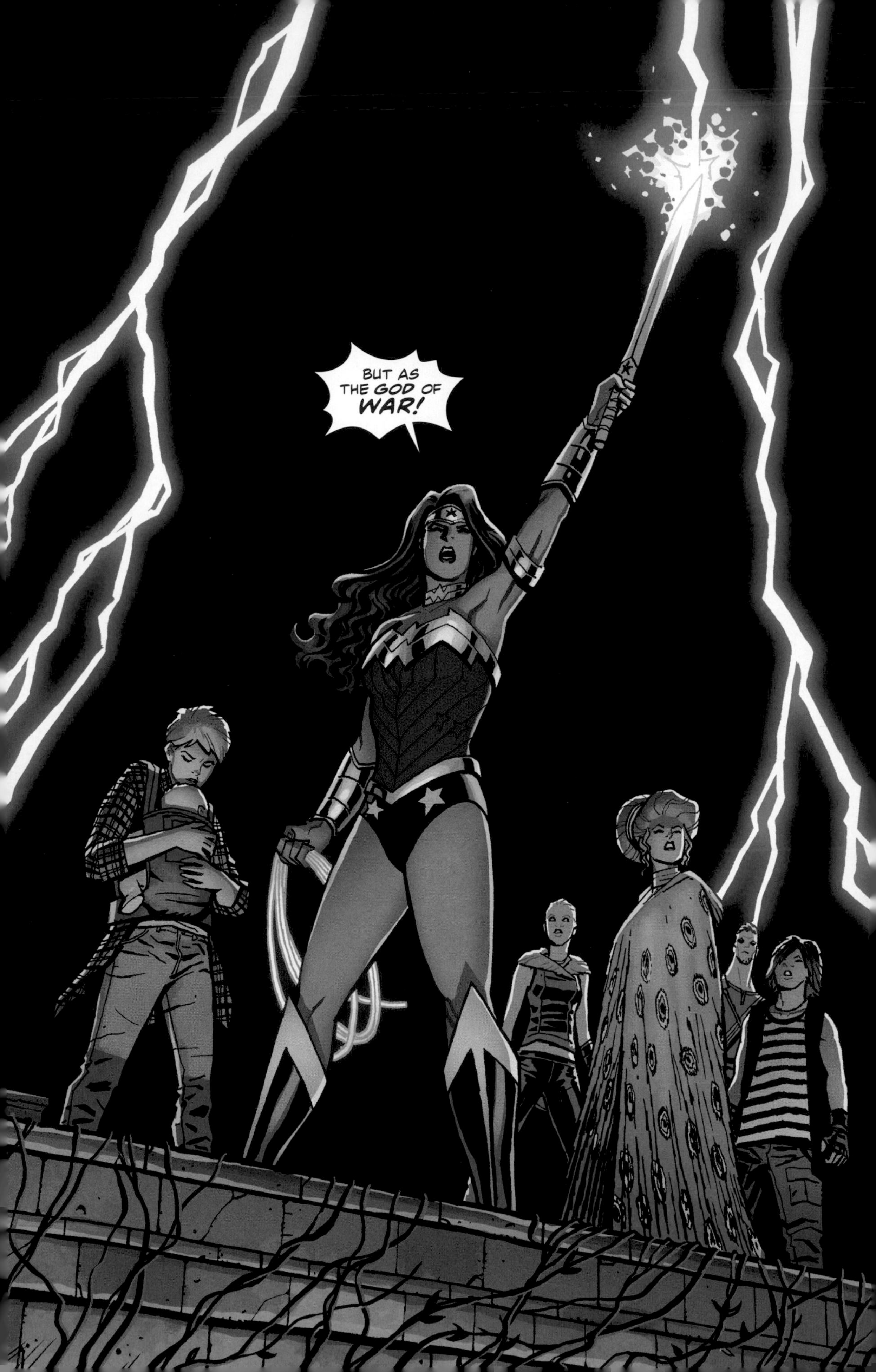
BUT AS THE GOD OF WAR!

Wonder Woman #27 Scribblenauts variant
by Jon Katz, after Cliff Chiang

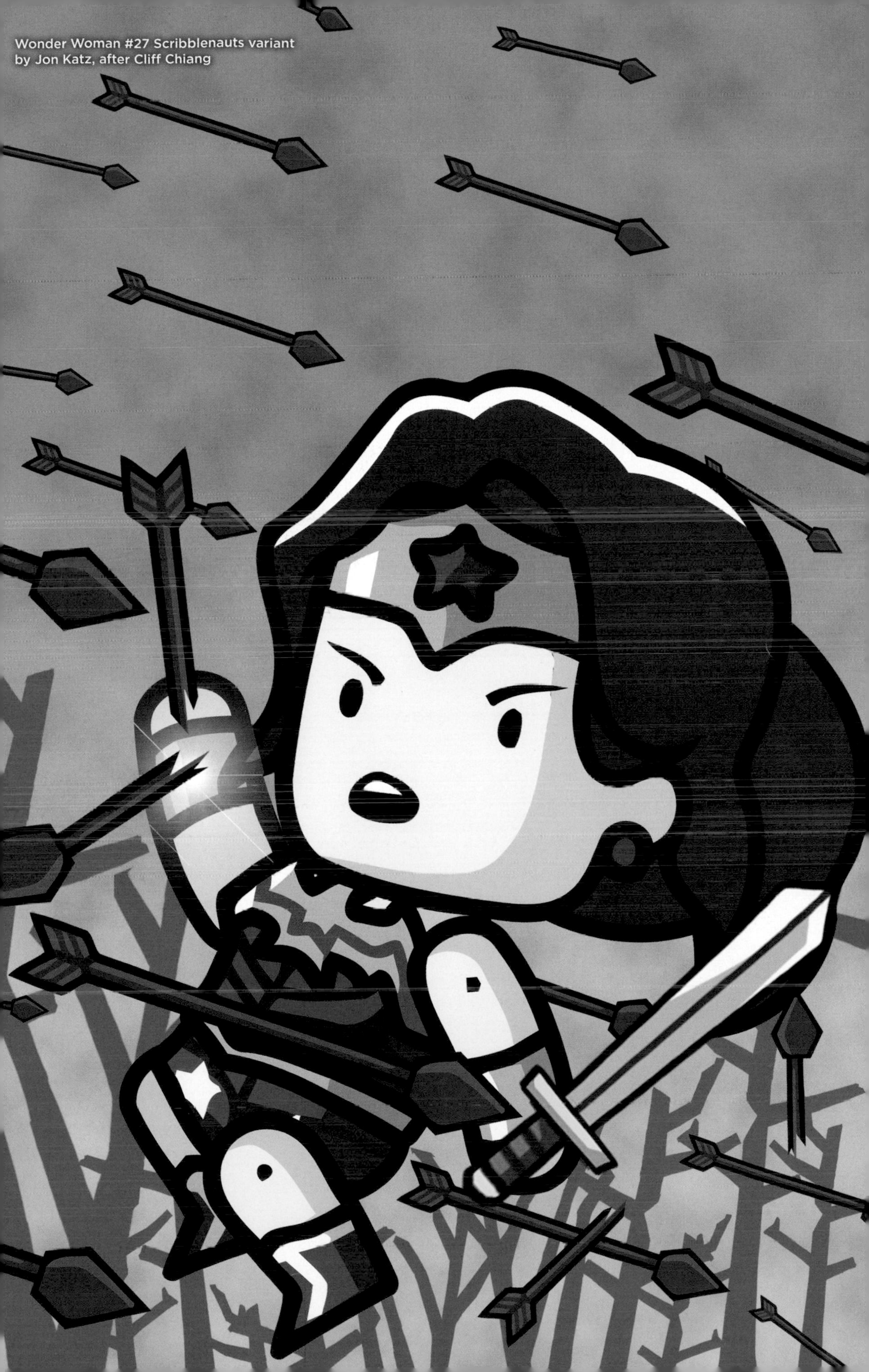

Wonder Woman #28 Steampunk variant
by J. G. Jones & Trish Mulvhill

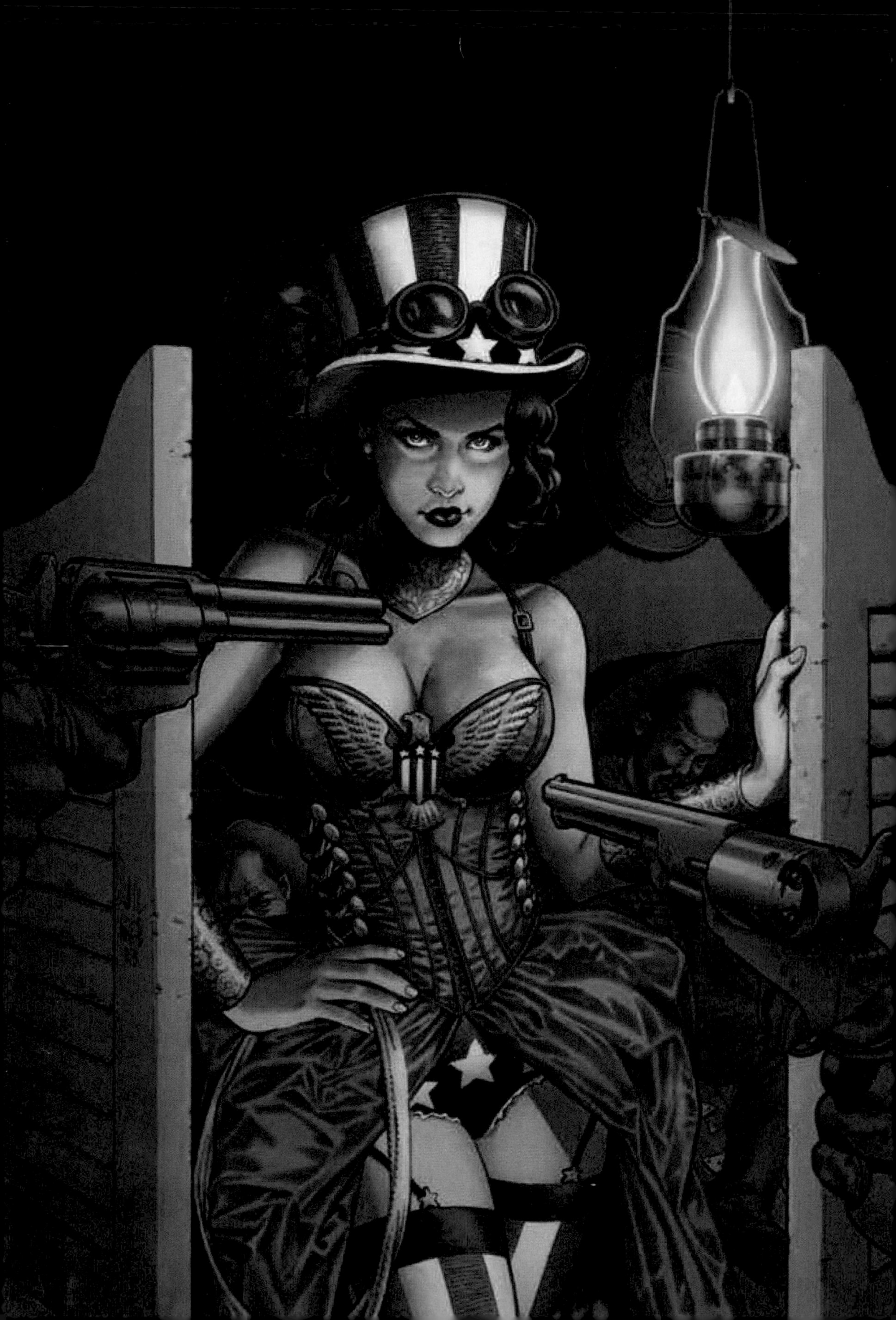

Wonder Woman #29 Robot Chicken variant
by RC Stoodios

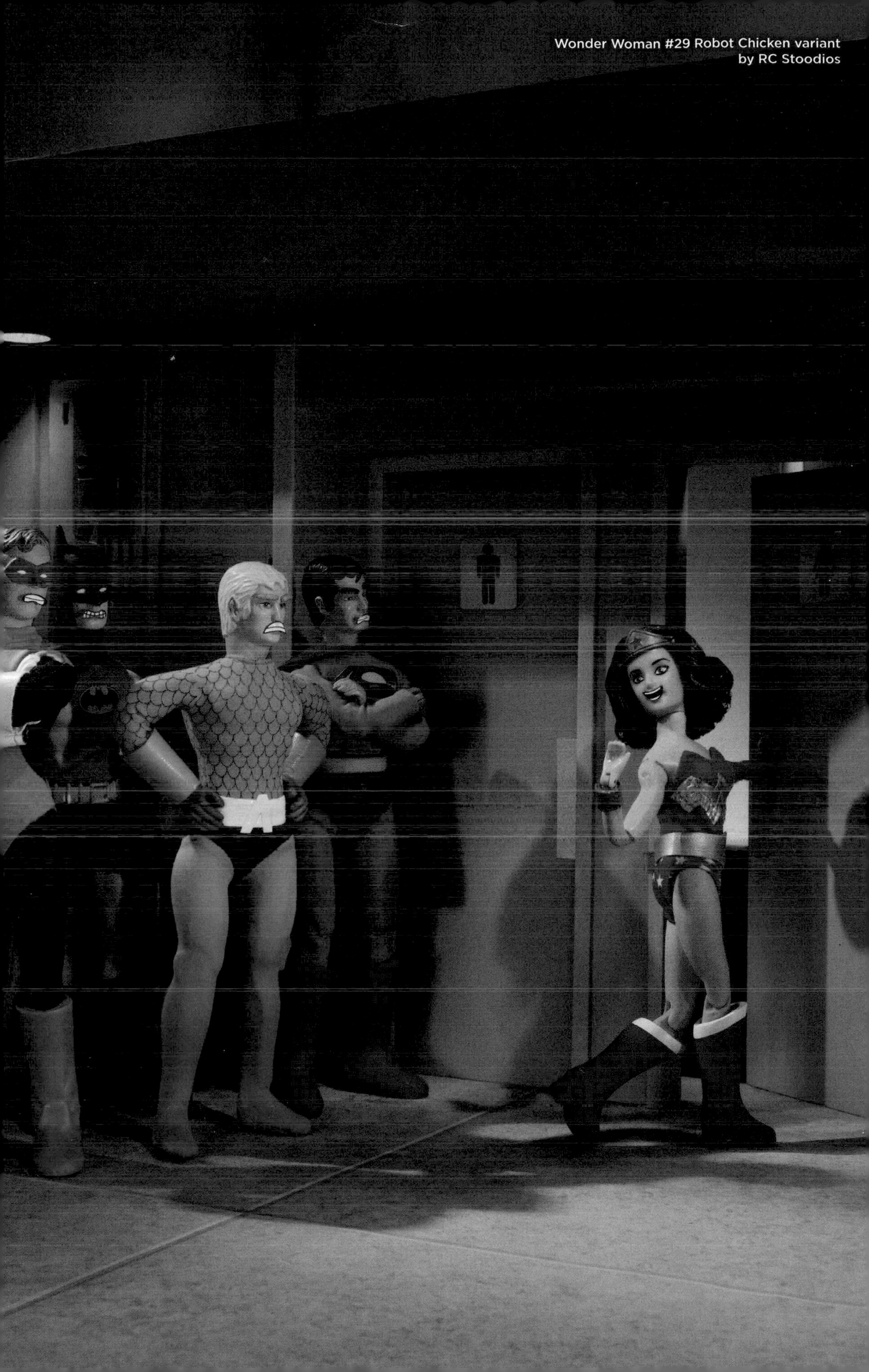

# WONDER WOMAN

## COVER SKETCHES BY CLIFF CHIANG

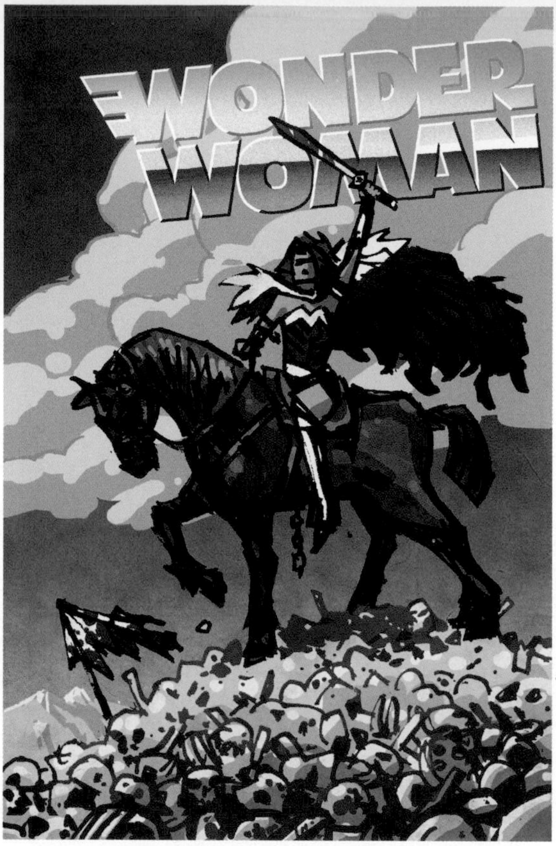
WONDER
WOMAN

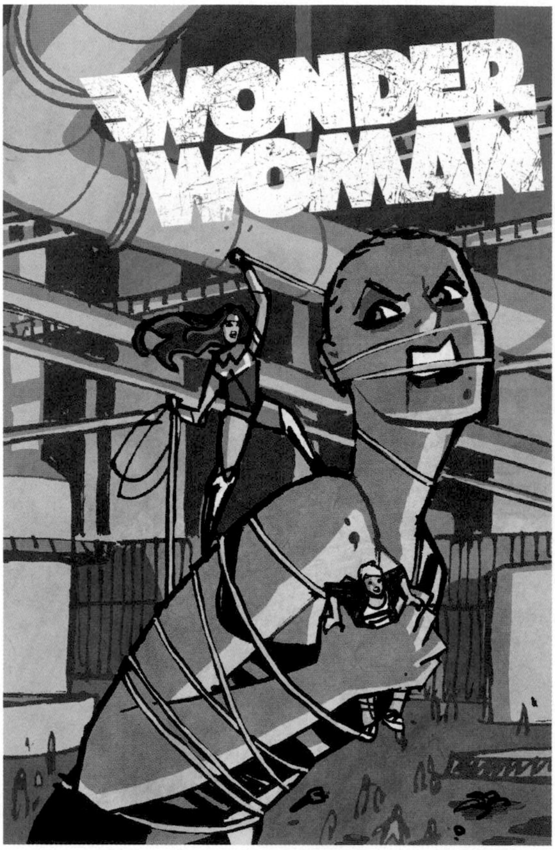
WONDER
WOMAN

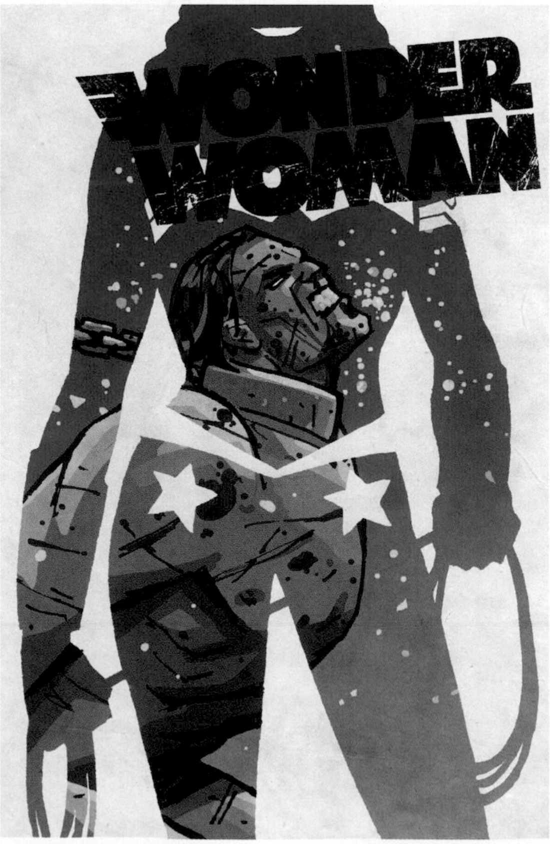
WONDER
WOMAN

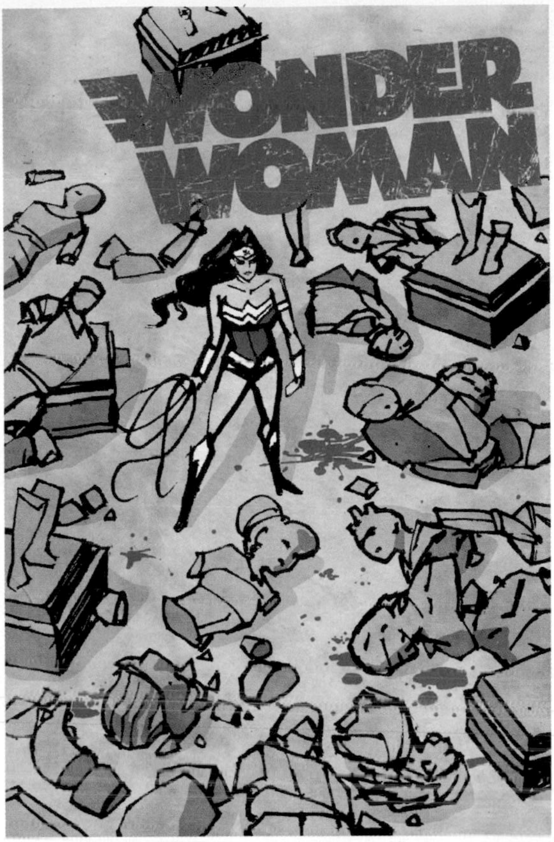
WONDER
WOMAN

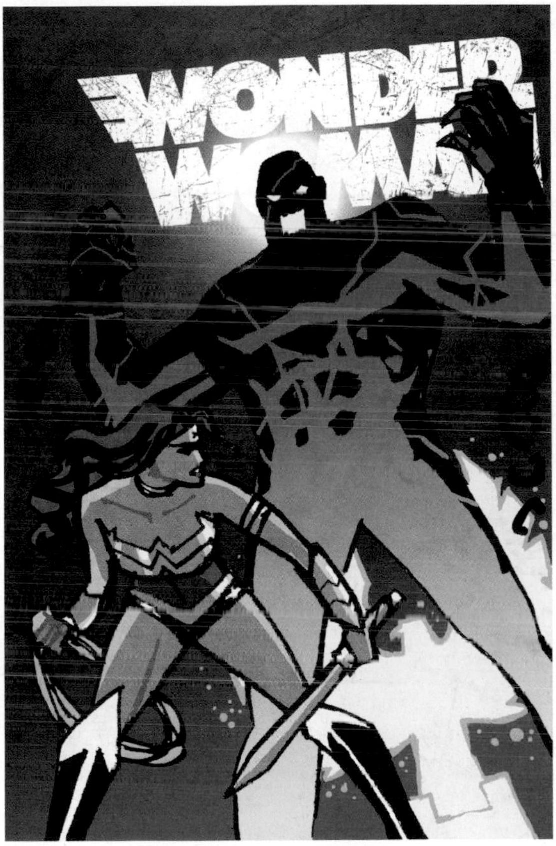
WONDER
WOMAN

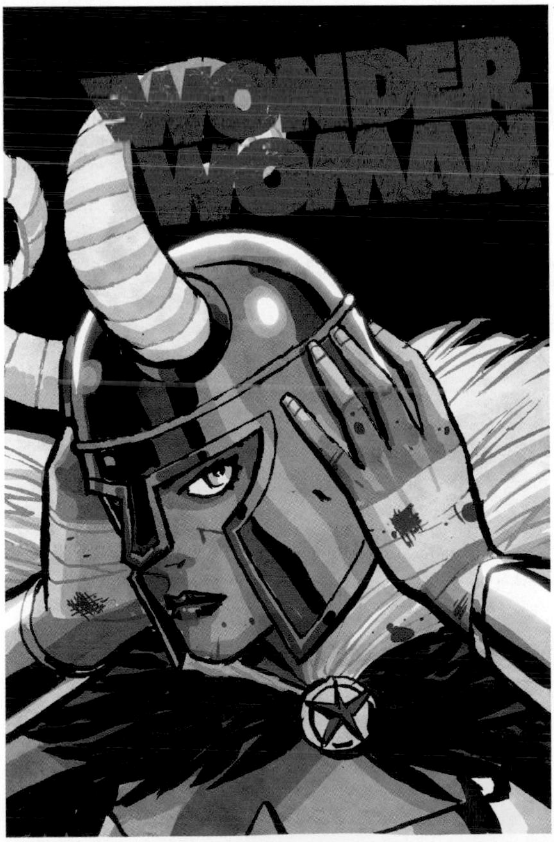
WONDER
WOMAN

# WONDER WOMAN

## ISSUE #24-25 LAYOUTS, PENCILS, AND INKS BY GORAN SUDŽUKA

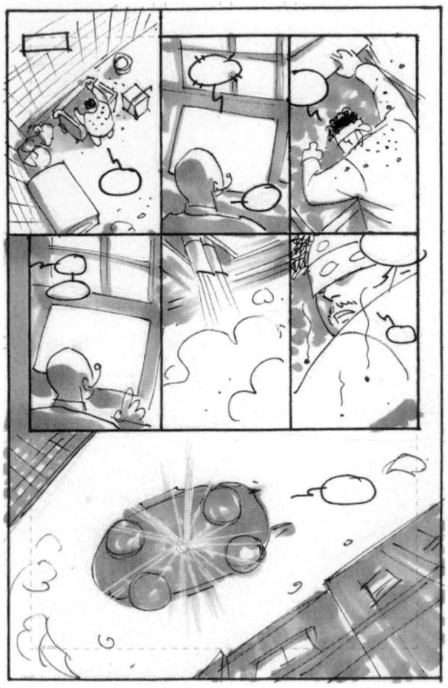

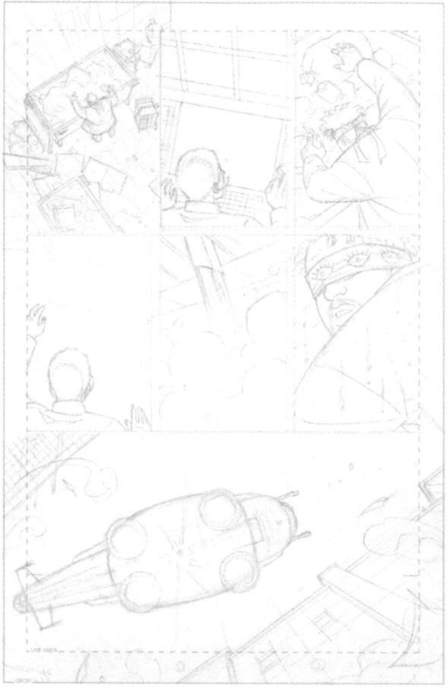

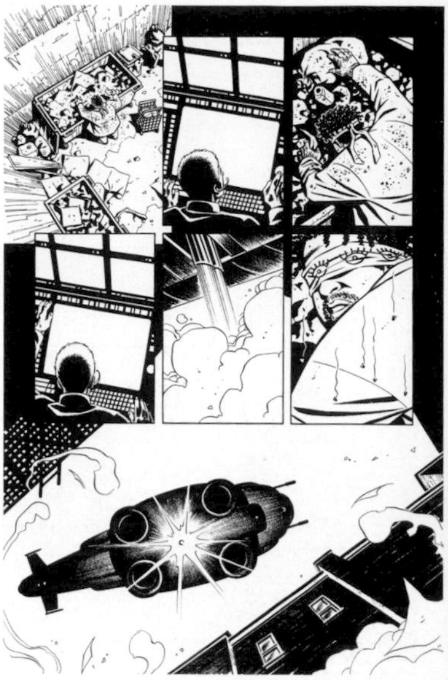

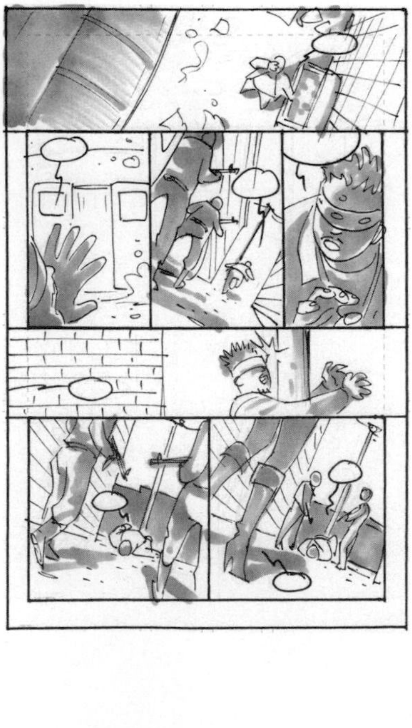

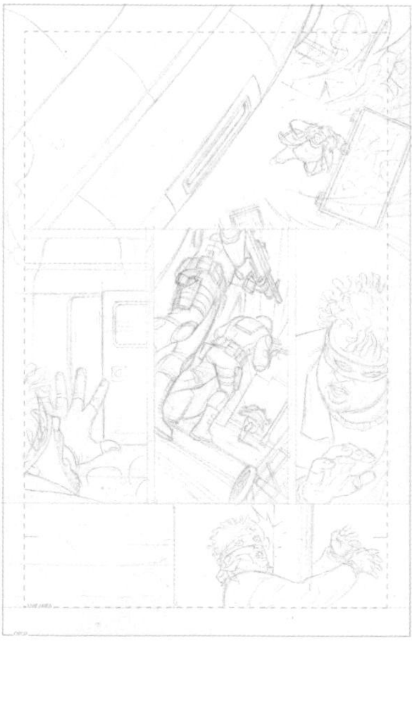

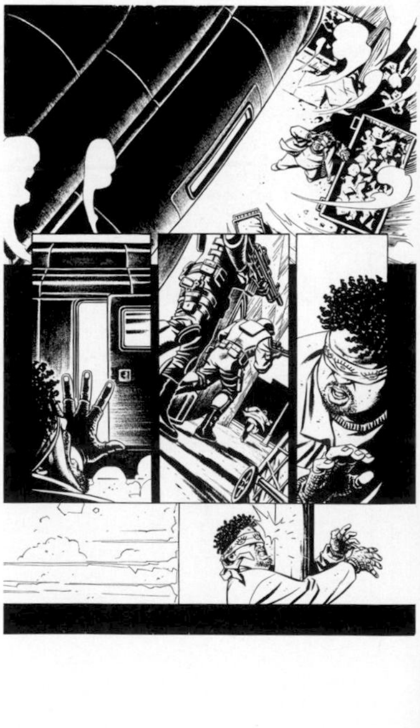

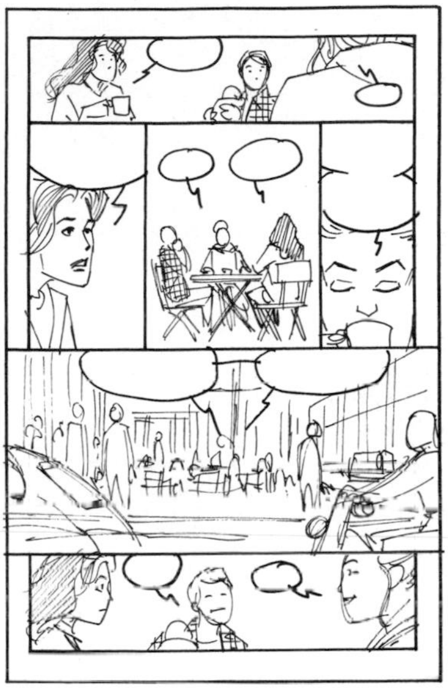
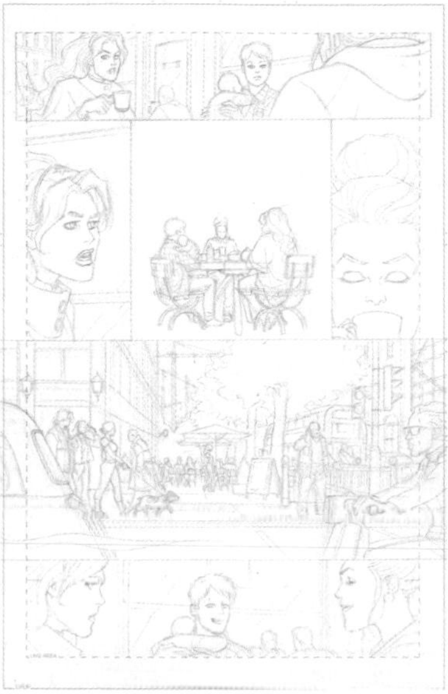
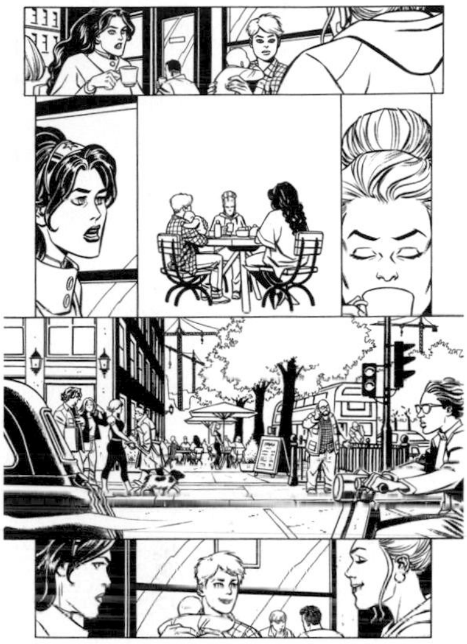
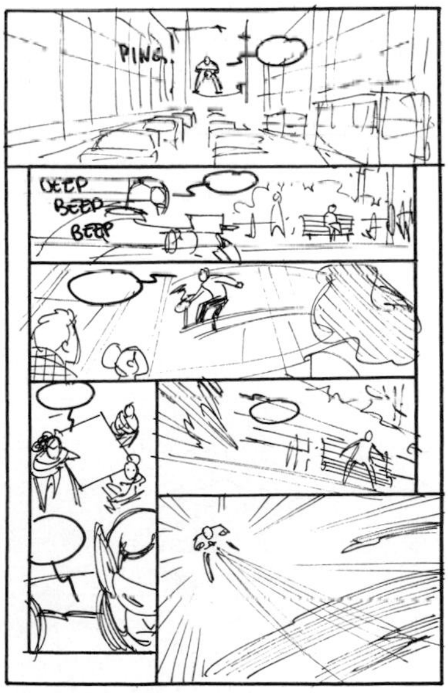
PING!
BEEP
BEEP
BEEP
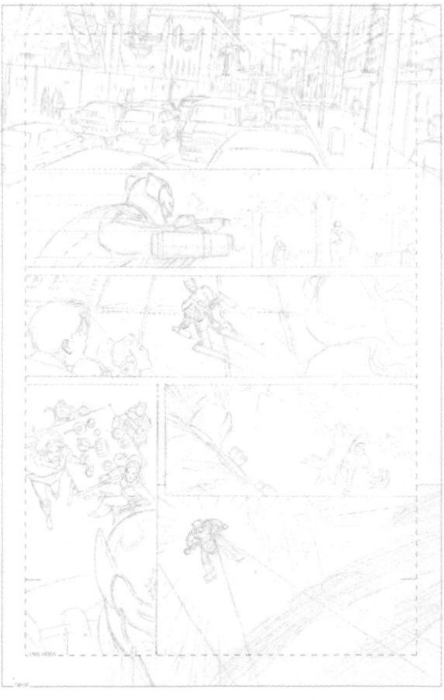
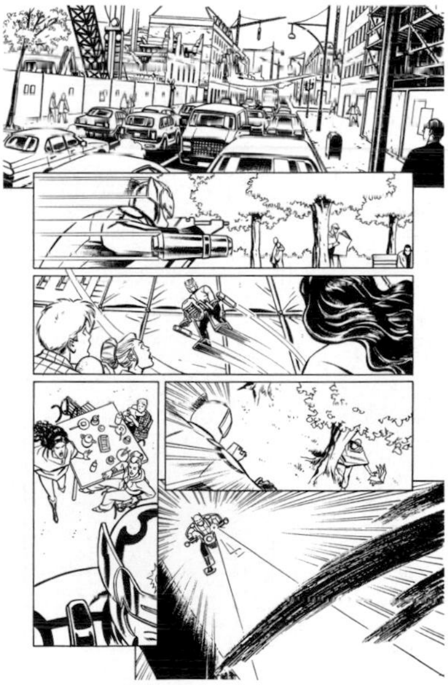

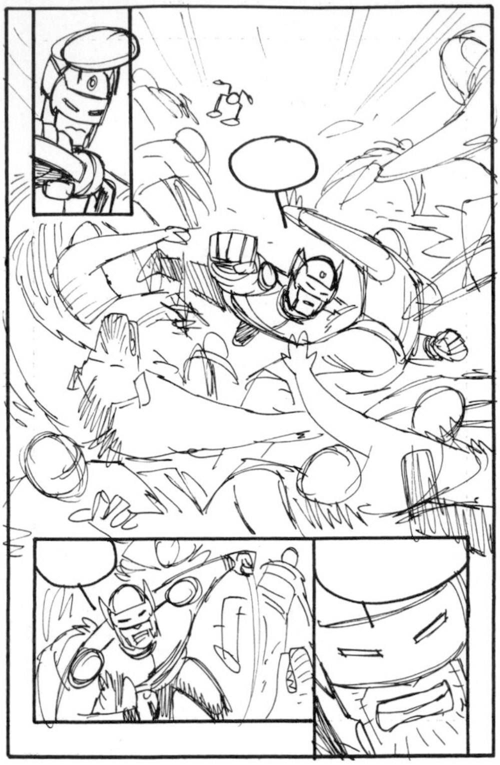

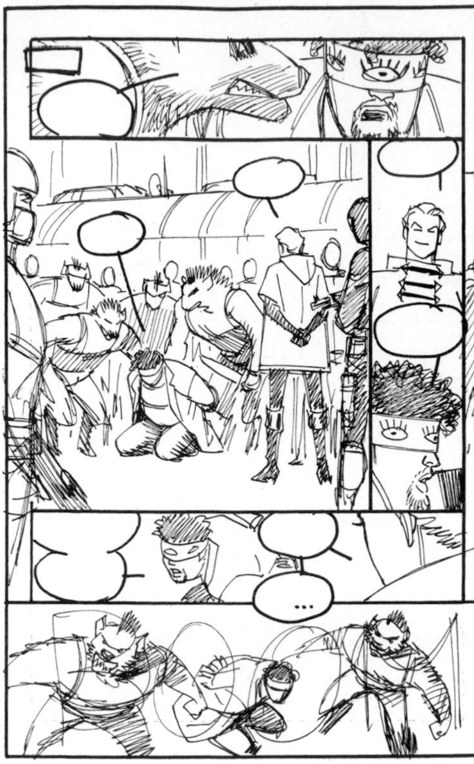
...

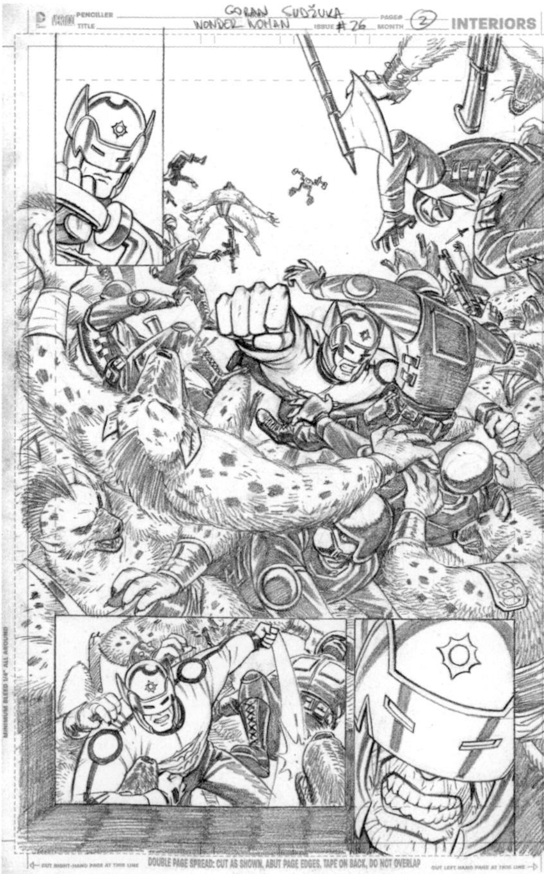
PENCILLER GORAN SUDŽUKA
TITLE WONDER WOMAN ISSUE #26
PAGE# 2
INTERIORS
DOUBLE PAGE SPREAD: CUT AS SHOWN, ABUT PAGE EDGES, TAPE ON BACK, DO NOT OVERLAP

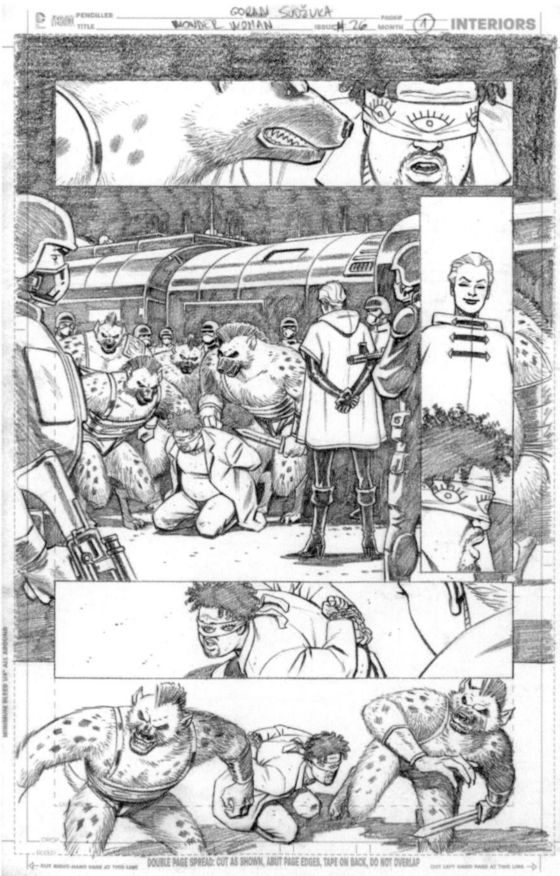
PENCILLER GORAN SUDŽUKA
TITLE WONDER WOMAN ISSUE #26
PAGE# 1
INTERIORS
DOUBLE PAGE SPREAD: CUT AS SHOWN, ABUT PAGE EDGES, TAPE ON BACK, DO NOT OVERLAP

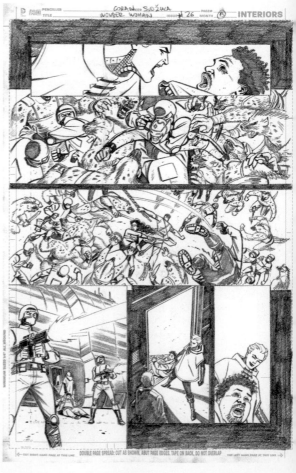

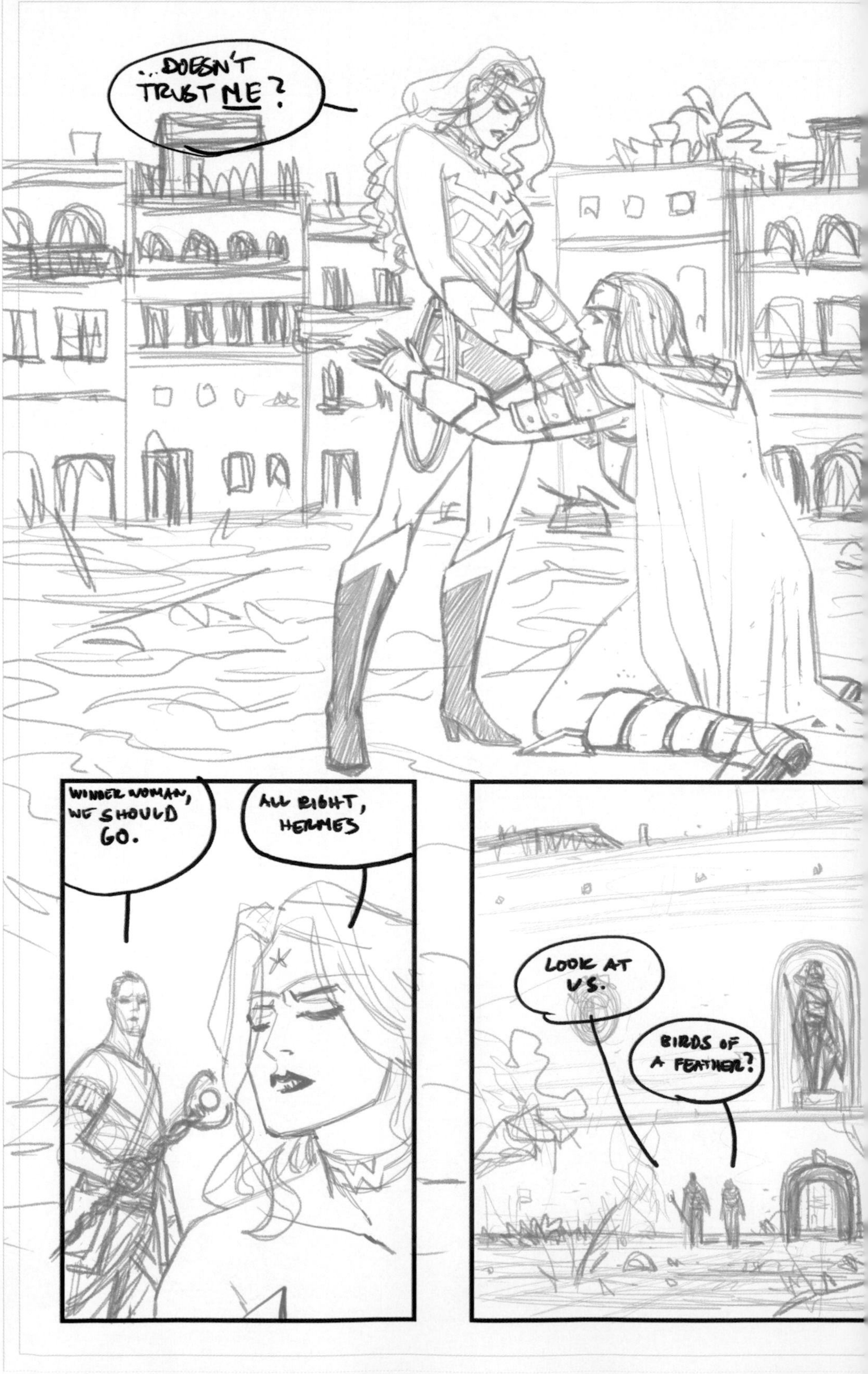
...DOESN'T TRUST ME?
WONDER WOMAN, WE SHOULD GO.
ALL RIGHT, HERMES
LOOK AT US.
BIRDS OF A FEATHER?

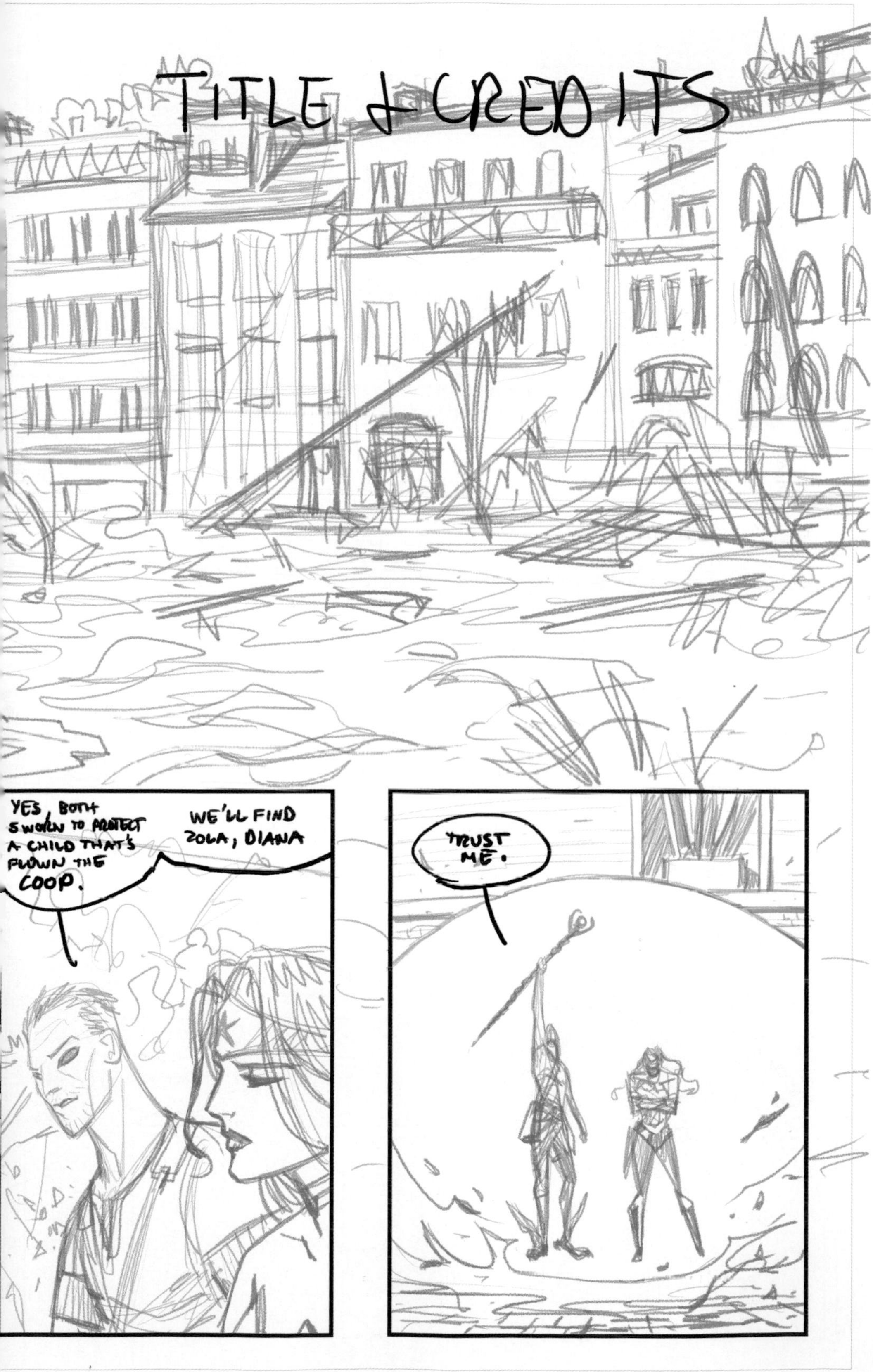
TITLE & CREDITS
YES, BOTH SWORN TO PROTECT A CHILD THAT'S FLOWN THE COOP.
WE'LL FIND ZOLA, DIANA
TRUST ME.

CLIFF CHIANG WONDER WOMAN ISSUE 27 PAGE 8

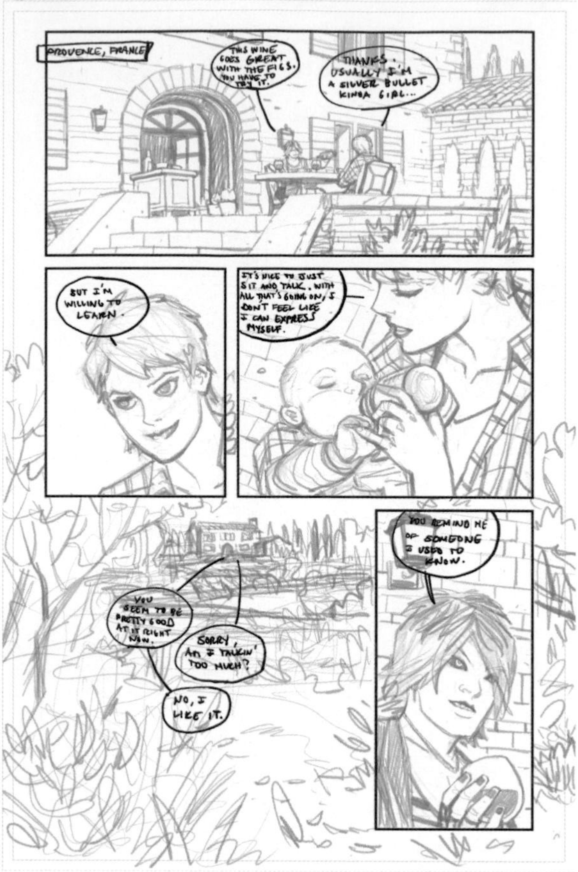
PROVENCE, FRANCE
THIS WINE GOES GREAT WITH THE FIGS. YOU HAVE TO TRY IT.
THANKS. USUALLY I'M A SILVER BULLET KINDA GIRL...
BUT I'M WILLING TO LEARN.
IT'S NICE TO JUST SIT AND TALK. WITH ALL THAT'S GOING ON, I DON'T FEEL LIKE I CAN EXPRESS MYSELF.
YOU SEEM TO BE PRETTY GOOD AT IT RIGHT NOW.
SORRY, AM I TALKIN' TOO MUCH?
NO, I LIKE IT.
YOU REMIND ME OF SOMEONE I USED TO KNOW.

CLIFF CHIANG WONDER WOMAN ISSUE 27 PAGE 9

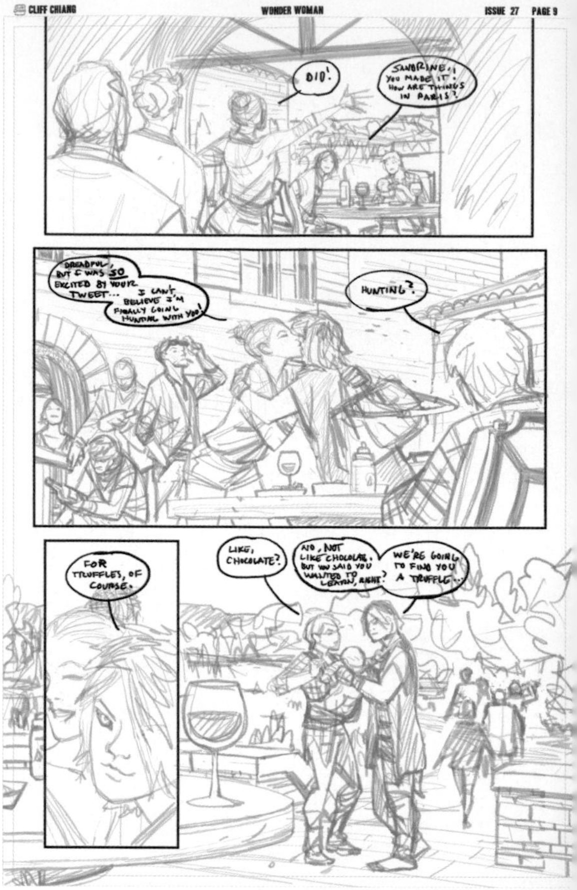
DID!
SANDRINE! YOU MADE IT! HOW ARE THINGS IN PARIS?
DREADFUL, BUT I WAS SO EXCITED BY YOUR TWEET... I CAN'T BELIEVE I'M FINALLY GOING HUNTING WITH YOU!
HUNTING?
FOR TRUFFLES, OF COURSE.
LIKE, CHOCOLATE?
NO, NOT LIKE CHOCOLATE. BUT YOU SAID YOU WANTED TO LEARN, RIGHT?
WE'RE GOING TO FIND YOU A TRUFFLE...

CLIFF CHIANG WONDER WOMAN ISSUE 27 PAGE 14

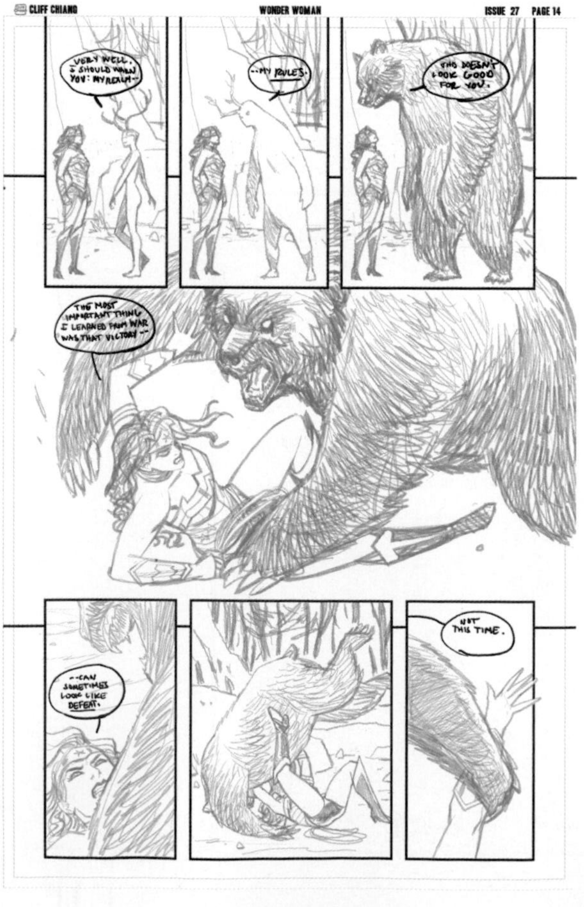
VERY WELL, I SHOULD WARN YOU: MY REALM--
--MY RULES.
THIS DOESN'T LOOK GOOD FOR YOU.
THE MOST IMPORTANT THING I LEARNED FROM WAR WAS THAT VICTORY--
--CAN SOMETIMES LOOK LIKE DEFEAT.
NOT THIS TIME.

CLIFF CHIANG WONDER WOMAN ISSUE 27 PAGE 15

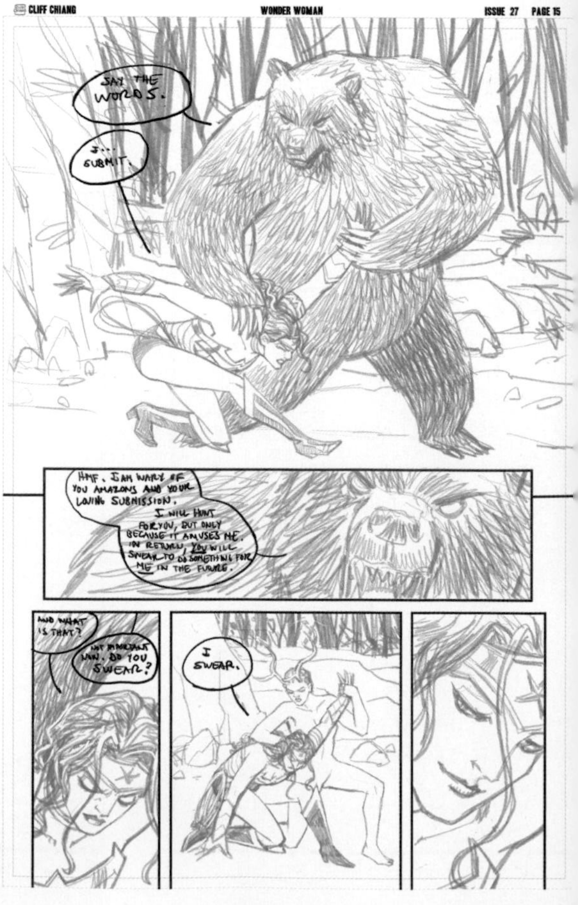
SAY THE WORDS.
I... SUBMIT.
HMF. I AM WARY OF YOU AMAZONS AND YOUR LOVING SUBMISSION.
I WILL HUNT FOR YOU, BUT ONLY BECAUSE IT AMUSES ME. IN RETURN, YOU WILL SWEAR TO DO SOMETHING FOR ME IN THE FUTURE.
AND WHAT IS THAT?
NOT IMPORTANT NOW. DO YOU SWEAR?
I SWEAR.

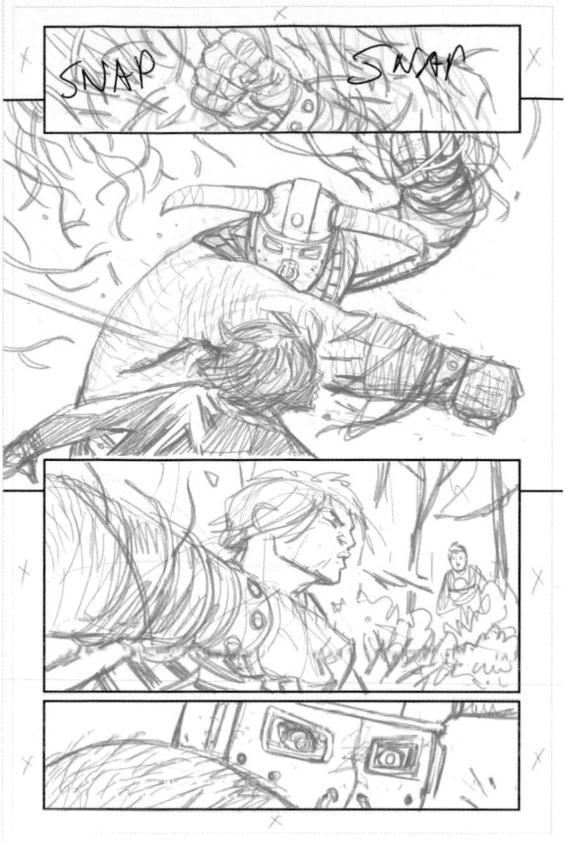
SNAP
SNAP



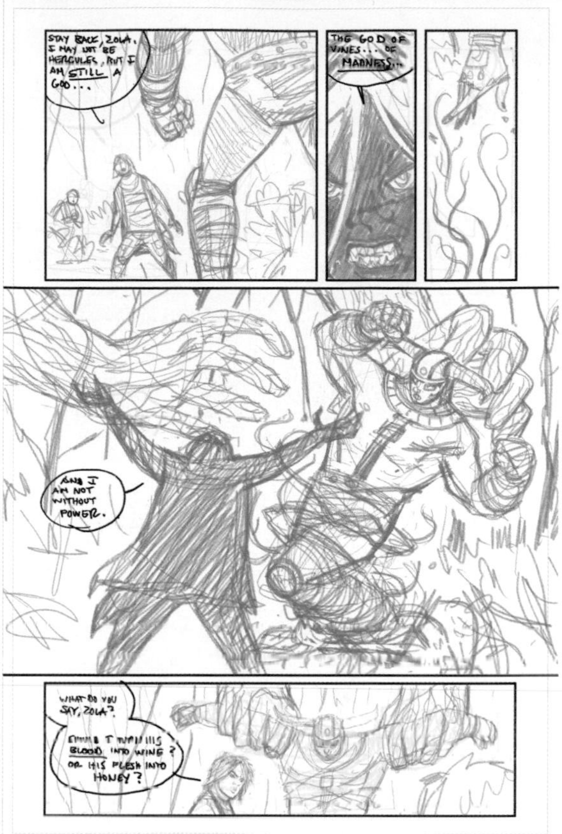
STAY BACK, ZOLA. I MAY NOT BE HERCULES, BUT I AM STILL A GOD...
THE GOD OF VINES... OF MADNESS...
AND I AM NOT WITHOUT POWER.
WHAT DO YOU SAY, ZOLA?
BLOOD INTO WINE? OR HIS FLESH INTO HONEY?



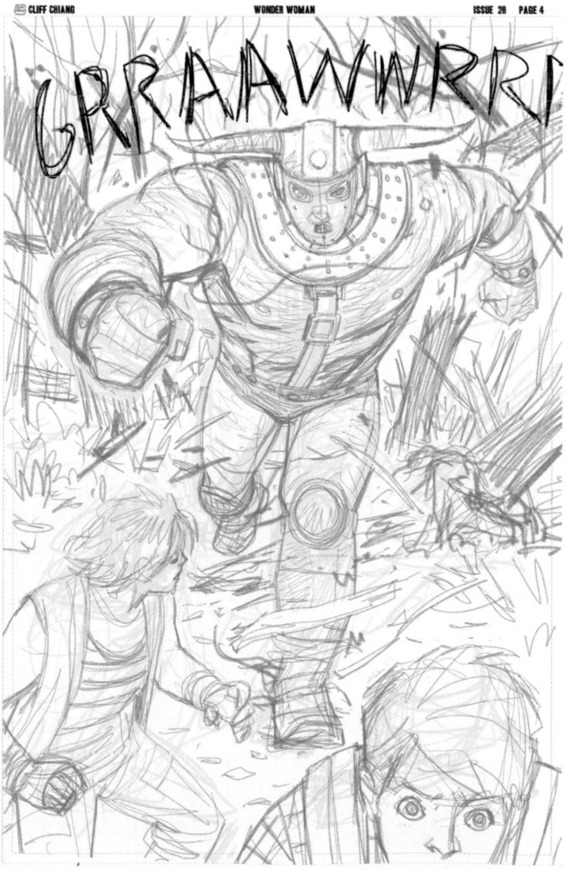
GRRAAWWRRR



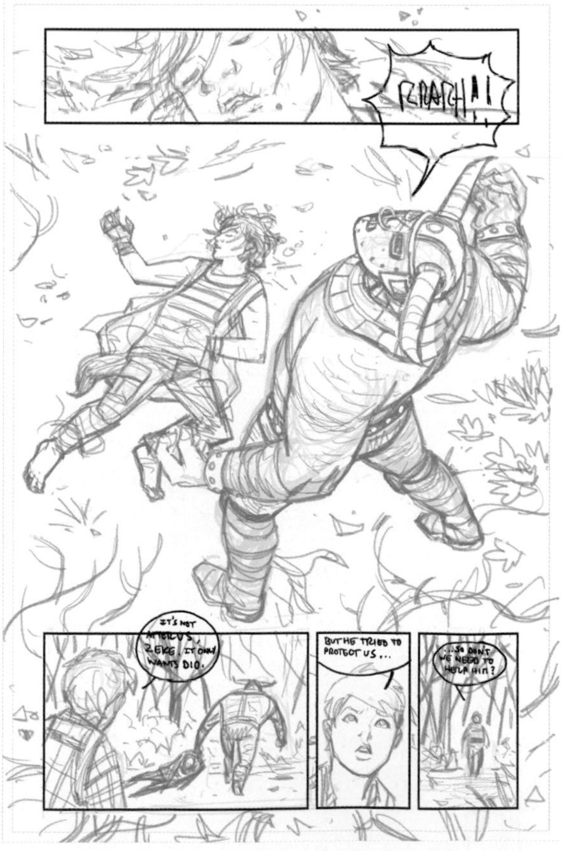
RRAAGH!!
IT'S NOT
ZEKE. IT ONLY WANTS DIO.
BUT HE TRIED TO PROTECT US...
...SO DON'T WE NEED TO HELP HIM?

CLIFF CHIANG WONDER WOMAN ISSUE 26 PAGE 14

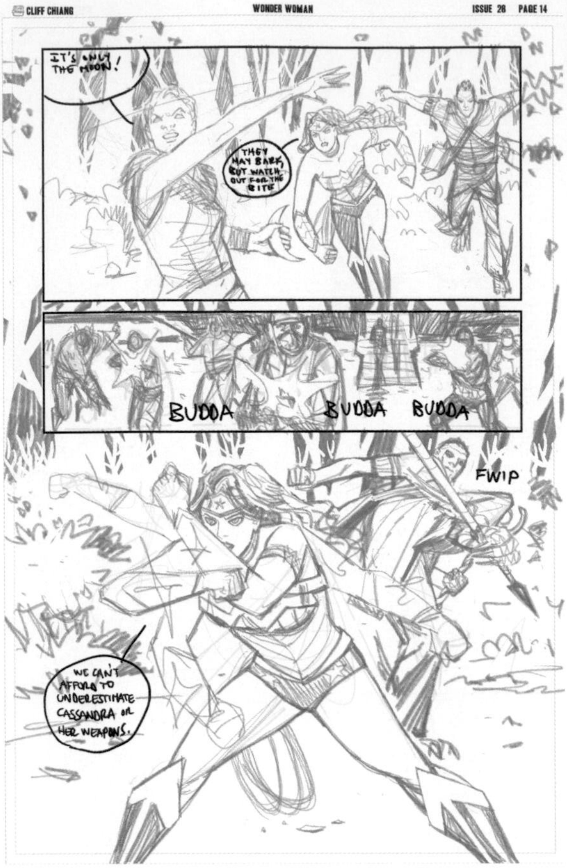
IT'S ONLY THE MOON!
THEY MAY BARK, BUT WATCH OUT FOR THE BITE
BUDDA BUDDA BUDDA
FWIP
WE CAN'T AFFORD TO UNDERESTIMATE CASSANDRA OR HER WEAPONS.

CLIFF CHIANG WONDER WOMAN ISSUE 29 PAGE 4

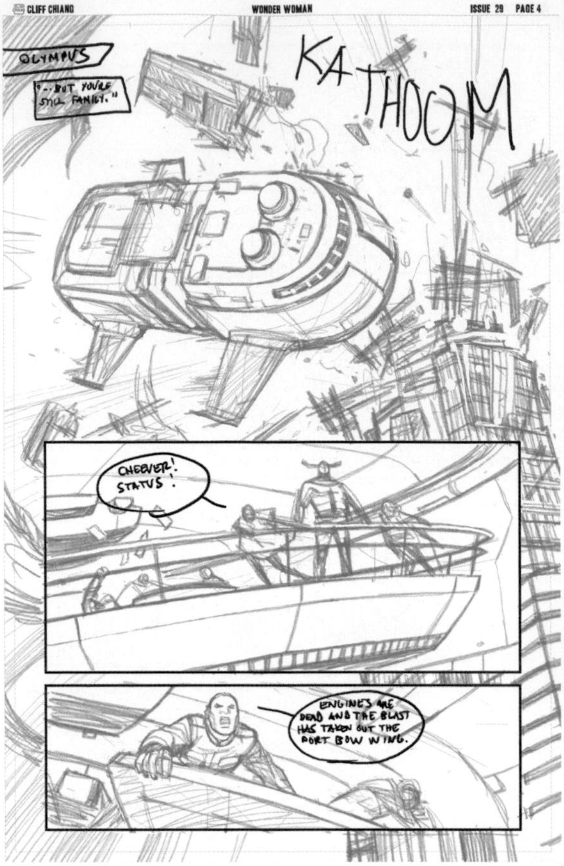
OLYMPUS
"...BUT YOU'RE STILL FAMILY."
KATHOOM
CHEEVER! STATUS!
ENGINES ARE DEAD AND THE BLAST HAS TAKEN OUT THE PORT BOW WING.

CLIFF CHIANG WONDER WOMAN ISSUE 29 PAGE 7

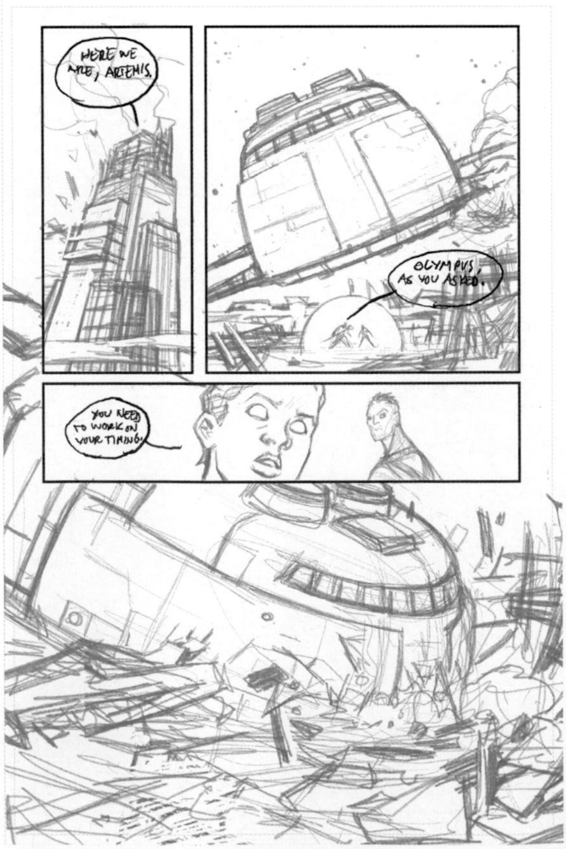
HERE WE ARE, ARTEMIS.
OLYMPUS, AS YOU ASKED.
YOU NEED TO WORK ON YOUR TIMING.

CLIFF CHIANG WONDER WOMAN ISSUE 29 PAGE 8

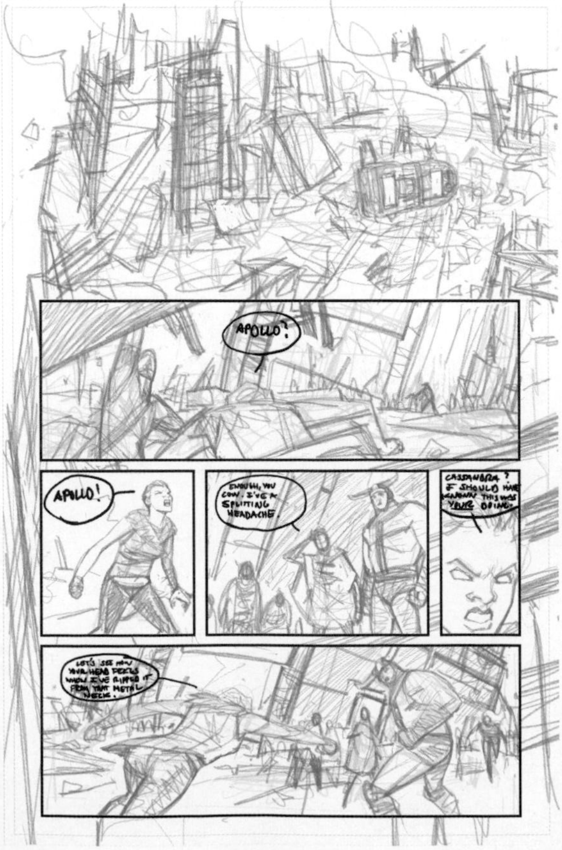
APOLLO?
APOLLO!
ENOUGH, YOU COW. I'VE A SPLITTING HEADACHE.
CASSANDRA? I SHOULD HAVE KNOWN THIS WAS YOUR DOING.
LET'S SEE HOW YOUR HEAD FEELS WHEN I'VE RIPPED IT FROM THAT METAL NECK.

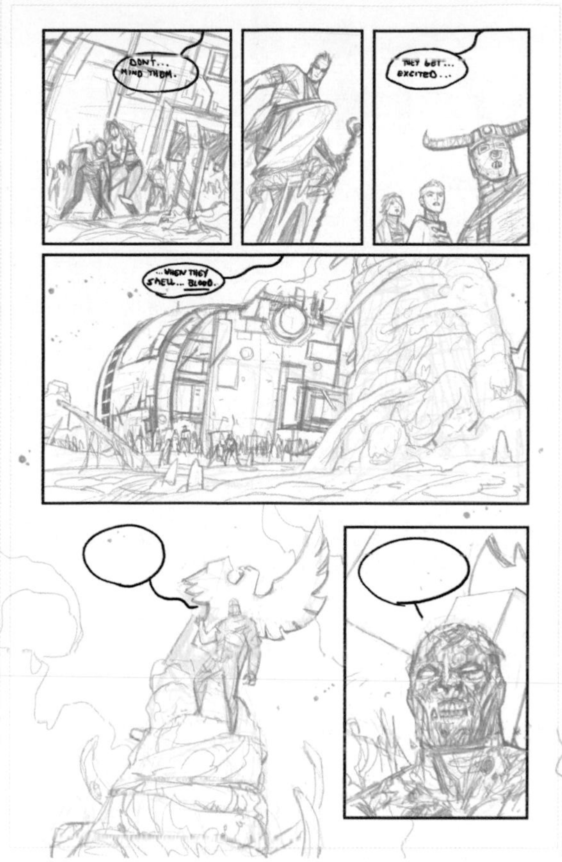
DON'T... MIND THEM.
THEY GET... EXCITED...
...WHEN THEY SMELL... BLOOD.



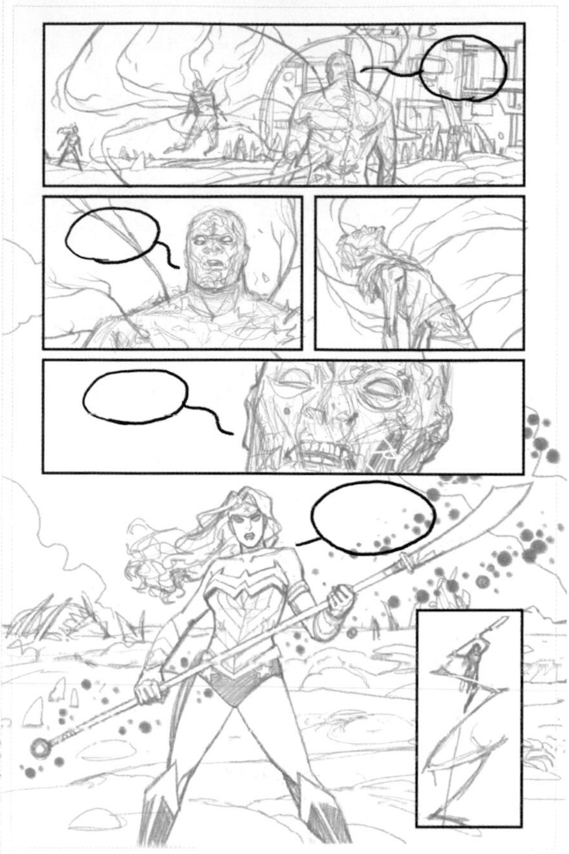



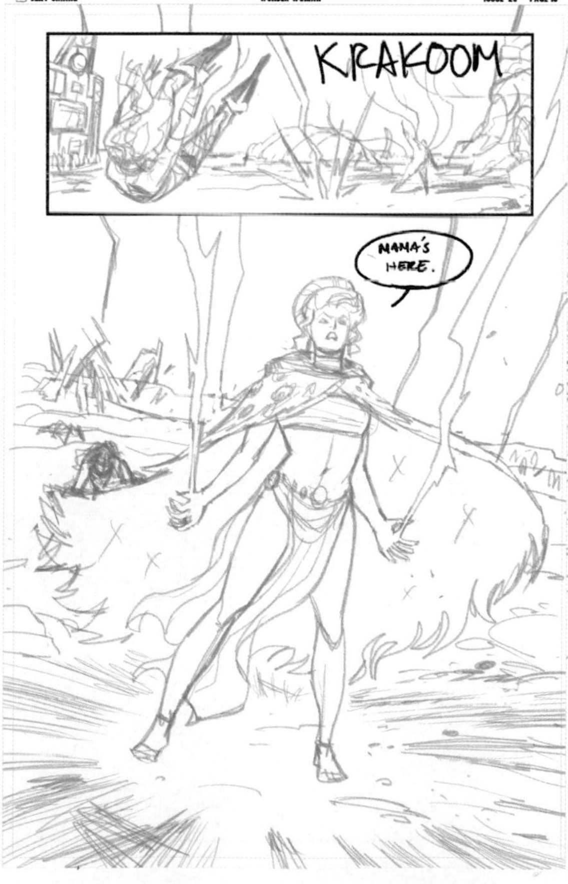
KRAKOOM
MAMA'S HERE.



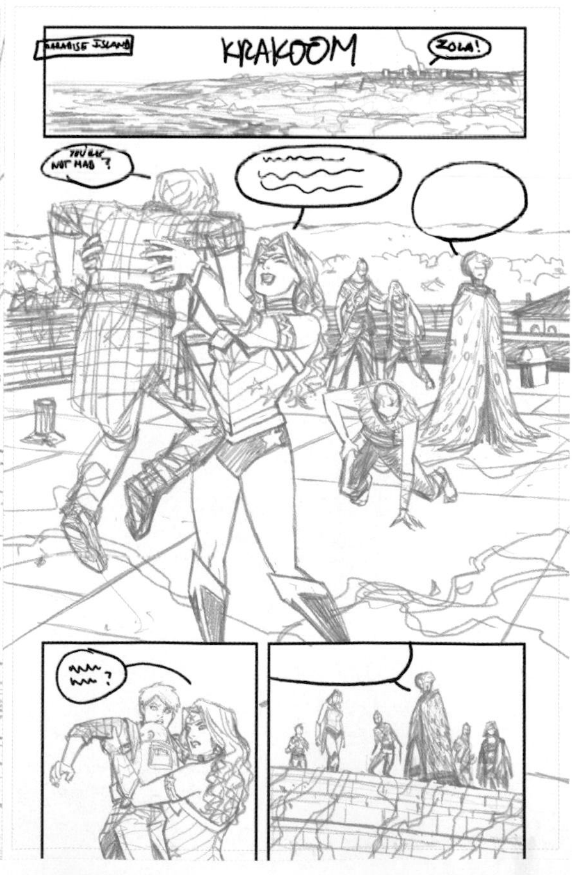
KRAKOOM
ZOLA!
YOU'RE NOT MAD ?

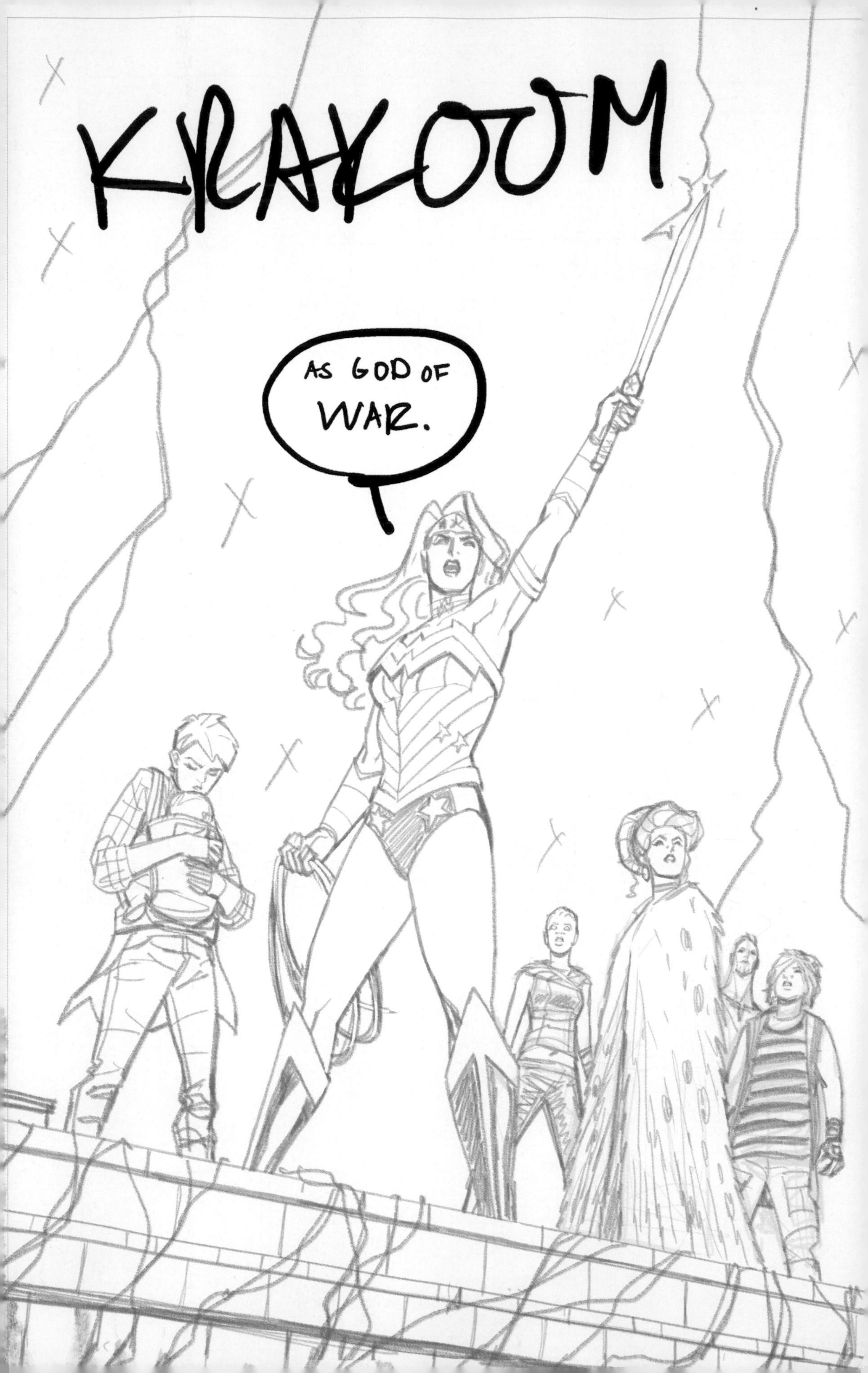
KRAKOOM
AS GOD OF WAR.